A CELEBRATION OF POETS

WEST
GRADES 7-9
FALL 2012

creativeCOMMUNICATION
A CELEBRATION OF TODAY'S WRITERS

A CELEBRATION OF POETS
WEST
GRADES 7-9
FALL 2012

AN ANTHOLOGY COMPILED BY CREATIVE COMMUNICATION, INC.

Published by:

creativeCOMMUNICATION
A CELEBRATION OF TODAY'S WRITERS

PO BOX 303 · SMITHFIELD, UTAH 84335
TEL. 435-713-4411 · WWW.POETICPOWER.COM

Authors are responsible for the originality of the writing submitted.

ISBN: 978-1-60050-548-5

FOREWORD

The ability to write has been a major influence on the progression of mankind. Unique to humans is this ability to learn from others and to share knowledge. However, it seems in an era of texting and Tweeting, that the value of the written word has been de-emphasized. Today's students are more versed in writing truncated, incomplete sentences and shortened or misspelled words that are corrected for them.

Writing contests give students an outlet that allows them to stretch and think in ways they normally would not do. In many schools, the assignment of writing an essay or a poem is one that has been lost to the pressure to include more "academic" subjects in the classroom. After meeting the demands based on the Common Core, teachers often don't have time to teach creative or expository writing. We are glad that the students participating in our program accepted the challenge and submitted an entry.

The entries that are published in this book represent the top 45% of the students who entered our contest. Every time you enter a contest, you are taking a risk. These are the students who took a chance and were rewarded by having their words published. Words that would have been left in a backpack or notebook are now permanently bound for others to read. We thank these students and their teachers and hope that you enjoy what they have shared. By sharing their thoughts, a part of these students is immortalized.

Thomas Worthen, Ph.D.
Editor
Creative Communication

WRITING CONTESTS!

Enter our next POETRY contest!
Enter our next ESSAY contest!

Why should I enter?
Win prizes and get published! Each year thousands of dollars in prizes are awarded throughout North America. The top writers in each division receive a monetary award and a free book that includes their published poem or essay. Entries of merit are also selected to be published in our anthology.

Who may enter?
There are four divisions in the poetry contest. The poetry divisions are grades K-3, 4-6, 7-9, and 10-12. There are three divisions in the essay contest. The essay divisions are grades 3-6, 7-9, and 10-12.

What is needed to enter the contest?
To enter the poetry contest send in one original poem, 21 lines or less. To enter the essay contest send in one original non-fiction essay, 250 words or less, on any topic. Please submit each poem and essay with a title, and the following information clearly printed: the writer's name, current grade, home address (optional), school name, school address, teacher's name and teacher's email address (optional). Contact information will only be used to provide information about the contest. For complete contest information go to www.poeticpower.com.

How do I enter?
Enter a poem online at:
www.poeticpower.com
or
Mail your poem to:
    Poetry Contest
    PO Box 303
    Smithfield UT 84335

Enter an essay online at:
www.poeticpower.com
or
Mail your essay to:
    Essay Contest
    PO Box 303
    Smithfield UT 84335

When is the deadline?
Poetry contest deadlines are April 11th, August 15th and December 5th. Essay contest deadlines are July 16th, October 15th, and February 18th. Students can enter one poem and one essay for each spring, summer, and fall contest deadline.

Are there benefits for my school?
Yes. We award $12,500 each year in grants to help with Language Arts programs. Schools qualify to apply for a grant by having 15 or more accepted entries.

Are there benefits for my teacher?
Yes. Teachers with five or more students published receive a free anthology that includes their students' writing.

For more information please go to our website at **www.poeticpower.com**, email us at editor@poeticpower.com or call 435-713-4411.

TABLE OF CONTENTS

STATES INCLUDED IN THIS EDITION:

ARIZONA
CALIFORNIA
COLORADO
IDAHO
MONTANA
NEVADA
NEW MEXICO
UTAH
WYOMING

Fall 2012 Poetic Achievement Honor Schools

*Teachers who had fifteen or more poets accepted to be published

The following schools are recognized as receiving a "Poetic Achievement Award." This award is given to schools who have a large number of entries of which over fifty percent are accepted for publication. With hundreds of schools entering our contest, only a small percent of these schools are honored with this award. The purpose of this award is to recognize schools with excellent Language Arts programs. This award qualifies these schools to receive a complimentary copy of this anthology. In addition, these schools are eligible to apply for a Creative Communication Language Arts Grant. Grants of two hundred and fifty dollars each are awarded to further develop writing in our schools.

Beacon Country Day School
Greenwood Village, CO
Catherine Roche*

Canyon View Jr High School
Orem, UT
Susan Astle
Brenda Favila*
David Lee*
Kathleen Moe

Chinese American International School
San Francisco, CA
Jake Sproull*

Christ the King School
Mesa, AZ
Janet Brown*

Daniel Savage Middle School
Modesto, CA
Sherry Chapman*
Amanda Harvey*
Nedra Voorhees*

Encore Jr/Sr High School for the Performing
& Visual Arts
Hesperia, CA
April McCue
Deanna Swank*

Falcon Creek Middle School
Aurora, CO
Laura Woods*

Gale Ranch Middle School
San Ramon, CA
Kim Carter
Nancy Dougherty
Sara Faidley
Pamela George
Jon Kontilis
Andrea Kopshever
Mary Joanne Loecher
Ashley Welch

Headwaters Academy
Bozeman, MT
Susan Schwab*

Joe Walker Middle School
Quartz Hill, CA
Brian Hurlburt*

John Adams Middle School
Los Angeles, CA
Linda Bolibaugh*

La Reina High School
Thousand Oaks, CA
Rebecca Adams
Nikki Blake
Kris Chisholm*

Lucerne Valley Middle/Sr High School
Lucerne Valley, CA
Linda Schlenz*

Meridian Elementary School
Meridian, CA
Pam Davis*

Monarch High School
Louisville, CO
Patrick Miskella*

Monte Vista Christian School
Watsonville, CA
Janice Renard*
Marcus Schwager

Mountain Ridge Jr High School
Highland, UT
Elizabeth Chynoweth
Amy McNeill

New Plymouth High School
New Plymouth, ID
Pierrette Madrid-Harris*

Palm Desert Charter Middle School
Palm Desert, CA
Jeff Ball
Nanette Davis-Kirchhevel
Kristin Wagner*

Pine Creek High School
Colorado Springs, CO
Jennifer Tews*

Pueblo West High School
Pueblo West, CO
Kelly Jackson
Janice Parker
Kati Wilson

Richardson PREP HI Middle School
San Bernardino, CA
Ms. McDaniel
Emily Tauffer*

Ripona Elementary School
Ripon, CA
Kim Johnson*

Rolling Hills Country Day School
Rolling Hills Estates, CA
Joyce Brown
Debby Corette*
Angela Favreau*
Peggy Johns-Campbell*
Ms. Shobert

Salida Middle School
Salida, CO
Jacque Fisher*

Sarah McGarvin Intermediate School
Westminster, CA
Cindy Ribeiro*

Sequoia Village School
Show Low, AZ
Amy Benzon
Paul Cryder*
Kim Robinson
Sherra Wahl*

South Lake Middle School
Irvine, CA
Azadeh Estrada
Kathy Holcomb

South Lake Middle School (cont.)
Irvine, CA
Allison Neser
Vincent Rico

St Francis School
Bakersfield, CA
Bronny Bowman*

St Helen Catholic School
South Gate, CA
Bernadette Windsor*

St John's Episcopal School
Chula Vista, CA
Connie Walker*

St Martin-in-the-Fields School
Winnetka, CA
Virginia Hessamian*

Stapley Jr High School
Mesa, AZ
Kathleen Holso
Julie Miller

Summit Middle School
Frisco, CO
Julie Fishman
Ashley Good Smith
Ms. Lowry
Brittany Wilson

Tenaya Middle School
Fresno, CA
Marie Meyer*
Tracy Owensby

The Mirman School
Los Angeles, CA
Wendy Samson*
Marjorie Zinman*

The Preuss School at UCSD
La Jolla, CA
Anne Artz*

The Preuss School at UCSD (cont.)
La Jolla, CA
Shannon Baird
Juliana Biersbach
Elizabeth Foulke
Jan Gabay
Alexandra Martinez
Allegra Mascovich
Oscar Ramos
Eric Romer
David Weber

Weldon Valley Jr High School
Weldona, CO
Robert Vance*

White Pine Middle School
Richmond, UT
Jessie Datwyler*
Evelyn Meikle

Young Scholar's Academy
Bullhead City, AZ
Jessica Dykes
David Martinez*

Language Arts Grant Recipients 2012-2013

After receiving a "Poetic Achievement Award" schools are encouraged to apply for a Creative Communication Language Arts Grant. The following is a list of schools who received a two hundred and fifty dollar grant for the 2012-2013 school year.

A E Arnold Elementary School, Cypress, CA
Benton Central Jr/Sr High School, Oxford, IN
Birchwood School, Cleveland, OH
Children's House Montessori School, West Dundee, IL
Crestwood Elementary School, Rockford, MI
Dixon High School, Dixon, MO
Dr R E McKechnie Elementary School, Vancouver, BC
Elbridge Gale Elementary School, Wellington, FL
Emmanuel-St Michael Lutheran School, Fort Wayne, IN
Great Expectations Academy, Sahuarita, AZ
Greeneville Middle School, Greeneville, TN
Harrison North Elementary School, Scio, OH
Holliday Middle School, Holliday, TX
Holy Cross Catholic Elementary School, Omaha, NE
Holy Cross High School, Delran, NJ
Howard DeBeck Elementary School, Richmond, BC
Kennard Dale High School, Fawn Grove, PA
Kootenay Christian Academy, Cranbrook, BC
LaBrae Middle School, Leavittsburg, OH
Mary Blair Elementary School, Loveland, CO
Menominee Jr High School, Menominee, MI
Outley Elementary School, Houston, TX
Pine View School, Osprey, FL
Poplar Grove School, Franklin, TN
Salida Middle School, Salida, CO
Shadowlawn Elementary School, Green Cove Springs, FL
Stevensville Middle School, Stevensville, MD
Thorne Middle School, Port Monmouth, NJ
Vacaville Christian Schools, Vacaville, CA
Victory Christian School, Tulsa, OK

Grades 7-8-9
Top Ten Winners

List of Top Ten Winners for Grades 7-9; listed alphabetically

Marina Bron, Grade 8
Swampscott Middle School, MA

Ashley Davis, Grade 7
Jim Hill Middle School, ND

Danielle Egan, Grade 8
Mill Valley Middle School, CA

Ellora Kamineni, Grade 7
Winburn Middle School, KY

Kayla Keener, Grade 9
Valley Christian High School, CA

Brenna O'Hara, Grade 9
Linn Mar High School, IA

Isabelle Page, Grade 8
Holy Spirit Regional School, AL

Taylor Pettit, Grade 8
Murray Middle School, FL

Noelle Santos, Grade 9
Westlake High School, NY

Olivia Wagner, Grade 7
Jefferson Middle School, PA

All Top Ten Poems can be read at www.poeticpower.com

Brave

I am brave and ferocious
I wonder what my prey thinks
I hear my stomach snarl
I see the grazing zebra
I want its tender juicy thigh
I am brave and ferocious

I pretend that hunting is effortless
I feel the fiery sun graze my back
I worry about my pack
I cry after every loss
I am brave and ferocious

I understand I can't do everything
I say "No man left behind."
I dream of elephant sized zebras
I try to nourish the entire pack
I hope after I die my pack will survive
I am brave and ferocious

I am the king of the animal kingdom
I am the brave and ferocious lion
Nick Johnstone, Grade 7
Falcon Creek Middle School, CO

Scrapbooking

All of my memories,
Tucked neatly away,
Into a scrapbook,
For all eternity.

For generations
Soon to come,
All that look will see,
The one and only,
Very plainly,
So imperfect me.

As silly as a turkey,
As grumpy as a bear,
As fitting as a sunset,
With my family always there.

The painting of my life,
May be the strange one that you see,
But that's what I am, I'm different,
And I always want to be.
Brigitta Clements, Grade 7
Canyon View Jr High School, UT

Our Love

Poems are like songs
As water falls to water
And you love our love
Nicholas Deckhut, Grade 8
Muirlands Middle School, CA

Where Poetry Hides for Me

Poetry hides for me
In the keys of my computer's keyboard
It hides
In the pictures in my hallway.
Poetry hides for me
In the closet with all my family's coats
And
In the emotions of my dad's passing.
Poetry hides for me in the bookcase's shelves in my room,
And
It hides in the big dog my dad gave me before he passed.
And
In the fun times with my uncles and brothers.
It hides in the best fun memories my Mom and I shared.
Poetry hides for me in the blue blanket my Mom's friend, Laura, knitted for me.
It hides in the screen of my television and in the family get-togethers.
Poetry hides in my Mom's stomach when my fraternal twin brothers kick.
It hides in the pen and pencil I write with an in the paper I draw with.
It even hides in the car with the family.
Khylia DeJean, Grade 7
Tenaya Middle School, CA

Death

Sitting in a room of darkness, thoughts going everywhere.
Feel your body growing dizzy as wind blows through your hair.
you slowly remember the playful rabbits and deer outside your house.
But your cold body is feeling numb as you rest on the bitter ground.
Remember climbing through trees as a child and almost soaring through the air.
Now your body is shivering cold, your feet ache with despair.
What happened to the comforting blankets on your warm, welcoming bed?
Everything that brought you joy is gone because your dead.
Now you've just grown old, cast aside in people's life.
Now your just an object and no one wants to waste their time.
If only we know what was waiting above.
Friends, family, people we love.
If we didn't say, "oh but this really can't hurt."
Tomorrows a new day.
It's then that I'll learn.
Then maybe we wouldn't be sitting all alone wondering,
Waiting, for our time to go.
If we all prepared and were ready to leave.
Perhaps death wouldn't be such a terrible thing.
Olivia Berhan, Grade 7
Monte Vista Christian School, CA

Spiritual Wind

For what you've accomplished, let it carry into the future.
Parting yourself to others' lives',
Until the time comes for them to forget about you.
Within the vicinities of the future, those of the past will never go.
The wind! Carry my message.
Nothing would best the life of a changed person.
For a new life, I would gladly accept.
Better yet, I shall remain alive, until the spiritual wind blows me away.
Andrew Nguyen, Grade 7
Sarah McGarvin Intermediate School, CA

Our Trivial Ways
Surrounded by inferior things
Encompassed by fear, isolated by my feelings

No one knows how hard it is
I'm better off than some creatures
Monsters of this gray, desolate world
Which we call home

Life, love, philosophy
Trivial to the big idea
How everything should be, how it shall be
When everyone is gone

Think of me
Not as an absurd evil, but merely wise
All this will come in meager time
Meek beings are nothing to me

I may seem too far away
To know what it all means
But take it easy now, be warned of what I see
Chilton Beasley, Grade 8
Campus Middle School, CO

The Sun's Shadow, the Moon's Light
The moon shines bright on a never-winter night,
But the sun shines dark on a hot summer light.
When the two collide, everything is black,
All but one, the bold stubborn attack.
As the two reset, none is dark,
The only thing that appears is a multi colored ark.
As the two rise again, nor day, nor night,
And all I can see is a powerful bright light.
They begin to fight again, they clash, they cry,
But it feels that both are about to die.
They retreat to the horizon, and wait there like stones,
They soon rise again after a night at their homes.
The sun fiercely attacks, the moon ferociously collides,
They seem evenly matched, but neither reside.
The final attack reveals a blinding light,
They now combine, but there is no day, there is no night.
Matthew Chartier, Grade 7
Joe Walker Middle School, CA

Memories
Sometimes we must say goodbye
To things we love, we sometimes cry
To friends or family, pets or toys
Sometimes we do not have a choice
But, new things will come
And old things that are gone become great memories
that you can tell to someone
So do not forget about your old memories yet
Trust me, you will regret
Haley Czapla, Grade 8
Canfield Middle School, ID

A Person I Know Who Does So Much
When you thought I wasn't looking,
I saw how much you cared about my little problems,
and I learned to look out for others.
When you thought I wasn't looking,
I saw you show love even when the favor was never returned,
and I found that love is unconditional.
When you thought I wasn't looking,
I saw how much you risked for me,
and I wanted to become that person.
When you thought I wasn't looking,
I saw you help someone learn,
and I decided that there is always time for others.
When you thought I wasn't looking,
I saw you come to my parties at school,
and I learned to make others happy.
When you thought I wasn't looking,
I saw you make dinner for those in need,
and I learned to be helpful.
When you thought I wasn't looking,
I saw what I wanted to become.
Isaiah Nimmer, Grade 7
Canyon View Jr High School, UT

A Normal Day for Me
Waking up at dawn, every day, while all the house is asleep
Waiting for my ride to school, fun deprived,
A normal day for me.
Learning every minute but nothing much is new to see,
Working very hard, writing on every card,
A normal day for me.
There she is that special girl, the one that's right for me,
She doesn't know, but still, although,
A normal day for me.
The last bell rings it's finally done time for fun and games
Get home and play the rest of the day,
A normal day for me.
Never something that is new always over again,
Always has been and always will be,
A normal day for me.
Ethan Holliday, Grade 8
Ogden Preparatory Academy, UT

Love
Love is like a piece of silk.
Delicate, fragile.
Though through thick and thin it holds its own.
You can see right through it,
or get lost in its complexity.
It can mask you,
convince you that it is all right.
Though it cannot protect you.
So be careful my darling.
For when you are neck deep in sorrow,
that harmless piece of silk will pull you under.
Emma Rodgers, Grade 7
Goddard Middle School, CO

Humans

Bang! Boom!
The cannons go off.
People fall and rise.
One side thinks the other deserves.

Bang! Boom!
What a great depression.
Also the people's expressions.
Who created this horrible idea?
Some folks say caused by want.

Bang! Boom!
Guns with powder have great power.
Bombs destruct the land.
As so does people who want more.

Bang! Boom!
Weapons may seem the danger of things,
But that's not true.
Guns and bombs may delete.
But humans are the real masters of destruction.

Alec Walker, Grade 8
Joe Walker Middle School, CA

Edge of the Table

When lunchtime comes and the kids get their food,
they split up into their separate friend groups.
Except for me, I'm sitting all alone
Here at the edge of the table.
I may get straight A's on all my report cards
but I get F's on my social grades
I try to act cool but they'll never accept me
I'm here staring at my empty social calendar
I can draw circles in mathematics and art
But there's one circle that I am unable to draw
Maybe if I had a social compass I could create
a circle made out of friends
My parties are always empty
no one will hang out with the uncool kid
I may not have any friends but I know everyone's name
I hear them speaking from the end of the table.
Maybe next year they will realize who I really am
and that I'm cool in my own way
I'm not just a wall, to be spray painted and covered with graffiti
I hope they see my view from the edge of the table

D. Andrew Nelson, Grade 8
Gateway Preparatory Academy, UT

Reflections on Rodin's Sculpture Titled "Thought"

The girl, stuck in a tough situation,
Thinks about her rough and bumpy life ahead of her
And knows
She will not be going anywhere
For a long time.

Noah Gonzales, Grade 7
Tenaya Middle School, CA

Hard Work

Football is a construction worker
hard working, never giving up,
and some bumps and bruises may come with.

If you get hurt or get some of those bumps and bruises,
it doesn't matter as long as you get the paycheck or the win
that's the most important thing.

You are begrimed and drenched in sweat. No worries,
it's all business, so no one minds.

Smack!
You strike as hard and as quick as a cobra.
And you never ever have any regrets.

Anger is common in both,
but that's all right
it helps you get the impossible done.

Strength is a must,
but you need to know how to handle it.
If you don't, it could be a hassle to have the strength
but not be able to use it.

You can't play football or be a construction worker for forever.
So once you hit that age or get that injury,
you need to know when to quit.

Tyson Hays, Grade 8
Falcon Creek Middle School, CO

Those Were the Days

Those were the days
Having parties that would never end,
Hanging out with my friends
Smiling, laughing, having a great time
Things that could never get replaced

Those were the days
Days that lasted forever
Days I would remember
Never could or would forget.
A part of me that always stayed in my head

Those were the days
No worries, just laid back
Everything was going to fall in place,
And if it didn't, a little push wouldn't hurt
Things that would get me on my way

Those were the days
Smiling, laughing, having a great time
My friends and I
No worries, no nothing
Those were the days, and now they're sadly over.

Kyla Johnson, Grade 8
Richardson PREP HI Middle School, CA

Life

Life is alive, life is cruel,
It may be hard,
But that's the rule.

Life is active, life is flourishing,
It cannot be avoided,
Even in conscious carousing.

Life is everywhere,
life is living,
At Christmas time,
We are all giving.

Life is unpredictable,
Life is never always controllable,
Like a blossom who gives off it's evermore scent,
We may or may not always relent.

Life has purpose, life has meaning,
We may lose our way,
Life in fictional reading.

Life is here,
Life is now,
And here ends my tale,
So I'll take a bow.

Julianna A. May, Grade 8
Mary Fay Pendleton Elementary School, CA

Your True Friend

When stuck in the eternity of sorrow, and hope is lost
Everyone leaves, hearts covered with frost
But a true friend comes to your aid
Never to leave and never to fade

Joyous, blissful, and content
Friendship surrounds like a tent
Distraught, sullen, and downcast
Only the best of friends will last

You know your secrets they will keep
And on their shoulder you can weep
With steadfast understanding you can confide
Always a listener, never a judge, and forever a guide

They'll travel to you from millions of miles
For cozy comfort, outstretched arms, and warm smiles
Together you are closer than a carefully crafted weave
They are all you need to have the strength to believe

The sacred treasure you find in a friend
Your sighing soul it will mend
One who loves you not from obligation but from choice
Having found the epitome of friendship, you rejoice

Diana Cristea, Grade 9
The Mirman School, CA

Not Just a Defender

The defender gets the ball, and quickly passes.
The opponent interrupts the pass,
Dribbles down the field and scores.
The defender feels like he has been burned into ash.

He thinks to himself
"How can I change to get better?"
"How can I change to be better?"

Unwilling to be defeated again,
Taking on the risk of failing.
He runs up to the ball, controls it
He does not pass.
He runs faster and faster.
Streaking past defenders like a comet on fire.

He runs all the way to the goal.
10 seconds left.
The referee with the whistle in his hand.

He shoots, scores.
He feels alive again!
The referee blows the whistle and the crowd cheers his name.

He is not just a defender;
He is a phoenix.

Gregory Brandt, Grade 8
Rolling Hills Country Day School, CA

True Laughter

What is the sound of laughter, you may ask.
Is it something special, or just a simple task?
Laughter is a special thing that makes people smile
No sad emotions come to their face for a while.

Who is the one laughing, you question.
What is their facial expression?
Laughter is full of joy
Everyone can do it, even a little boy.

When is it time to laugh, you say.
Is it once in a while, or every day?
Laughter can be at any time.
Any time would be fine.

Where does laughter come from?
Does it come from the throat or a strum?
Laughter comes from the heart,
A heart, with a happiness part.

How do you laugh, is your last question.
I smile and say this suggestion.
"Laugh with love, joyfulness, and with a shining bright.
Then let your laughter take off in flight"

Noor Mumtaz, Grade 8
The Guidance Charter School, CA

Desire

Desires spill from my pen as my heart navigates the vast realm in which my desires are yet to be revived. This common vast place is detained with the lowly word of "mind."
This magic sorcery amuses me to the most tear plunging, eye prying, deadly madness that breaks the chains that the world and reality restrain me by.
My eternal thirst for the desert; which is where God himself brought down the first heaven to earth, is where my breath is never in tune with the soft knock of my heartbeat. And where the great majestic desert blooms with nothing but my sheer thirst for it.
Messy untamed blotches stain the white of my canvas in the very center of my "mind." The sound of my inner voice makes me flinch as the delusional blotches take flight into beautiful shapeful dreams.
"Clouds, sky, dirt, sand."
The list goes on for eternity as I create a work of art that is both worthless and priceless…
Yet, here I sit, a dreamer with a pen and paper that burn reality to a ghastly black ash, and give me only a sliver of a glimpse at the fiery globe in which my real life is stolen, restrained and held in eternal captivity by the fiery and icy chains.
Or
What
Is
Commonly
Known
As
Reality

Yasmeen Allie, Grade 8
South Lake Middle School, CA

The Dark Side

The house on the left of a dead-end street
holds a dark side to it.
A side that left us in mourning.
A side that filled us all with hate.

The house on the left of a dead-end street
had many joyful times — until the dark side was revealed.
A side that killed us a little inside.
A side that filled us all with hate.

The house on the left of a dead-end street
had many depressing moments — the dark side showed us the worst…
A side that made us fear death just a little more.
A side that filled us all with hate.

The house on the left of a dead-end street
was never the same the day my grandmother died — they day the dark side reared its ugly head.
A side that changed our view of the world.
A side that filled us all with hate.

Irad Leon, Grade 8
Richardson PREP HI Middle School, CA

What Is War?

A struggle of power, man trying to rule another.
A fight between cultures when, in the eyes of God, we are all equal.
What drives us to execute our fellow humans?
They say it's about freedom, power.
But is that a valid reason?
A valid enough reason to destroy the lives of those who are only innocent victims in the midst of all this cruelty?
We are cold, we are cruel, but shall we let it consume us? Or rise above it?
We ask ourselves what we did to deserve this, it is not us entirely. No, only our hatred, greed, and pride.

Jennifer Valencia, Grade 9
Patriot High School, CA

Lacrosse Is a New Shoe

You go to practice with an open mind
Like walking into a shoe store
Not knowing what to expect.

You tie the laces
Or learn the rules
So you won't trip and get hurt.

You learn how to cradle and pass
Or make sure the shoe has enough support
So if all else fails, that will always be there.

You figure out what position fits you best
Like wearing the shoe consistently
It will fit you better.

When the season is over
Or the shoe wears out
You go back wanting more shoes or another chance to play.

Kaleigh Southern, Grade 8
Falcon Creek Middle School, CO

The Musician's Mind

It starts out simple, clean and mild,
And turns to chaos, fully wild.
Scratch that line, add a new,
So many things I want to do.
No limit at all, no boundaries set,
Nothing at all can stop me yet!
A few more notes, no that's not enough,
I need this, and that, to patch that up.
New inspiration always comes in time,
To change, revise, and keep in time!
Add a sharp, maybe a flat or two,
Let's make this piece dynamic too!
Softer here, until this line,
Then boom with sound, shake the heavens this time!
At last the piece is finally done,
I will admit it was rather fun,
To make and spin a musical piece,
Where the musician's mind never sleeps.

Gabriel Martinez, Grade 7
Christ the King Catholic School, AZ

The Trees

I smell the Evergreen leaves.
I see all the animals running around.
The wind blows and moves all the trees.
It looks as if all the giant trees are going to fall.
The wonders of how they are still standing tall.
All the needles they leave are everywhere.
All the animals that are living in them are so hard to count.
Trees are why we are alive.
Trees are everywhere.

Cole Brennan, Grade 7
Christ the King School, AZ

Last Goodbye

I sit here waiting
Waiting for you to see,
that time is running out, come on and save me.

It's not your fault I'm crying
so don't you think that at all.
Don't feel guilty for something you didn't do
just hug me and don't let me fall.

Your arms are so soft and cozy.
The look in your eyes, I can't forget.
I wish you didn't have to leave,
but I know the date is set.

I let the tears fall down my face on the sides,
but you tell me not to cry
and that everything will be fine.
I know its all a lie.

I know you can't stand it either.
For the best we say our last goodbyes.

Brianna Mormile, Grade 8
Yolo Middle School, CA

Don't Cry

Don't cry little baby
mommy's only gone for the moment.
Don't cry little baby
listen to the words that've been spoken.
You've been through pain all your life
so sleep away this night without any tears.
Don't cry don't cry.
I promise I'll make the pain go away.
Mommy will protect you from all this hate.
I know daddy ran away
from what could have been a happy family.
I know he left us broken hearted
not knowing what to do
but mommy will love you for daddy too.
One day soon things will get better
and you won't have to wear this painful sweater.

Hannah Smith, Grade 8
Pentecostal Way of Truth Academy, CA

Sandstorm

The dark endless falling of blinding sand
people running
but many not knowing where they are going.
Many loved ones looking for each other.
The physical damage was very bad
but the mental damage was worst.
Many were lost in the endless storm of sand
buried alive, never found
No sun or anything to guide anyone out.

Tyler Jury, Grade 7
Monte Vista Christian School, CA

Curiosity

Curiosity, seeking knowledge not known
Looking beyond the window of understanding and possibility, the unquenchable thirst for more

Without inquisitiveness, development will remain stagnant
Civilization grinds to a halt, daily life turns repugnant

A powerful principle, one that changes the future of existence
Breakthroughs in medicine and technology come from man's curiosity and persistence

Bing! The cure for cancer. Ding! The first man in space
Ideas are made possible through the curiosity of the human race

Curiosity leads to learning, traversing the treacherous, tumultuous trail
One step at a time, we get there without fail

Constantly we push and struggle for answers, accomplishments accumulate into an immense mountain
Satisfaction within us shines bright like the brilliant sun with curiosity, success is certain.

Elliott Sina, Grade 8
The Mirman School, CA

Black

Black is the night consuming our once lively sky.
Flooding the world from place to place.
Engrossed by loneliness and the lost faith, forgotten long ago.
Black comes from the dark ashes of death, and the helpless feeling of depression and tragedy.
Black comes from fear and nightmares that haunt you, ready to catch you at your weakest state.
It materializes from bad luck and utter disappointment.
It is the monster that conceals in your closet.
It is that misunderstanding that breaks close relationships into pieces. Ruins. Devastation.
Black is the weak and forgotten.
The lost and defenseless.
Black is the defeating moment of bad news.
It is the hurt and betrayal of shattered trust.
Black is the never ending darkness of outer space.
The untrustable,
Unforgiven,
And unknown.

Alexandra Hernandez, Grade 7
Gale Ranch Middle School, CA

Winning

"Hey kids, wake up!" My mother yells.
Awakened by the bright sun and the smell of bacon, I get out of bed quickly and scramble down the stairs.
In the kitchen is my mom, frying bacon in a pot, and my dad, drinking his daily cup of coffee while reading the daily news.
"Hey kiddo, look at this," my dad says suddenly and tosses the paper at me.
I read the first few lines out loud:
"Mr. Max Brown, 86 years old, wins the multimillion lottery of ten million dollars!"
"Oh, wow." I say. "Lucky man."
"Now, wait." My dad replies while flipping through a couple of pages. "Now read this."
I eye him suspiciously and glance at the newspaper.
In the obituary section, is a picture of a man, and I scan the caption quickly.
"Max Brown, it says, 86 years old."

Megan Lee, Grade 8
South Lake Middle School, CA

Everything About Me

Everything about me.
I am different. I am odd.
No one is like me.

I am overly clumsy.
One moment I'll be balanced, the next I am on the floor.
When I fall, I laugh it off.

Sports are a big part of my life.
Volleyball, basketball, softball. I love it all.
It has become a part of me.

The odd part of me is obsessing
Over celebrities who don't even know me.
I support them like they're my friends.
I don't care if people judge, it's who I am.

I'm protective and caring of my friends and family.
I will always be loyal and loving to them.
Even if they are mad at me.
It's a quality I have.

I like to think I'm crazy and odd.
Some people will agree, others won't,
But it doesn't really matter because it is
Everything about me and no one else.

Genesis Villafan, Grade 8
St Helen Catholic School, CA

Where I'm From

I'm from a big dark hospital in Arizona,
Heavy as a rock,
Laying there in my pink blanket,
Wrapped all snug and warm.

I'm from two wonderful parents,
Vaughn and Dale,
Both with bright blue eyes,
Bright as the blue sky.

I'm from grandma and grandpa coming to see
The beautiful little baby,
Holding her like a tiny fragile glass,
Sitting there looking into her blue crystal eyes.

I'm from green grass all around my house,
Enormous gray barn with gigantic hay,
Thousands of cows grazing and drinking,
In the hot warm day.

I'm from dry, hot summer days in Arizona,
The place with the cactus as tall as a giant,
Pretty green, yellow, red forests,
Animals everywhere here.

Brooklyn Newman, Grade 9
Seligman High School, AZ

I Miss You

Tears went down my face when I saw you that way.
I love you grandpa, I will love you every day.

As my tears raced down my face,
I knew you'd soon be in a happier place.

My love will be with you wherever you go.
Oh, how I loved you so.

Although I know it was late,
You can't fight fate.

You told me everything as time passed by and by
I never wanted you to die.

We did a lot together throughout the years.
It's time to let the tears go away.

I want you to know
I will never let you go.

I know you loved me too.
My heart will always be with you.

Now it's time to say goodbye,
Until I see you again someday.

Jesseca Saavedra, Grade 8
St John's Episcopal School, CA

The Truth About Fire Girl

If you could see my insecurities
Beneath all the pain and suffering
If you could live one day with my tears
You would be so worried about all the petty voices

You all need me
But maybe just maybe
I need some of you, too
Laugh at my tears
Snarl at my happiness
Could this be the end of the one and only
Poised and practiced
Fire girl?

No, I put on a smile
Stand tall and proud
And hope
That no one could ever see that imperfect me

A blank smile to hide
All the nights I've sat up and cried
So please
I'm begging on my knees, help me
Just once, through my insecurities.

Kiana Roberts, Grade 8
Campus Middle School, CO

A Struggle to Understand

A beloved President of an entire nation, killed by the bullet of one man,
this I cannot comprehend.
A young mother, death with cancer, helplessly leaving children in a world alone,
this I cannot comprehend
A firefighter charging a burning building saving the life of a small child but later loosing his own,
this I cannot comprehend
A hurricane violently washes through a community mercilessly stealing the large home of a troubled family,
this I cannot comprehend

A wife finds peace through forgiveness and helps a nation heal,
a comprehension of the heart.
A daughter grows to become a doctor and tirelessly finds a cure for cancer
a comprehension of the heart.
A small child grows to be a firefighter and saves a burning school bus
a comprehension of the heart.
A family becomes whole as they work together to build a humble home
a comprehension of the heart.

Blake Yarak, Grade 8
Rolling Hills Country Day School, CA

His Legacy

On the 9th of April, 1898, a child was born in Princeton, New Jersey
He would grow to be a giant, standing tall for the equality of all people

They say his eyes were like fire and his voice was an ocean
Washing over all who dared to listen to his vibrating, voracious, and voluminous voice

He had no shame of his rich heritage, feeling that his fellow Negroes shrunk and retreated from it
He began to embrace his culture through his incredible, indestructible, intellectual prowess

His controversial speeches permeated the stillness like arrows piercing the sides of his enemies
The CIA revoked his passport in an attempt to silence the great voice of truth

Living, loving and laughing were important to this American giant, who spent his life defending his race
He strode calmly through the sordid streets with his head high and his honor and ideals untouched

Paul Robeson, never faltering in his beliefs, working for the good of all, passed from this world on
January 23, 1976, leaving behind a legacy that all mankind would be proud to inherit

Sayahn Mudd, Grade 9
The Mirman School, CA

What I Learned from You

When you thought I wasn't looking, I saw you kiss my puppy and I realized you need to be kind to animals.
When you thought I wasn't looking, I saw you take care of my sister when she was sick and I knew it was good to take care of others.
When you thought I wasn't looking, I saw you stay up late working and I learned you need to work to get what you want.
When you thought I wasn't looking, I saw you crying during a movie and I learned it's okay to cry.
When you thought I wasn't looking, I saw you walk into my room and kiss me goodnight when I was asleep and I felt loved
When you thought I wasn't looking, I saw you wrapping my Christmas presents and I quickly ran away
When you thought I wasn't looking, I saw you playing the piano and I learned that to get good at something you need to practice
when you thought I wasn't looking, I saw you clean the house and I learned you need to keep your house clean
When you thought I wasn't looking, I saw you making scrapbooks and I knew you need to keep the memories.
When you thought I wasn't looking, I saw you kiss my dad and I knew you really love him.

Maggie Donaldson, Grade 7
Canyon View Jr High School, UT

Storm

You hear thunder when he runs
You see lighting when he fights
He watches over us when a storm comes
Sometimes he brings destruction, sometimes life
Other times he just passes over us

He let plants grow and waters forests
Some believe he's some type of god
He travels to every part of the world

There was more of them at one time, but they meet the sun's ray
The sun is his natural enemy
If he meets the sun's rays, he will die
His kind will be forever gone

He roams around the world looking for a safe place
He is Storm, last of the phantom horses
Storm bringer of the clouds

Vivien Hall, Grade 7
Monte Vista Christian School, CA

I Should Have Stayed

Oh God how you are so kind
You changed my life in every way
You changed me and my mind
I am thankful you have not left me astray
Why do you still forgive me no matter what I do?
I will always somehow commit a sin
Do you think I will carry through with you?
I was born in this accursed skin
Have you really always been near?
Do you enjoy seeing me in pain?
God I love you, please help me not to live in fear
Please God, break these chains that constrain
I am sorry I have left you alone
I am sorry, I should have known

Andrew Aguiñaga, Grade 9
Heritage Christian School, CA

Music

What is the best art form in my whole life?
All the band members have a microphone
A man could write a love song for his wife
Singers should have a very perfect tone
Anyone can write any type of song
Sometime soon I want to be in a band
All guitar solos can be very grand
There is a mixture of music like rock
Besides guitar there are drums and a bass
There might even be music done by Bach
There are many types for everyone's taste
I believe that music can be the key
That's why music's the best art form for me.

Courtney Dority, Grade 9
Lucerne Valley Middle/Sr High School, CA

Afraid of Letting Go

All I want is someone to express who they are,
Someone to be a risk-taker.

All I want is for someone to express who they are,
Someone to go beyond their horizons,
Someone to pick up a paintbrush and go crazy.

All I want is for someone to express who they are,
Someone to never be timid,
Someone to never be afraid of letting go,
Someone to love what they do.

All I want is for someone to express who they are,
Someone to never be ashamed of their work,
Someone to be proud of what they do and say,
Someone to be creative with their personality and
Someone to never despise their creations.

All I want is for someone to be a genius and create!

Carly Schwulst, Grade 7
Falcon Creek Middle School, CO

The Chirping Sound

This morning when I woke up,
I heard a quiet chirping sound,
but when I looked out my window,
there was nothing to be found.

I went to go eat breakfast and there it was again,
that annoying sound,
that couldn't be found,
was louder than it had been.

I waited at my window to see if it would chirp again,
and when it did,
I found it had been,
two baby birds that looked like some really ugly dogs.

Laura Pagliaro, Grade 7
Joe Walker Middle School, CA

The Civil War

Slavery tears North and South apart,
the country is breaking down,
the army is breaking down,
the Union is breaking down.
Southern states begin to secede,
officers resign and go back to their homes,
one by one, 11 states secede.
Young men are all quite eager for a war.
The uniforms are fresh and sharply creased,
companies of clean-faced boys marching to war,
they are all proud and excited,
marching on......
They must all do what they believe is right.

Howard Wang, Grade 8
Las Flores Middle School, CA

Mute

The poor boy could not see, all he wanted was to read.
The only sound he heard was the turning of the pages.
Then she came, the deaf girl.
Her muted ears matched his empty eyes.

Silence and grief followed by the hating of imperfection.
Depression knocks them down, and they envy all who are perfect.
Word spreads of rumors that are pretty ugly.
As they accept themselves they find compromise.

They find that, like them, no one is perfect.
Everyone has their flaws, and that makes them who they are.
This is normal, for we are only human.
Acceptance of what we are makes us strong.

Their lives go on as a cheerful hymn.
Like humans who need oxygen,
They need each other.
He is her ears,
And she is his eyes.

Isaac Inocentes, Grade 7
Joe Walker Middle School, CA

Slave Ship

Three fourths of the population enslaved
Robbed of one's identity, torn from family
Desolate, pain, misery, agony, desperation
Quiet whimpers, snap of a whip
Why do they have to suffer?

Does it matter what color?
Everyone is white, just a different shade
Yet beat, whipped, chained even killed
Why does only the black shade have to suffer
All you hear are cries of helplessness
Snapping of whips and the crack of gunfire
Don't try to run it just gets much worse

Worthless, helpless, used
And only little is paid for their service
Confused, sad, petrified
Hair cut, names changed
Who are they now?
Slaves

Kendra Yanak, Grade 8
Ripona Elementary School, CA

Disgust

He occupies uneducated communities
Dirty, scrawny, ugly and unwanted
Moves rigidly, silently in the dead of night
Cold black eyes shape his chiseled face
His raspy whispers remind us of things we want to forget
Stealing us of our innocence and comfort

Morgan Gray, Grade 9
Monarch High School, CO

Love

Love, love,
you look me in the eye;
I'm always hoping that you'll be mine.

Love, love,
you've won me over.
You make me feel special like a four leaf clover.
Oh what love does to me.

Love, love,
you put me in a trance;
it always reminds me of our first dance.

Love, love,
when you are away,
I never know what to say.
Oh what love does to me.

Love, love,
all you need is love.

Samantha Rafeedie, Grade 8
Joe Walker Middle School, CA

I Meant To

Time is like a stream
You can't touch the same water twice
Because the flow that just passed
Will never pass again

I meant to be your friend when nobody else would
I meant to pick you up when you fell
I meant to appreciate your positivity and confidence
I meant to understand your sense of humor and
Ponder upon your unique and wondrous conception of life

I meant to laugh at your stupid jokes
And I meant to tell you how much you were worth
I meant to express my great need for your reassuring presence
And I meant to tell you how much you meant to me

Some people dance in the rain
Others just get wet
One thing that I meant to do was dance like you did
Not worrying about a single droplet

Erin Berglund, Grade 9
University Preparatory School, CA

Friends Are Forever

Friendship is a firework bursting in the sky.
Friendship is like a seed growing every day in the sunlight.
Friendship is as lasting as a child's love for his/her mother.
Friendship sounds like a warm heart beating forever and ever.
Friendship feels like a hug that could never be forgotten.
Friendship looks like a pair of shoes walking together for life.

Audrey Kroeker, Grade 7
Daniel Savage Middle School, CA

The World of Books
I picked up a book,
One of my favorites I see!
Time do dive in and look…

So I open the cover
Into a world filled with a lover.
The sea of grey
Forms to become a beautiful array

The story unfolds just fine,
First full of terror and hopelessness
Last overflowing with tears and happiness
All in between the bold line

So if you ever see a good book,
Go check it out!
Or at least, take a look.
Because you may never know what you could find
In that sea of grey…

Holly Rounds, Grade 7
Canyon View Jr High School, UT

Basketball
The crowd is on its feet.
Could they take on this impossible feat?
The offense is dribbling.
The defense is nibbling at the ball.

The player runs the ball up the court.
The defense sets up like a fort.
He shoots for the hoop.
A miss, the rebound comes down with a scoop.

The rebounder makes a shot.
The ball is bounced off the backboard and is caught.
The next shot comes up short.
Basketball is a difficult sport!

Ryan Anderson, Grade 7
Monte Vista Christian School, CA

Twins
She and I are like twins in disguise
We can collide or coincide
With her it's like a roller coaster ride
It's one big fun time
What would people see if they saw what we see
What would we become and be
What is real sisterhood
Is it something bad or good
Sometimes we think we are so witty
To others we may seem so giddy
Thick or thin we have been though it all
Even though we are so small
She and I are like twins in disguise

Erin Cahill, Grade 9
University Preparatory School, CA

Trees
Fall means the soft rustle of dewy leaves
Shifting, fluttering, dancing in the breeze
Fall snatching the life off a tree that grieves
Trees who groan and creak, nearly silent pleas.

Winter means frozen, icy, bare fingers
Exploding through the dull shade of cold
Causing eerie crawling shadows to linger
Trees, imprisoned by winter's old, shaky hold.

Spring means life leaking, seeping, pushing out
Green lightly tugs at branches, fighting
Green, merely a small, quiet, barely there sprout
Taking bits of winter with it, biting.

Trees, life, life supporting, life everlasting
A reminder in the haze, outlasting.

Ambree Campbell, Grade 9
Monarch High School, CO

Love Is a Never Ending Movie
Love is a never ending movie
You stay always wanting more and more
Until it becomes a part of you
Dragging you in hoping there would be a future
Watching hour after hour
Day after day
No ending could ever be enough
Sitting there, you rewind every special moment in your head
Over and over again until you will never forget
You treasure every moment of each scene
Wanting it to last a thousand more years to come
It keeps you in wonder, guessing where you will end up
Will it drag you in, making you into a Hollywood treasure?
Or just another ordinary person to be loved?
There will be no way of escaping once you fall in too deep
The thrills and chills will take you under
But the ending will always stay a mystery for you to figure out

Thuy Nguyen, Grade 8
Falcon Creek Middle School, CO

Reflections on "Bond of Union"
Honestly,
When I first saw this piece,
I thought it was disturbing
But as I look closer, and closer, and closer,
I see two people in love
The way they look at each other is…
Well…magical
They are connected
It seems as if they love each other more than anything in the world
They are together
They are happy, really happy

Megan Elower, Grade 7
Tenaya Middle School, CA

Acceptance

We humans have a habit
Of making others feel small
Like they're lost and alone in the world
Like they don't fit in
Most people are guilty of this
Some don't realize it
But it's all around us
We're all just people
There is no "fitting in"
Because if we were all the same
The world would be a boring place
We need to learn one lesson
Acceptance
Acceptance of others
Tall or short
Brave or afraid
Because in such a cruel world, who wouldn't be afraid?
And more importantly
Acceptance of yourself
Because an original is worth so much more than a copy

Lillian Wood, Grade 7
Salida Middle School, CO

Sunset

All you can see is the tip of the sun,
The sky is pink with wispy clouds of purple,
You watch in awe as the sun disappears before your eyes,
And realize the beauty in this world.
You sit, thinking, how everything on Earth has an important role,
That the sun's role is to give us light and warmth,
So what would my role in this world be, little me?
What could I do to benefit this world?
Now the sun is completely out of sight,
All you have as a light now is the bright pink and orange sky.
It's still warm out but you are feeling tired,
So you go inside and think, and think, and think,
You think about this huge world and how little you are in it,
And how you can't wait to have a wonderful sunset tomorrow
And what your mind will do with its crazy thoughts.

Chase Arenal, Grade 7
Monte Vista Christian School, CA

Seldom Tears

As the telling signs of aging rain down
A single tear is dropping
Through the valley of an aging face
That this world has forgotten
There is no reconciliation that will put me in my place
And there is no time like the present
To drink these draining seconds
But seldom do these words ring true
When I'm constantly failing you
Like the walls we can't break through
Until we disappear

Lance McCabe, Grade 9
Canyon View Jr High School, UT

The Broken Horse

It was a bright warm day
When I broke the horse
I was playing with a piece of foam
I threw it into the air
And the sound of something about to fall
Rang clear through the house
Then with a crash and a bang
The horse was broken
Strewn in several pieces upon the floor
My mother came into the room, crying at the sight
I felt so bad, I didn't know what to say
Though it is harsh, all horses must be broken
Much like a shoe
You must break it before it can be worn
For this reason, I fear horses
Their size marvels me
If they saw fit, they could kick me once
Just once and I would be dead
I now respect horses for the dangerous creatures they can be
And for the beauty they can behold once broken
Only once they have been broken

Tyler Angel, Grade 8
Headwaters Academy, MT

I Am Scared of My Best Friend

My loving, comforting, cozy friend,
Scares me to pieces, screams, and shreds,
Leaving me shivering in my seat.

She is silky smooth, and very strong,
With graceful strides so incredibly long,
Sending chills of panic down my spine.

Soft and cuddly like a lullaby,
Sleepy yawns and cute little sighs,
Charging towards me, alarmingly slobbery.

She can be a whimpering, little fur ball,
Or a lunging beast, all teeth and claws,
Fickle as she is, my dog is still my best friend.

Belinda H., Grade 8
Gale Ranch Middle School, CA

My Musical Love

M y love for you is a song,
U sually like a tree swaying in the wind.
S ometimes I sing along.
I am ignited by the song,
C all it what you want I call it love.

L onely and for a long time do I listen.
O utstandingly does the song play over.
V anishing from time to time,
E ntering my life again without warning.

Melissa Soliz, Grade 8
Mary Fay Pendleton Elementary School, CA

The Western Plains

The Western Plains
seem to stretch forever,
like an everlasting dream.

The Western Plains
are where cowboys ride
and where gold-diggers hide.

The Western Plains
are where you can ride into the sunset
on a golden horse.

The Western Plains
are where camp fires glow
and where wolves howl.

The Western Plains
have no trees
but have lots of grassland.

The Western Plains
have many memories
where heroes came first.

The Western Plains
are where villains
die by the minute.
Eva Froese, Grade 7
Plainview Jr/Sr High School, CO

Guernica

Hark! The world so painted black
And in the sky no day;
The Earth you painted grey with hate
And left us to decay,
And demons, through your vengeful plight,
You dare look past your theft—
But we, the people less the might,
We sing the hymn of death.
But alas! the fire spears our Earth
And trembling do we see:
There is nothing but our shaken Earth
And beloved, loved tree.

But victory is in our hands now;
You had never torn us 'part
For when you left our shaken Earth,
You let live Guernica's heart.

Now man watches with his aging eyes
And sees the muted wrath,
With flaying hands, so held outstretched —
Paint;
Our aftermath.
Naomi Pham, Grade 9
La Quinta High School, CA

Just Be Yourself

Just be yourself, don't
Be somebody that you
Are not, just be yourself

Just be yourself, no matter
Whether you are small, tall, big, or
Gigantic, just be yourself.

Just be yourself, who cares
If you're weak or meek? Just
Love yourself, just be yourself

Just be yourself, you can
Make friends better by
Just being yourself

Just be yourself, no matter
Whether you are weird or popular,
Just be yourself

Just be yourself, who cares
If you are different,
Just be yourself
Jesus Oros, Grade 7
St Helen Catholic School, CA

God's Creations

I wish I could fly
Like a bird in the sky
I'd fly all day long
And sing a beautiful song

I would see the creations of God
That were created with one tiny nod
I would see the beautiful trees
And the honey collecting bees

If I could fly in the sky
I would fly very high
And see all the white clouds
And below them the crowds

I would fly very low
And see the blue ocean flow
I would fly very high
And see all the birds that go by

All the wonders I'd see
And of course it would be
The most amazing thing
So praise the High King
Sveta Starovoytov, Grade 7
South Sutter Charter School, CA

Stray

They look at me,
I look at them,
Who is she,
And they condemn.

I watch and wonder,
I wait and pray,
Then I ponder,
Around I'm stray.

They interrogate and ask,
Peck and pick,
They remove my mask,
With one click.

Why do they care,
What is it to they,
I am not aware,
That's why I'm asking you today.

What do you want,
To snicker and taunt,
I am a child of God,
So you should not.
Tori Stout, Grade 8
Stapley Jr High School, AZ

The Girl

This girl is athletic;
This girl is sympathetic.

This girl is insecure;
This girl is pure.

She is different,
Not so confident.

She is a nerd,
Not always heard.

She is usually the odd one out,
The girl who people talk about.

She is only plain: thoughtless: wide-eyed,
The girl who everyone leaves outside.

This girl can't blame anyone else,
Only she, herself.

This nobody nothing girl secretly,
She is me.
Victoria Mendoza, Grade 8
Joe Walker Middle School, CA

My Chickens

My chickens, on cool, crisp mornings, are very noisy
Like a flock of geese flying above my house on a cool autumn day
Rooster crowing crow after crow, calling to me to let him out
Hens softly squawking and clucking inside the coop
Still sleepy, not awake, open the door, all run out
Flapping their wings, and running, getting where they want
I drop a small white egg, they come running, devour the egg in 30 seconds
I think "cannibals"
They have beautiful feather patterns; green, blue, brown, all other colors
My chickens gather at the garage doors, waiting to be put in and get treats
I go in and come back with some grain
Behind me the entire way to the coop, other hens near straw bales come running
Flapping their wings, rushing to get their share
At night, they are all perched on their roosts, resting for the next day
They really are more human than animal, they speak to me, softly clucking, telling me how their day went
My chickens are truly amazing creatures, how they speak
Clucking or squawking, crowing or just cocking their little heads
Those chickens, very curious, wanting to know everything, following me wherever I go
Looking in my house at what I am doing
I really wonder what they are thinking in those little heads of theirs
My chickens are truly curious and fascinating creatures.

Michael Cline, Grade 7
Weldon Valley Jr High School, CO

Perfect Mom

The happiness you give to me on a daily basis has touched me inside my heart more than words can say.
People search the world for the perfect mom, a person's happiness lies in the hands of her; as before, she is the perfect mom.
Fate has brought me to you, so you can love me like one of your own and the love you have given me is like I'm the only one.
I swear before the end of our time, if you will believe I'll do nothing, but make you as happy in return.
Your lips upon my head, and just a simple touch across my cheek has opened my heart for many years to come;
to the woman I call my mom.
When around you I feel like I'm six, and nothing can go wrong.
In my heart there will be your image, on my face there will be a smile.
Even if we don't have long, the time is worth the wait.
So take my hand like a child and hold me tight for just a while;
and the day will come where you teach me to be the perfect mom.

Kaianna Gonzales, Grade 9
Colorado Connections Academy, CO

Sweatshirts

It catches my eye as I wander past my closet,
The oversized, smoke-gray hoodie is a symbol of wear.
Looking at it brings back all the good memories, all the adventures.
Forever 21 introduced me to the sweatshirt, the beautiful, velvety black, the candy scent of the store.
But now diminished to the spot at the very back of my closet,
Gray and shedding, pilling, the seams loose, and threads pulled from boring classes.
Examining the cloth, a splattered, orange stain as big as a clementine,
Sends the memory of paintballing with my friends back into my mind.
The remembrance of me crying in the warm covers in my bed, from knowing that my grandpa had gone to a better place.
Then comes a picture of the future, myself all grown up.
A family portrait adorns the side table, a small Justin Bieber backpack hanging from the doorknob awaiting tomorrow's school day
And the oversized sweater warming my skin, soft to the touch.
And I see the world in a different way,
from the past, present, and future.

Gabriella Martinez, Grade 7
Rolling Hills Country Day School, CA

My Puppy's Death

My tears came pouring down as rain,
While I kept thinking in my brain
Why did she have to go away?
But she didn't have to live her life in pain.

Part of me died that day
When my puppy passed away.
She was my friend and pal,
But she had to leave anyway.

She was my friend, she was my all,
She would have been there after my fall
To help me get up and feel better.
And at the end of the day we played ball.

Her green eyes stared right at me.
She closed them and it was her time to leave.
My world crumbled just like pastries
I always loved her and let her free.

Jaqueline Moranchel, Grade 8
John Adams Middle School, CA

Fido the Dog

Each paw had a built in spring,
With that he would bring,
A horrid smell that burned any nose,
And a smooth coat of black and brown fur that shows.

Then my happiness broke to pieces,
As if being eaten by leeches.
My eyes were to burst in tears,
For now I had my fears.

Worry sprung out at me,
I spread his photo for all to see,
But where would he flee?
Would he come back to me?

The memory, forever kept it shall be.
Days got brighter for me to see,
To give a dog a chance,
A chance, with joy, to freely prance.

Karen Rosales, Grade 8
John Adams Middle School, CA

The Mean Across the Room

She constantly makes fun of me
Calling me four eyes and giving me dirty looks
I don't think I can take it anymore
She will not stop spreading rumors
I tell her to stop but she won't listen
I'm now leaving for the day
And will never return
Because of the meanie across the room

Dylan McPhillips, Grade 8
Monte Vista Christian School, CA

Good Friends

Good friends are hard to find,
there aren't many that are kind.
When choosing friends you must look hard,
you must be very on guard.
Some people are mean,
some aren't very keen.
Some are kind of nice,
and aren't cold like ice.
You must look hard when searching for friends.

Some might never have enough.
It may be kind of rough.
Some will never have friends,
that add up by the tens.
It's a pretty ugly act,
and such a sad fact,
that some people will never have friends,
whose friendship never ends.
If only good friends weren't hard to find.

Daniella Huerta, Grade 7
Joe Walker Middle School, CA

Loss by Betrayal

At a new school, the first day of second grade
I felt really worried, I was very afraid
She came and started talking to me
From then she was my best buddy

I used to think she was very nice
I didn't know her heart was cold as ice
I thought that we had so much fun
Playing together under the sun

After a while we started drifting apart
There was a yearning in my heart
The leaves were changing color
The days were long and duller

Now there is coldness in the air
As I remember the color of her hair
She used to act kind to me
Now she is just a memory

Lizeth Garcia, Grade 8
John Adams Middle School, CA

Night Protector

Living in the dark
I'm always watching you
With the stars, moon and shadows
The stars will be your path and eyes
The moonlight is your armor
The shadows will always be your shield and sword
But once the sunrise comes, I'll be locked in your heart
Waiting for the stars to shine again

Alexis Garcia-Vega, Grade 8
Young Scholar's Academy, AZ

The Beach

The beach is a wonderful place
With water blue and so clear
And the sun in your face,

With children playing in the water
Jumping the high tall waves
Like there's no tomorrow,

All kids playing shark
With waves getting stronger and stronger
And the sky getting darker,

It's about time to start a fire
Everyone gathers around
Very warm but so tired,

Roasting marshmallows and singing songs
Telling scary stories and funny jokes
Everyone is happy and jolly singing along,

I love the beach, there's no doubt in my mind
That the beach is so much fun
Just to think of all the seashells I will find,

Driving home is the saddest part
I know I'll be back again one day
With all my friends and family.

Maria Beltran, Grade 8
St Helen Catholic School, CA

To Be Free

Soaring, high above the clouds, full of life
The wind rushing past my face; I am its master
A comforting fire raging throughout my body
The sun glinting on my illustrious scales
This is what it is to be free

Deep in the ocean, lost beauty hides
The sea is mine, to explore and to be
My body, sleek and smooth, moving gracefully
I am here, I am now, where I cannot be found
This is what it is to be free

My legs pumping, I feel the soft earth
I am the wind that flies across the plains
Joy, pure joy; the sun warms my back, filling me with strength
I cannot contain it anymore: my exalted roar fills the sky
This is what it is to be free

Never to fly, gallop, or delve in the deep
Caged, society all around
Work, obligations, expectations, judgment
Always a watchful eye
Is this what it is to be free?

Dylan Johnson, Grade 9
Golden High School, CO

The Lights of the Nights

Lights of the nights in the midnight clear.
All the ringing bells is all you can hear.

As you clatter and chatter about the kingdom,
The arches attached to doors, leads you to freedom.

The animals on the fountain,
Surrounded by steps,

Represents the pennies,
Thrown for the deaths,

The statue of King,
Watching the seems,

Of the lights of the nights,
In the midnight dreams.

Catelyn Baker, Grade 7
Daniel Savage Middle School, CA

Seasons Change

Apple is cider poured in champagne flutes,
and a blanket of snow covers the trees.
White powder tracks in on the soles of boots
and bike racks are used for transporting skis.

On New Year's Night the ball drops in Times Square
as the people raise their glasses and cheer,
but I'm much happier at home than there
with no massive crowd welcoming the year.

It's January and the lights are gone.
Christmas trees have long since been taken down.
Quite soon, the days will begin to grow long
and the grass will be green, not faded brown.

Now the winter snow is melting away
and spring gets closer and closer each day.

Simone Nadel, Grade 9
Monarch High School, CO

Ode to the Willow Tree

Under the willow tree
falling from the top of the tree,
leaves
like chocolate chips falling onto the cookie
melting into the ice cream of joy
sticking to the ground like green sprinkles on ice cream.
Branches,
drooping down like caramel on the cake of delight
reaching to touch the ground with the branches of bliss.
The tree,
glistening like a pile of dessert
That is the willow tree.

Heather Stoddard, Grade 7
Mountain Ridge Jr High School, UT

Success

Success is a word.
A word used when people feel accomplished and content.
Success is more than a word.

Success is a feeling.
A feeling that is felt when your goals have not only been attained, but conquered.
Success is more than a feeling.

Success is a value.
A value that people cherish in their everyday lives because it makes them feel different or distinguished.
Success is more than a value.

Success is a goal.
A goal that is only accomplished when you try your hardest and are happy with your level of work.
Success is more than a goal.

Success is a direction.
A direction for people to follow when they have lost their way and are looking for the path to enlightenment.
Success is more than a direction.

Success is a mindset.
A mindset that is used when people change their normal ways of thinking to doing above and beyond what is required.
Success is more than a mindset.

Success is a lifestyle.
A lifestyle that people live by when they have accepted confidence and determination instead of fear and giving up.
Success is more than a lifestyle.

Colin Gavin, Grade 9
Pine Creek High School, CO

A Girl Asks Her Mother

Where is the glory of the night?
Where are the diamonds and the pearls? Where is the dancer dancing gayly?
Where are the colors that twist and whirl?

There is the glory of the night
Among the twinkling stars, that shine and wink as they dance
While the moon shines from afar
The glorious blue and the shining white provide the glory of the night.

Where is the glory of the night?
Where are those majestic swans? Where is the hunter and the lion?
Where is the treasure that disappears at dawn?

There is the glory of night
In the picture that stars make; that form swans, and hunters, and lions; the treasure that cannot be fake
You cannot see it in morning light, when the sun steps up and the moon alights.

I see the glory of the night
Among the stars that dance and wink,
Forming pictures all the while;
The swan that glides and the lion that winks
I see the glory of the night
Now good night, Mother; I see the glory tonight!

Anushree Thekkedath, Grade 7
Stratford Elementary/Middle School, CA

Woodward

Camping at Woodward
tents, campfire and blue water
green bushes everywhere
the smells of burning fire wood
ducks in the water,
people sitting around a campfire
singing those campfire songs
swimming in the lake, going jet skiing,
with my family,
yeah that's the Woodward
Woodward reminds me of
a forest, calm and restful
Woodward means peace and
happiness to me
Yeah that's Woodward
Samantha Beasley, Grade 8
Ripona Elementary School, CA

Nature

Water crashing down
Down the waterfall it goes
It is full of peace

Plants are very nice
They move as the wind blows through them
Plants are a beauty

Baby birds hatching
All beneath the willow trees
New life will start soon

The north wind is blowing
Rolling over hills of sand
Imitating waves
Ani Rashe, Grade 7
Monte Vista Christian School, CA

Squataholic

Dear Volleyball Coach,
I would like to tell you
Squats are ridiculous
You tell me
Go lower
You tell me
I can do better
I would like to tell you
Squats make me sore
So during our next encounter
When the ball falls short
And you raise your deep voice
Say you owe me a minute
I'll remember when
Yours didn't go over either.
Rachel Wachter, Grade 7
Falcon Creek Middle School, CO

Everyday Adventure

I woke up in the morning
Feeling happy as can be
I went down to the kitchen
Looking for something to eat

We were out of cereal
So I ran out to the store
But the clerk at the counter told me
They too needed more

I went from town to town
Looking in every place
Eventually I asked myself
If there was any left in the human race

It turns out the people
Who made cereal had left
They went back to their planet
And they took all of their chefs

We moaned and we sobbed
Our hearts were all beat
Breakfast just wasn't breakfast
Without cereal to eat
Nolan McCool, Grade 8
Young Scholar's Academy, AZ

In the Backyard

The mulberry tree
Bare
Verdant buds sprout
Blossoming into emerald leaves

A swing
Dangling from two ropes
A girl laughing
As she soars

Branches
In a pile
Built into a ladder
Leading to the sky

Sitting high
Sunset golden
Talking among the leaves
Soft breeze blowing

Laughter, peace
Accomplishment
All my best memories
In the backyard
Pearl Zhou, Grade 7
North Star Academy, CA

Love

Love is a piano
it can be
soothing
calm
loud
You might need a rest from it,
but it always gives you a melody
You might have a minor or
Major
Fight
Maybe you need a staff
to settle things
There's always going to be those
Black and white
Moments
in a relationship
It can last forever
or
Break in half
Lily Le, Grade 8
Falcon Creek Middle School, CO

Time

In a blink of an eye
From the autumn leaves
'Till the summer breeze
The hand ticks by

Developing friendships
Whispering secrets
We've been writing fairy tales
In our fantasy book

Chasing stars and reaching out
To capture our dreams and about
The world is shaking
My heart starts racing

A tear drops from my eye
I remember all those times
From the autumn leaves
'Till the winter sky
Christine Nguyen, Grade 7
Sarah McGarvin Intermediate School, CA

Blue Is...

Blue is like the ocean.
It reminds me of
the cold breezy
days in the winter.
Blue
Hailie Bangloy, Grade 7
Daniel Savage Middle School, CA

Dear Dora

Dear Dora the Explorer,
I would like to tell you,
you're foolish.
You tell me:
"Where's the mountain?"
You tell me:
"Backpack, backpack, backpack, yeah!"
You tell me:
"Vamanos!"
I would like to tell you:
You make me furious!
So during our next encounter
If I turn on the channel and see you in front of a mountain
and you ask a question you can answer yourself
and if I see your introduction for "Dora, Dora, Dora the
Explorer, Vamanos!"
That will truly be the end!

Ariel Kennedy, Grade 7
Falcon Creek Middle School, CO

Home

Through the sliding door and into the backyard are good times.
The good times with friends and family in the backyard.

The backyard has lots of fun and knee scraped memories.
Where people enjoy life.

The place where the dogs dig their holes.
Where people enjoy life.

Moms have these rules while in the backyard.
To be careful and dogs not to be digging.

Obviously the rules are bound to be bended.
With all of this, it contains memories.

Their unforgettable memories.
The backyard, that was the place.

Brandon Arias Jr., Grade 8
Richardson PREP HI Middle School, CA

Wishes

What if people could fly?
I might actually see the whole world.
What if people never died?
I could do everything I wanted to do.
What if everything I touched turned to gold?
I would be rich.
What if everything that occurred in fairy tales
came true in real life?
I could live in a castle.
What if bullies stopped bullying people?
The world could finally be peaceful.
What if everything I wished for came true?

Reychel Morris, Grade 7
Falcon Creek Middle School, CO

Ageless

How old am I?

I am older than adventure,
younger than danger.

Old enough to know reality,
young enough to still imagine.

I am old enough to share my knowledge,
yet still young enough to learn something new.

I am old enough to cry for a reason,
too young to deal with the pain.

I am old enough to be big and tall,
But young enough to still grow.

How old am I?
For I have no age...

I am forever young,
Everlasting aged.

I am everyone's age,
5 to 92

Everyone is my age,
which is no age at all.

Sandrine Nguyen, Grade 7
Our Lady of Fatima School, CA

A Dog Is a Car

A dog is a car.
It needs expensive fuel for energy
And it may "honk" at people who encounter it.

You have to control it
Or it gets out of control.

When it gets in a crash or gets in trouble
You have to be like an adult.

It destroys things
Which you're supposed to fix.

When it leaks oil
You have to be in charge and clean it up.

Some hate it,
But some like it.
The car can be out of control
Or it can be smooth on the road.
You have to be responsible for all of it.
A car can be a real pain.

Tyler Nguyen, Grade 8
Falcon Creek Middle School, CO

If You Vanished?

What would you do
if your friend won't acknowledge you?
What would you think
if nobody noticed you?

How would you feel
if you were ignored?
If you were insulted?
if you vanished to the background?

No one noticing
nobody caring,
that you were broken inside and out.
Their lives going on without you.

But soon there will be this one special person.
A person who will make you laugh,
who will make you smile forever,
who will be there when you need them.

That one unique, amazing, beautifully, special person
who is just for you.
For you to depend on for you to count on.
They are there for you

Forever and always…that person is your special LOVE.
Tiana Lohmiller, Grade 8
American Heritage Academy, AZ

I Am Who I Am

I am Georyet Alexandra Corsey Uribe Stopani
And I am who I am.

I am James and Veronica's daughter.
I am from Ensenada, Baja California, Mexico.
I am from the beach and from the sand and the waves.
I am from the cold breeze of the ocean early every morning.
I am from churros, locos, and fish tacos.

I am a writer and a dreamer.
I am tall and I am stubborn.
I am from the stories of my father's childhood.
I am from the stories of how my parents first met.
I am from cold snowy days in Denver.
I am from the memories of my first pet, now gone.

I am from the breezy warm afternoons spent with my cousin.
I am from the adventures at Puerto Escondido, "the hidden cove."
I am from the shadows of my own sister.
I am from dirt roads, graffiti walls, and mosquito bites.
My name is much more than a title, it is me and it is all that I am.

I am Georyet Alexandra Corsey Uribe Stopani
And I am who I am.
Georyet Corsey, Grade 9
Colorado Connections Academy, CO

Ode to Dance

Above the girl's dance
light drops from the ceiling,
dance, like a swan,
swimming gracefully through glassy water,
skirting the edge of the stage,
leaping into the air and floating down like petals from a rose.

They watch, with wide eyes and gaping mouths
as she jumps across the stage.

Her skirt bounces like a floppy Frisbee
as she turns perfectly as if she was a top,
her head whipping around
her eyes like an arrow meeting its target.

The soothing music slows,
as she finishes the wonderfully choreographed dance
with a pose, her white teeth forming into a smile.

The applaud echoes throughout the whole building
as she stands up to bow, the clapping crescendoing,
her glittering golden costume reflecting the stage lights
over her head, like glittering gold stars.

Her shining face beaming at her accomplishment,
she turns and gracefully runs off stage.
Aubrie Aagard, Grade 7
Mountain Ridge Jr High School, UT

Runaway Love

My Justin Bieber doll he meant so very much to me
That doll made me feel as if we were the only ones
I treated that doll fair and it might've felt care
At night I'd make sure it was perfect like a square
When it was, I'd squeeze it hard and hold it tight

I never slept alone, it would be with me
The doll was as handsome as the real Justin
It was so lovely and realistic
Something you would like to cherish way past forever
I'd look at my doll, I saw it bright as ever but I'd doze off

My whole family knew I loved that doll, it was so obvious
The doll and me were like two peas in a pod
The doll was unbelievably cute
It might've taken you're breathe away if you've seen it
It was imperfectly perfect

My last days with my doll were so beautiful
It was so intense, I was shocked at a horrible scene
One lonely evening, I went into my room, no doll was at sight
I cried and tried looking for my doll
I sniffed and wiped my last tear away
It was a silent night
Caroline Rodriguez, Grade 8
John Adams Middle School, CA

We Are Marines

We are marines,
Rough and tough,
Violent and unclean

We are marines,
Great fighters
Work as well as a machine

It is the perseverance
That makes us tough
We lead our lives with guidance

It is the humility
That makes us great fighters,
Serving for our country

It is the Obedience
That makes us concentrated
To lead our nation to brilliance

We are the eyes in the military,
We are the hands of the nation,
We are the police of the world.

We are marines that serve our country,
We are marines that serve our world,
We are marines that serve our God.
Immanuel Kyun, Grade 8
Falcon Creek Middle School, CO

Time

Time brings us many things
Like the past into the present
My future in my hands
Or a memory stuck, spread across the land
Fade away, fade away
Far Far from the past

Tears and sorrow
Not today, not tomorrow
Laugher to cries
Dreams into lies
Fade away, fade away
Do not stay in the present

Our minds digging deeper
Rage, passion, love and hate
Open as a book
Yet locked in chains
Tangled in my own vines
Wondering about what's next
But to never forget what happened
Fade away, fade away
Do not come soon, future.
Sabrina Zahid, Grade 7
Gale Ranch Middle School, CA

The Journey

Though my heart was set on being the best
Trying to impress and be like the rest,
I loved the sound of my own tune
And followed it and was not to ruin

The dream I set my heart on firmly
Was not going to make me worry
No matter the names nor stick nor stone
I decided to let my free heart roam.

The journey taught my mind the most,
To be kind and loving and not to boast
The fears of my past were now behind me
It was easy to follow my pure hearts plea

Don't give up my dear friend
For like a seed you're not close to the end
And everyone has a dream to pursue
Discovering is half the work for you

Although my heart was set on being the best
I decided to follow my dream to success
And the product was worth so much to me
It filled my heart with a love like the sea
Eleanor Persing, Grade 8
Monte Vista Christian School, CA

The Love They Leave

To love someone in life,
is to love someone in death,
for it seems we love them stronger,
when from this world they've left.

In time the spirit passes,
balance is in view.
Memories will heal,
or memories undo.

With love comes pain,
that loss of life borrows,
because it is replaced,
by weight of lover's sorrows.

In the stars we see their faces
in the wind we hear them sing.
We are carried through this life,
by the love they bring.

Each generation passing,
the love they leave takes flight.
We have the greatest tools,
to make our future bright.
Matthew Pimley, Grade 8
Meridian Elementary School, CA

Rainstorm

"Pitter-pat"
Gentle sound,
Rain come near;
Hear my cries,
Burn my tears.

"Stomp! Slam!"
Doors slam in
Your untimely haste;
Hear my screams,
Blow away my fears.

Rumbling skies,
Flash of light:
You bring me fright,
My never ending fears.

"Crash!"
Trees frantically
Obeying your dubious plans,
"Slap!"
The hard bark
Against the wet concrete,
You've left now.
Taylor Motley, Grade 7
Stapley Jr High School, AZ

Lost

Mistreated as a child
Confused from the start
My hands deepest black
My heart broken and lost

Misjudged by the outside
Mislead by my color
Why can't I be understood
Or be the sweet color of butter

By dawn I work
By night I read
Always alone my voice unheard
I cry out in pain and need

As my soul begins to whither
And my voice begins to quiver
I try to buck up my spirit
For the end near to come

But I fight for my race
Never backing down
For when you're one of a kind
You get used to feeling all alone
Trace Webb, Grade 7
Brentwood School, CA

Kindergarten

The first day of kindergarten
In the middle of August.
New backpacks, new lunch boxes,
And numerous new faces.
The bell blares and gives us all a jolt.

Some kids are crying, not wanting
Their moms to leave their tiny hands.
What will we do?
Is the teacher nice?
These are the questions I ask myself.

We creep through the door
Of room ten, and see
Colorful books, pointy crayons,
Shiny desks, and a young teacher
Who greets us with a reassuring smile.

"Hello class," Mrs. Hatos says
With a voice as soft as silk.
"We will have a lot of fun this year,"
She says with a twinkle in her eye.
I let out a sigh of relief.
My road to education has just begun.
Brigg Trendler, Grade 7
Stapley Jr High School, AZ

Music

Music is meditation to life.
It is what keeps me calm.
My sweet release to freedom
from this psychotic world we live in.

Music is meditation to life.
The mantras I need
to keep me striving forward.
But sometimes these mantras
lead us to believe
the most absolute bizarre things.

Music is meditation to life
but can also be a sin
if you give in to the wrong genre.
Some music will talk about God,
and the little things that make us happy.
Other music will distribute death,
drugs, sex, and hatred.
The foul things of which
ruin our very minds and soul.

Music is meditation to life.
It is what completes my person as a whole.
Alaura Stepina, Grade 8
Falcon Creek Middle School, CO

Forgotten

Am I that rag in the corner
Or a piece of forgotten dust?
Then I'm noticed I'm loved!
Then they forget again.

I wish I was a dog,
A cat — or even a bird
But I'm not!
I'm just forgotten.

They treat me like a pet rock,
Or a decoration.
Sometimes I'm fed,
Sometimes I'm forgot

All I've done all my life
Is watch and swim…back and forth?
That's why it sucks to be me…
Just a fish.
Nathan Davis, Grade 7
Joe Walker Middle School, CA

My Silent Crimes

I close my eyes and I see it,
Standing there…staring
Looking into my soul
Warning me of my silent crimes

I shield my face, yet I still see it
Shaking it's head back and forth
Looking into my mind
Threatening to reveal my silent crimes

I fall asleep…is it gone?
No…it is still there, moaning
I toss and turn to avoid it
My paranoia overwhelms me

I reveal my silent crimes
Suddenly, it disappears
The weight it has left vanishes
Guilt is my silent crime
Andrew Nelson, Grade 9
Eaton High School, CO

Come Along

Sometimes I stroll along a street,
Seeing scenes someone else has seen.
Sucking on the sweet-sour smog of the city,
I seize the news and make my segue
Singing songs no one else dared sing.
Seldom do I select another soul to share
These walks, but I seize the moment
And ask you to come along.
Jenny Chiu, Grade 9
American High School, CA

Little Miss Giggles

She's always giggling,
We even call her Ms. Giggles,
She cracks jokes as fast as cheetahs,
Always smiling silly smiles,
The laughter you hear is probably hers,
Forever jolly and grand.

She's the light to the darkness,
Whenever we feel down,
Clowns could use her advice,
To not scare kids at night.

No wonder Ms. Giggles is always laughing,
Her mind's always filled with jokes,
I wonder what it would feel like,
To be Little Miss Giggles for a day.
Meredith Quintana, Grade 7
Daniel Savage Middle School, CA

The World of Books

I am battling fierce dragons
I am in a forbidden romance
I am riding on a magical unicorn
I am a unsolvable quarrel
I am transported through time
I am in a hot air balloon going
Higher and higher
I am in a world of magical spells
I am solving a murder case
I am dancing in the clouds
I let out cheery guffaws
I am in a different year,
A different time
I am in my own surreal world
Until I close the cover
Instantaneous reality
Gianna Giorno, Grade 7
Salida Middle School, CO

The Barnyard Blues

In the summertime it gets very hot
I have to go work the animals for awhile
I have to work with them with a smile
I have to work with them if I like it or not

The cows need to be watered and grained
The horses need to be fed
These chores are such a pain
They make me feel dead

Then after it all the dogs need to be walked
And the cats need to be petted
The goats need to be tended to
The barnyard blues.
Hanson Brudevold, Grade 9
New Plymouth High School, ID

A World of Written Word

Crackling pages sigh in relief, oily hands skim through the paper
Its cuts are nothing compared to words that cut your hard shield with a fictional saber

You can fight with daemons and soar with eagles, drift to destinations in descriptive dreams
Only there you see the magic of reading where nothing is ever what it seems

Books are the bridge between fantasy and reality, where thoughts and dreams splash in its water
A whole new world behind old tattered pages brought to life by a palatial author

You feel the sting of ice-cold water and taste the hot desert air
Printed text will spring to life when seconds shall be spent and spared

It speaks in a whole different language, one that all readers can comprehend
The electric touch of paper and words to a higher level your mind transcends

When you feel life could use a fresh look, just close off reality and open a book

Camille Roberts, Grade 8
The Mirman School, CA

Rain

There's darkness all around me, and I catch that last glance of the shining silver moon above me.
Dark gray clouds roll in, teaming up and covering the sky, looking down at me with powerful but promising expressions.

As the first few raindrops fall, I see there's only the rain and me outside enjoying ourselves.
In front of my eyes, the raindrops seem as if they are falling diamonds, making their journey to earth, and then rest undisturbed.

I stand there, on the wet ground, letting the rain water soak me, cooling and refreshing me.
I stand there, inhaling the aroma of fresh water all around me.
I stand there, listening to the constant drumbeat of the rain splashing to the ground.
I stand there, and feel the cold air around me, mingling with the rain.

When each little drop falls on me, I feel happiness from within, never wanting to move from this place in time.
When each little drop falls on me, I turn a few years younger, am carefree, and simply enjoy myself.

But when the last few raindrops fall to the ground, and the rain stops all together, I stand there, all wet and dripping.
I stand there very, very, still…

Krupa Prajapati, Grade 8
South Lake Middle School, CA

In the Woods

We sit on the rocks and watch day leave and be replaced by night.
We all go quiet and listen to the night creatures as they come out to play.
Everyone gathers around and the adults tell stories about the *old days* back in their home towns.
I tilt my head up to the sky as the words of the adults begin to take me away,
And I see the moon is full and beautiful, the warm, inviting night is dotted with brilliant stars,
And then I realize something.
All of us are gathered here together under the watch of the moon,
Protected by the water and the forest around us.
Everyone is at ease,
And for the first time in a long time,
We all are at home.

Karla A. Carcamo, Grade 9
Oak Hills High School, CA

Where I Am From

I am from cookies, cake, and ice cream.
I am from recitals and music.
I am from talkers, and under-exaggerators
I am from parades, and big holiday dinners.
I am from hot cocoa, and sweets filling my house.
I am from the popsicle eaters and campers.
I am from four-wheelers zooming along.
I'm from, "Be quiet I can't hear the T.V!"
I'm from the football watchers.
I'm from swimming in water.
I'm from funeral potatoes, warm and cheesy.
I'm from loudness, coming from everywhere.
I am from warm beds, cuddly and soft.
I am from Super Bowls.
I am from Diane and Beverly.
I am from Mike and Juli.
I'm from Smithfield.
I'm from Greece.

Will Weber, Grade 7
White Pine Middle School, UT

Serenity

On a dim, obscure night,
the gray clouds are forming.
There is scarce moonlight and it is darker at dusk.
The foaming water rushes and crashes on the shoreline.
Tumbling waves are raging with disordered turbulence.
The wind is rough as it carries the foul salt.
As the tide rises, it curls, collapses
and collides with a rapid downfall.
The wild storm is nearer
and upon the assault,
there's a flash and a rambunctious clash
of electric discharge at the eye of the outbreak.
Although there is the onslaught of the violent disturbances,
there comes an opposing contrary of unstoppable stillness.
And deep down inside, amid the aggression
is an indestructible state of harmony and
tranquility called…
Peace.

Blake Olsen, Grade 8
Payson Jr High School, UT

The Ride of Life

Life is like a roller coaster
There are ups and downs and loopy loops that make you nauseous
So imagine,
There you are at the beginning of the ride
You're feeling carefree and have nothing to worry about
But as you go up, your stomach feels hollow
As you're at the tippy-top, you just think
"Do I really belong in this world? Just let me die."
Then whoosh
You dive down, just going with the flow
But you just wish you could just get off this wreck
Then comes the loopy loops with all the complications mixing in
As you continue, everything starts slowing down
You reached the end, everything stops here.
That's it.
Nothing Left.
It's the end of your journey.
Life may not be perfect, but live it well because you only live once.

Katherine Tran, Grade 7
Sarah McGarvin Intermediate School, CA

Pressure Point

Game point;
Twenty-six to twenty-five.
I am serving.
The pressure weighs down on me like a ton of bricks.
The crowd's eyes are all on me.
I watch the ref.
He blows his blue whistle and motions for me to serve.
With no more thought, I toss the ball high in the air.
A perfect back spin.
I move toward the ball.
'SMACK.'
I watch it go flying;
Soaring over the net right to the libero.
'No...'
She shanks the ball to the right.
Dropping to my knees, the crowd forms around me.
I am speechless.
We are champions.

Emily Olson, Grade 7
Mountain Ridge Jr High School, UT

Green

Green is the grass, touching my shoe
Green is the leaf, falling on my head
Green is the marker, staining my paper
Green is a salad, covering my plate
Green is a four-leaf clover, giving me luck
Green is my Christmas tree, sitting in my living room
Green is money, filling my wallet
Green is a tennis ball, getting hit my by racquet
Green is the M&M, being eaten by my dog
Green is the frog, getting kissed by the princess

Ximena Posada, Grade 7
St John's Episcopal School, CA

Bullying

Bullying can be as little as one word
And no matter if it spreads or not, it is always heard
People think, "oh it's just one sentence…what is the damage?"
But forgetting the words that have been said is a challenge
Almost 3 million students are being bullied each year
And sometimes the consequences of their words are severe
So from now on, think of life as one big plate
One side is love
And one side is hate
Now which side would you rather take?

Kelsey Gehl, Grade 7
Monte Vista Christian School, CA

Good Bye

My dog was a chocolate Labrador
Her name was Libby she was there from the start
In my heart I love her so very much
She had allergies and played all day
And she broke in to trash cans and ate all the garbage

As she grew she slowly started losing her eye sight
And started moving slower and slower

Until finally one day she left my world forever

Doesn't mean she's now gone forever, I still love her
She still in my mind and my heart
It was hard, I did cry, I didn't want
To say good bye

Life goes by, day upon day
We laugh we cry
Even if we don't know it we
We all hate to say, "Good Bye."

Delilah Steinmann, Grade 7
Monte Vista Christian School, CA

Reflecting

Returning from a day
Of red-marked blunders,
I remove my drenched coat, settle down
On the couch to watch the rain keep pouring.
In gloom I ponder the drops smacking the window,
Overflowing the gutters, and reflecting my tearful hours.

Returning from a day
Of sleep-inducing lectures,
I remove my damp jacket, settle down
On the couch to watch the rain keep dripping.
With fatigue I brood over drops sliding down glass,
Mirroring charcoal skies, and reflecting my tired times.

Returning from a day
Of mind-opening headway,
I remove my dewy sweater, settle down
On the couch to watch the rain keep sprinkling.
At ease I revel in drops disappearing on the panes,
Leaving rainbow sparkles, and reflecting my sunny seasons.

Michelle Shen, Grade 9
Saratoga High School, CA

Friendship

Friendship is like a Christmas morning
Friendship is a orange red sky on a summers night
Friendship is as fragile as a thin glass ball
Friendship sounds like ocean waves
Friendship feels like you accomplished the impossible
Friendship looks like children playing in the leaves of fall.

Ryan Higginbotham, Grade 7
Daniel Savage Middle School, CA

Never-ending Journey

The night darkened by, as the time wore on.
The dim light of the moon, the dim light of the stars;
The night was never more dark than tonight.
Tomorrow, it shall be brighter.
For they will not carry the sorrow that they do now.

The sound of the clock, the small movement of the pendulum,
All — all ticked slowly, for it had not been slower —
As if it was too heavy to move,
As if it had too much burden to carry;
Hearken; it carried the sorrow that will be no more forever.

Yes, I now saunter around the place,
The place where I must weep over, no matter how blithe I am.
I must weep; for my own sorrow tells me so
For I cannot withstand the scene
But I could not prevent it, for I am merely a mortal.

Facing the never-ending journey that separated my second self,
I could not reach, not even to grasp him for the last time.
Yet, all I could do; within my power
Was to weep over, to cry out in despair.
Now I carry a burden forever, for it torments my heart.

All I can say, all I can manage to say is "In pace requiescat."

Seungil Lee, Grade 8
Huntington Middle School, CA

Dark and Light

I am Brandon, Dark Dragon of the White Fortress

Son of David and Fey, their only heir
Brother of no one and everyone
I worry I will not accomplish what I set out to do
I cry for no one and everyone
I dream of dragons

I am Brandon, Dark Dragon of the White Fortress

I wonder about the circle of life
I need a day of free time but I'll take an hour
I hear my friends laughing in delight
I want to be in the circle of warmth and light
Protected and shielded from the fire

I am Brandon, Dark Dragon of the White Fortress

I love my mother with a thousand hearts
I depend on my father's faith and allegiance to me
I'll fight for my dad's steaks and world peace
I know at the end of the day,
I have accomplished one good deed

I am Brandon, Dark Dragon of the White Fortress

Brandon Wu, Grade 7
Rolling Hills Country Day School, CA

Life as a Fashion Designer

I live in a penthouse
Of my fashion house in Paris
Where my new collection is made
While in magazines
Trends fade and fade
Those who are critics
Who say my work will never go out of style
Are lying
Designers like me spend hours
Searching for the perfect textiles
Back in my workshop
I put together pieces
On a live model
Who can pose and give feedback
Backstage of a fashion show
Stylists fix up hair and makeup
While I am proud of my designs

Baomy Van, Grade 7
Sarah McGarvin Intermediate School, CA

My Magnificent Mother

Oh, my dearest mother
You know I love you so
I know you love me too
There is no need to show.

I love what you do for me
Anything you can
I couldn't return the favor
Even if I ran

And did all these things,
Whatever you want
It would never make up for
Times like you taking me to restaurants.

In conclusion, I have to say
You are always there, night and day.

Jason Christensen, Grade 7
Daniel Savage Middle School, CA

Grandma

Looking around
wondering why?
She was so…perfect.
Kind, loving, impossibly understanding
Completely selfless
I know she is in a better place
But can't help wishing she were here
I've never seen Grandpa cry before today
And as we let those pink balloons float
Out of our sights
I know in my heart I will never forget her.
Grandma

McKenzie Ray, Grade 9
New Plymouth High School, ID

That One Love

That one love,
the one you think about,
every second of every day

The one you say is true,
and let nothing get in the way,
of how you feel and what you want to say

Because you think
it is everything you could wish for,
until it comes crashing down.

That one love that never lasts,
and just becomes
another part of the past.

That one love,
adults don't believe is possible,
because in truth, you are too young.

You think that one so-called love
will be forever,
but in the end it wasn't really ever.

That one love,
that young love,
the one that doesn't exist…

Yatzyl Lajud, Grade 8
St Helen Catholic School, CA

Moving Onward

In a world filled with changes
each and every day,

I feel I'm being judged
for what I do and say.

I remember back to preschool
and play days at the park,

When I didn't give a though about
other people's remarks.

Now I'm looking in the mirror,
I see to my surprise,

A completely different person
staring in my eyes.

The care free boy
I knew at age of 4 and 5,

Is now becoming a teen,
just trying to survive…

Gabe Arciniega, Grade 8
Christ the King School, AZ

Not My Brother's Keeper

I have an annoying brother
whom I'd gladly trade for another.
It's really not my fault at all
that we share the same mother.
Why, I even have a number to call
in case we ever run into each other

"Help, you're my brother!" He yelps.
"Aurghh please don't remind me!" I say.
But when no-one else comes and helps
I'll be there, to take the troubles away

I have an annoying brother
whom I'd gladly trade for another.
Seriously, I really do mean it.
Don't give me that look!
Excuse me, I'll be back in a bit
after I help him with homework.

James Yang, Grade 7
South Lake Middle School, CA

Silver Stallion

Silver stallion moonlit hill,
Gray ghost standing still.
Rustling leaves make him prance.
Hooting owl, he starts to dance.
Wild eyes make fiery pools,
Flinty hooves like dancing jewels.

Running across the grassy plains,
Herd of mares flowing manes.
Waving banners, tails held high,
Galloping under the midnight sky.
silver stallion in the lead,
Forever freedom is their creed.

Single stallion galloping fast,
Hoping the moment will forever last.
Rising sun in the air,
Stallion does not give a care.

Dane Nelson, Grade 7
Joe Walker Middle School, CA

Red

Red is a strawberry, filling up my stomach
Red is a rose, growing in my garden
Red is an apple, falling off my apple tree
Red is a bird, flying across the sky
Red is a starfish, living in the ocean
Red is a fire truck, saving people's lives
Red is a heart, pumping inside your body
Red is a ladybug, crawling on the grass
Red is a cherry, topping my ice cream
Red is a Crayola, coloring my paper

Regina Valenzuela, Grade 7
St John's Episcopal School, CA

Saying Goodbye

I watched through tearful eyes as she packed her bags and life away from me
My heart felt so heavy I could barely stand to see her off
It felt as if I was weighed down with bricks and weights and words I should have said
but when the time came, all I could say in a creaking was goodbye
I cried, but my tears had run dry, so all I could do was watch helplessly as she walked away
but suddenly she turned and said to me, "I could travel the world, even to a different planet,
but there would never be anybody like my family, and you remember that, I'll always be coming
  home." And thus my sister went to the exotic and dangerous life of college, but I always
remember her words and say goodbye with a lighter heart.

Beth Lopez, Grade 7
Christ the King School, AZ

Christmas

As the cold wind blows and the snow falls the warmness of the room warms my heart
Simple pleasures become life treasures and soon stay locked in your heart and mind forever

Like the Christmas star finishes the last touch on the Christmas tree, you top my life and complete it with joy and happiness
Like the bright lights outside shine threw out the night, you brighten my life
Like the snowflakes fall and make you want to play in the snow, you make me want to smile
Like the Christmas gifts under the tree make you want to give, you bring to me the most valuable one of all —
Having you here next to me on this cold December night

Flor Cancino, Grade 7
Isbell Middle School, CA

The Volleyball Court

The volleyball court, ivory tile with hard concrete underneath, a metal pole covered with padding,
a sky scraping net, and a daring black line warning you not to trespass,
The smells of teenage sweat, no longer the smell of bleach,
The taste of Snickers as the children watch intensely,
I feel, as it is my home, a place to just play the game without worrying,
only the fear of losing keeps us rambunctious and ready to win,
All I hear is the silence of the crowd when ready to serve,
then the ecstatic voices as I got the point leading us to victory!

Jennica Baldwin, Grade 8
Ripona Elementary School, CA

Idaho

With winding roads through the hills, bears teaching their cubs, and lakes sparkling in the sun.
Open spaces of natural green, and waterfalls you can swim under.
One last thing is the change of seasons.
Dad and family take a place, but so does the smell of barbecues on weekends, and friends I count as family.
Dad works to fix his truck and friends go about doing their regular school work.
The sun peeks over the round hills. It transforms the land into a menagerie of different sights.
This place represents home and where my life began.
This is a place where I feel I fit in.

Jessie Estrada, Grade 8
Ripona Elementary School, CA

Reflections on Rodin's Sculpture "Thought"

The lady in this sculpture
Looks sad
And alone in her own world,
Trying to fight
The pain.

Manuel Ayala, Grade 7
Tenaya Middle School, CA

Halloween

As night time approaches the tiny little town.
The round yellow moon hangs bright in the sky.
It lights up the trees all around.
Excited little children are getting in gear to gather
candy on the scariest night of the year.

Annie Carpenter, Grade 7
CA

Loss of a Dog

oh friend, do you recall
when you came to this house and made it yours
you were just a ball of fluff
not even halfway grown

but there won't be any thunderstorms,
and no vets with shots up there,
you won't even need a leash
you could run free in the air

and when my time on earth is done
and at heaven's gate i'm near
i don't won't any harp or harps
just…your barks to hear

so, see you later, little friend
i'm glad your now pain free
and i'm glad your up there with Jesus
now…you wait for me over there i'm not too far from there

Gerardo Ramirez, Grade 8
John Adams Middle School, CA

Silence of Deep Snow

I sunk deep into the snow,
So deep I forgot light.
But in the depths of eternal darkness,
There was no warmth in the silent night.

Thrice, I tried to light flames to life,
But was again put to death by ice.
Seconds, minutes, hours, days, weeks, years,
Yet never, did summer arrive.

I waited and waited in the cold, cold night,
And kept walking down the sea of snow,
Until a faint voice whispered to me,
"Turn back now and you'll make it out alive."

But too late did I realize,
And never, will I love again,
For love is like a double-edged sword,
Yet without it, the world is at its end.

Warinthorn Chuenbumrung, Grade 8
Joe Walker Middle School, CA

Love Fades

Some people say that love is forever
Some people say that love is doomed
I do not care what those people believe
Because I believe that love fades
Some people say that it's not true
Some people say that no words have been truer
No matter what those people say
I will forever believe love fades

Elisia Medina, Grade 9
Arrupe Jesuit High School, CO

The Last Song

Their favorite song was on as she cried
Her tears fell like water droplets and hoped they lied.
She sat alone in her room, the air was dense
They say her father had died.

As night started to fall,
She couldn't bear it at all.
Her eyes sparkled in the dim light
Yet her smile was not so bright.

At his funeral she smiled
But she only stayed a while.
The warmth of the sun fell upon her
From that day on she became stronger.

After her father's death
With every breath
Everyone took one look
As she played, the last song.

Blanca Marquez, Grade 8
John Adams Middle School, CA

My Grandma

My grandma was sweet as honey,
Beautiful as a peony;
Skin white as snow and lips red as blood.
When she left me I filled with agony.

When I think of her my heart is light.
She was a special person a steer delight.
Thoughts of her drive the darkness away.
The thought of her smile makes me feel alight.

She was always there,
There for my affaire.
I always felt safe.
Aye to say beware.

Even after she left I felt secure.
Someone to make sure scars cure.
Even though I miss her a lot,
I smile or at least I procure.

Alitzel Cervantes, Grade 8
John Adams Middle School, CA

The Movies

She is the loud boom of the surround system.
She is the quick pop of the popcorn.
She is the double ping of the pinball machine.
She is the babble of the people entering and exiting.
She is the obvious crumpling of candy wrappers in the silence.
She is the piercing scream of the seat as you pull it down.
She is the crunch of nachos as they break between your teeth.
She is Hanna.

Ellen Bake, Grade 8
Lewis & Clark Middle School, ID

Nobody's Flawless

Computers think they're so great
Because they always get things right.

Humans are like lopsided tables,
They can hold things up there,
But there's a chance they fall out from the side.

Sometimes I feel like
I'm the only lopsided table there is.
But I know that
Nobody's flawless.

One wrong step
And you can end up with
A mouthful of grass.

One false move
And you can end up
Ruining something and breaking a heart.

But mistakes can lead to greatness.
Like, inventing something new,
Or simply cheering up a friend.

Making mistakes seem like
Nothing.

Armida Calderon Quezada, Grade 7
Canyon View Jr High School, UT

Best Friends

Through ups and downs they say
That best friends are forever
But where were you that day
Or any other for that matter

You changed yourself because a dream
That we used to see together
But times, like you, have surely changed
And to go back, I wouldn't ever

It's not my fault you see
I tried to make this work
It was you who pushed and pulled
On your face, a sinister smirk

I think you should stand down
From that pedestal you praise
And look at who your friends are now
Your new boyfriend, and the lies he lays

We are now like broken glass
That will never be picked up
Both damage beyond repair
I hope you're happy in your world of despair

Jessica Lewis, Grade 9
New Plymouth High School, ID

My Best Friend Forever

I lost a friend today
My little dog that used to lay
Her tiny head upon my knee
Who shared her thoughts with me

High up in the sky of heaven today
A dog angel waits
I wish I had you back again, to fill this empty space
But one day we'll be together in a better place

Although my eyes are filled with tears
I appreciate these happy years
For spending time down here with me
After all your love and loyalty

But on the other hand I wish I could tell you
How empty I feel
Therefore a part of me went with you
Indeed a part of time that can't heal

Oh I just wish I could hear you again
To touch your fur again
To see your goldish fur
And to hear your purr

Bye Princess

Kelly Ramirez, Grade 8
John Adams Middle School, CA

Anthem to Hope

Under the dark dampening veil of oppression
A light shines above like the summer sun
Glimmering on all who choose to see it
But not without a willing risk

The lost turn to this in their time on need
Looking for warmth in the eyes of the light
And once they find it they all but pray
For that shining shimmer of freedom

Hope is more than just a word on a page
It can unite a people together, as one
To fight the entire tyrannical world
And fly off if on the wings of doves

But hope can carry us out of the silence
With that feeling of warmth we all desperately desire
Away from the mocking limits of cruelty
And to taste the sweetness of freedom

Hope has us believe in things that we doubt
The ideals and convictions that we have always had
Hope guides and nurtures you toward your everlasting goal
Whatever it may be just have hope

Josh Knoller, Grade 9
The Mirman School, CA

Chitter, Chatter

"Chitter, chatter!" quips the cardinal, merry,
Perching in the wide oak tree—
Refusing to eat ev'n one berry,
But chirping a haunting melody.

Blue eyes twinkle in the sunlight
As red, feathery wings take to the sky.
She slowly glides like a flying kite,
Letting out a contented sigh.

Orange flames color the air,
Sinking with the fading sun.
She alights on her branch with care,
Acknowledging that the day is done.

The cardinal happens to be you —
Free, wild, and strong.
Soaring above and beyond in all you do,
To guide me and my day along.

Kathryn Abraham, Grade 8
Lewis & Clark Middle School, ID

My Life

Before school
I'm like a sloth
Walking slowly to each room.

On the bus
I'm like a bookworm
Reading and reading.

In school
I'm like a grandma
Listening to every word.

During lunch
I am like a caterpillar
Eating slowly.

After school
I'm as bored as a snail doing homework,
Talking to myself to keep my sanity.

Cari Redmon, Grade 7
White Pine Middle School, UT

Black

With fur so soft and eyes shining,
You look at me, loud meowing.
   I ruff up your fur
   I will miss you, sir
Giving you to a friend, little thing.

LyKae Frates, Grade 9
New Plymouth High School, ID

Judge

I am who I am;
you are who you are;
I don't need any judgment;
because it will just leave me scars.

When I talk to my friends,
it's like talking to a wall;
they want girls with pretty faces;
which leaves me quite appalled.

I just don't understand,
why people say what they say,
I don't need any judgment;
because without harsh words I'm okay.

I am who I am,
and I won't change a bit;
one day everyone will love me,
but it's too hard to admit.

Kayla Bame, Grade 8
Joe Walker Middle School, CA

Lady Like No Other

Oh grandmother,
Beautiful grandmother,
You were wrinkly as a raisin,
But also beautiful like a rose

You were my leader,
You used to guide me.
If something ever happened,
You were always right beside me.

I go back to the time,
Where I would always see your face.
There isn't a woman alive,
That can take your place.

To keep me happy,
There were no limits to the things you did.
I'm thankful that you raised me,
And the entire extra love that you gave me.

Victor Esteban, Grade 8
John Adams Middle School, CA

Oh Me!

The clouds of pain in the sky,
Oh! Why can't I fly.
The fears of future
Brings tears to my features.
The emotions would not bring me down,
Oh! I will not stay like this being a clown.
I'll will not let shadow of sadness fulfill,
Wait for me I will be in a dollar bill.

Deodatta Baral, Grade 9
George Washington High School, CO

Mile Beyond Mile

She, thin and small,
Lines up to start,
Ready to defeat all.

She, trained and ready,
Begins the long run,
Keeping her speed steady.

She, powerful and strong,
Tires as she sprints,
Endurance prodding her along.

She, hopeful and great,
Pushes toward the end,
Her path now straight.

She, champion and winner,
Recovers as others finish,
Their chances forever thinner.

Faith Tsou, Grade 8
Joe Walker Middle School, CA

Dew

Dew kisses a rosebud,
It nestles in the grass.
The starry tear of the clouds,
Is as clear and smooth as glass.

Dew touches the lavender,
It welcomes morning breeze.
The glittering drop from the heavens,
Is gliding down the trees.

Dew embraces the starlight,
It glistens and it shines.
The sun is slowly rising up,
And it is almost time.

Dew cries on a daisy,
The flowers are in full bloom.
The sun reaches out to take her back,
"Don't worry. I'll be back soon."

Lauren Oliver, Grade 7
Ocean Grove Charter School, CA

Color

Red is...
Red is the color of roses.
Red is the color of love.
Red is the color of apples.
Red is the color of Christmas.
Red is the color of blood.
Red is the color of the heart.
As you can see red is my favorite color.

Brianna Selfridge, Grade 7
Daniel Savage Middle School, CA

Rain

Pitter Patter,
Softly on the window,
Droplets scatter,
Filling the house with taps.

The plants huddle,
Thirsty and greedily,
Leaving puddles,
Scattered across the ground.

It starts and stops fast,
First sprinkling here and there,
Abrupt at that,
Just left with some more clouds.

Goodbye, good friend!
Please come back once again,
During frosts' reign,
How I wish to see rain.
Helen Hoang, Grade 7
Sarah McGarvin Intermediate School, CA

Dreams

I am invisible.
I wait and listen,
quiet and patient,
I am like the air.

I do not cause trouble;
I do not inflict pain;
I never speak my mind
because I live there.

I live in my dreams,
never in my reality.
In my head it is prefect;
In my dreams I am perfect.

I sit in my solitude
and write of my dreams.
Because dreams
are my improved reality.
Jordyn Baccus, Grade 8
Joe Walker Middle School, CA

Taunting Fire

The bright flickering light
Drew me in;
Its golden claws so bright
Held the logs.

The bright flickering light
Lulled me softly,
With its red wings of flight
Fluttering in the breeze.

The bright flickering light,
Held images of playing
Into infernos of blight
Running onto the coals.

Oh, that bright flickering light
Made me think wildly of
Dancing with flames in night,
But only in far-off dreams.
Samantha Vogel, Grade 8
Joe Walker Middle School, CA

Last Memory

I saw him smile
I saw him wave
Through the hospital window
Then I remembered

I remembered
All those happy
Memories
That I would remember forever

I never thought
That this would be
My last memory
With him

But it was
And it is
The last memory
I have with him
Ana Paula Alcantar, Grade 8
St John's Episcopal School, CA

Infection

I can't wait until
You happen to see
That my love for you
Is never ending

Your eyes, smile, and laugh
Never leave my mind
It's like an infection
It haunts me all the time

The spaces between my fingers are empty
It's where yours fit perfectly
I long for your hands to hold
Your feelings to be told

I'll be here waiting
Until I can be with you again
Because not only are you the love of my life
You are also my friend
Brooke Saum, Grade 9
Santiago High School, CA

Sports

Kick a round, white ball,
You shoot and you score,
Do an epic cheer,
This is soccer.

Hit the ball with a bat
Over a gigantic, green wall,
Run around the bases
This is baseball.

Hit the puck with a strange looking stick,
Get a penalty
Hit the post and score,
This is hockey.

Run around and fake,
You better catch the ball,
Get a touchdown,
This is football.
Collin Shaeffer, Grade 7
Joe Walker Middle School, CA

Baseball at the Park

I go to the park on a nice day,
Ready to start to play.
As I get my glove and hat,
And I put on my dirty hat.
I know I am going to have some fun,
Oh, how I love to play baseball
In the sweet summer sun!
Diego Ramirez, Grade 7
St Martin-in-the-Fields School, CA

Winter Storm

The wind is blowing all around,
The snow is falling to the ground,
When I walk out into the storm,
I feel as if I'm frozen in time,
All I can hear is the wind chimes,
Then all of a sudden in the distance
I see a beam of light shine
Through the clouds
Mekenna Boehl, Grade 8
Meridian Elementary School, CA

Winter Time

Winter time is big and bright.
It is a very satisfying sight.

Neat lights hung up high.
Tables filled with cookies and pie.

Eager children waiting for toys,
Regretting being naughty boys.
Pamela Hogu, Grade 7
Silver Hills Middle School, CO

The Gift of a Best Friend

I hear her coming,
Down the hall
I stop and wait,
And start to call.
I see her face,
That beautiful face,
With a sparkle
In her eye.

When I see her,
Sparks fly!
She's like a piece of heaven
Falling from the sky.
She comes closer to me,
As far as I can see
She starts to come over
Her ears flapping in the air
How I love her golden hair,
She's my best friend
Nobody can compete,
We are as happy as can be!

Caitlin Ritter, Grade 7
Joe Walker Middle School, CA

Fire's Ballet

Crazed flames are burning
In a beautiful, eternal dance
The flames move to a silent song
In a fire's great ballet

Crazed flames are burning
Forever bound together
They move and sway alone
The rhythm soft and sweet

Crazed flames are burning
Their song is soon to end
The flames sip back through the cracks
Only the embers are left to watch
The remnants of a fire's ballet

Reece Huff, Grade 7
Monte Vista Christian School, CA

Winter

Winter blows in, bringing the ice.
Trees quake, shaking in the cold.
Snow sets in, creating a mold.
Stinging winds, slicing, dicing.
Gone is the sun, white quite bold.
The quiet starts stories
That were left untold.
Later will come the biting frost,
And soon every color that we know
Will be lost.

Melissa Arnoldsen, Grade 8
Canyon View Jr High School, UT

Christmas is Baking

What is Christmas?
Christmas is baking.

Everyone has a different perspective on it
It brings excitement to some
And stress to others
It's a time for giving,
a time for family and friends,
It's a time for letting go.

We all have to shop in order to prepare
Whether it's presents or just ingredients, anticipation can't help but to fill the children
When it's time to unload, curiosity swims into the mind
What is going to be the outcome?

Now it's time to decorate
Everything has to be just right
spending time with the ones you love is all that matters.

It tastes delicious.
The Christmas was perfect.
The best present of all,
Family.

Christmas is baking.

Susan Wilson, Grade 8
Falcon Creek Middle School, CO

I Am from Open Sesame

I am from those old, knocked-over plastic pigs in the front yard,
and those Buddha heads in the backyard, staring into my eyes.
I am from a big white gate — OPEN SESAME! —
that welcomes me every time I enter my home.
I am from the chirping birds that awake me every morning,
the hoot of owls that lull me to sleep each night.

I am from Persian carpets covering our entire floor.
I am from antique cabinets, tables, chandeliers, and more.

I am from jumping over a flame of fire, letting misfortune burn.
I am from seven S's at the Noruz table, celebrating a new year of beginnings.

I am from crossing, turn out, arms and more;
the spectacular world of dance.
I am from trophies and injuries, dresses, shoes, bobby pins,
and that wonderful feeling of winning.

I am from the roots, branches and flowers of the family tree.
Everyone growing higher and higher, reaching towards the sun;
everyone including me.
I am that leaf that is small, but still growing.
I am from the long-gone leaves of the family tree, but still growing;
blooming into flowers.

Anais Ovanessoff, Grade 7
High Tech Middle School, CA

First Kiss

We were apart
From one another
Then one day
His lips brush mine
I am drunk with his love
Pink, silky
Smooth lips
No longer me
No longer him
We are as one
Together
Forever
A couple

Kandice Knapp, Grade 7
Weldon Valley Jr High School, CO

Catch

A happy memory,
throwing a ball to my dad
and getting it right back.

He makes me dive,
he makes me slide.
He throws it right to me,
or he makes me run.

No matter where he throws the ball
we always have fun.

This is a happy memory.
Antone Fanucchi, Grade 8
St Francis School, CA

Success

What is it like to get everything you want?
Everything and anything,
To be given everything you need,
It is not what we want to be,
We want to be free,
Not held captive by a king,
But as free as a birds wing,
We want to see our own,
Success you are not alone,
In that fight,
For right,
Success is the best,
To have success is to beat the rest.
Mariah Ricks, Grade 7
White Pine Middle School, UT

I'm Proud to Be Thirsty

Late July. Montana. 4:00 in the afternoon.
The thermometer soared to 105 degrees.
Little puffs of dust rose
From the cattle's feet as
They moved slowly along
Like they had for generations.
My lips so dry every time I spoke
Little droplets of blood appeared
I tried to lick them
But my tongue was so swollen
I could barely move it
But I was as happy as could be
None of us minded not being able to drink
We all knew a good cowboy
Doesn't drink until his horse is watered
Or until the job's done.
I'm proud to be thirsty.
Mimi Weber, Grade 8
Headwaters Academy, MT

Ashley Maki

Ashley,
athletic, spunky, outgoing, friendly
sister of Matthew
Lover of volleyball, the best sport ever
Who loves to be with friends
Lover of the water
Who feels accomplished after a long day
Who feels welcomed with friends
Who feels great after a good serve
Who fears imperfection
Who fears saying 'No'
Who fears not making the grades
Who would like to see perfection
Who would like to see more joy
Who would like summer year round
Resident of the galaxy,
Maki
Ashley Maki, Grade 8
Daniel Savage Middle School, CA

Deer Hunting

Deer flee from me
Especially when I search for them
Excited for the chance to hunt
Running up the hill

Hiking over the next ridge
Until I am so tired
Never giving up
Taking all of the time I need
I love the crisp feel of the air
Noticing the beautiful colors of autumn
Grateful for the memories made
Levi Austin, Grade 9
New Plymouth High School, ID

Glorious

It saw it's
Last days while
It soared past
The endless
Trails of leaves
Which would
Soon become a
Fresh blanket of
Clear, white snow,
Signaling the
Return of a
Special awakening.
The snow is
A
Barren
Abyss
To the owl
Who now must
Struggle to
Find food.
Ariel Goldstein, Grade 8
South Lake Middle School, CA

Practice Makes Perfect

I am strong
I wonder how strong
I hear the ball bounce across the court
I see the ball made for a shot
I miss
I am strong

I yell, "Shoot it!"
I have the ball somehow
I am dribbling
I shoot it
I swish it
I am strong

I dream
I know I won't get in the NBA
I try
I play
I am not so good
I am strong
Alex Montes, Grade 7
Falcon Creek Middle School, CO

Phantom

His hooves pound the earth,
Turning up soil while he gallops.
What is on his mind?
Curiosity, shame, helplessness.
He's concentrating on me,
I am fearful of this animal.
Gemma Forshaw, Grade 8
St Martin-in-the-Fields School, CA

Stranded

With the sand underneath my feet
The waves are whispering to come
Breezes will urge me onward
As the blazing sun above
Made harmony with the clouds
Soaring over head would be the seagulls
Calling to one another
The monkeys are chattering to each other
While I lie in the shades
Within the palm trees
gazing in the blue sky
Wondering if someone
Will look for me
For I am trapped
On this lonely island
Full of sadness.

Tiffany Nguyen, Grade 7
Sarah McGarvin Intermediate School, CA

I Will Not Back Down

Every day I go to school,
And I wonder what she'll do,
Push me down,
Make me frown,
But I will not back down.

Make me bleed,
Make me cry,
Enough is enough.
I will stand my ground,
I will not back down!

I went up to her,
And I told her so,
I will stand my ground,
And I will not back down!

Gisselle Acevedo, Grade 8
Joe Walker Middle School, CA

Baseball

What is my most favorite sport to play?
My favorite sport to play is baseball
If I could, I would play baseball all day
If I can't play baseball, I cry and bawl
The Angels are the greatest baseball team
My dream is to be an Angel player
If I could do that, I'd fulfill my dream
I would be doing the best job ever
There are nine innings in a baseball game
When the game is over, someone wins it
Most of the time, the games are really tame
To score, you have to get a real good hit
That is why baseball is the most fun sport
People that say different, I'll take to court

Matthew Rodriguez, Grade 9
Lucerne Valley Middle/Sr High School, CA

Monster

She heard a scratching
A whisper in the night
A ghostly shadow passing
She tore apart the light
Ripping the veil
In search of her curse
Wrist trickled red dewdrops
Her invisible hurt
A knife blade controlled
By an unforeseen foe
A creature still
Gnawing at her soul
It's talons groped
Wildfire spreading
To darkness succumbing
Her mind was catching
No hands reached out
Too late to realize
The claws were raking, tearing
The monster was inside

Annie Wang, Grade 9
Dougherty Valley High School, CA

Oh What a Place

My aunt's house is a place
A place to dance, sing, run.
The patio was a garden full
Of roses, flowers, bees.

My aunt's house is a place
Thanksgiving was memorable.
Turkey, potatoes, stuffing
Mmm mmm mmm pumpkin pie.

My aunt's house is a place
Christmas eve, New Years eve
Wrapping paper on the floor
Ohh the good old memories

My aunt's house is place
Summer time in the pool,
Beach balls everywhere we look.
My aunt's house is a place
Ohh what a place.

Jaqueline Cardenas, Grade 8
Richardson PREP HI Middle School, CA

Hailee

unstoppable, undefeatable
graduating, accomplishing, acknowledging
hardworking, achiever
accessorizing, organizing, teaching
brave, courageous
teacher

Hailee Weathers, Grade 7
Daniel Savage Middle School, CA

Owls

Above in the sky
they have nothing to fear
they are the kings of the night
as they glide to and fro
some are tiny
some are gargantuan
but all are the owls

By day they stay in their assorted branches
all waiting for night
when they will spread their wings
and soar into the darkness
from their humble abodes
in search of their dinner
and to frolic and play
these are the owls

Marcus Burton, Grade 7
Salida Middle School, CO

Eraser

Smooth as cloth
Pink as a pig
Oh eraser
What would I do without you
Big and bold
Small and handy
What will I do without my dear eraser
So many colors you can be
Pink, green, blue, yellow…
Oh eraser
You help me on all my mistakes
But the more I use you
The smaller you get
You sacrifice yourself for my mistakes
Oh eraser
What will I do without you

Armando Felix, Grade 7
Daniel Savage Middle School, CA

Drowning in a Sea of Lost Souls

I drowned myself in a sea of souls
I've tried to breach the surface
But always manage to sink again
I've always been told that hitting the
Bottom is a good thing 'cause there's
Nowhere to go but up
I found this to be untrue…
Every time I sink, I go further down
Making it impossible to swim back up
But I was never the one to quit
I've always fought to get back up
Even if I get knocked back down
It still hasn't changed the fact that I
Drowned in a sea of lost souls

Heaven Young, Grade 8
Mountain View Jr High School, CA

My Sport

Picking up the orange, bumpy ball.
Shooting free throws.
My passion for the game is as big as a hot air balloon.
Playing my favorite sport,
With my favorite friends.
Blocking the screams
And the cheers out,
I'm in my own zone.
Dribbling,
Dribbling,
Dribbling.
On a fast break away,
Running as fast as I can,
Going in for a layup.
I am out of breath,
Panting for more oxygen.
The buzzer goes off…
We won!

Shelbie Scherff, Grade 7
Salida Middle School, CO

Why?

On the ground,
seeing movement.
Hearing screams and cries for help!
Feeling some sort of liquid run down my head.
As every single muscle shuts down and stiffens.
In my head,
I ask
"Why is mom crying?"
Hugging me as if I was her one and only child.
Hearing the words of "don't die!"
While looking up at the ceiling
moments of my life flying away from my memories.
Faded sounds
The darkness consumes me.
Silence
And only

Silence.

Noelia Evangelista, Grade 7
Salida Middle School, CO

Bye Friend

Why did you have to go
You were a great friend
Felt like yesterday
When we watched Sunday Night Football
We talked about universities and colleges
We had fancy dinners together with our families

Well, hope you enjoy your time in heaven
We had lots of great memories
Bye, friend

Gahan Ritonga, Grade 7
St. Francis Parish School, CA

Rainbows Are Life

It's a beautiful thing
but never lasts forever
Each color is a stage in life

R ed is the start
O range right after,
 the beloved toddler years
Y ellow is basic elementary
G reen is when the parties are endless,
 but the homework still unbearable
B lue is when you have a family of your own
I ndigo, when more years have passed
V iolet is the end

the last of the rainbow
Then…
It fades into nothing
as if it never existed.

Sonya Tran, Grade 8
Falcon Creek Middle School, CO

Everything Is Better with Chocolate

Everything is better with chocolate
Schools, beaches, even supermarkets
Without chocolate, life would be boring
Kids would have nothing to look forward to each morning

Everything is better with chocolate
For example, let's try school
Chocolate pencils, now wouldn't that be cool?
You would also have chocolate desks
Let's face it, chocolate is the best

What about the beach?
Imagine a rich and creamy sea
You can also play with chocolate sand
Look at that beautiful chocolate land

Everything is better with chocolate, can't you see
Anything is better with chocolate, believe me

Kelvin Nguyen, Grade 7
Sarah McGarvin Intermediate School, CA

Seize the Day

If I could seize the day
I could run away and never look back
London India Canada all fly by
Its all me and no rules, it's my day

I would watch the sun set from the top of the world
I would watch a snow storm devour a town
I would dance with the queen of England
I would ride the longest train in the world
That's what I would do if I could seize the day

Elizabeth Prouty, Grade 7
Sequoia Village School, AZ

Home Is My Place to Be
Home is my place to be.
To relax and just be free.
Making me feel safe and happy,
Home is my place to be.

Rooms filled with laughter and joy,
While sitting there playing with my toy.
Smelling the good food from the kitchen.
Home is my place to be.

Going outside to play with my dogs,
Hopping over the large logs.
Having fun and being silly just like frogs.
Home is my place to be.

Home is my place to be.
To relax and just be free.
Making me feel safe and happy,
Home is my place to be.
Bianca Garcia, Grade 8
Richardson PREP HI Middle School, CA

The Last Sight
I will never forget him.
He was like a dad to me,
So loving,
So caring.

He always brought joy into the room.
Even in those difficult moments,
He always knew what to say,
He always knew what to do.

Ever since he left,
Nothing has been the same.

I miss him all the time.
Sad songs make me think of him.
And all I can remember,
Is my last sight of him through the glass.
But at least now he's in a better place,
And my uncle remains in my heart.
Juan Carlos Meave, Grade 8
St John's Episcopal School, CA

Adoration
I am kneeling in a pew.
The faint sound of cars driving by.
I am deep in prayer with the Lord.
God's love and peace fill my heart.
A very peaceful moment.
Kaia Rummelsburg, Grade 7
St Francis School, CA

Free
The big tree on Freedom hill
is where I'd rather be
with the wind whipping my face,
the tall grass lapping at my feet
instead of here, the school house
with the witty teacher
the fly on the board
and kids throwing paper
I try and try and try
but it's not where I want to be
my mind drifts to that tree
up on Freedom hill with
the wind and the grass
it's where I want to be
it's where I want to be
Free, Free, Free
ZZ Cranford, Grade 9
Home School, CA

The Key
God has the key to my heart!
The devil cannot tear us apart.
My faith for him must be strong.
And I know it will last long!
I know he's done a lot for me.
Trust in Jesus, then you'll see.
He gives life that never ends.
Jesus is the perfect, true friend!
How can you ignore something so true?
Trust him, God's got a plan for you!
Give God your key,
And he will set you free!
I know God won't lose my key.
And I know he really loves me!
God is love, God is free.
Trust in God, give him your key!
LeAnne Bedford, Grade 9
Salome High School, AZ

Remember
Remember the fun,
Remember the frights.
Remember the love,
Remember the fights.

Remember the gore,
That we could all bare?
Remember the friendship,
That we used to all share?

Yet we still care for each other,
In our own special ways.
I wish I could go back,
Back in time to those days.
Deseree Serenko, Grade 8
Canyon View Jr High School, UT

Softball
Softball isn't just a game,
It's a lifestyle.
Well, for me anyway.

Day and night,
Rain or shine,
Every day from six to eight.

Every day,
Or once a week,
Either way I play.

I step onto the field,
All my troubles go away,
I'm there to play.

With determination in my heart,
Strength in my arm,
I stay focused on my game.

Outfield, infield,
Pitcher, catcher,
Those are the positions I play.

This game is a part of me,
It's who I am,
It's my one true love.
Gina Marie Esparza, Grade 8
St Helen Catholic School, CA

Someday
He's the reason for my smile
The light within me
The one I can't seem to live with out
…And yet he doesn't know it

He's the reason for my happiness
The reason for those butterflies
The reason for this poem
…And yet he doesn't know it

My heart says yes, but my mind says no
I hesitate which to follow
I choose a path that affects the other
When he doesn't even bother

Maybe so? I don't know
Maybe never? Hopefully no
I want to take a chance
But I'm afraid I might regret it

I'll just wait for that day
I'll take caution
…So maybe someday
Julie Ann Lane Sumalpong, Grade 7
Sarah McGarvin Intermediate School, CA

My Grandma

Know her, I did not.
Love her, yes I did. A lot.
But just like the bees, trees, and other things.
The time came for her to sleep.

Although my mother wept.
Memories of her she had kept.
I told her there was no reason to cry.
For she now has her wings to fly.

My brother who did not know,
Asked why we were crying so.
And although he did not cry,
We could tell he was destroyed inside.

My grandma went to a better place.
She went to God's place.
A very wonderful place.
Oh, such a nice place.

Manuel Gonzalez, Grade 8
John Adams Middle School, CA

Lost Sister

What you mean to me,
Is more than I can express.
You see, I had no sister when I was a little kid
To call when I was depressed.

When we first met,
I had no clue,
What was getting ready to happen,
It was completely out of the bloom.

God had a plan,
Throughout the years,
He was making us for each other,
To share life's smiles, and tears.

I never could have imagined,
What a sisters love was all about,
Until I met you,
And then I really found out, what it was all about.

Aurelio Chavarria, Grade 8
John Adams Middle School, CA

Legos

O how I love to build Lego sets;
I guess it's because I don't have a pet.
If I had a pet, it would take all my time.
But the Lego set is all mine.
There are Lego themes of all kinds.
In building these sets, I use my mind.
When the product is finished, it is one of a kind.
I'm so glad the Legos are all mine!

Gregory Noorigian, Grade 8
St Martin-in-the-Fields School, CA

Shallow Grave

Intolerance is a crime scene:
A body found in a shallow grave
Buried beneath the dirt of hidden truths and darkest lies
Enshrouded within the mysterious folds of an untold story

Intolerance leaves deep muddy footprints
The dry white bones of a death dance
Performed puppet-like at a fast and furious pace
Ending in a sharp cry for help

In the dead of night, intolerance lurks like some wild beast
With razor-sharp claws and iron jaw
Holding its prey in a death grip of hate
Extinguishing its last breath of life

In the cold, stony silence of an unmarked grave
Intolerance clings to shadowy secrets and bloody wounds
That seep deep into the earth and join a dark underground river
That runs to some unknown, unearthly destination

David Duncan, Grade 7
The Mirman School, CA

The Old Me Is Still There

I've been on this road for so long
Can I turn around?
Wondering who I am
Who am I destine to be?
I won't be like the other guy
He comes out the other end of me
So it's time to straighten up
Stand strong and never lose sight of my destination
But no matter what happens
Keep that drive don't lose that determination
Get back to the old me
He's the one who cared
He's the one who lived life
Longing for honesty
He wanted to be
Everything he could be
Honestly no matter what no one says
I am still he
He's still a part of me

Orion Drake, Grade 8
Pentecostal Way of Truth Academy, CA

Ode to My Hero...

My hero.
She is always there, and has been all my life.
I love her to death and would do anything for her.
Many may have a hero, but mine is the best.
She fights every day and pulls through every night.
My hero she loves, and loves with all her might.
Some days she struggles, but I know it's okay.
When I come home and see my mom every day.

Natalie Hilton, Grade 8
Daniel Savage Middle School, CA

Dear Political Ads

I would like to tell you
that you are an abomination against
mankind.
You tell me
dirty lies.
You tell me
that your party is right for America.
You tell me
that you approve this message.
I would like to tell you
your existence infuriates me.
So during our next encounter
In my living room watching TV
And you appear on my viewer
I will thank God that they
end in
November.

Ben Humphries, Grade 7
Falcon Creek Middle School, CO

By Your Side

I stand watching
Not knowing what to do.
I ask myself
If I should do something.
My mind screams,
but my body does not do anything.

I comfort my friend.
Thinking, what if.
Still having the rank smell
of his words.
The painful wounds of his insults.
All you can hear is his breathing
full of vengeful pants.
I calm him down,
only to have it happen the next day.
That's what happens every day.

Marco Solis, Grade 9
New Plymouth High School, ID

At 12 O'clock

Exactly at twelve
The creatures will dwell
Under your bed and your closets
And you will sleep tight
And hope that night
You don't doze off in a nightmare
But at the hint of the light
The good light will shine
Upon of your bed and your closet
And the creatures descend
Back under your bed
For their next nightly descent

Quan Ngo, Grade 7
Sarah McGarvin Intermediate School, CA

Shh!

Shh! Listen to that sound,
It is as melodious
As Bach playing Minuet.
Oh, how beautiful.

Shh! Listen to that sound,
Oh, so beautiful, then it stopped,
And there was crying,
And there was dying.

Shh! Listen to that sound,
Of everybody crying.
Then the piano player
Started playing again.

Shh! Listen to that sound,
Now there is no more crying,
And there is no more dying.
Oh, how beautiful.

Leah Wilson, Grade 8
Joe Walker Middle School, CA

Daddy's Little Girl

Daddy's little girl
Dressed in pretty white.
Wearing Grandma's pearls;
It was love at first sight.

Daddy's precious angel
Grew up way too fast.
The sweet sound of her bangles,
Reminded him of memories past.

Daddy's lovely rose
Had sparkling eyes like him.
She had a pretty pose,
And her light was never dim.

Daddy's gracious gift
Had the most beautiful smile,
And the tears began to shift;
As he walked her down the aisle.

Tiffany Caram, Grade 8
Joe Walker Middle School, CA

Camping

On September 2nd
As I saw my father
With his handy axe and box
He swings his axe at a tree branch
It falls dead in a box
As it gets darker and cold
He starts a fire and sings campfire songs
And that's how I spent my weekend

Andrew Ha, Grade 7
Sarah McGarvin Intermediate School, CA

Boredom

What to do?
Don't have a clue

Where to go?
I don't know!

Who to see?
Don't ask me

I need a life
Without much strife

Something to do
Something new

Need something more
'Cause my life's a bore

Josie Sorensen, Grade 9
Gunnison Valley High School, UT

Mr. Whiteout

Dear Mr. Whiteout,
I would like to tell you
that you don't work very well.
You tell me
it will erase all my mistakes.
You tell me
you'll blend into the paper.
You tell me
I can write over you.
I would like to tell you
Whiteout makes me furious.
So during our next encounter
when you are the color of a lion's tooth,
and you won't dry,
and you get all over the paper,
and I have to start over,
I am switching to erasers.

Carlee Edge, Grade 7
Falcon Creek Middle School, CO

Winter Rabbit

Here,
Leaping to and fro,
In the frosty air,
As its paw meets the crisp snow,
Its stretched ears stick up,
Followed by a small head,
Wiggling its whiskers,
It senses a carnivorous predator,
Sneaking in the shade of the trees,
The rabbit vanishes,
Silently,
To a more secure area

Ryan O'Connor, Grade 7
Salida Middle School, CO

'Tis God's Will

These people cause great suffering. They revive but on occasion. These people don't have any empathy for those who do their work. They watch and laugh while the slaves wipe away the painful tears, tears they are now adapted to. A prince who lost his crown. A king who lost his heir. A wife who lost her husband. A son who lost his father. It's all a part of God's will. Tis God's will, tis God's will.

Does it help to think that? Or is it frightening to face the music when you don't like the tone? The painful blood shed, burns and aches that come with this life, it's all worth it when you hear the angelic comforting voices in the everlasting one. It's all a part of God's will. Tis God's will, tis God's will.

Marissa Poyorena, Grade 8
Ripona Elementary School, CA

Free of My Memories

Stuck in my past, where my memories will always haunt me
Remembering that time, and wondering when I'll ever be free

Still I must grow my wings and fly
To the place where I will no longer cry

I look back at my sorrow, but still I try
To do my best to grasp the sky

Oh what it is to be free, to be able to fly
To be with those who own the skies?

With the sun, comes the light
But we must first brave the night

Even though the pain has left an unbearable mark
Light will always shine brightest in the dark

What I dream is to be able to fly
With no more sorrow, and no more being shy

I must linger no longer, for yesterday was history
And I must not worry, for tomorrow will be a mystery

I have no fear, for the past can no longer hurt me
The only thing is regret, because I always start with "If only"

I now belong to the present, my past now behind me
And it will remain this way, for the truth has set me free

Khang Huynh, Grade 8
Robert E Peary Middle School, CA

A Giant Leap of Faith

A noteworthy date in space and time
July twentieth, nineteen sixty-nine

A challenge was set, and dreams were made
Farewells Armstrong, Buzz and Collins bade

They boarded that rocket, and with three, two, one…
White, hot fire launched them to the white, bright sun

Through the deep, dark void, cold and vast
In three days, touching the moon at last

Families gathered in their homes and off the streets
United by one man and his pair of giant feet

And his words were uttered into the books
Leaving listeners lost with awed looks

The crackle of the radio filled our ears
Every ocean and river was then filled with tears

For each one of us, that boot meant so much more
A bright shining example that we can look towards

And though dead may be the heroes of the past
The American spirit will eternally last

For the flag will forever fluttering be
A symbol of the brave and the land of the free

Brandon Fong, Grade 9
The Mirman School, CA

Thoughts on Escher's "Bond of Union"

I see a man
Intertwined with his past self
Going through time and space
A man wishing he could change everything he has done
A man wanting his parents back
Wanting and wishing he could be a kid again
A man regretting his choices in life, in his career, in his childhood.
What did he do? Why does he want to change his past?
I see a man
Intertwined with his past self.

Brooke-Lynn Crews, Grade 7
Tenaya Middle School, CA

Colors in the World

Colors are found wherever one looks,
even inside the tiniest nooks!
From the color peach
found on the beach,
to shades of green
in a forest scene!
Lift your eyes for a fleeting second,
to you the millions of colors will beckon
for your mind to see
the world's colors from the perspective of me!

Macie Miller, Grade 8
Monte Vista Christian School, CA

Emotion Is Our True Weakness Yet It's Our One Greatest Power

Emotion makes us human, yet it also makes us weak
There are people in this world who feed on hatred and greed
Yet there are others who live on love, kindness, and friendship
These people are the diamonds that hide among the pebbles
Without these emotions, we are mindless, we are weak
We are robots, empty shells that cannot be filled
There are people in this world who have given in to their emotions, to madness, to despair, to longing or need
Yet there are others who think only of kindness, and joy, and leave every moment of despair behind
Emotion may be a weakness no one can hide
But it is also the thing that keeps us alive, that keeps us human

Katherine Stearns, Grade 7
Hillside Jr High School, ID

Friends

A friend is one who believes in me when I have ceased to believe in myself,
no matter how far apart I am from them, they are always there in my heart.
They cheer me up when I am down,
They share a smile and not a frown.
They are always close to my heart and there for support,
and they bring out the best side of me.
Friends come and go, but the true friends are the ones that never leave your side,
no matter what happens in life.
A true friend is one of the greatest of all blessings.
They will be there every time you need someone to lift you up or to celebrate your joys with each other.

LeeAnne Wirth, Grade 8
Christ the King School, AZ

Monsters

Remember when you were four and monsters hid in your closet and at times under your bed
Furry monsters maybe with three heads
Purple and green and big-eyed and mean
Giving you nightmares and ruining your escape to magical dreams
Hiding under your blanket and in the arms of your mother, knowing that everything will be fine
When you grow older, you may see that the monsters have only been in disguise
Looking like ordinary people, being blinded all these times
But these monsters are actually real and can be such a harm
Unfortunately your blanket may not be able to help you
Especially when the monsters come and set off the alarm

Aileen Maranan, Grade 8
Robert E Peary Middle School, CA

San Francisco

I remember going to San Francisco
The wind blowing
The sound of the tour buses driving past and the people screaming from the top
The smell of the sourdough bread from the sourdough factory
The fog so thick I can only see about a hundred feet away
The cool wax of historical and present day figures from the wax museum
The amazing street performers
Going to Pier 39 and watching the performer stick a needle up his and nose and walk on broken glass
Seeing a street performer balance on a ladder as he walks up and down
I remember having to walk so far my legs were about to collapse.

Sean Franklin, Grade 8
Daniel Savage Middle School, CA

Unexpected

Footsteps pounding on the burning road, echoing of the sand
Beads of sweat glisten, as they slide off my cheeks
My lungs hurt as if they are on fire, eager to burn everything inside
I make shallow, ragged breaths trying to keep up
My legs so sore, they almost collapse from exhaustion
A sharp pain jabs me in the chest, making every step agonizing
I was afraid to look back, to see some monster catching up to me
I was running for my life as if my life depended on it
The end of the journey seems so far, and distant
This dreadful experience never seems to end
I should have seen it coming
But I wasn't prepared
Not at all
But I was almost there
Almost
There
By
A few
Footsteps
And…that concludes how horrible my P.E. period was.
Scariest. Thing. Ever.

Hailey Zhu, Grade 7
Carmel Valley Middle School, CA

My Room

My room,
Mirrors, white vanity, white bed,
Bright yellow, floral, bed spread.
Pretty paintings painted by me,
On every wall that you can see.
A place where I go to blast the music and feel free,
But also a place that I go to relax,
Just my bed and me.
Smells of sweet,
Body sprays,
And
Smells of fragrant
Perfumes.
All come together and make a place
That I call my room.

Rebecca, Grade 8
Ripona Elementary School, CA

The Flight of Freedom

You can fly anywhere you wish
You can get things on your own like fish
There is no one to tell you what to do
No one to make your feelings turn blue
On your journeys you will learn new things
You can see many things while you fly with your wings
There are things you must see
Things you cannot just believe
You are an Eagle
A symbol of our country.

Ajia Cuevas, Grade 8
North Middle School, CO

Forest

With moans so selfish and forgiving
Love is life, but naught is living
Darker, darker, shadows lie
And fall asleep to Death's lullaby
The trees, they grow old, bare branches a perch
For every poor bird who is weary with thirst—
For no water is found in this deep, darkened forest
And those who are fearless can't bear to ignore it—
Bliss would mean ignorance in this silent, dead wild
Where cruel, dying trees cannot be reconciled.
They tear and they scratch, and can't help but catch
An old woman peasant's lost child.
With screams and with cries,
At her bravery's demise,
The girl struggles to run far away,
But Prince Charming is lost in this cold, bitter frost
And his face bears a look of dismay.
Running far from the trees, branches grasping with greed,
He tries hard just to find the young maiden,
And if not for the trees, he'd have journeyed with ease;
On a tombstone his name has been graven.

Shelby Smithouser, Grade 9
The Classical Academy, CO

Growing Older

I remember long ago,
I used to watch silly shows,
Like SpongeBob, Arnold, and Camp Lazlo.
But now, my childhood has now been done,
There's no time for television, games, or fun.
I have more homework, and less time for games,
Now I've been boring, and also quite lame.
I can't eat candy, for I'll get cavities,
Unless I pay the dentist financially.
Now, I'll have to work most hours of the day,
Then, I'll continue doing that until I'm all old and gray.
But now, I'm only twelve,
I don't have to care.
I don't have much homework, and a lot of time to spare.
Overall, I like the feeling of being young,
You get to sleep in, play games, and also have fun.

Millie Nguyen, Grade 7
Sarah McGarvin Intermediate School, CA

Ode to My Bed

Dear sweet bed,
Who for some youngsters is a dread
You cradle me when I'm sick
And welcome me when I'm tired
Who is sometimes overlooked
As nothing but a cushion
Who allows me to think without interruption
Oh comfy bed,
It won't be long 'till I see you again

Marisa Fenter, Grade 7
Daniel Savage Middle School, CA

Turn of a Day

Green hills shot with a ball of fire,
Yellow, red, and orange is all that is shown.
The joyful birds sing their song,
And welcome morning, as it will come.
A hazy mist begins to dissipate,
And a bright blue sky emerges.
A gentle breeze begins to blow,
Bringing all of the lush trees to a rustle.
Then as the sun hits mid-day,
It begins its gradual descent.
And as it becomes closer to the smooth flowing water,
The sky becomes a fluffy orange and pink,
Lighting the horizon up.
And as the sun falls below the horizon,
The cool, icy moon makes its first appearance.
Bringing along with it the darkness of the night.
Until the morning time when,
The green hills will get shot with a ball of fire.
And the darkness will subside.

Brendan Craig, Grade 7
Westside Neighborhood School, CA

Candy Shop

My closet is a candy shop,
With many different flavors.
My purple tank is a grape Jolly Rancher,
My blue jeans are blue rock candy,
My black, white, and pink Toms are salt water taffy,
My polka-dot Toms are Smarties,
My black jeans are black licorice,
And my pink T-shirt is bubble gum.
It's hard to choose which candy to wear.
Do you agree?
I do like having a candy shop for a closet.
It makes me feel sweet.
I do wonder, though,
Are all closets this sweet?

Katherine Canellos, Grade 8
South Lake Middle School, CA

Choose

The feeling of peace,
It is great.
Until you realize
It can control you.

The feeling of freedom,
It is wonderous.
It dwells within you,
It never dies,
And even when your physical freedom is gone,
Your spiritual freedom lives on,
It harbors in your soul,
For longer than your heart is beating.

Natalie Rubio-Licht, Grade 8
Gale Ranch Middle School, CA

Rain

Drip, drop, drip,
I feel water streaming down my face,
It comes from above.

Where did it come from?
Did it just appear from nothing?
Again I feel it.

Drip, drop, drip,
I look up and see where it comes from,
It comes from the heavens!

The gray, fluffy heavens!
Are they the joyous tears of God?
Or are they sad tears?

Drip, drop, drip,
I can't explain its softness on my skin,
It just feels as if I'm in a happy place.

I feel overwhelmed,
For I don't know whether I should hide from it,
It seems harmless, especially to nature.

Drip, drop, drip,
Then it hits me,
This wonderful gift is called rain.

Liliana Vasquez, Grade 8
St Helen Catholic School, CA

Desk 33

Every day I hold you up, not going to let you fall
Never ready to collapse, not going to let you down at all

Books, pencils, folders, too, all are piled on me
But I am strong, proud and tall, never for help will I plead

Bored, you scratch me, write on me and doodle
Then you listen to the teacher, abandoning your picture of a poodle

Your water bottle leaks, your tummy isn't feeling so well
All your problems I already know, no need for you to tell

Notes are passed, read and written
It's sad to see you doing things forbidden

One day you'll leave, pack up your things and go
One day it will happen, I'll be prepared, you know

But I still feel empty inside, as I imagine how you'll graduate
I really wish I could cry, as you go from 7 to 8.

I've seen millions of kids, all special and unique
I wonder if they remember me, Desk 33

Lavanya Singh, Grade 7
Thornton Jr High School, CA

Distinctive Delicacy

Many think,
Ballerinas are a fragile thing.
Reduced figures,
Elegant makeup,
Fine structures.
I think,
Ballerinas are athletes.
Persevering players,
Devoted teammates,
Triumphant jocks.
I believe,
Ballet is a sport.
Ambitious competitions,
Strenuous activity,
Booming applause.
Stereotypes are meaningless.
This is a new generation,
Gracefulness is
Action of the future.
Emme Morin, Grade 9
La Reina High School, CA

All I Can Do Is Ride

Tacking up
I prepare to ride
Mounting up on my horse
I feel excited and joyful
My horses pace quickens
I Try to maintain a good seat
But all I can do is ride

My horse approaches cross rails
My nerves stiffen
But I get in my two point
I hope it will be accurate
But all I can do is ride

I dismount
Untack
Groom my horse
And think about what I could do better
But in the end all I did was ride
Gemma Guzman, Grade 8
Monte Vista Christian School, CA

The Color White

White
is the color of the snow
on the ground. Like the
big clouds in the sky or
the whipped cream on my
pie. W-H-I-T-E spells
the color white for me.
Kelsey Davis, Grade 7
Daniel Savage Middle School, CA

Yellow

Yellow comes from
The shining sun at the dusk of dawn,
And the chirp of a newborn chick awakening the neighborhood,
and a lemon just ripe enough to eat.
It comes from the smile of a child on Christmas morning,
And a lion that roars for protection.
It comes from the fresh smell of tennis balls fresh out of the can,
And from glistening gold as blinding as the sun,
It comes from the curiosity of a student eager to learn,
From a post-it note stuck to the shy white refrigerator,
It shines lights of hope down on us like a strong sun beam leading the way,
As a rubber ducky sails across the acrylic bathtub.
It comes from the pucker of lemon heads as you lick your lips from its sweet temptation,
It comes from the coating of a unsharpened #2 pencil,
And the bright city lights of a wide-awake city,
It comes from treasure buried deep waiting for a child to uncover,
And the sand burning your toes on a hot summers day,
It means yield and slow down and have a moment of solitude.
Yellow is the color of
Wisdom.
Claudia Menziuso, Grade 7
Gale Ranch Middle School, CA

Music

Music is majestically fantastic
The broad and beautiful sound of it so slick
The sound of music gives you an everlasting harmony
In everything a gorgeous Do, Re, Me
Music is heaven coming from a radio
The sound of it as white as the whitest snow
It flows out of an instrument soft and delicate
It gives you your peace, the candle is lit
A song, a grandiose dove's flight
It moves off the page and creates a stunning light
A rap, a trip to a journey a-far
With rhyme and time and moves smooth like a brand new car
An instrument, the king of melody
This king makes it possible for every Do, Re, Me
The tools, a pick, a stick, a bow
Get plucked and struck and rubbed across to make the noise of every song you know
The sound, oh a truly indescribable noise
So justly and faithfully striking that none but music itself could poise
Music, the dove above all doves
Truly the only sound that EVERYONE adores and loves
Aundrea Keenan, Grade 7
Colorado Connections Academy, CO

Happiness

Happiness is knocking on my door, it crashes its way inside.
Happiness feels a lot like sorrow.
It smells like rain on my windowsill.
It sounds like a violent roar in my ear.
Happiness tastes like the sweet honeysuckle in the spring.
It projects itself as bright, and warm, but I see it as a shadow in my past.
Madison Martin, Grade 9
Monarch High School, CO

Summer Is Over

Why is summer over so soon?
I never wanted it to end. I
Would play with my brother
Or go out with my friends.

It was the best to
Just sleep in and rest,
But now it's all over
And we're back to school.

School can be fun
But summer is better.
I especially like the hot weather.
We would get wet to get cool.

I don't like when it rains.
I feel I can't do
Anything outside that I love to do.

I miss summer because I love staying up late,
And being with my friends.
And I also made cakes with my cousins.

Summer was the best and I'm sad
That it's gone but I guess
I will have to wait till next year.

Brenda Batres, Grade 7
St Helen Catholic School, CA

Shipwreck

Our elegant schooner glided across the water,
The captain stood proud at the helm.
He treated this ship like a daughter,
This ship made of strong elm.

That morning we left silently,
In fear of a hurricane down south.
It was blowing ships quite violently;
Rearing its ugly dragon's mouth.

In the beginning, disaster seemed averted,
But that was truly not to be.
So when the wind whipped up, our fears were asserted,
I knew this ship was going to go undersea.

I knew this voyage was doomed from the beginning,
Our captain though, he tried to reassure us,
But we needed no attempt at reassuring,
I realized that the captain was not trying to impress.

Our crew all began to flee,
Yet our captain only tightened his grip.
I saw a tear in his eye, but he could only oversee.
I asked him to leave, but he said only, "I will go down with my ship."

Wesley Domsalla, Grade 7
Joe Walker Middle School, CA

My Dad Will Always Be There for Me

As my dad looks at me,
I realize what he's done for me.
He taught me how to ride my bike,
and to make sure I knew, that when you turn a screw to the right,
bam, it makes the screw tight.

As my dad looks at me,
I realize that I'm not just three,
but now I'm ten.
Ten was a big age for me.
I learned that volleyball was the sport for me,
and when I thought my life was going to end because I hurt my toe,
my dad was there to make it stop bleeding.

As my dad looks at me,
I realize that I'm not just ten, but thirteen.
I'm learning that Geometry is difficult for me,
but I'm glad my dad's been there for me.
My dad's always told me I'll be his little girl,
and that he'd be there to pick me up off my feet.
My dad will always be there for me.

Megan Taflinger, Grade 8
Joe Walker Middle School, CA

You Only Get to Live a Life Once

You only get to live a life once!
So let's live it to the fullest,
And appreciate all that we have
Make everything count, no matter what you do!

Life is full of beauty and love.
So go take advantage of what you can.
There is so much more to life than just sitting on a couch,
Now go out and explore the world
You might even notice the things you never realized before!

Life may have its difficulties,
but no matter how hard it is.
Take a deep breath and enjoy it,
Because you only get to live a life once!

Georgtte Moreno, Grade 9
Lucerne Valley Middle/Sr High School, CA

Purple Dress

I have a purple dress
It brings me stress when my mom wants me to wear the purple dress
It is a big mess
I try to wear it less but I know I am blessed with this purple dress
I confessed that I don't like the purple dress
It gave my mom distress
When she found out I dislike the purple dress
She accepted it with glee
And now you can clearly see
You would like my mother and me.

Jack Pearson, Grade 7
Monte Vista Christian School, CA

The Country

The country has beauty you will never see anywhere else.
Trees and grass that are always green and growing.
Lush green forests and animals roaming everywhere.

In the country at night there's always cold clear air.
Nothing breaks the quiet stillness.

In the city you see no stars,
and you always hear the roar of cars.
But in the country you can watch,
the specks of light dance and wiggle in the night,
and very few cars pass.

How come it is that in the country,
there are no strangers.
Everyone seems to know everybody.
It's nice to know that if you ever need help,
there's always a hand to hold on to.

A country snow floats softly to the ground.
It's perfect for a snowman or fort.
It's not dirtied by cars nor people,
and stays untouched for awhile.

The country is special to me and always will be.
It's my place to be.

Megan Bartschi, Grade 8
Bear Lake Middle School, ID

Dance

Ceaseless freedom of emotion
A dwelling aside from relation
A sanctuary solely of solitude
Serving attainment of a peaceful mood

Unremitting, unblemished movements
Extending into unlit boundless space
Unabridged sensations of training
Purely perfectly peerless

Anguish of balancing on distant extremities
Gradually unsteady faintness becomes you
Twirling on frayed silk and broken battered wood
Blood blisters form faster than crystal ice melts

The virtuous side of grace
Elegance fulfilled only here
Through the Thriving thrill of performing
To pulsations of my thumping heart

Dance is a prestigious art
A form of savage beauty
My wanton supreme dignity
Simply my cup of tea

Delilah Roberts, Grade 8
The Mirman School, CA

Mother's Hands

Mother's hands have always been there
Soft, caring, and gentle.
The day I opened my eyes to the world,
Mother's hands are the first to hold me,
After nine months of pain and worry.
If I am hurt or to shed a tear,
Mother's hands will hoist me up to a higher place
Until we are face-to-face.
Her hands are my seat as she carries me around.
My pain quickly fades after those hands had soothed my wounds.
Mother's hands button up my shirt with great expertise.
Hands that reach far out with effortless ease.
Although they may not always be fair,
Still…mother's hands have always been there.
A mother's love is expressed through her wonderful hands.
Reassuring and always enduring,
Compassionate, forgiving, and forever believing.
Nurturing me, mother's hands work day and night, night and day.
Worn hands that are etched with love and pain.
For this child, her hands always had to bear…
For me, mother's hands…will always be there.

Richelle Tran, Grade 9
La Quinta High School, CA

Pirates of the Sea

Pirates of the sea, with your pointy swords
And biggest ship, raced to the sea
Of the trapped dead and furious beast
Taking a troll in the water
Looking for the dead treasures

Stealing, robbing your neighbors ships
Threatening, capturing with your dangerous swords
Wanderers of the seas
Warriors of the oceans

Though having a bad name at land
Acted as true warriors at sea
Bravely charged into the deadly storm
Courageously fight the furious beast
Dead or alive, fate will decide

Helping a friend when they are down
Saving a companion's life at the rebellious sea
Looting a ship, needs a great fight
Never enter the battle without a friend

Bich Nguyen, Grade 7
Sarah McGarvin Intermediate School, CA

Sunshine

The sea is blue like your eyes
The sun is bright like you every day
You are perfect like the sunset
When I see you, it makes the clouds go away from my day.

Tony Smith, Grade 8
Young Scholar's Academy, AZ

Man's Curiosity

The descendent of Spirit and Opportunity arises after a long, lonely journey
To unmask the Red Planet and all of its disguises. Will Curiosity discover that we are not alone?

Launched on Thanksgiving, it must travel over 36 million miles,
the mission will end before it starts if there is the slightest of errors
Designed to detect, discovery and describe the barren rocky red surface,
Curiosity will expose us to the sights, sounds and smells of Mars

Curiosity enters Mars' atmosphere, traveling almost as fast as light, it lands using special effects
taken from the pages of science fiction thrillers
Everything has to work perfectly or Curiosity will suffocate and die
the world experiences seven minutes of sheer terror

The keen anxiety turns into tears of joy, curiosity lands perfectly in the dark shadow of Mount Sharp
And rumbles to life as it sends news and pictures from its new Martian home
demonstrating man's ability of overcoming even the largest of challenges

As it begins its mission to try to detect the building blocks of life,
the small SUV will transverse the Martian landscape for one Martian year
Being carefully guided by shrewd and sober scientists on Earth,
its unbelievable capabilities generating infinite possibilities

Curiosity will likely answer many of our questions about life on other planets
and perhaps lead to people walking on the Martian surface
Curiosity reflects the best of our spirit and our quest for opportunity,
we celebrate our imagination and creativity, bounded only by our curiosity

Michael Hatch, Grade 8
The Mirman School, CA

Puppet in the Darkness

You are sitting there, minding your own business.
The small booth empty. Just you and the empty cup of coffee. The
Warmth and joy now gone. Drunk and disappeared. And
Suddenly you can't see. You can't see the red pattern of the
Cushion. You can't feel the plastic underneath your fingertips. You are sinking.
Quickly now. No intention of stopping. Nothing to grab on to.
Then when you reach the bottom, you see the scratches on the walls. The dried…blood.
You remember the fear. The hate. The disbelief.
There is no light. No sound but the beating of your heart. But, somehow,
It is comforting. Knowing that this darkness may be the only constant in your life. You would
Have never seen it this way. The happiness sitting with
You in the booth can't compare with the constant. You no longer want to feel like a puppet.
Especially in your own life. You open your eyes and the darkness melts into the stage.
Your entire life depends on these next choices…But
You can't move. You try everything. To pull, to inch forward or sideways.
You look up. And you see why everything has stopped.
Your strings are being pulled in opposite directions. Your limbs are on fire.
Your joints feel like they are being torn, ripped from each other.
The stage lights flicker. And everything darkens.
You gasp for air as you see on the table, a message has been written on the napkin.
"Who do you believe? Who is right?"

Aiden Jacobs, Grade 9
East High School, CO

Christmas
Snow is white
Trees are green
Colorful lights around me
Gleam
Santa wears Red
While he flies in his sled
While we're all snug in bed
Dreaming of him
He fills the stockings with candy and toys
But only for the good girls and boys
He eats the cookies and drinks the milk
Picks up the toy bag that is covered in silk
All the kids get up so happy
They love Santa Claus
They're so joyful and clappey
Then sit by the fire and take a pause
Christmas is the best
Can't wait for next year
Santa will come again
My favorite time of year
Abby Kimball, Grade 7
Mountain Ridge Junior High School, UT

My Best Friend
We are going to different high schools
I know it will be hard
We were best friends
And now we are ripped apart

I remember the good days we had
Throughout these three long years
You were there when I was sad
Even when I was in tears

But now it's all changed
We can't be together anymore
No more notebooks to exchange
Or laughter to adore

I will never forget that smile of yours
And how it made me glad
Just remember you'll always be
The bestest friend I've ever had
Elvin Vazquez, Grade 8
John Adams Middle School, CA

Weather
Weather is light as a feather
If it is warm it is better
When I'm cold I'm in the shelter
I love the weather
Wind blows away the leaves
Wearing a jacket on my sleeve
Weather brings the best out of me
Nathan Hoang, Grade 7
Sarah McGarvin Intermediate School, CA

I Am Thankful For
my family that cares
great life which I love
clothes to wear daily
necessary things in life
functional body that works
caring parents which love me
food that is doing justice to my needs
brother and sister who care for me
not getting abused or worse
getting fed everyday
a house that is decent
all the things I get in life
Dayton Samarin, Grade 7
Daniel Savage Middle School, CA

The Ocean Lives
Seaweed flutters in the breeze,
Otter dips and twists.
Starfish twinkles and she shines,
While oyster shows off her pearls.
Shark swims 'round a school of fish.
Eel lights up the night.
Fish darts through the coral reef,
And octopus waves hi.
Turtle stays with the current,
Dolphin dances with the tide.
I could watch this all day,
But it's time to say good-bye.
Samantha Scampone, Grade 8
Ventura Missionary School, CA

I'm Thankful For
I'm thankful for…
A roof on my head
clothes to wear
amazing food to eat
parents who love and care
amazing teachers to learn from
real friends that I can't trust
being alive right now
having school and learning
money to buy things
a bed to sleep on
I'm thankful for everything
Breshna Shoja, Grade 7
Daniel Savage Middle School, CA

A Step into My Past
I am from an old bedroom
Where as a small child
I played with brightly colored
My Little Ponies and
Plastic Barbie dolls
In Bullhead City, Arizona

I am from my first love
Who turned into my
Brown-eyed heartbreaker

I am from my hazel-eyed savior
Who comforted me and
Wiped away my tears of sorrow and pain

I am from the ancient
Photo album, where memories are kept

I am from the
Quiet, dusty town that
Others just call Seligman, but
I call it home

I am from
The good and the bad
The happy and the depressed
Alexa Schreiner, Grade 9
Seligman High School, AZ

The Magic of a Moment
The first drop of rain,
falls into my outstretched hand.
The rainbow displays its glorious colors,
just for me.

The full moon glisters brightly above,
winks at me as I long for it.
The sun is up there, providing warmth,
just for me.

The ocean is a mystery,
mystically intoxicating me.
The waves rush in and dance in glee,
just for me.

The magic is in the air,
lurking, playing hide and seek with me.
The fragrance of it stays there lingering,
just for me.

I cherish these moments and thoughts,
and tuck them safely into my heart.
The magic of these moments resonate love,
just for me.
Resha Panda, Grade 7
Windemere Ranch Middle School, CA

Mommy

Mommy,
I love you.
You will never understand.
To explain to you
Is like trying to catch a wave upon the sand.

Mommy,
How can I thank you?
You will never understand.
To explain to you
Is like trying to hold a ray of sunshine in my hand.

Mommy,
You are my best friend.
You will never understand.
To explain to you
Is like trying to reach a rainbow on the land.

Mommy,
I need you.
I hope you'll understand.
You are my Mommy and my best friend
We go hand in hand.

Riley Atrops, Grade 7
Joe Walker Middle School, CA

Anger

Anger is red, blood red,

It tastes like a burnt cookie,
Where every imperfection is shunned,

It smells like fires,
Licking hatred inside you,

It sounds like yelling,
Denting your shield of pride with every blow,

And looks like another dimension,
where you inch closer to the edge with every word.

Anger feels like a time bomb inside your heart,
Just waiting to go off.

Maya Vannini, Grade 7
Tenaya Middle School, CA

But Now...

When I was little, the snow was a place of fun,
A place of refuge, to hide from the wiles of the world.
But now I realize, the cold bite, the sting of frozen limbs.
There's a lot of the world I didn't understand,
But if it snowed, that was good enough for me, cold enough for me.
There was a lot to you that I didn't understand,
But now I do, now I understand.

Joseph Budge, Grade 9
Canyon View Jr High School, UT

Crystal Clear

His raspy voice reflects the cruel world,
That has tortured him since childhood.
While his father drank,
His mother sank, deeper into depression.

It wasn't fair for his father,
To take his aggression out on him.
The abuse began,
When he was ten, a pantomime to the world he had become.

He had a hard life,
And all could tell.
His pain,
Would reign, within him forever.

Until the day he met his wife,
Life was forever changed.
He had much joy,
When he held his baby boy. His voice was crystal clear.

Brennen Boulger, Grade 7
Joe Walker Middle School, CA

Sparky

My dog Sparky was so white,
He looked as bright as the snow white.
Sparky had very great traits,
He could run faster than a train.

Sparky woke me up one morning,
With a very loud howling.
He was a German Shepherd,
But had the eyes of a leopard.

Cars passing by in the busy street,
All I heard was a very low scream.
Sparky's white fur soon turned muddy.
From his head to feet.

Dark, dark the sky went,
My feelings went along with the sky.
Cats meowing, dogs crying I could hear.
Worst of all, it was a shame I didn't shed a tear.

Jimmy Juarez, Grade 8
John Adams Middle School, CA

I Love You!

I love you more then words can say
I love you more every day
A broken heart torn right in two
Is now complete and belongs to you
You picked me up when I was down
And gave me a reason to never frown
I'm yours for life I swear its true
Just like the promise that I will always love you!

Mia Hendrix, Grade 9
New Designs Charter School, CA

Gymnastics

Gymnastics is a rubber band
You can make a mess, like in a drawer
Just like when you mess up your routine.
When they are combined
And wrapped together
It is like when you are on the floor and do a rebound.
You can stretch them
Like when you have to stretch your brain
To handle school and your routines.
There are different colors and sizes
Just like there are different events and tricks.
You can stretch it further
Like when you stretch at practice.
So you can prevent injury.
When you try too hard,
Stretch it too far,
Or push yourself past your limits,
The rubber band snaps
And your career is done.

Colette Martinez, Grade 8
Falcon Creek Middle School, CO

Fun with the Family

How is racing on the Wii possibly fun?
Making each other laugh makes us all very proud.
Jumping bikes with the kids is like a run.
Chasing each other is lots of fun but loud.
Going to choose a dog or cat is nice.
Racing each other is fun and entertaining.
When we wrestle, the dogs are protective.
Playing a game is fun for the family.
Riding horses can be very dangerous.
Watching movies is fun when we agree.
Mark and Dana like to ride bikes with us.
Jumping rope does not require a degree.
Summer time brings lots of fun to stay late.
That is why summer time fun is so great.

Marissa Decker, Grade 9
Lucerne Valley Middle/Sr High School, CA

What Happened to the World We Lived In?

It used to be a safe world.
Anyone could go outside and never have to hide.
In this new world there are missing little boys and girls.
Leaving loved ones upset, with tears in their eyes.

What happened to the world we lived in?
I've searched and searched but it's not here.
What happened to the world we lived in?
I guess that world is just fiction.

There's no peace, the world's at war.
Why can't we all be friends?
And maybe, just maybe, this world we lived in will come back again.

Juli'Anne Easter, Grade 8
Robert E Peary Middle School, CA

Plague

Conceited are you who are under the impression that
you are the only one to have suffered hopelessness or fear.
Those souls passed on,
with emotions just the same.
Their significance lost forever,
in the flame lit for all.

The darkened, dim shadows, surged like wildfire.
Slowly, weakened souls slipped into that obscure fog,
one by one, 'til there was no one to close the vacant
eyes of those who couldn't bear to stay alive.
No one there to mourn the lost,
agonized in their last moments.
Souls suffocating, gasping
through choked lungs,
whispering to silenced loved ones.
Evidence, stories of the
unmourned lost.
Lost forever,
in the flame lit for all.

Kathern Crockett, Grade 8
Indian Hills Middle School, UT

Poetry's a Girl's Best Friend

When Mimmy had first started middle school,
She wasn't known for being cool,
She didn't have many friends,
They didn't care about her in the end,
So she was usually all alone,
But she stayed quiet and never moaned,
But one day, she found her special gift,
She was great in poetry, her sadness started to lift,
She became the top of her English class,
And every subject after that,
She began to make new friends,
And her quietness started to end.

Mimmy became top professor at Stanford,
And this time, she was always heard,
She looked back at her old memories,
When things weren't always at ease,
She thanked everyone in the end,
But mainly poetry, because to her,
Poetry's a girl's best friend.

Tiffany Yu, Grade 8
Taylor Middle School, CA

Thoughts on Edvard Munch's Painting, "The Scream"

The man might be invisible
Or even worse,
Nobody cares about him
Because they think he is crazy.
Nobody
Cares.

Eric Franco, Grade 7
Tenaya Middle School, CA

The Four Seasons
A leaf falls from the tree
The wind blows
Piles of leaves are found on the ground

A hot chocolate sits on the table
You take a sip
Of the creamy and chocolaty milk
While looking at a blanket of snow outside

Flowers bloom with the sun shining down
Rain drops fall on the ground
More flowers start to bloom

The sun shines
People eat ice cream
While sitting by the pool
Julia Morales, Grade 7
Carmel Valley Middle School, CA

Cliff Jumping
Jumping into the icy cold water
Swimming to the rocky cliffs
I step onto the sharp rocks
The cliff awaits me
I walk to the edge and look down
Big mistake!
Suddenly it hits me —
Literally it hits me —
My friend pushes me
And suddenly I'm faaallliiing —
SPLASH!
Time to do it all over again.
Ryan Moltz, Grade 7
Salida Middle School, CO

Words Unsaid
sharp, shooting arrows of pain
running their course
around your body.

intense despair
threading through you.
cold darkness
surrounding you.

he's gone, ascended to heaven.
you're here, feeling all alone.
the worst thing is
you never got a chance to say
goodbye.
Kate Stokes, Grade 9
Canyon View Jr High School, UT

The Mystic Woodland
Enveloped in a green canopy
Entangled in ancient mystery

Folded into mossy sunshine
Making the wood something sublime

Ringing with elfin whispers
Covered in ethereal glory

Majesty unheard of
Rippling with aerial beauty

Darkness steals in in velvety silence
A chill settles through the wood

The stream is laughing its way downward
Calling old tales of yore

And yonder off the hill
A dream is sprouting because of it
Eythana Miller, Grade 7
Eagle Valley School, MT

Hardships
They said, "Get to the back of the bus."
I sighed.
They said, "You don't belong here."
I sighed.
They said, "Get away from him."
I sighed.
They said, "Use the other fountain."
I sighed.
They said, "Why is your skin like that?"
I sighed.
They said, "You're not allowed to…"
I sighed.
They said, "Nobody cares."
I sighed.
They said, "Where are you from?"
I sighed.
They said, "You're so weird."
I sighed.
They said, "You have nothing to say."
I said, "I have a dream."
AmirParsa Arefian, Grade 8
South Lake Middle School, CA

Snow
The snow is white
and very bright.
It sparkles under the sun
while you are having fun.
It's something we all should share.
Everywhere.
Adanna Bekverdyan, Grade 7
Sierra Charter School, CA

Be Thankful
Go inside a poor child's home
Observe the way he lives
See what he has gone through
See its emptiness like an
Old abandoned fairground with its
Junk food strung about the furniture.
Perhaps you'll find
That ripped mattress
In the corner
Perhaps now you should be
Thankful for what you have
And help those
Who haven't.
Hailey Jenkins, Grade 9
New Plymouth High School, ID

Make a Connection
I heard her story,
I couldn't make a connection.
She had much glory
I couldn't make a connection.
She was a survivor,
I couldn't make a connection.
She was much wiser,
I couldn't make a connection.
She loved everyone,
I couldn't make a connection.
She found her freedom,
I couldn't make a connection.
She got the lucky breaks,
I couldn't make a connection.
She made mistakes.
I made a connection.
Savannah Griffin, Grade 8
South Lake Middle School, CA

Reflections on Escher's "Relativity"
In this drawing I see an illusion.
I see people without expressions,
people without faces, people without race,
Walking
In every direction;
Up, down, sideways on stairs with railings.
In a big old building
Leading
To a new path in life.
Some are with others,
Some are by themselves.
But all are choosing different paths in life.
Jake Newman, Grade 7
Tenaya Middle School, CA

I Love

Loving is so different,
So complex and strange,
Yet it brings the best of me.
I love him,
Oh so much.
And I miss him,
Oh so much.
When he speaks,
I shiver,
When he works,
I watch.
My heart sings when I see him,
Sighs when I do not.
One day I will tell him,
The words I utter not.
The words that form a barrier,
From me,
And him.
Yet I think he knows I love.
I love.
The most dangerous thing of all.
Katy Wickberg, Grade 7
Mountain Ridge Middle School, CO

Emotions

They call your name
Like a bullhorn
Sometimes scream
In your face
They have
A bittersweet
Harsh sound to them with a slap
Of hardcore honesty
And or like a bubbly feeling
Yet you hate them
You still go
Back and use them
For guidance
With more trust than the first time all these
Big, little, small, huge, strong, weak
Emotions like a bullhorn
It seems so clear
But makes you so deaf and unaware
To your surroundings
But in the end
They're pretty handy
Miquela Black, Grade 8
Falcon Creek Middle School, CO

Captain Hook

There once was a captain named Hook
He had taken what he shouldn't have took.
He tried to fly for a while
But then got eaten by a crocodile.
Quinn Seawalt, Grade 8
Beacon Country Day School, CO

Bright Lightning

Falling golden leaves,
Burning, melting.
Flowing into a rigidly ice cold stream,
Mixing ashen gold with trickling brilliant blue,
Moving, forming,
Creating a mound of black sludge,
Slithering across the damp ground,
Inhaling, exhaling.
Hearing the sound of tears shattering against the floor,
Trying to move away from the deafening pain only to find another fire,
Scorching every dream and happiness,
Sucking the breath of life away.

Grasping frantically around the terror to find strength,
Knowing it is there but blocked by a numbing blindness,
Fearing, fighting.
Lightning cracking showing the destruction around you,
Allowing for the slightest chance,
Hoping, doubting.
Straining for the possibility of changing the open future,
Remembering forever.
Taylor Lofgren, Grade 9
Pine Creek High School, CO

A New Winter

Winter, a foreign feeling that embraces me like an old friend
A pure white lining of fallen snow crosses the gentle horizon
An admirable sky blends its refined colors of pinks and purples and baby blues
A chill runs through my skin, concealed in bumps indicating the coldness in the air
I drape a blanket over my shoulders and watch the day pass quickly and swiftly
A warm cup of hot cocoa heats my throat as it slips past my tongue
I savor the flavor that creates a dance among my taste buds
Dim lights surround a humble tree like an artifact in an exhibit
Like a statue it stands proud, proving true a Christmas soon to come
A season of affection for one another, a season for offering and giving
A season that brings people together as neighbors, friends, family.
The blazing moon illuminates the freezing sky
I feel a sense of rightness in the air as I prepare for a deep slumber
And as I sink into my sheltered bed, I wait patiently
Waiting for a new dawn to awake.
Alexandra Capelouto, Grade 8
Vail Ranch Middle School, CA

Best Friends

It's hard to think back to the time we met,
So long ago,
You were my very best friend even though…
I hid your phone and put mayonnaise in your hair,
And while on our camping trip I slipped a worm in your sandwich right then and there,
I took care of your dog and frog even though they were a chore,
But at least it wasn't a bore,
Even though I did those things,
We are best friends, because we find the best in one another,
And that's exactly why we're best best friends with each other.
Lauren Verna, Grade 7
Monte Vista Christian School, CA

A Wonderful Time of Year

There's a park with light green grass and
Little kids running and playing for the first time since snow.
One boy wearing his Avengers t-shirt and his Superman pajama bottoms
Yells, "You're it!"

Boys are tossing a baseball around, preparing for the season.
And many are playing with their dogs.
The oldest black and white bulldog doesn't understand the game and refuses to return the ball.

There's a bench with teenagers with the most "stylish" clothes
Talking, laughing, and telling stories.

There's a picnic
With ants creeping up
And stealing pieces of dropped Mac-n-Cheese and bits of crust from a peanut butter sandwich.

Mothers pushing yellow strollers
Show their year old babies the bright green nature in the world they live.

No one is lonely,
Everyone has a friend to talk to and have fun with.

Gabriella Campbell, Grade 7
Rolling Hills Country Day School, CA

The Fall of Summer

The taste of fall, the smell of fall, the sound of fall
It's rich pumpkin pie, hot apple cider, and black bean chili
It's the smell of the warm soup, the new leather jacket, and a pile of old books
It's the crackling of leaves, a knock on the door, the sound of a mouse skittering across the floor
It's radiant colors of the trees, the cold damp ground, the bright orange pumpkins
You feel the whirling wind in your ears, and feel the chill creep up your back
You see the bright yellow moon, the ash-colored sky, and the fading green grass
There's a sense of newness in the air
Something leaving
Something coming
As the season before is disappearing, fading

Tessa Lindley, Grade 7
Mountain Ridge Junior High School, UT

Be Heard

Once you're on this earth, you are known for something
Being someone's daughter, relative, friend.
Or something you're good at.
Or being heard.
Once you're heard you will never be forgotten.
Once you speak your mind to the public, you can live freely, passionately.
To live with passion is to live by your choices and your own actions.
To live freely is to be free minded and to do whatever pleases you.
I chose to be heard and to live passionately.
I spoke my mind to prove my point to the world that once you say or do something nobody will forget it.
It will be stuck with you like your genes or facial features.
I chose to live passionately to show people that its not about how you live your life but who's in it with you.
Once you're put on this earth you are known for something
I was heard and will never be forgotten

Cheyenne Johnston, Grade 8
Palm Desert Charter Middle School, CA

Penalty Kick

I step up to the line
the pressure is on; everyone is watching
holding their breath
I pick my head up high
with my nose to the sky
I take a step back and pull my leg up
I look at the goalie
then at the ball
I launch like a rocket get ready to swing
my leg goes out fast
my foot hits the ball
though the ball is in the air
for less than a second
it seems like an hour
the ball goes up to the corner
away from the goalie
he springs like a tiger so agile and free
the ball hits his gloves
but it slides by like butter
the goal of the game, the score of the season
everyone's cheering and the pressure releases

Caleb Bartel, Grade 7
Salida Middle School, CO

Ode to Chocolate Milk

O', chocolate milk you're essential to my life.
Your addicting chocolate touch
And your refreshing milk
Give me joy.

As soon as I pour you into my glass,
My mouth waters,
And I am instantly taken under your control.

After a long day,
I can rely on you to be there.
Like my dog,
When I come back from school.

Some prefer soda or lemonade;
But me, I savor you and your coziness.

Katie Gould, Grade 7
Rolling Hills Country Day School, CA

Be Like Water

Be like water, help life live.
Be like water, fit any situation.
Be like water, soothe the burns of others.
Be like water, let your mind be still.
Be like water, welcome all into your life.
Be like water, let your emotion and movement flow.
Be like water, be in everyone's life.
Be like water, constantly give to others.
Be like water, for to be like water, is to be at peace.

Aidan Healy, Grade 7
Petaluma Jr High School, CA

People in Shadows

Sitting here in the park on this bench, my arms on its arms
It's legs old and rusted, the paint falling off
Thinking why must people
Follow each other
When they could
Inspire
Or start a new era
Of many things
Dance, fashion, technology
They don't know
That they could stick out
And not have to blend
They could be the icicle falling not
Hanging
They could be the delicate balloon that people see,
Floating around like a cloud
Watching it rise until
POP
It just tears at the inspirers, making them blend.
Everybody
Wants to be black and white

Vincent Flores, Grade 8
Weldon Valley Jr High School, CO

As a Child

When I was young I danced all day,
Always wanted more time to play,
Couldn't wait to get out in the sun,
Somehow managed to always have fun,
Laughed at my own cheesy jokes,
Loved to spend time with my folks,
Always called my brother mean,
Since I was such a drama queen,
Had fun playing in the park,
Always tried to stay up till dark,
My favorite food to eat was candy,
I liked to play with my little turtle Dandy,
On long car rides I liked to hum,
Tried to blow bubbles with bubble gum,
I most definitely loved to talk,
And write on the sidewalk with colorful chalk.

Rachel Jeet, Grade 9
University Preparatory School, CA

Ode to Lovely Dog

I saw her with the owner who sold her to my dad,
her fur is like mixed coffee,
with the coffee creamer falling in darkness,
her fur feeling soft like a blanket,
when she's hungry it's like she can eat everything,
after her bath she smells like raspberries,
she loves to play with me,
licking wildly on my face,
my dog is the best

Zakiya Williams, Grade 8
Daniel Savage Middle School, CA

Amen

The ache of a cold winter spent alone,
A heart breaking for the love that is lost.
All of the long nights waiting by the phone,
If only I would have known of the cost.

How can I do this to myself again?
The salty tears streaming from my hurt eyes.
It's over, nothing, no more, gone, amen.
I don't have what it takes to win the prize.

Somewhere along this time, I lost my heart.
I would've followed you 'til the world's end.
We would've loved 'til we were forced to part.
Every turn, I think of you, every bend.

If only you knew the pain that I hold.
If you will listen, my love will unfold.

Anna Marie Myra, Grade 9
Monarch High School, CO

Confidence

I watch you walk through the maze of the hall,
You hold your books, rushing to make the bell.
Your deep-set, big, brown eyes; they say it all
I see right through you, I am shy as well.

But we are not in any way the same.
I wish that your confidence would grow.
Do you constantly have to play this game?
You hide inside yourself, even you know.

You are always trying to impress me,
Faking smiles even when you are sad.
Can you not be happy and let things be?
You're a beautiful girl, why are you mad?

Why can't you see that I love you for you,
And look in the mirror and see that too?

Georgia Reis, Grade 9
Monarch High School, CO

Ballerinas

It is rare that you see them work.
You think they don't practice at all.
Yet, they practice every day.
If you look at the stage you will see their sweat.
Their magic is their grace, the way they move their body.
You see romance. It is real in that moment.
Their turns and leaps tell a story.
You never hear them land.
Even at curtain call they are in character.
They live to do this for you.
They live to dance.

Cassandra Hope, Grade 7
Christ the King School, AZ

The Spring

The cold is gone and the sunshine is here to stay.
The flowers and the bees are here to play.
Now it is the time to go outside,
but the sun shall stay it will not hide.

We shall once more feel the breeze
of the ice of a new cup of icee freeze.
The children are playing in the parks,
and they have one dog to play with that barks.

The spring makes me smile in joy
like when I was a boy and I would play with a toy.
The spring is coming to a end,
and the weather is starting to bend.

The summer is almost here.
The extremely hot weather is near.
the spring is at its end it is out of time,
and the summer is here but it is not a crime.

David Venegas, Grade 7
Joe Walker Middle School, CA

The Unicorn

A majestical creature in the forest,
its horn is long and strong,
I've been looking for it all my life,
and as it stands before me, nothing can go wrong.

Fourteen years I've waited for this,
and the time has finally come,
that large, white horse in front of me,
is a magical unicorn.

I took a step forward,
snap! I broke a stick,
it glared at me with fierce eyes,
and then it did a trick.

It flew away like a beautiful song,
off to infinity and beyond,
I've been looking for it all my life,
and in two seconds it was gone.

Eva Fink, Grade 7
Joe Walker Middle School, CA

Friendship

Friendship is like a sailing ship,
on a journey to cross the sea.
It can be a smooth sailing ride on a sun kissed day.
Or it can be as if there was a terrible storm
with lighting thrashing, destroying everything in its way.
Friendship is a mysterious and phenomenal thing,
nevertheless it can be a pain.

Adrianna Oliver, Grade 7
Daniel Savage Middle School, CA

Where Poetry Hides for Me
Poetry can be found anywhere
But this is where poetry hides for me;
Poetry hides in my music and in my beat-up soccer ball,
It also hides in the soccer field at which I played my first match,
Poetry hides in my old beat-up uniform,
It hides in the fireplace of my old house,
Poetry hides in my bed where I always stay warm,
It hides in my dreams,
Poetry hides in my pencil and all the paper it has marked,
But, most important, poetry hides in me.

Nico Medina, Grade 7
Tenaya Middle School, CA

One Day...
Have you ever thought that maybe...
One day, you'll be able to live your dream?
One day, that's all it takes,
If you worked hard enough...
You've got to take action for what you believe in.
Make it work for yourself, even if...
You've tried your hardest.
The next thing you know, that slightest moment, that one day...
You could've possibly given up, you'll be sitting in the
Hall of Fame.

Ivy Nguyen, Grade 7
Sarah McGarvin Intermediate School, CA

Reflections on Rodin's Sculpture, "Thought"
In this sculpture
I see a head
With no legs or arms;
Trapped in a carved
Molten rock.
She can't get out,
She's hopeless,
She's sad.
She doesn't have a friend.
She is a lonely, miserable being.

Jarron Vasaure, Grade 7
Tenaya Middle School, CA

Books
Books are a wonderful thing
They take me to another world.
To the past or future,
To a magical place,
Or a time of warfare.
Their words keep me engaged.
The characters fascinate me.
The images they put in my head are amazing.
There is nothing I love more than a good book.
Books are truly amazing things.

Gianna Nicolich, Grade 7
Daniel Savage Middle School, CA

Unwanted Flames
Cancer is a fire
that burns up the memories you would've made
but will let you cherish all that you have

It will be a painful burn
but will always heal in time

Some can be put out fast
others last until nothing else can be destroyed

Fire consumes the body
it drains you of all that you were
it leaves you with just a shell

It can do so much
just remember it can be good
think of the positives

Never let that fire bring you down
put it out with all your love

If that fire decides it's your time
let it be
for only you will know

Brooke Robertson, Grade 8
Falcon Creek Middle School, CO

Music
Music — Full of laughter
Talking to himself
And talking to the world
Weaving a song
A unique song
Full of playfulness and joy and even contention

Music — He is full of power and wonder
Full of strength
Full of happiness and excitement
But also filled with sadness and weeping
And hatred and conflict
With sorrows untold
However
The beauty that he brings to our world
Is truly better than any earthly possession

Music — He has the power
To unite countries
Into peace and to rid the world of rebellion

Music — Life wouldn't have meaning without him
Thank goodness he's here
Hallelujah

Caleb Durant, Grade 7
Tenaya Middle School, CA

Fall

A time for preparation
As birds fly south in migration,
While bears prepare for hibernation,
And squirrels gather nuts in preparation.

For soon it will be Thanksgiving
And food the harvests will bring.
For Christmas bells will ring,
As joyous Christmas songs we sing.

Garret Dupper, Grade 7
Intermountain Adventist Academy, CO

Drawing

As I draw on a sheet of paper,
I let my imagination flow free.
Using color pencils or paint,
I love to draw with any coloring item.
As I draw, I feel like Leonardo Da Vinci.
I create art from my mind
Without rules or exceptions.
Sometimes my creations even surprise me
As they come to life for others to see.

Gabriel Rangel, Grade 7
Christ the King School, AZ

Ode to Lip Gloss

You come in different colors
So bright, so glamourous
Matte, gloss, sheer, and shimmer
Fun, and chic you always glimmer
I find you at night
Or sometimes in plain sight
I get you on my birthday
You make me feel like a shining star
You take me far, you are lip gloss

Matula Kakridas, Grade 7
Daniel Savage Middle School, CA

If

If you can breathe then you can whisper
If you can whisper then you can talk
If you can talk then you can yell
If you can yell then you can scream
If you can scream then you have a voice
If you have a voice then you have a brain
If you have a brain then you can dream
If you can dream then you can do…
ANYTHING!

Destany Little Bird, Grade 8
North Star Charter School, ID

The First Time I Played Violin

I picked up my first instrument
The shoulder rest on my shoulder,
Strange to the touch, like very hard uncomfortable pillow on my shoulder.
My teacher placed the bow in my hand
And the magic started.
I placed the bow on the string and
Listened. The music flowed into my ear.
The mesmerizing melody, sweet as melting chocolate and sugared strawberries,
And as graceful as a dancer.
The music entered my world and changed it. It came to
An end. I was amazed. My teacher played beautifully,
But all I could do was "Twinkle Twinkle Little Star."
Months passed, then a year and I improved, but every time I play the
Music becomes magic again. Even though it's not as
Beautiful, it's still magic. The harder the piece got the more magical
And frustrating it got. It would always move me again.
My violin now is the thing that sets my soul,
   Free

Marissa Morimoto, Grade 7
Rolling Hills Country Day School, CA

Poetry Hides

In my hands…under the place I stand,
Poetry hides
In my very first roller coaster ride, where I made twists and turns upside down
Poetry hides in me,
Poetry hides where I first moved into my first house.
Poetry hides where my sister gave me a hug for the first time,
Poetry hides where my niece took her very first steps,
Poetry hides
Between me and my best friend's friendship,
Poetry hides in my box with my most valuable treasure,
Poetry hides where I had my happiest moment,
Poetry hides under all the fun toys my mom bought me when I was two.
Poetry hides where my family has their family reunions.
Poetry hides in my favorite book, in my TV, and most of all
Poetry hides
Where
My older brother
Died.

Stefanie Lopez, Grade 7
Sierra Charter School, CA

Global Diversity of Light

Light gives us life and provides us happiness.
It bring us knowledge and insights.
In light of our differences in our society and in our nature,
it makes us human.
All forms of light provide both sources of light and heat.
Different amounts of light appears to us as diverse colors.
Light traveling at various frequencies appear to us as assorted colors.
We too travel at different rates and speeds.
As humans, we are as a ray of light.
Our light shines in different colors and gives us a global diversity of light.

Luke Merrill, Grade 7
Canyon View Jr High School, UT

Those Memorable Moments

I am from pitching in my backyard
Feeling the softball
Rolling off my fingertips.
I am from friends and family
Smiling and laughing till it hurts.

I am from a house of many children
Little kids running around
Playing with their SpongeBob toys.
I am from being the oldest of 7 children
Having to take the responsibility of watching my siblings.

I am from listening to Justin Bieber
Believing every step
Of the way.
I am from those San Francisco Giants moments
Waiting for Emmanuel Burriss to get a base hit
Hearing the fans cheering.

I am from those memorable
Most-wanted moments.

Kiana Alvarado, Grade 9
Seligman High School, AZ

The Unknown in the Closet

The closet door creaks open
Like a coffin welcoming the dead
Smiling, daring us to see what's inside
As we lean in to glimpse,
The unknown obscures our senses

Every step is a stride
In an abyss of desolate darkness
Not knowing what will be around the corner
The unknown clouds our reason
And takes advantage of our blindness

The unknown controls our lives
Manipulating us through constant fear
It follows us through our life
Until the largest unknown of all

Nicholas Song, Grade 7
The Mirman School, CA

Red Rocks, Red Sands

I see acres of smoke.
Death is at hand.
Red Rocks Red Sands.
I see cut hands and bruised skin.
The fog of war has soiled our land.
Red Rocks Red Sands.
I see nothing but ruin.
We have all fallen victim to the beast that is man.
Red Rocks Red Sands.

Sawyer Cliff, Grade 7
Salida Middle School, CO

Dandelions

As I walk through the plain
I see nothing but shame
No flowers to smell
No trees to hide under
All I see are small weeds
Some plain green
Oh great, more green
But others are white
What a weird color for a weed
So I ask myself
Why are they here, they are no good
They do not smell, they do not blend into the grass
So I turn back and see other kids blowing on them looking for them
With expressions that look as if they have found gold
Like it is their most prized possession
So I think and think and I realize
Those are not weeds
But beautiful flowers
That do not need big pink or blue petals to be beautiful
That flower is beautiful all on her own
With no effort to fit in

Kaisha Serrano, Grade 8
St John's Episcopal School, CA

I Do Not Understand

I do not understand
Why people make hasty decisions
Why some presidents are elected
Why change can't always be good
But most of all I do not understand
Why middle school girls like to gossip
Why some people are shy
Why good grades are hard to achieve
Why my friends think its weird to hang out with guys
Why guitar strings are hard to push down on
What I do understand is singing
The trills, slides, turns, feel wonderful in my mouth
The melody makes its way into my chest
Lyrics form images in my head, and
Give me ideas about life.

Mykelle Coats, Grade 7
White Pine Middle School, UT

Meeting

The golden moon shining brightly, meeting the gray ocean.
The gray ocean meeting the cold sand.
Me, on the cold sand watching the waves leap onto the sand.
Waiting, I listen for the footsteps of my love.
I quickly turn and see my love still a field away.
Running toward each other, her golden hair flying in the wind,
The warm breeze hitting my face like a warm kiss on my cheek.
We meet, talking in hushed tones.
Two lovers, meeting in the night
Face to face.

Kimberly Richard, Grade 7
Mountain Ridge Jr High School, UT

I Was

I was always a mysterious child,
I always wanted to be alone for a while.
Gatherings would always seem eternal to me,
I did not like being with my family.
My relatives wanted me to play with them,
But I asked myself when are they going to leave, when?

I was always a mysterious child,
The kitchen was the room I most disliked.
I fiercely wanted to run out the door,
When I wanted to have silence behind my tree,
I found out it was just a dream.

I was always a mysterious child,
I still remember when my plants died.
The expression on my face was blank,
Then my tears shrank.
I had to put on a fake smile on my face,
And pretend everything was okay.

Kimberly Eileen Mejia, Grade 8
Richardson PREP HI Middle School, CA

Life Lesson

Life is a high, rocky mountain
Which you need to climb up
Reaching for dreams
You'll think you might not make it
And just give up
But every hope you get
The more stronger you will be
Courage will lead you through
To every step of the way
When you succeed
Life changes for you
And becomes a cool, sunny beach
You can walk your way and not be afraid
With courage and hope, you can do anything.

Jesenia Alonso, Grade 8
La Presa Middle School, CA

Is the Relationship Worth It?

Every relationship is an emotional roller coaster
It's that one crazy theme park ride
Everyone is scared of
But once you ride it you
Either loved it or hated it
Afterwards you either feel sick to your stomach
Or have butterflies
Every relationship has a price
But is it a price worth paying for
Some say yes, others say no
Relationships have an emotional toll
Sometimes good, sometimes bad, sometimes both
But never the same

Mykayla Branscomb, Grade 9
New Plymouth High School, ID

December

The shivering season has come,
As we saw the change in weather,
We were outside viewing the colorful bright lights.

We all wait for the time to come,
Slowly green branches come out,
One by one.

We all cheer for our neighbors have come,
A meal for twenty appears,
Also some hot cocoa to warm up the day.

Once we all fell asleep,
We dreamt we heard a,
Ho, ho, ho
And a,
Ha, ha, ha
Plus a,
Merry Christmas!

Catherine Tran, Grade 7
Sarah McGarvin Intermediate School, CA

Love Is Winter

love is like winter where it's cold and rains
how the wind taunts me making it worse to bare
shivering place waiting for warmth not pains
when will it go away just waiting near
as night falls where there's hardly light or warmth
then in the morning there falls white powder
here in the middle of a shower of smooth
it just blew away pain not making it matter
why is love bright and awful its too much
to take but you fight through it and light
comes around making your day a lunch
like I said winter is love day and night
never let it go for it is like hope
love also can hurt but try not to mope

Arleen Quevedo, Grade 9
Lucerne Valley Middle/Sr High School, CA

Freedom

Freedom is hair blowing in the wind,
Freedom is expressing yourself in your own way,
Freedom is being creative and making something new.

Freedom is speaking for your rights and others' rights,
Freedom is fighting for everything you're for
and what you think is right for others.

Freedom is willing to love who you want to love,
Freedom is something we all have when we are born,

But without freedom,
We're nothing but American slaves locked away without a key.

Clarence Manakaja, Grade 9
Seligman High School, AZ

Life's Journey

Life is an unimaginable journey
It's the craziest thing in all of man kind
The funniest of all and horrible
But loved, not fair life is
Life is a journey for birth to death

Life does not have a meaning it's a endless journey
Life is an adventure that goes on endlessly
You experience everything you can possibly see and learn
Life's journey is to learn love hate trust learn live
Life is a journey there is nothing else to it

You learn you live you experience
You feel all these different emotions inside yourself
You explore all the emotions in a different ways
You love some of them others you hate and wish to never feel again
Life is unexpected it's a journey
Cole Brownlee, Grade 8
Palm Desert Charter Middle School, CA

My Wonderful Aunt Stephanie

Warm heart filled with love and compassion.
Hugs and kisses fill the air.
With care she would share.
The sun shines bright whenever near.
She walks by singing lullabies.
The birds sing along as they hear.
The heart breaks.
The seizure erupts.
Everything is destroyed.
It's quiet.
Cries ands shouts
Of despair scream out.
The clouds are gray.
The carriage is set to take her away.
Every part is burned and placed in the wind.
Her spirit is gone, but it shall return again.
Good bye and farewell to a long, yet short term friend.
Faye Mensah, Grade 7
Monte Vista Christian School, CA

The Life I Love

I walk onto the field
as dust flies from the cleats of my teammates
I continue my march into the white, chalked circle
I'm surrounded by my screaming fans
but I only see one person.
I gently scoop up the scratched, yellow, leather ball
as I go into my windup and hear the snap of the glove
and then the yell of the ump "strike one!"
Now I know
deep in my heart
that this is what I love.
Cheyenne Stallions, Grade 9
New Plymouth High School, ID

A Place Called Home

The place I call home
Is where dogs wag their tails and bark,
Where my brothers make silly jokes,
And the smell of yummy food filling your nose.

The place I call home
Is when there is music calling out to our ears,
When guests and relatives come over to hang out,
And eat together as a big family.

The place I call home
Is where everyone can feel beautiful in their own way,
Feeling happy around each other,
And making good and bad memories.

The place I call home
Is where my family turns up the music
And dances all night long.
So be glad you have this place which we call home.
Nathali Torres, Grade 8
Richardson PREP HI Middle School, CA

The Inflation of an Overdo

In an instant of making your heart desire
You become a dull shadow
A space of loneliness that fills your distant heart
Forms a road to an ashy cell
We emphasize by the beat of the belt
The pain washes away rather then the scars
As you give all you have
Not surprised what you give is not enough
You become used to screwing up and unfamiliar to being noticed
To the point where you become uncomfortable with yourself
The scratchy noise pounding on your heart
Fades with the thump of a dark boot
Your fear is no longer in existence
For it had just become life
Cheyenne Aragon, Grade 9
Bear Creek High School, CO

My Best Friend

Camryn Willis is my best friend
singing and dancing is how she expresses
her personality is surely one of a kind
as beautiful as a flower
as graceful as a swan
her smile oh how she hates it
loves One Direction they make her feel pretty
yet she hates when people give her pity
she is as strong as a rock
remember there is a inside and its funny, talented, and sweet
Camryn Willis who is she…
my other half, my twin, you might say my sister
Aarynn Jones, Grade 7
Daniel Savage Middle School, CA

Future

Put the future
In a box
Tie it up with
Lots of knots
Hide it under
Rocks and clay
To save it for
Another day
When the past
Has gone away

Izzy Dent, Grade 7
Monte Vista Christian School, CA

Don't Give Up

Don't give up,
Things will be just great,
You're just out of luck
Just don't be irate
Good things are meant to come
Ignore all that hate
Until those feelings are done
Not everything is rainbows and unicorns
Don't give up,
And keep your head up.

Madeleine Hill, Grade 7
Monte Vista Christian School, CA

I Believe

I believe in Santa
I believe in magic
I believe in fairies
I believe in miracles
I believe in fairytales
I believe that dreams can come true
I believe that…
If we work together, we can do anything
I believe!

Kaylee Chang, Grade 7
Sarah McGarvin Intermediate School, CA

Water

W hat will the world be like without water?
A mazingly pure
T rouble without it
E veryone needs it
R ising, evaporating, raining

Respect water,
Don't tolerate it.
Use it wisely as it lasts.

Long Trinh, Grade 7
Sarah McGarvin Intermediate School, CA

Personification

The weather tonight…has come alive.
The wind is blowing as hard as it can.
You can hear the deep rumbles of his roar of frustration,
Then, you can see a flash of anger in his eyes.
He starts to cry,
At first it's just sobbing, then
All of a sudden he's crying showers of tears uncontrollably.
Soon, the sun calms him down,
Talks him through his problems, helps him and wipes away the tears.
Now, he's all smiles, he shines bright.
A rainbow appears showing all his colors;
All is right in the world.

Marissa Middleton, Grade 7
Tenaya Middle School, CA

My Kitchen

Dishes everywhere, flowers spread upon the cabinets
And a refrigerator that I can see my reflection in
Lots and lots of food
The smells of cooked meals
And yummy desserts
Mom, dad, and especially me spend a lot of our time searching for food
Mom cooks for all of us
Although, dad and I wait impatiently and decides to snack
Sun sets slowly through the shadows of the curtains
Makes it look like a moonlight evening
Many wonderful memories, too many to remember
My kitchen

Alexandra Gonzales, Grade 8
Ripona Elementary School, CA

The Way We Do Things

Some people say it's just a sport,
It's more than just a sport.
The way you learn things, or the way you listen to people.
The way you walk or talk, all depends on one sport.
It teaches you more than a few skills,
Not only do we use the skills we learn on the court, but also in the real life.
The way you respect other people's choices.
This sport has brought me more than just something to do,
It has brought me family, friends and a way of doing something.
It's more than just a sport,
It's a way of life.

Robi Salisbury, Grade 9
New Plymouth High School, ID

Winter Air

I love the smell of winter air
Fresh with smells of rainy ground
I love the feeling of wind blowing through my hair
Every day I wish it would snow
I love snow the white falling down to the ground
It is so beautiful
I know one day that it will end but wishing every day that it didn't have to

Mekaylynn Boehl, Grade 7
Meridian Elementary School, CA

Love

The first time you see your puppy,
Love.
The smiles of the children,
Love.
The last time you see your grandmother,
Love.
The time you say goodbye to go to college,
Love.
The first day of 7th grade,
Love.
The first day of kindergarten,
Love.
The first steps you took,
Love.
The first person you saw, mom,
Love.
The most powerful thing you will
Ever have,
Love.

Ashton Martinez, Grade 7
Salida Middle School, CO

The Universal Projector

I am small and loud
I wonder how I sound to others
I hear feedback from myself
I see millions of screaming fans
I am small and loud

I pretend people come to see me
I feel the trembling inside
I touch many different hands
I worry about getting dropped
I cry when I am no longer needed
I am small and loud

I understand all languages
I say what I hear
I dream of moving all around
I try to sound clear
I hope I will live forever
I am small and loud

Carol Johnson, Grade 7
Falcon Creek Middle School, CO

Reflections on Escher's "Relativity"

I see stairs of a never-ending path,
A path that leads to the future,
A path that works in any way
Upside down, sideways…good or bad,
The path never stops.

Joseph R. Alvarez, Grade 7
Tenaya Middle School, CA

Nightmare

My pajamas push in on me,
Damp with sweat
Icy after-images
Flash through my head
Dread is running through me
Continuing to rush
No rest for me
Tonight
Coming closer
Weaving itself
Through my mind
I beg for someone —
Anyone —
To wake me up
To save me
From this
Nightmare.

Gwen Boyack, Grade 7
Canyon View Jr High School, UT

Ode to My Dog: Kole

Oh my handsome dog Kole
He is as black as charcoal,
His eyes are as blue as the ocean,
Oh how he loves to chew up all
of our socks, not his squeezer toys.
Whenever we say the key words
like walk, bath, or bye bye
how he just jumps up and down
because he is so excited,
after his baths he tries
to get the good smell off
and that just terrible smell back
by rubbing his whole body on
our carpet and just going
crazy running everywhere.
But oh how I love his tiny,
caring body so much!

Sophia Weldon, Grade 7
Daniel Savage Middle School, CA

Chilling Flavors of Ice Cream

The cold flavor
dances on my tongue
It makes me feel
calm and relaxed
Its colorful varieties
capture my eyes
mint chip fills me
with happiness
and relieves the stress
building up inside
ice cream can
always bring me up

Ramina Lazar, Grade 7
Daniel Savage Middle School, CA

Stage Fright

Behind the curtain,
waiting in darkness,
nervous tension builds.
Breathing faster, heart rate rising,
fear is coming.

Name is called,
mind is blank,
searching for how to start, what to say.
Used to know the words,
stage fright.

Brain triggers,
first line comes, breathing eases,
mind is working, words returning.
Attentive crowd,
fears forgotten.

Words ringing,
growing stronger every verse.
Final line bouncing off the back wall.
Crowd waits, then explodes in cheers,
finally done, confidence restored.

"Next!…"

Melissa Labnow, Grade 9
La Reina High School, CA

The World

The world is a palace
And you are the king.
You can rule it how you choose,
Or let it rule you.

To some,
The world is as overwhelming as it seems
And to others,
It is a measly spec of dust
Longing to be remembered.

Why let the world rule you?
It has too much to offer
To take for granted.
There is too much world
To just let it sit and wait.

If you choose to make the world wait,
The opportunity shall never expire.
You can relieve yourself
Of your forgotten deprivation.
All you have to do is decide
And the world will forever become
Your palace.

Stephanie Kerby, Grade 8
Frank A Miller Middle School, CA

Fake

It is fake, that smile is
I can tell it is
An actor you may be
But I can tell
It might fool many
Thinking your happy
Or find something funny
I've only seen glimpses
Of the real one
At least your real smile
Shows when least expected
But goes right back
To a fake smile

Ashley Kumar, Grade 7
Sarah McGarvin Intermediate School, CA

Hero

My hero
Is strong, loving,
And courageous.
My hero
Is
My older brother,
Bobby.
Whenever I'm sad,
He comes and helps me through it.
But, now,
I can't talk to him;
He is in
The military.

Emily Thompson, Grade 7
Tenaya Middle School, CA

Penguins

They flap their wings and waddle,
Slide on their bellies and toddle.
Wear their black and white suit,
Which looks very cute,
And dive to get fish for the family.
Penguins live on the ice,
Which must be very nice.
Penguins like to play in the snow,
While gliding to and fro,
Under the sun's glistening glow.

Isabel Wirth, Grade 7
Christ the King School, AZ

Snowplow

So much depends upon
A gray snowplow
Covered with a veil of snow
Resting peacefully
Beside the big tree

Susan Wadsworth, Grade 7
Salida Middle School, CO

Hidden Behind the Lines

Hidden behind the lines, is a strong mind. Without it, we are weak.
Hidden behind the lines, is a smart move. Without it, we are nothing.
Hidden behind the lines, is a child's heart. Without it, we cannot love.
Hidden behind the lines, is a dream. Without it, we are directionless.
Hidden behind the lines, is a wish. Without it, we have no pull.

Hidden behind everything, is a mind, a move, a heart, a dream, and a wish.
Our lives are run by the drive to reach our dream, the need to grab our wish,
The want for love, the craving for intelligence, and the initiative for change and movement.
We strive for our lives to work the way we want and for the respect for our lives.
Every aspect for our lives relies on the characteristics that are hidden behind the lines.

Hidden behind the lines, must be a strong mind. For without it, we are weak.
Hidden behind the lines, must be a smart move. For without it, we are nothing.
Hidden behind the lines, must be a child's heart. For without it, we cannot love.
Hidden behind the lines, must be a dream. For without it, we are directionless.
Hidden behind the lines, must be a wish. For without it, we have no pull.

Jessica Anderson, Grade 9
Edison Jr/Sr High School, CO

Turquoise

The cool ocean waves, my soccer cleats, and
My favorite Converse shoes look turquoise
The pitter-pattering of drizzling rain, the rush of a waterfall,
And wind chimes tinkling in the breeze sound turquoise
Turquoise feels soft and fuzzy like a warm blanket, cool and
Refreshing like cucumbers, but also comfortable like sweat pants
Turquoise makes me feel like I'm drinking a glass of
Ice cold lemonade, spending a day at the beach
With my friends, and camping under the stars
Blue raspberry Jolly Ranchers, Hawaiian Shaved
Ice, and yummy popsicles taste turquoise
Turquoise is under the sea where the fish are, in Hawaii
Where the sun shines bright every day, and at home, where I
Spend time with my family and friends
Purification, smiling, and living life to the fullest are turquoise ideas
Turquoise flies through the air, spreading peace, love, and happiness

Yuna Kim, Grade 7
Rolling Hills Country Day School, CA

Who I Am

Brinlee
Smart, athletic, kind, tough
Daughter of Jeff and Heidi
Lover of friends, my family, chocolate, the Denver Broncos
Who feels happy, tired, bored
Who finds happiness in playing sports, watching football, and taking naps
Who gives good laughs, fun times, and great advice
Who fears a world without cheese, burgers, and Sunday Night Football
Who would like to see Hawaii, the Eiffel Tower, and Mount Everest
Who enjoys hanging out with friends, having money, and playing soccer
Who likes to wear the color blue, sweats, and pajamas
1600 West in Lewiston, Utah
Hall

Brinlee Hall, Grade 7
White Pine Middle School, UT

The Pain

Her slimy, slick tongue beats me in the face, disturbing my TV show
I am up
I let her outside
She digs up her rusty bone from 2 weeks earlier
She high tails it inside
She drops the bone, then waits by the door
I know what she wants
I grab a leash
Click, it's on
The second I open the door
She takes off running
I lose my balance and hit the ground
As I am getting drug
I look ahead
She is about to enter the sticker infested pasture
I tell myself, get ready
The next thing I know, I am walking inside covered in pain
Shrieking stickers with a dog happy as a horse
That's what I deserve for being a loyal master

Trey Branom, Grade 7
Weldon Valley Jr High School, CO

The Flying Muffin

There once was a muffin,
His name was Puffin.
He wanted to fly,
but he didn't ask, he was too shy.
Then one day he saw some wings that were nice,
but his parents said no because of the price.
Later that day he saw his friends flying,
he was so sad he was almost dying,
but then he prayed and God gave him wings.
He was so grateful he said many things.
Then he went to his friends, and started to fly,
but no one flew with him, he started to cry.
It turned out that they were out of style,
but hopefully only for a little while.

Kepler Dawes, Grade 7
Monte Vista Christian School, CA

Brennan Maestas

Brennan,
Crazy, fun, sleepy, hyper,
Son of Steven and Jodie,
Lover of God and my country,
Who feels tired and hungry,
Who needs money and my own room,
Who gives happiness and joy,
Who fears heights and buzz cuts,
Who likes to wear bracelets, watches, and clothes,
Who would like to see a flying squirrel,
Resident of Earth,
Maestas.

Brennan Maestas, Grade 8
Mancos Middle School, CO

My World

In my world, I am queen
No one can replace me
No one can change me
I do what is right

In my world, I know what I want
I fight for what I believe
It's not always easy
But I will conquer in the end

My world is beautiful, just how I plan
Often it is rent with storms
And invaders from strange lands
But it stays beautiful throughout it all

In my world, a brook of laughter babbles
Curious creatures search for new knowledge
Silent, secretive trees stand proud
And small critters long to be noticed

I am this world
This world is me
It's always changing,
And it will change others

Allie Hill, Grade 8
Lewis & Clark Middle School, ID

Sky

Suddenly the wind rushed up
And the most beautiful flower was a victim of chance
It whipped to and fro like a hapless doll
Until the great sky finally swallowed it whole

I would look up at the great blue sky
And marvel at how blue a blue could be
And think of a flower, feeble as a fawn
Wondering exactly where it had gone

After a while the sun began to shine
But that only made the light seem harsh
And no matter how healing a smile could be
I could not with that sky hanging over me

One day I saw a flower
Wilted with lack of care
I pitied it, and so with love
I once more picked up my gardening gloves

So I learned I must try and do my best
For memory of what is beautiful
And I know I can look up now and not cry
At that beautiful great blue sky

Jess Keller, Grade 9
Billings West High School, MT

Don't Forget

Black comes from
the evil inside you
the darkness in
your soul
the fear in your eyes
the tears of fright
the screams of Halloween
the night sky at dusk.
Do you have something to say to black,
because it has something to say to you,
Don't forget me.

Sierra Gard, Grade 7
Gale Ranch Middle School, CA

Pink

Pink is love
Pink is my color
Pink is paint
Pink is cake
Pink is a store
Pink is makeup
Pink is color
Pink is shoes
Pink is a dress
Pink is strawberries
Pink is me

Katherine Tejada-Rodriguez, Grade 7
Daniel Savage Middle School, CA

Realized

Make a wish,
And I close my eyes,
Seeking for what I want,
In this fantasy world of mine,
That I love;
Wishing for the things,
That I want,
As I open my eyes,
And just realized,
I just miss the bus,
Once again.

Tristen Yazzie, Grade 9
Sequoia Choice School, AZ

Away

Blue skies of satin blue
Clouds lining the silver carpet
A sun above all
Falling into a sunset of scarlet
Stars come out to play
Puncturing holes of light into the sky
Raising my arms
I hope to fly
Away from here, and into the night

Samantha McFadden, Grade 8
Katherine Delmar Burke School, CA

Slave

Gunshots fired and I heard my voice moan
I had 2000 men and now I have none
Tied together by ropes I hear the silent cries
In the dark of the ship, only one bucket of water a day.

Slaves at my side as I worked in the hot sun
I dash for freedom, but fall short, hopeless
I work in cotton, producing many tones
Proud of my abilities but still not back home.

A lovely lady I train in cotton
Love is a sweet ray of hope in my life
The reward of marriage and the treasure of children
Released to grow potatoes for my own
With my family by my side, I seek success.

America's impressed by my Arabic reading
I find more success as a translator

In great sorrow, again released from my loved ones
Torn from my children, we cry again
As one king to another I help the President

I find some honor restored, but still children are denied to me
Ah, the sorrow, the madness; all we ask but cannot receive
As I return at last to Africa I feel the evening of my years come up on me.

Courtney Slamon, Grade 8
Ripona Elementary School, CA

The Artist

Silence abodes an opaque, quiet night,
A writer briskly places down a beautiful white.
The scurrying sounds of a conductor's delicate pace,
A simple stroke of a smooth, rich pen.

The eyes of the painter visualizing a heavenly land,
The ears of a composer listening to a cricket's chirp.
The graceful fingers of a pianist running through fresh keys,
The inspiration has been freed.

An idea slowly expounds out like a flame slowly igniting.
A dab of gold paint, a knock on the drums, and a gentle pluck of a string.
The sketch artist ferociously scribbles, the conductor raises his baton.
A beautiful magic has begun.

A whirlwind of notes, voices, and sounds with intensity and color,
The expression, emotion, and ideas rupture with vigor!
The blare of brass and the pounding of waves are delivered to a forte,
The indescribable feelings flood! The excitement! The drama!

The painter flamboyantly signs his name in the darkest hue of black,
The conductor signals the final climax to his beautiful masterpiece.
The world rests in a calming silence,
The writer has finished his final composition.

Justin Zhu, Grade 8
Santan K-8 Campus, AZ

Our Lovely Cat's Story

I was at school that day
And you were at the doorway
Lying down like you had no life
You didn't see it coming, but neither did I

You were so quiet and innocent
Yet you weren't patient
You were wild when you were hungry
Like a lion wanting a zebra

My life has changed
My love for you cannot be rearranged
Because without you
Nothing will be the same

You came without any notice
And when you passed away
It was like my heart broken away
But when my time has come, we will surely meet again

Xelha Puc, Grade 8
John Adams Middle School, CA

Finding You

I miss you oh so much,
Please tell me where you are.
I will one day find you.

Looking for you,
Through cats and dogs rain.
I will one day find you

If I have to,
I'll search in marshmallow snow.
I will one day find you.

Whether I walk one million miles,
Because you are important to me.
I will one day find you.

I ran out of places to look.
Until I looked on my shelf and found my book.
I have finally found you!

Daniel Morin, Grade 8
Joe Walker Middle School, CA

iPod

At the beginning of the song,
a soft, extended note drifts into my welcoming ear.
The barrier of peaceful sound
is shattered,
and a stream
of intense beats and tunes
block out all other existence.

Sam Tameler, Grade 7
Salida Middle School, CO

My Dear Sister

It comes every year,
The time for her to leave me;
My sister that I love so dear;
It is her right to be free.

It comes every year,
Tears are crawling down my cheeks for,
My sister that I love so dear;
I cry like this for endless weeks.

It comes every year,
The drive is a trip to the gallows;
My sister that I love so dear,
All of her packed bags look like marshmallows.

It comes every year,
She hugs me as if she was a python;
My sister that I love so dear;
I think of that hug until the new dawn.

Emily DiPressi, Grade 8
Joe Walker Middle School, CA

Time

Time is a circle that will never end;
It will never be a helpful friend.
Time leads to people walking with canes;
It eats away the last of our remains.

Time gives people the chance to hope at first;
It leaves them with a result of nothing but the worst.
Time makes almost everything grow;
It sometimes seems to go by slow.

Time is something nobody can beat;
It always meets people with great defeat.
Time brings about complex imperfections;
It, yet, lets us make accurate projections.

Time is a circle that will never end;
It is not something a person could suspend.
Time is not easy to explain;
It only expects us; always to be game

Ismael Medellin, Grade 8
Joe Walker Middle School, CA

Reflections on Escher's "Bond of Union"

In this picture,
I see a man
Looking back at his wife
While they are on a different Planet;
Together in their own little world,
It's like no one else can separate them from being
Together.

Kiara Haynes, Grade 7
Tenaya Middle School, CA

My Neighbor's Christmas Lights

Dear Decoration Enthusiast,
I would like to tell you
your Christmas lights are horrible.
You tell me
the lights are beautiful.
You tell me
the horrifying song is jolly.
I would like to tell you
the lights are too bright and Santa is frightful.
So during our next encounter
your lights will go dim
and the reindeer will run away
and your Santa will sink into the ground.
Then I'll stroll off laughing into the distance.

Nick Campagnari, Grade 7
Falcon Creek Middle School, CO

Beaches

Feeling the sand between my toes,
Hearing the ocean's waves crash on the beach,
I watch the dogs run by,
Trying to catch each other in the sun,
The dogs, not so smart, chase the sand sharks
And bark as they swim away.
I hear little kids splashing in the water
And I see them building sand castles,
But the fun has to end at night when the sun sets
And all of those little kids leave,
But don't fear, it's not done, the older ones still have to come.
I see the flames from the fire wood burning.
I smell the marshmallows melting over the burning fire.
This is the end, but don't fear, there will still be tomorrow.

Emily Brey, Grade 8
Christ the King School, AZ

Montana Seasons

Wind and snow, fire and ice,
Montana winters are so nice.

skiing, hunting, tubing, snowball fights,
winter can be fun even with long nights.

sun and moon, day and night,
Montana summers are full of light.

fishing, swimming, hunting, hiking,
summer can be hard if light is not your liking,

summer, winter, fall and spring,
all Montana seasons make me want to sing.

Taggart Griner, Grade 7
Sequoia Village School, AZ

Music Is a Test

Music is a test,
Leading to a bright path or
A dark road for your future.
Music questions,
To grow, study.
Music helps one learn new things,
Opening doors to wonderful opportunities.
Music challenges,
A constant, creative work.
You sometimes don't know the answers,
But if you practice and persist
Music will lead you to passion and excitement.
Passing tests can make your dreams come true,
But music can make your dreams come alive!

Cierra Vigil, Grade 8
Falcon Creek Middle School, CO

Free Together

Ethereal clouds form in the sky;
Angelic white puffs against the clear blue,
Delicate raindrops that splatter on the meadow
As they cascade down the blades of grass silently.

Angelic white puffs against the clear blue,
Their feathery lightness, untouchable from where I am;
They seem very light and free together
As the delicate raindrops splatter on the grass.

Their feather lightness, untouchable from where I am,
As the birds spread their wings and envelop the gentle breeze;
All nature is one, united forever,
As they are very light and free together.

Madhumita Ramesh, Grade 7
Stratford Elementary/Middle School, CA

Glowing

Glowing throughout the night
Shining in between the stars forever
Feeling like it's never-ending light
Always drawing your attention
It's quiet and calm like no ones there
It's golden it shines bright
Sometimes it may be kind of dark but
It shines bright
I feel like I can touch it
It's glowing right now and it's better than ever

Haley Reddick, Grade 7
Daniel Savage Middle School, CA

Death

My eyes like stones,
My hair like wire,
I do not feel,
And I am dead.

Carolina Ramirez, Grade 8
Canyon View Junior High School, UT

Love

Love is like a mountain
The journey starts off fun as you go along
You realize what it is you've signed up for
Steep slopes seeming sincerely impossible.

You try to climb—you think it's safe
Then suddenly you find yourself
Falling — lost trust
Afraid to try again yet trying a new route

It's hard to be brave
to make good judgment
After awhile you take a short break
Think about if you really want to go on

You realize what's at the peak is worth trying for
Continue onwards
Forwards Upwards
You keep pushing and soon find yourself
At the top

The view is everything you'd imagined it would be
You realize the journey was difficult
But it was fun. It was worth trying
You realize it was an experience of a lifetime.

Madison Byczynski, Grade 8
Falcon Creek Middle School, CO

Ode to Paper

Always there when you need it,
Ready to act as a helpful reminder,
Or the canvas for a drawing,
Or a message to a loved one,
Or to be used to make a simple little craft.

Many people overlook this tiny part of life.
They take it for granted,
Not thinking about all the ways it helps them through their life,
Seeing it as a nuisance,
A way for work to be shoveled on them.

Nowadays it has been turned away from,
In favor of the future of electronics,
But they forget,
If not for its existence,
We wouldn't have all their cell phones and whatnot.

Even with all the electronics,
It is still used in tandem with them.
It brings the ideas from the screen and out to the world,
So we can all see the glory,
Of what has been made.

Never forget it — Paper.

Everett Earles, Grade 9
New Plymouth High School, ID

Heartbreak

This feeling you can't put into words,
thoughts race through my mind,
I toss and turn every night.
Sometimes the darkness of my room takes me over
and I get sucked into
a black hole of pain and sadness.
My heart is beating,
But why does it hurt so bad?
When the sun comes out,
I just want to run and hide.
This is reality…
this is just a dream,
But then I open my eyes
and it's all laid out in front of me.
Every time I think
It always comes back to you.
The things about you come and go,
and all you are
is a memory and a smile
left in my old photo.

Shelby Martin, Grade 7
Salida Middle School, CO

Midsummer's Eve

I know of something that will give you a fright
The eyes in the darkness of Midsummer's Night
When spirits of all shape and size
Peer through the trees with their glowing red eyes
Once, a girl at the age of fourteen
Decided to go and have a see
Armed with a wrench and a candle for light
She left for the forest in the dead of night
She soon saw a flash, and another there
And bravely blew out her candle with care
A voice in the trees whispered, "We've been watching you."
And the girl of fourteen replied, "Who?"
The spirits of Midsummer's Eve came out
Some with a mumble, some with a shout
These fairies and creatures of magic were the cause
That into their realm, the girl of fourteen was forever lost
So, my friend, I give caution to you
For believe me, this story is true
Do not, I tell you, or you will get a fright
Do not enter the forest on Midsummer's Night

Mckenzie Moore, Grade 9
Cedaredge High School, CO

Stars

Staring at the stars above
Twinkling their precious gleams
Feeling the tenderness of my mother's loves
As she wishes me sweet dreams
Angels watching over me through the night
Until the sun awakens me with its morning light

Courtney Butler, Grade 9
New Plymouth High School, ID

Ode to Soccer Ball

Dear my sweet fellow soccer ball,
You are the best thing that has
ever been invented.
Oh how I love you so!
You have been there for me
Through rain and shine.
Soccer is a thing you can
play or do and if you
practice you can be good at it too.
Oh thank you soccer ball,
Thank you.

Shelby Martin, Grade 7
Daniel Savage Middle School, CA

Music

The music
Lifts me up
Morning till night
Everywhere I go
Keeps my soul in rhythm.

The sounds
Make me dance
Every day
All around me
The noise is beautiful.

Samantha Keane, Grade 7
Monte Vista Christian School, CA

Soccer

It's 3-2,
He dribbles into the box,
I sprint at him as hard as
My body can muster,
He kicks it to my right,
I dive to the ball as it
Sails at the goal,
I hear the whistle blow,
I punch the ball and it
Goes out,
We won!

Samuel Denwalt, Grade 7
Salida Middle School, CO

I Cheer

All my life,
I have been competing,
I am addicted to the dedication.
I crave the feeling of accomplishment.
At times it's frustrating,
But the motivational words pick me up.
Performing like its my last,
Every time.
I cheer.

Anna Murphy, Grade 8
Daniel Savage Middle School, CA

My Puppy's Death

I've lived empty lonely years.
With gray skies and hopeless nights,
Dying inside little by little.
Feeling lonely more and more every day.

I haven't slept in weeks.
Hoping you were here,
I know you won't be back.
I'll do anything in return to have you right by my side.

A million times I needed you.
A million times I cried for you.
Although my eyes are full with one thousand tears,
Am glad for all the happy years.

I see you bright, in the sky,
You're that star that shines at night, the star that makes up the night.
I will keep all these good memories with love,
Until we meet above.

Jacqueline Armijo, Grade 8
John Adams Middle School, CA

Drip, Drop…Drip, Drop

Drip, drop…drip, drop
Split, splat…split, splat
Trickle, trickle…trickle, trickle
Flowing down the window, crashing onto the sidewalk, washing away the world

Yesterday, the world was stained, with the red that crashed from the skies
Today, the eye of the storm, calm and numb, mere water pouring down the windows
Tomorrow, comes the pain, salty tears will surround us and crush us to the ground

But today, it is calm, today, all that happens is
Drip, Drop…Drip, Drop
Trickling down the window pain

Washing away pains that will never be washed away
Hiding sins that will never be hidden

Somehow, the cold, wet water
Crashing and pounding down is calm and soothing
Relieving everything, that cannot be relieved

Elyse Owen, Grade 8
Santa Cruz Montessori School, CA

California

Home to surfers, travelers, and beach-goers
Disneyland, earthquakes, and family;
Towering Redwoods, blistering Death Valley,
Legendary Hollywood, and the connective Golden Gate Bridge.
Mild temps, seemingly endless miles of coastline,
Seagulls, vineyards, and Spanish missions that play "Connect the Dots."
From sea to ski, from desert to farmland.
This is radiant California.

Ian Helfrich, Grade 7
Christ the King School, AZ

Awakening
Confusion drowns the conscience of each adolescent mind
Making the thoughts and the actions imperative to be done faster and faster and faster
Until it seems that all the time in the world could not be enough.

Never satisfied, always hungry and longing for what each of us cannot have,
The dying oak paid its price and allows us to remember each arrow that is embedded in our green earth
Circling arrows cry out for help as us young ones carry on without realizing their deafened screeches

Help, help, save our world and keep all creation alive!

Natalie Lavacca, Grade 9
La Reina High School, CA

Ollie and Sammie
My awesome dogs.
They lick me to death with their bad breath.
They are fluffy, soft, and Sammy is skinny and Ollie is fat.
When I throw a toy to them they start to play tug-of-war.
Ollie is the smarts because he knows how to get what he wants and Sammy is the trouble maker because he steals food off of desks and trash cans.
Sammy takes cupcakes from people while Ollie just wants a simple belly rub.
I love these dogs with all my heart and they are like my little brothers.
They are like my little brothers because I have to look out for them, clean them when they are dirty, and give them baths.

Matthew Meskin, Grade 7
Rolling Hills Country Day School, CA

The Feeling
The liberating feeling of stepping into the fresh chill of the early morning darkness.
The subtle, toasty-smelling fourwheeler exhaust; wafting through the frozen air.
The complete solitude and utter beauty of the outdoors at sunrise.
The empowering feeling; sitting high upon your throne like a powerful emperor glaring down upon your subjects.
The complete cold during your never-ending wait; chilled to the bone despite your many various clothing layers.
The heart-pounding, brain-boggling adrenaline as the trophy comes upon you.
The feeling of being a victim of chance; hungry for an opportunity at the prize.

It's called whitetail hunting.

Cole Sites, Grade 7
Salida Middle School, CO

I Am From
I am from early morning, a table full of dice, cards, and candy wrappers.
I am from unswept hardwood floors and a family of four.
I am from a bed covered with fuzzy warm blankets and two TV remotes under a polka dot pillow.
I am from if you know it just do it.
I am from my family's frozen smiles on a large clock.
I am from whiskers, a wagging tail, and small, slimy fish fins.
I am from furniture covered with popcorn kernels, crumbs of greasy BBQ chips, brown throw pillows, and small blankets.
I am from mashed potatoes steaming on a table on the third Thursday of the month before Christmas.
I am from a loving family with smiles of love and laughter

Aurora Joham, Grade 7
White Pine Middle School, UT

Hourglass

Spellbound by the sound of the sand.
Slipping,
Spilling,
Never stopping.
Ever surging.
Filling the glass cage around me
Mocking my foolish attempts
My struggle
My pleas

The sand continues to pile up
Burying me
Suffocating me

Time waits for no one
Yet it enslaves all.

I cry out,
But I am chained

What will become of me
When the hourglass turns?
Hannah Gonzalez, Grade 9
Maranatha Christian School, CA

Fantasy

What if winter
lasted an entire year?
I might finally learn how
to snowboard.
What if being lazy was
a sport?
I could be a
gold medalist.
What if listening
to music
made you smarter?
I would be
a genius.
What if the fantasy in
your mind could be reality?
Malia Kim, Grade 7
Falcon Creek Middle School, CO

The Most Exciting Thing

This is one of the most exciting things
That will happen to anybody
It's not going to school
It's not drinking
Can you guess what it is?
It's driving!
When you drive, it feels like you're
Free from everything in life
And it's only a few years away.
Assad Zeinaty, Grade 7
Young Scholar's Academy, AZ

The Mysterious Figure Within Us All*

I am a mystery…
I see a boy, who screams for help, and mercy…
I hear sobbing, and hatred toward others…
I feel tension, and stress of who wants to be freed from their prison…
I am a mysterious figure, with compassion…

I dream of the perfect time, for one person to figure out their mistakes…
I worry that one will not see their mistake, and make a bigger …
I want a world, where everyone would be happy, and peaceful…
I hope for this boy, to figure out his own figure, like within us all…
I am a mysterious figure, with hopes and dreams…

I understand this troublesome feeling, and want to help…
I try my very best to heal, and purify this boy…
I command the soul, to figure out the path that it will take…
I touch the soul, as if it has already changed…
I am a circle, and I helped change this boy's life forever…
Billy Gargan, Grade 8
Palm Desert Charter Middle School, CA
*Inspired by the book Touching Spirit Bear

Two Trees

Two trees, rooted in the grove that is our family
Mine short and young, my grandmother's older and tall
Like Aspens, we look different, but on the inside, we are the same
The roots interwoven, the branches far apart

On the banks of Lake Michigan, our cottage
Strung between two sturdy oaks, our hammock, where we watch the sunset
Enjoying family dinners
Strolling the sandy beach
These roots deep and intertwined

Savannah and mountains for me
River and lake for her
These branches each seeking their own light
Her family around the corner
Mine around the world
For both of us, family that we love
Our grove growing for generations
Henry Coppolillo, Grade 8
Headwaters Academy, MT

Softball Is Life

There is always an opposing team.
You will have errors.
There are winners and losers.
Strikeouts are the bitter taste in your mouth.
Coaches are like undesirable bosses.
Teammates are the best friends that you've known since kindergarten.
Umpires are like the guiding road to tell you what will happen.
Memorizing signs is like studying for a semester exam.
Sliding and getting a strawberry is a slap in the face when you do something wrong.
Softball is life.
Audrey Pickett, Grade 8
Falcon Creek Middle School, CO

Candles*

Our lives are much like candles
They burn bright, sometimes flicker, and bring warmth.
Sometimes we do not see candles for what they are worth,
or the warmth, light, and comfort they give us.
But once the candle's flame is gone, we truly realize what they gave.
Death, with her breath cold but welcoming,
may extinguish the flame of a candle tall and bright
Leaving only a wisp of smoke where a strong flame once was.
Ah! But that sweet smoke contains in it's depths
the memories and good times of the flame.
The other candles huddled around that candle extinguished
may flicker or quiver with the shock of their lost companion,
but the smoke that is left they must cherish
and use to burn brighter than ever before.
That is how they will burn, bright, strong, and true
until Death invites them to rejoin their companions

David Nelson, Grade 8
Gateway Preparatory Academy, UT
*Dedicated to Brittany Lacy.

Good Video Games

I think a good video game is like a cool soda
in the summer's heat.
A good video game is like the center
of a PB&J, all mushy, but sweet.
A good video game releases all worries
for the time being.
A good video game excites you
and can make you jump sometimes.
A good video game lets you connect to other people
and communicate with them.
A good video game can let your imagination
fly free and explore new things.
A good video game can make you feel like
you're the only person in the world.
A good video game can do all of these
but the most important is that a good video game
knows when to end.

Nickolas Nikaydo, Grade 8
Ogden Preparatory Academy, UT

Lions

Fierce and ferocious,
With eating manners quite atrocious,
It's always roaring,
And sometimes snoring.
Hunting with vigor
And always bigger
Than its fleeing prey.
With a mane like a crown,
And a face with a frown,
A lion is something you might not want to meet.

Alexander Wozny, Grade 8
Christ the King School, AZ

Voiceless Girl

I once knew a girl that would never talk.
With not a word, nor a whisper, nor a sound or thought,
She stood silently in the background,
Blending into the crowd without a rebound.

I tried to speak with her and smiled.
Her eyes told me that I was extremely vile.
What had I done to wrong you?
Her silence was something I could not break through.

Sometimes, however, I went to sit beside her.
We never spoke and that was how things were.
People pushed, tripped, and hated the girl.
They told her she was ugly, horrible, and stupid.

Looking into a mirror, I realized that girl was me.
I hated that part of me that said I was worthless.
I pretended to be happy, perfect, and overconfident.
But that girl was me and I was her.

Gaining strength she finally had a voice,
And she told the world how it was like to be wronged.
In a swirl of confessions our hands connected
And now that girl is a part of me.

Anh Nguyentran, Grade 9
La Quinta High School, CA

Strong Ties (Ode to Friendship)

Friendship, how you readily reach out
With steadfast understanding, extended arms,
And a warm, sincere smile that speaks of a new comfort,
Providing a hope that finds its way into one's heart,
Coiling cozily around a newfound trust

Friendship, how your warmth shields
The oppression of hate, the error of exclusion
Showing, with a gleaming glow in your soft expression,
That you are as tight as a carefully crafted knot
That you are unstoppable; undeniable unwavering

Friendship, how you break unfortunate solitude
And show one how to embrace company,
A fully focused and true sense of belonging,
And strong ties that undoubtedly make
For an unworried, contented existence

Friendship, how you grasp the hand of completeness
Piecing together a string of fond memories —
Memories light with joyous laughter
Memories heavy with the weight of love
Memories upheld, forever

Gabriella Fooks, Grade 8
The Mirman School, CA

I'm Sorry

I'm sorry for causing you pain
I'm sorry for ignoring you
I'm sorry that I didn't listen
I'm sorry that I wasn't there for you

I have regrets of these things
Hoping that you'll come back
Staying up all night waiting for you
I've never really understood

Now that you're gone, I see it clearly
Missing you every second of the day
Wishing that I could have done something
I don't know why I couldn't see the signs

I wish I could have been there
I wish that I wouldn't take advantage of you
I wish that I could hug you one last time
I just want to say that I'm sorry

Marissa Meadors, Grade 8
Young Scholar's Academy, AZ

The Day My Bird Died

It was a sunny day and I was at home
Then I started to play with my bird
He was flying and flying
Then I noticed he hit himself at the door

He started to walk then stayed still like a block
He fell while trying, then I started crying
I stood up hoping I could help him
Then decided to call my mom

We decided to lay him down
He looked tired like my sister when she got fired
He looked scared
He started falling asleep

I noticed he was no longer breathing
We decided to bury him in our garden
Which was his home
Our play place

Annie Oliva, Grade 8
John Adams Middle School, CA

The Flag

With its shining stripes and stars,
With its sad tears and scars.
With its bright red, white and blue,
With its meaning of liberty and do.

The souls pouring out of the seams,
The flag holding tears and beams.
The shining white stars,
The feeling that it is ours.

With its freedom that is to show,
With its head held up high, its colors flow.
With its own county that is proud,
With its own country of heads bowed.

The gold, shining eagle on top,
The symbol of freedom won't drop.
The flag whistling in the wind,
The American Flag to lost soldiers we have pinned.

Dalton Harvey, Grade 8
Joe Walker Middle School, CA

Growing Up

Raised in a funny, crazy town
Where there were plain, cruel people,
We miss the days we children were unruly, loving louts,
And as we grow we're silent, dreadful people.

Let's bring back outrageous, hilarious days
Where we can play funny, duddy pretend;
We'll have endless, relentless chase
And we'll long for a perfect, enjoyable end.

When everything was merrily, barely easy,
The world began to sorely, morally change;
New eyes were open to the plain, cruel world
And innocence was horribly, sorrowfully maimed.

We'll put away our plastic, cheap guns
Then bring out the silver, sharp swords;
The things we'd grown to wield with mean, determined shuns
And let go of the habits of the little, loving ones.

Elena Smaltino, Grade 8
Joe Walker Middle School, CA

Surfing

The waves crash,
Beating the sand like it's done something wrong.
I wait, dead silence, until I see it.
I paddle faster and faster,
Until I feel it lift me.
Like I'm floating on a cloud,
So at peace, riding.

Annie Arriola, Grade 7
St Francis School, CA

Popcorn

P op! There goes the popcorn!
O h my! Oh my! Mouth watering!
P op! Pop in my mouth.
C orn so salty.
O h my! Oh my! Making me hungry!
R unning down the side of the bowl is butter.
N ow the popcorn is gone.

Samantha Hay, Grade 7
Sequoia Village School, AZ

Athletic Me

I am funny and athletic
I wonder how hard baseball players work
I hear a chirpy noise
I see a baseball
I want to be in the MLB
I am funny and athletic

I pretend that I'm not hurt when I really am
I feel the baseball bat
I touch the grip of the baseball bat handle
I worry about health as if I'm a doctor
I cry when I get an F on a test
I am funny and athletic

I understand I don't get what I want
I say work your hardest to get what you want
I dream to be in the MLB
I try to do great in school
I hope to be in the MLB as a starter catcher
I am funny and athletic

Alex Hammock, Grade 7
Falcon Creek Middle School, CO

Mountain Biking

Flying over the hills
Diving through the trees
When I'm mountain biking I am happy as can be
Splashing through the streams
Tearing across the mud
And then I stop for a moment
And hear a giant "THUD!"
Surprising that my heartbeat
Is so loud and strong
It sounds to me
As if it's singing a song
Climbing, climbing, climbing
Up to the top
Then I fly down
And screech to a stop

Tristan Ricci, Grade 7
Salida Middle School, CO

Pet Love

The pets I own all live in my house;
First there was Hershey who was quiet as a mouse.
Then came Jo, my cat, who scares my dogs so;
She is cranky and big like a huge clump of dough!
Then along came Chloe, who tries to attack Jo as a joke,
But the cat is not amused and always gives back a poke!
My goldfish we call "Orange Treasure" and is my cat's main dish.
Jo always stares at "Orange" like she's never seen a fish.
Now we have Orange, Chloe, and Jo;
The question is "when will they love each other?"
I guess I'll never know!

Andrew Ludwick, Grade 7
Monte Vista Christian School, CA

Ten Bad Boys

Ten bad boys, watching the sun shine,
One watched too long, and then there were nine.
Nine bad boys trying to find a mate,
One got lucky and then there were eight.
Seven bad boys, trying to get to heaven,
One succeeded and then there were seven.
Seven bad boys, bought some Twix,
One ate too many and then there were six.
Six bad boys, trying to stay alive,
One of them failed and then there were five.
Five bad boys, walking through a door,
One door left out and then there were four.
Four bad boys were sailing the sea,
One got seasick and then there were three.
Three bad boys bought a bat that was new,
One used it wrong and then there were two.
Two bad boys, trying to have fun,
One did not and then there was one.
One bad boy, ate some dip,
The dip was spicy so then there was zip.

Benjamin Jones, Grade 7
Canyon View Jr High School, UT

Anger

Do you even try to understand?
Do you even try to care?
I'm just a walking problem.
You can't expect me to be normal.
It's just not who I am since you.
Since you gave up on me, I gave up on you.
So please don't pretend to understand.
I'm just a walking contradiction.
Failing the lives of everyone you know.
So just leave me alone.
I don't need anyone or anything.
I can make it on my own.
You gave up on me, so don't try to come around now.
Stay out of my life,
And I'll stay out of yours.

Tanner Fisher, Grade 8
Bear Lake Middle School, ID

Dreams

Dream, dream, dream away
Fall asleep to the time after the day
Close your eyes to a place darker than night
Take a journey like a plane on first flight
The dreams start as your brain starts to unwind
Images and colors flash in your mind
Visions more impressive than stars themselves
Dreams that shine brighter than the sun itself
Then it all ends as soon as it began
Awake to first light to wait for again
Dreams shall come next night

Dylan Vuong, Grade 7
Sarah McGarvin Intermediate School, CA

My Favorite Season

The leaves all change color;
They turn red, orange and gold.
My favorite season comes after summer
When it finally turns cold.

The smell of sage and pine;
The feel of warm, cozy sweaters.
This season is a favorite of mine;
It brings so many pleasures.

Families gather around warm fires;
They celebrate Thanksgiving.
This season is what I desire;
It makes life worth living.

This is my favorite season;
Everyone's favorite should be fall.
I gave you so many reasons,
And it brings joy to all!

Magenta Money, Grade 8
Joe Walker Middle School, CA

What If

If I walked away today,
Would you follow me?
Or would you play pretend,
And act like I was never there?

If I walked away today,
Would you miss me?
Or would you not care,
Just like I was never there?

If I walked away today,
Would you remember me?
Or would you burn the memories,
As if I was never there?

If you walked away today,
I would miss you,
Because I care,
And I hope you do too.

Aubrey Knittel, Grade 8
Joe Walker Middle School, CA

Magnets

they are helpers by clasping up…
notes for teachers,
a shopping list for your mom,
showing your siblings good assignments
and pictures for memories,
they help almost everybody,
they go by the name,
magnets!

Ashley Leopold, Grade 7
Salida Middle School, CO

I Am

I am a black Chihuahua dog
I see my dog food
I love the food I eat
I want more dog food
I am a black Chihuahua dog

I dream to be in *Beverly Hills Chihuahua*
I worry for not having enough talent
I feel I should be the superstar
I hope to be the best
I am a black Chihuahua dog

I understand I need talent
I try my best
I say, "I will be the superstar"
I feel joy to be in *Beverly Hills Chihuahua*
I am a black Chihuahua dog

Jason Samperio, Grade 8
Palm Desert Charter Middle School, CA

Elodea: King of the Ocean Floor

When I look at you
I think of the sea
With the crashing waves
Of foam and dark blue water
And the fish so plentiful
Swimming along the ocean floor
I see your bright bending body
Flowing alongside them
Leaves, stem, body and all
Elodea candensis
Chlorophyll dancing around
Just like the celebrations
In an underwater grotto
From a long time ago
And thus the journey ends
As you float away
To a different home

David Miron, Grade 8
The Mirman School, CA

Fall

Just fall and you will see,
That life can go on for eternity
Like dark skies and warm days
Just fall and be happy.
Don't frown or
Even be upset
Just fall and succeed
Like diamonds on a ring
Just fall and let go
You have to know
That you're going to be
All on your own

Anna Ouzounian, Grade 8
Theodore Roosevelt Middle School, CA

Braces

Braces are prison for teeth.
Many sets of teeth visit court
to see if they are guilty of being crooked.
Many are convicted
and will serve four years of pure torture.
Security guards are glued to each tooth
to make sure they don't run away.
Metal wires wrap around the teeth
for extra protection.
Security guards and the wires claim to be
putting
teeth
into
line.
But they hardly seem to change.
But once their time is up
security and the wires leave
and the teeth are finally free.

Micah Mindoro, Grade 8
Falcon Creek Middle School, CO

Two Separate Places

Each house with two parents
Struggling —
to function
to say calm
to live a normal life
Two separate places

Being a kid
Is harder with two separate places
Now in one, now in the other
Finally able to function
Two separate places

Learning to cope with it
Loving them both the same
Having them both there for me
Loving those
Two separate places

Samantha Reeves, Grade 8
Richardson PREP HI Middle School, CA

Time

Time time
Time is all around
Things we need to do
Things we need complete
All has to do with time
Time is a beautiful thing
You can read or sleep or do homework
Or brighten up someone's day
So why are you wasting your time
Reading this?

Damian Haro, Grade 8
Monte Vista Christian School, CA

Beautifully Blue

Blue is calming,
it is quiet,
like a summer sky,
or a new baby's eyes.
It is beautiful,
and amazing,
it can be dark,
like a stormy ocean,
or it can be light,
like a clean morning sky.
Blue is comfortable,
like my jeans.
Blue is innocent like a kitten.
Blue is beautifully blue.

Aarian Crowder, Grade 7
Daniel Savage Middle School, CA

My Personality: A Brick Wall

I am a brick wall
I am indestructible
But sometimes I fall
I'll build myself up
To be stronger
But when something
Hits me I am no longer
As stable but my wall still stands
I have battle scars
From friends of the past
I have holes to be mended
By those who are here
I am a brick wall
I am indestructible

Lexi Lapp, Grade 9
Eaton High School, CO

I Do Not Understand

I do not understand
Why people can't fly
Why turtles are slow
Why grass is green
But most of all I do not understand
Why kids are bullied
Why people murder
Why others don't try their best
Why there is sickness
What I do understand is friendship
That true friends always believe in you
That they will stand up for you
True friends never let you down.

Rachael Williams, Grade 7
White Pine Middle School, UT

Nobody Is Perfect

I am a little bird.
I will sing forever.
I'd want some hugs and many love
and I'll never say never.
I'd fly and soar so high
'til I can touch the clouds
my dreams are also way up there
and I will not back down.

The wind pushes me back sometimes,
but people make mistakes.
The sight is pretty ugly
but trying's all it takes.

Nobody is perfect.
We all have flaws, you see.
But in order to succeed in life,
hard work is the key.

Brianne Allen, Grade 7
Joe Walker Middle School, CA

Where I'm Found

I'm from a historic town
Where I always see lost tourists
Come and go.

I mostly see them come and go
At the Chevron gas station
My family runs.

I'm from a family that cooks
Delicious food.
The yummy soft, spicy tamales
Soft, fluffy fry bread with
Cheese, beans, or powdered sugar.

I'm surrounded by Natives from
The Walapai nation, saying
Words in the Walapai language
To each other.

Falisha Johnson, Grade 9
Seligman High School, AZ

My Dreams

What if humans could fly high
in the sky? I might visit Canada
for the very first time. What if
mammals could speak the language
of ours? I would carry on a
long and vivid conversation.
What if ice cream gave you super
powers? I would be stronger than
the Hulk. What if, someday…this
poem came true?

Kyle Tatlock, Grade 7
Falcon Creek Middle School, CO

Together We Can

Together we can stop bullying
Together we can heal the sick
Together we can stop animal cruelty
If together we will stick

Together we can feed the hungry
Shelter the homeless, and give to the poor
Together we can do this little
And they will suffer no more

Together we can stop all the fighting
Together we can stop all the wars
Together we can stop all the crying
Together we can heal all the sores

I know we can do it together
I know we can if we try
If we do it together
There'll be no more reason to cry

We just need to stick together
To make the world a better place
Then everyone will feel happy
Like a member of the human race.

Kiersten King, Grade 9
Highland Sr High School, ID

A Hero Falls

"A job well done, a war well fought.
Let's treat ourselves today,
And ride down to Ford's Theater.
To watch a lovely play."

"Sounds like fun, we'll leave at eight,
We could use some fun my dear.
And ride down to Ford's Theater,
You've worked so hard this year."

We sat right down to watch the show,
A bird's eye view we had.
I wish that we could have known,
That the evening would turn bad.

A shot rang out, screams all around!
A hero falls today!
The gunman had a master plan,
That changed the U.S.A.

Who is the man that did this deed?
Does anyone really know?
We have to find out who he is,
And wherever he will go.

Charlie Falcone, Grade 9
Woodbridge High School, CA

Sun

The sun is always shining
Like a diamond in darkness
It will appear when it's the right timing
It is very easy to seek
But hard to reach
The sun helps us every day
By warming the cold earth on it's way
In space you look like a huge ball of fire
I sometimes wonder if you're tired
Thank you sun
Without you, time will be done
Peter Phaminhung, Grade 7
Sarah McGarvin Intermediate School, CA

A Friend

So much depends upon a
friend

A lost tear
gone

A light giggle
escaped

The touch of love
gone
Abby Scott, Grade 7
Mountain Middle School, CO

Grandpa

Your smile is as sweet as a lollipop
And your personality is unusual
You talk to me about your childhood
To give me tips on mine
I love your stories you tell me
And how you tuck me in at night
Saying "Don't let the bed bugs bite,"
This poem is dedicated to you
I know it's kind of late
And how it's not great
Just remember that I love you.
Phoebe Nguyen, Grade 7
Sarah McGarvin Intermediate School, CA

Christmas Year

What if Christmas lasted all year?
I might drown in a room full of hugs.
What if stockings were bottomless?
I might be able to pass it off as
a genie in a bottle.
What if everyone could wake up
every morning with the same excitement
as on December 25?
I might get really bored.
Jackson Kibbee, Grade 7
Falcon Creek Middle School, CO

LA Angels of Anaheim

The Anaheim Angels, that's the team for me.
A team that scores runs, and is interesting to see.

Albert Pujols steps to bat, and is wanting a home run.
And he swings, and that ball is going, going, GONE!

Jered Weaver steps on the mound, and is ready to make his pitch.
The batter swings, and he misses, and the sides now have to switch.

Mike Trout is given a walk, with happiness in his face.
The pitch is gone, and so is Trout, and he stole second base.

Mark Trumbo is at bat, with the bases loaded. The pitch is gone, and Trumbo swings,
Hitting a double, scoring three runs, while the Angels fans begin to shout and sing.

Mike Sciocia is happy, that is so true.
Anaheim Angels is a team for me and for you.
Fernando Sedano, Grade 8
St Helen Catholic School, CA

The Classroom

The tapping of pencils creates a strange beat set off by the walking and shuffling of feet
Hands brushing pencils and papers away whispered words like, "what's the date today?"
The only sluggish movement is from the clock students looking, it seems to mock
Thoughts of sleeping and beds at home more pressing than the "Roman Dome"

The chattering of kids behind the door feet jittering against the floor
Backpacks zipped up in advance heads nodding in a trance
Paper crinkled into balls a notebook and a binder falls
27 minds trying to think 27 pencils moving in sync

The teacher shushing, students hushing lights shining, kids whining
Papers turn, try to learn

Tapping, snapping, thoughts of napping sneezing, wheezing, whispered teasing
Mumbling, fumbling, minds tumbling

The clock jumps forward with a beat, rush out, switch classes, and then repeat!
Danielle Egan, Grade 8
Mill Valley Middle School, CA

And Wait for You

I rejoice at the life before my eyes; I weep at the pain that comes in cries.
I laugh at the butterfly that tickles my nose; I shun the sins that cause my woes.
I follow the path that leads to light; I pity the road that is full of spite.
I strive for integrity; I shy from jealousy.
I try my best to be like you, I do the best I can do.

But a canvas offers the world; only to show me what you can't do
A light welcomes me in; only to burn my skin.
A smile lightens my heart; only to come and take it apart
And a person says they love me; only to take it back.

But I never give up, I believe in the good, I pour a cup of tea, and wait for you.
Sarah Fletcher, Grade 7
Horizon Charter School, CA

Volleyball

bump, set, serve, spike
returning the ball
receiving the ball
six girls on the court
gaining and losing points
more girls on the bench
cheering on teammates
volleyball is a team effort
no girl on the court
is more important
than the one on the bench

Bridget Hodges, Grade 7
Christ the King School, AZ

High School

H orrifying
I ncredible
G igantic
H arder than elementary

S witching more than five classes
C ramped lockers
H orrible lunches
O ver full classes
O ver achievers and under achievers
L ots of homework

Bridget Mac Donald, Grade 7
Young Scholar's Academy, AZ

The Death Raven

The battle was quick yet bloody,
The man was far too wounded,
To go home to his beloved,
As he lay dying,
A raven rested on his arm,
No mercy was shown that day,
As the bird of death hath pray,
"No one should ever see,
What I have today."
And with that final caw,
The warrior had left his world behind…

Gretchen Blackburn, Grade 8
Taft Alternative High School, CA

The Welcome of Winter

Under the gray sky
snow drifts through the branches
snow
like powdered ice
being crushed by the clouds
snuggling
onto the flowers that are slowly dying
gliding down
like a bride walking down the aisle

Brittany Jones, Grade 8
Mountain Ridge Jr High School, UT

Labyrinth

Ears ringing, adrenaline racing, no point in looking back,
I'm to far, to close.
Running though the shadows, I hear but can't believe,
Am I going crazy?
Footsteps, closer and closer, as it seals my fate, I cannot escape.
The thread is cut, my life is gone, it's set in stone.
Can stone be broken?
I'm lost in a daze, what I know has not caught my grip.
I slowly start to understand.
Tears drip down my face, sadness is creeping in, hopelessness, hopelessness,
No, I must keep the blood pumping,
Hopelessness shall be my fatal flaw,
Hopelessness shall seal my fate.
Slowly the rope is bonded back,
My fate, my fate generations, to go on.
As I face a wall, I realize there is no where, to face my fear, and die dignified, sounds good.
I slowly turn, and find myself facing, the wall?
A new door has opened,
It's happening again, it's happening again,
Shall I take the path chosen, or shall I sit?

Sarah Barrett, Grade 8
Bryant Middle School, UT

The Holocaust

One powerful perpetrator, Hitler had Europe in the palm of his hand.
Bystanders watched in terror, they were too afraid to take a stand.
Fierce, fiery, and fearful, the Nazis swept away the Jews,
They were in desperate need of a refuge.

Starved and tortured,
It was like the Jews were butchered.
Hitler the hypocrite,
He was the one, who should have been thrown in the pit.

No master race,
The Aryans were a disgrace.
Blonde haired, blue eyed, in Hitler's eyes, you carried much pride.
While he himself had the opposite, brown hair and brown eyes.

Death and concentration camps,
Left the earth bloody and damp.
Death opened his arms in welcome, to the thousands that died every day.
Europe was a tree in autumn, its leaves; over 11 million fallen to the clay.

Sophie Clarke, Grade 7
Hamilton Middle School, CO

What if Aliens Did Exist?

What if green, slimy aliens did exist?
I might become an astronaut just to see if it's true.
What if every single time you laughed, it added one more hour to your life?
I could live forever, well at least to when I'm too old to laugh.
What if pigs could fly?
I would seriously get me one of those.
What if life was just an everlasting dream waiting to end?

Cole Crader, Grade 7
Falcon Creek Middle School, CO

For the Girls

This is for the girls on Saturday nights,
Who sit in their rooms,
With tears in their eyes.
This is for the girls who love with their heart,
Who let it get torn out,
And broken apart.
This is for the girls who despise their complexion,
That stare at the mirror,
Hating the reflection.
This is for the girls with their heads in the clouds,
That fall hard for a boy,
But come crashing back down.
This is for the girls with cuts on their skin,
Who can hide every feeling,
With polyester and cotton.
This is for the girls who hate what they be,
This is for the girls,
Just like me.

Kelsy Begin, Grade 9
Roundup High School, MT

Our Leading Light!

Small, but standing strait,
On it's base, a small black plate.
Dripping white string cheese.

Around it is heat.
A yellow glow surrounds it
In it's glare, I'm beat.

A bright red fire,
It's blazing never tires.
Eating oxygen.

Light out of the fright!
Guiding us through the dark night
Full of light, light, light

Leading us to see
Who, our true creator be ever this candle lights

Aveen Mostafa, Grade 7
National University Academy, CA

A Companion's Comfort

A great companion, an old friend,
Always there in times of need,
Whether it be words of comfort,
Or help on an assignment from school,
They are always there for a fellow in trouble,
When family is unable,
A friend is able,
Words of anger may be spoken to enrage,
Words of peace will be spoken to comfort,
In the end a friend is always there

Dennis Tran, Grade 7
Sarah McGarvin Intermediate School, CA

Fast and Powerful

I am fast and powerful
I wonder how the next game will proceed
I hear the crowd hollering and screaming
I see my opponents skating, rushing toward me
I want to score a goal
I am fast and powerful

I pretend I have no fear
I feel the sweat rush down my face
I touch the goal post
I worry I will get severely injured
I cry and fear that my team will lose
I am fast and powerful

I understand when to strike and when not to
I say I am the best
I dream to play NHL
I try to play my hardest
I hope we win
I am fast and powerful

Isiah Maldonado, Grade 7
Falcon Creek Middle School, CO

Christmas Memories

Waking up late at night,
hearing sleigh bells, jingle jingle.
Staring at the smiling moon, wishing I was on the roof.

When morning starts, it's presents all round.
the Christmas lights,
oh so bright.
The angel on the tree,
staring down at me.

Laying there in my pajamas,
mother taking pictures with her camera.
eating breakfast at the table,
laughing at Christmas past.
Slowly we go down to one present each,
night comes and we are beat.

Megan McDonagh, Grade 7
Joe Walker Middle School, CA

The Ocean

The sea…
So vast and graceful.

As I stare into your unforgettable eyes I calm
As light shines upon you, you form a glittery
Complexion.

I wish I was there with you
But sadly…
My life differs from yours.

Jack Mavrakos, Grade 7
Monte Vista Christian School, CA

Hope from the Ashes

Tired and weeping, the lonesome boy collapsed on the sidewalk.
Was his father really gone? Could it be true?
He prayed it wasn't.
He had seen the news images of his father's red fire engine
Screaming, speeding through the streets,
Rushing toward the Twin Towers.

He yearned deeply to find his father.
He ran and ran across the city to reach him.
His father is a hero to many, but most of all to him,
Not only as a firefighter, but also as a man.
A kind and loving man, ready to save others,
Always risking his life, no matter what the cost.

Now the ashes engulfed him.
He pulled his shirt up to his face and put his head down,
He could hardly breathe.
The Towers were down, would he find him alive?
He felt a hand on his shoulder.
The sun was breaking through as he looked up.
He gasped for air and cried out with joy, "Father!"

Austin Gatons, Grade 8
Palm Desert Charter Middle School, CA

Become Who You Are

Become who you are
Any dance makes me fall into a trance.
The way it allows you to express yourself in many different ways.
Let dance excel you to a whole new world.
If you get caught up in a rhythm dance dream it may come true.
The way you sway to different rhythms.

The way you put yourself down only makes it worse.
Let your body feel the beat.
Become the beat, you are the one and only interpreter.
You must become who you are, show emotion.
Don't be afraid to show emotion the beat will guide you.

Dance is beautiful you can become whatever you choose.
It is a Goddess and I am its Zeus.

Lizette Silva, Grade 8
Palm Desert Charter Middle School, CA

To the One I Love the Most

She is the most beautiful human I've ever seen
How her eyes light up my morning sun
Her smile inspires me to try my hardest
And her hair is like a waterfall cascading into a river
Also her body is shaped to perfection like an angel's body
Whenever she talks I get lost in here words of inspiration
Her laugh makes me smile every time she laughs
Her smell always smells like strawberries
Here skin is as soft as bunny's fur
Her personality is what I love most about her

Andrew Torrentera, Grade 7
Monte Vista Christian School, CA

Easier with You

Do you sense the feelings, bouncing through your head?
Acting like a waterfall wanting to be said,
Do you catch the stares, walking down the hall?
Do they stop you in your step, acting like a wall?
Do you feel alone, do you feel afraid?
Do you feel like a no one, while others have it made?
Do you know the reason, the reason for this pain?
It's because you aren't popular, a player of its game,
But sometimes that is better, it is always great,
When you aren't a hater, 'cause haters have to hate,

I am here beside you, you are not alone,
see yourself in my own eyes, see how you have grown,
You are strong, you are brave,
You are making a shockwave,
I see the light when you're around; I see it in your eyes,
I'm the moon and you're the sun, starting now to rise,
Rise to fight the shadows, plaguing all your dreams,
Fight them with your smile, not fighting with extremes,
Life is sometimes hard, life may seem askew,
But it is much easier; if I'm here with you.

Savannah Tanner, Grade 9
Vision Charter School, ID

Baseball

Baseball will teach you a lot about life.
It can raise you up to heaven,
then cut you like a knife.
I think that I'll appreciate it once I am grown,
those dirty rotten curve balls that got past me, when thrown.
Baseball demands you adapt
and correct all your bad habits.
When a fast ball whizzes past you
you must adjust your stance,
so that home run that's waiting for you
gets another chance.
In nine short innings
win or lose,
baseball will teach you
all you ever need to know.

Daniel Glenn, Grade 7
Monte Vista Christian School, CA

My Animal Names

My dog's name is Reef,
and he eats lots of beef.
Lexi is my other dog,
even though I wanted a frog.
My sister's horse's name is Cruz.
He thinks he's a cow so instead of neighing he moos.
My cat's name is Karma because she is black.
My bird's name is Harper and he's bringing sexy back.
I once had a goldfish whose name was Joe,
But he passed away a while ago.

Zev Gragg, Grade 7
Monte Vista Christian School, CA

Grandma Mabel

While sitting at the kitchen table
Trying to be strong and stable
Not letting a tear fall from my face
Remembering my grandpa Mabel

Life is more like a race
Don't let it get out of trace
My love really grew
Especially not in outer space

Everything makes sense when I'm with you
But I really had no clue
I will love you forever
I don't know what to do

We will always be together
I will forget you never
I will remember you whenever
I will remember you whenever
Jazmine Mejia, Grade 8
John Adams School, CA

Are You Really Gone?

I wish you were still here
Not far, but near
You didn't care
It didn't seem fair

We had so much fun together
I thought our friendship was forever
We had lots of trust
And everything was discussed

I miss you, and wish you were by my side
There's no need to hide
You have lots of respect
That I will protect

I hope we can still be friends
And make sure our friendship never ends
I'll be there for you
But will you be there for me too?
Elizabeth Gonzalez, Grade 8
John Adams Middle School, CA

Trampoline Fun

As soon as you get on,
you feel a little bounce.
And if you get higher,
you hear a great sound!
Do a flip here and do a flip there,
I'm doing flips everywhere.
Soon I am as high as the sun,
I like to call this trampoline fun!
Caleb Drake, Grade 7
Salida Middle School, CO

The Mystery Box

I go downstairs to the living room
During the time of early morning gloom
And find a big box, filled with old things, I assume.
I shake it this way and that, hear a tinkling sound.
Like Tinker Bell trying to tell me something that I don't understand.
I have a feeling that I am not supposed to look inside.
Perhaps in there are marbles, clear and crystal white like chilly ice;
Or maybe it is an abandoned lamp, discouraged with no more light.
Probably it's an aged photograph of my mom and dad and me,
Or an old and unused CD of a beautiful ancient symphony.
It may be some important painting of some sort of fruit
Or my mother's fluffy, white wedding dress, and her smooth vanilla pearls.
Whatever it is, I want to find out.
It's a prehistoric treasure, I'm sure;
But it will not be discovered just yet, I hope.
However long time ticks quietly on a clock,
It will be as silent and unspeaking as a rock
I so badly want to rip it open and find out what's inside.
But people have their secrets that they want to hide.
And it's not mine, so I have no part to play
In this mysterious game of take-apart.
Daisy Lee, Grade 7
St. Joseph of Cupertino School, CA

Dead

I looked away for a second
But by the time I saw it was to late
It was devastating
Unprecedented
She was kind person
And I was right there the whole time
In the same room
It only took a second
But someone did this
It wasn't her
It's impossible
She wasn't depressed in anyway
And with her happy go lucky attitude
No one could help but befriend her
And she was the most loyal and trusting friend anyone could hope for
Also very vulnerable she was
But why
Who would want to betray her
Who would want her killed
Who would want her dead???
Swathi Ramaprasad, Grade 7
Merryhill School, CA

Rocky Waters

The water is bright like the sun, the clouds are beaming orange,
and the mountains are greener than before.
The water is misty like a cold night, it sounds like wind running in your face
The rocks are gleaming orange, the sun is setting.
The clouds are floating and the water is flowing again.
Daniel Rodriguez, Grade 7
Daniel Savage Middle School, CA

Baseball Is a Long Day on the Farm

After playing three agonizing hot games in the sun
sweating so much
I feel like I am in a rain storm
smelling like a pig
I refuse to quit until the job is accomplished
Bang! The ball is hit
I take off as quickly as a bullet from the rifle
I feel like a plow circling the field as I head toward home plate.
It would be a job well done if I made it in time

Sliding into home plate
a dirt devil rises over me
fans squawking and squealing
the call is safe
I spring up from the field

Finally the day is over
my hard work has paid off
a moment I will remember forever
Max McCoy, Grade 8
Falcon Creek Middle School, CO

You Are Not Musicians — Just Singing Brits

Dear One Direction,
I would like to tell you
that you are an unintelligent boy band
You tell me
"You got that one thing!"
You say
"That's what makes you beautiful"
You chant
"Live while we're young"
Well let me just say
You are not musicians, just singing Brits
so next time my sister blasts your music
I will put my headphones on and listen to
Justin Bieber
and whenever you sing
I will slap that British accent right out of you.
Ashley Raymond, Grade 7
Falcon Creek Middle School, CO

Adrenaline Rush

Waiting in line as thirty minutes go by
And I finally arrive at the gate.
As I hop in the train and buckle my belt
I hear a pop and a click and we are ready to go.
The train lurches forward and we start moving
As a chainlift lifts me to the top of the drop.
With no turning back, the trains begins to drop.
10, 20, 30, 40, 50 mph.
As we hit the first loop and hit a sharp turn the train begins to drop
Wind is rushing through my hair, and before I knew it, it is over.
I get off the train and walk away with a smile.
Gabriel Velazquez, Grade 7
Las Flores Middle School, CA

Athletes and Who We Are

An athlete is competitive and strong
Always willing to go to the extreme
Tenacious they are, to prove doubters wrong,
Being undefeated is the big dream

Long practices take great strength to get through
To overcome every wall encountered,
To be aggressive and determined too
One day, when we win, we'll be undaunted

Every single sacrifice we have made,
Every day, every second of practice
Every wall we ran past and over came,
For that one moment to stand in first place

Everything will be paid off, soon, someday
When the title is claimed and there to stay
Tiffany Shyu, Grade 9
Monarch High School, CO

Sun: Our Guardian

A bright orange, yellow dot gleaming in the sky,
It brings warmth to our soul and soothes our minds.
A fireball, or angel's light, united life to fly,
up in the distance, stuck in the air's bind.

Grabbed and dropped for our safety of heat,
only to realize the coming of dark shadows.
The bright light vanishes leaving traces of dark sheets.
Growing and growing mystical to cause sorrow!

A dark hand moving closer, and closer,
out of the shadows with a fearful gloom.
But then a ray of light banishes her.
Darkness slowly creeps away from the room.

The bright light scares away the dark from us.
The dark has gone and the Guardian watches us.
Calvin Mak, Grade 9
Monarch High School, CO

Reflections on Rodin's Sculpture "Thought"

Trapped
In a world
Only thinkable for her.
she is as still as death;
Being observant of each and every thing
In sight and in sound.
Bang! Pop! Smack!
Those are the noises in her head
Which may cause her pain.
But at the end of the day
She's still a structured statue.
She's Rodin's masterpiece, "Thought."
Porshay Mays, Grade 7
Tenaya Middle School, CA

A Present Day Nerd

I am a girlie nerd who loves crafts and music.
I wonder about anything having to do with any kind of math.
I hear rivers running past me.
I see a cabin I helped build.
I want a family full of crazy, cute kids.
I am a girlie nerd who loves crafts and music.

I pretend that I am a pioneer.
I feel excited about this school year.
I touch the soft feathers of a chick.
I worry that people won't like me.
I cry for those who don't appreciate school.
I am a girlie nerd who loves crafts and music.

I understand that everyone thinks differently.
I say people can't learn to their limit unless they want to.
I dream about my bright hopeful future.
I try to be nice and help others.
I hope to be better and smarter tomorrow.
I am a girlie nerd who loves crafts and music.

Alyssa Johnson, Grade 7
Canyon View Jr High School, UT

A Story

Everybody has a story
So think about what you say
Don't ignore trust
Acknowledge the key they have given you to their life
What if it was your story
That no one wanted to know
Don't pity them for their past
Admire that they are strong today
Everyone has a story
There is no "more interesting" or "saddest"
There is a story
That has entwined with millions of others
And might not even know the impact
So pay attention to those details
And remember all of those times
Because everyone has a story
That changes every other
So continue telling, and living yours
Everyone has a story
What impact will yours have?

Maryfher Villarreal, Grade 8
North Middle School, CO

The Person I Admire

My mom, Katina, is as beautiful as she can be
Started off with a bad start, until she had me.
I brought joy to her life and she changed her ways.
Then she became the beautiful person she became.
She is a wonderful person and it's all because of me.
I changed her life just like she changed me.

Azalea Jimenez, Grade 7
Daniel Savage Middle School, CA

Once Upon a Time

Once upon a time, in a world where
My candy-coated life consists of
Teddy bears preferring two sugar cubes to one,
And leaping from couch to couch being the only way
To avoid being scorched by carpet lava.
Once upon a time, in a world where
My eager life consists of
Wanting to grow up; clomping around in my mom's heels,
And longing for the day that I can buy
All the lollipops I had ever wished for.
Once upon a time, in a world where
My confusing life consists of
Time waning and stress building,
Wondering if it'll ever end, and —
Wishing I was five again,
When I could spend an entire day with my best friend —
Even if they didn't exist.
When I didn't need to know why
Leaves change color
Or how — because I was a kid.

Karlye Hankins, Grade 9
University Preparatory School, CA

Reflections on Rodin's Sculpture, "Thought"

I see
A woman
Trapped and forlorn,
She looks like she has been
Laughed at and scorned.
I see
A woman
Trapped in stone,
Trapped in her thoughts,
Eternally alone.
I see
A weathered, heartsick woman,
Knowing that
She will never escape
Her eternal prison.

Fabian Samano, Grade 7
Tenaya Middle School, CA

A Melancholy Sea

In the sorrows that drown you,
A dark despair arises.
You swim, you fight,
But sink farther into the deep blue.
A deep blue, soon to become black.
You sink to the bottom,
Where you have given up.
You feel peace, but remember all those you leave behind.
You swim faster, you fight harder.
You reach the top, your depression left behind in the bottomless sea.
Joy and happiness burn ever brighter with the glowing sun.

KhyLeigh Claunts, Grade 7
Vallivue Middle School, ID

Sights Never Forgotten on a House Boat

This thing jetted past me quickly,
With a hiss
Its tongue like a raging, fiery sting
That hits you so fast in the face,
So fast,
That you barely even notice it
Water snake

This thing swam away from me,
With graceful,
Breast stroke like movements.
Its green, slimy, spotted skin
Looks like an illusion
Toad

This thing basked in the sunlight,
Moving very, very,
Slowly, but steadily. Its rock-like
Shell on top of it.
Turtle

These are the things I
Remembered while going
House boating

Jenna Yamada, Grade 7
Rolling Hills Country Day School, CA

Seeing Through New Eyes

I am like a computer
Intelligent and deciphering
I realize how great it is to say "I"
I am my own person choosing my own
To speak, to think, to wonder, to roam

I play like an artist
Listening to song the colors dance in my head
How lucky I am to hear like I do
I wish everyone could have this chance too

I can be as loud as a roaring dragon
Or sometimes I'm a mouse
It kind of depends on if I'm at my house

I watch as the ball gets kicked into the sky
Then I see the players run by
The ball under my feet it rapidly rolls
And before I know it
I've made five goals

It seems like I'm always hungry
I am not really sure why
If I was a bird I wouldn't be able to fly

Nathan Baker, Grade 7
Canyon View Jr High School, UT

Music

Music is a noise, playing in my head.
Music is love, in search of a word.
Music is my world, revolving around me.
Music is art, hanging in a museum.
Music is a flower, blooming in the sun.
Music is a diary, holding my secrets.
Music is a light, brightening my day when I'm down.
Music is my armor, protecting me from harm.
Music is a prize, making kids smile.
Music is a river, flowing downstream.

Kaiya Alvarez, Grade 7
St John's Episcopal School, CA

White

White is a horse, running free in a field.
White is the moon, coming out every night.
White is a piece of paper, being written on.
White is a rose, making my garden beautiful.
White is a dog, playing in the backyard.
White is a white board, helping teachers to teach.
White is a blanket, keeping you always warm.
White is snow, covering the ground.
White is a candle, sustaining the fire.
White is an angel, taking care of people.

Veronica Bustamante, Grade 7
St John's Episcopal School, CA

Endings

Even though they end and don't always end well
Even though they can be sad or happy
Each has a story behind it
A story with a golden age and a downfall
This story becomes a past we don't forget
A memory
It follows us and we remember how it made us stronger
Even though they all have endings
Each different
Each started a beginning

Anik Boyadzhyan, Grade 8
Theodore Roosevelt Middle School, CA

City Life

The tower ticks as the night goes on
The water has calmed, the water is asleep
As the boats drift to the dock
The city lights turn off the tower lights remain
The sky is gray the city is hush, hush
As you hear grasshoppers and frogs the city gets
Covered in clouds and fog
The bridge is still not a sudden move
The people are asleep but not the quiet, not the
Water, not even the towers that remain still…

Tasneem Yasin, Grade 7
Daniel Savage Middle School, CA

A Letter to My Lovely Stalker

Sometimes you're see-through, others you're filled in.
You mimic my moves as I copy yours.
Sometimes you are thick, sometimes you are thin.
When I can't find you, I look on the floors.

In different shades of light, you shift and bend.
Where do you hide when I cannot find you?
You are my stalker and my closest friend.
Everything that's said about you is true.

They say you go hand-in-hand with darkness.
Everyone has you, but you are unique.
You're as large as me, but remain noiseless.
You hide so well, I believe you are meek.

You've been my follower since long ago.
You are my lovely stalker, my shadow.
Asha Wiltshire, Grade 9
Monarch High School, CO

Aspirations

Our dreams and goals to which we aspire
How important are they to you and me?
It truly helps if one is inspired
Into the future, how far can we see?

You find out what you are truly made of
You can do anything if you believe
Everybody wants to do what they love
Set your mind to it and you will achieve

You are responsible for your own fate
If by chance, it's your dreams you do not chase
In the end, it is yourself you will hate
There will be challenges for you to face

Try to accomplish your goals if you would
Who wants to look back and wish they still could?
Nathan Davis, Grade 9
Monarch High School, CO

Light and Dark

The water is warm and misty
People fishing along the sea
Big Ben is lit up and shining
The air is dark and cold
One castle is brightly glowing
Cars and buses honking through the night
Waves crashing on sandy shores
Salty air running through the night
The whole town is lit up by a mystery
Everything is lit up but two building
They create beautiful light and shine so bright
Sabrina Murillo, Grade 7
Daniel Savage Middle School, CA

Grandpa

I know we are all feeling a little bit sad.
That we've lost our grandpa, our friend, and our dad.
Together we have cried tears,
Such as we hold many fears.

But he would want us to know,
He is in a good place.
And he sees us with a beautiful smile,
Just how we spent time for a while.

Thinking back now I must say,
I feel lucky to have met my grandpa to this day.
He has played a special part,
In my heart.

I know you loved me too.
My heart will always be with you.
Now I have to say goodbye,
Until I see you again, when I die.
Prisila Alvaro, Grade 8
John Adams Middle School, CA

Ode to the Creamy Goodness of Dreyers

Chocolate, strawberry, or vanilla?
Too much of it can be a killa!
It is tasty and creamy,
And it makes my insides feel dreamy.

The ultimate dessert for one or two,
Just grab a bowl, no need to chew!
Ben and Jerry's, Dreyers, or Haagen Dazs,
In the end, I will never need to floss.

It makes me happy; it relaxes my muscles,
It can even calm my throbbing blood vessels!
Ice cream is a treat well deserved,
I'm sure you have thought and observed!

The delicious goodness cannot go to waste,
Ice cream can never be replaced!
It's been recorded in books since 1722,
Ice cream, just wanted to say, I love you!
Camille Daszynski, Grade 9
Archbishop Mitty High School, CA

The Majesty of Letters

The young artist paints,
As all his viewers faint.
The splashes of colors are precise,
So small, it could only be done by artistic mice.
He shows away all skill,
As the blank canvas fills,
And reveals a large letter "A."
Deekshita Kacham, Grade 7
Young Scholar's Academy, AZ

Dragons

They are majestic,
Uncurling huge wings.
They are beloved by children
And can assume any shape imaginable.
They can be huge with blue scales and sharp fangs
Or be red and have huge wingspans.
They can breathe fire or other elements.
With all those things, they must be one thing.
They are dragons.

Andrew Le, Grade 7
Sarah McGarvin Intermediate School, CA

4th of July

4th of July
Pop, pop, pop of fireworks
They light the grin upon my face
The lights casting hazes over the landscape
Boxes, plastics, laying there giving off smells
Of sickly intoxicating old rotting wood
I'm like a firefighter watching for trouble
I'm dousing the spark
Finally in control

Karissa Schulte, Grade 7
Weldon Valley Jr High School, CO

Sleeping

The old saying is unleashed,
"Time for bed!"
I sense my eyes closing
while I pull the sheets up.

Imagining.

My mind is dragged from the present,
and pulled to the past or the future.

Waiting.

Anxiety and excitement wash over me
as mysterious lands appear from blackness.

Dreaming.

Worlds fly past
as one dream finishes and another arrives.
My mind whirls round and round.

Finished.

I finally have had enough.
My mind is empty and tired.
And deep, dark sleep creeps over me.

Sleeping.

Rebekah Earhart, Grade 7
Salida Middle School, CO

Black Waters

The black waters of life
Trickle slowly down the gorge

The day is young with
Sunshine.
Laughter radiates off the walls in heaps.

Dark clouds…
Creep into view above the gorge

Time ticks away and the laughter
Fades

Thunder booms
Lightning flashes
Water droplets

Fall…
Until they are a tsunami

Ripping away at the
Stone walls

Then the canyon is
Simply…

Gone…
And the journey is over

Kyler Sengsavath, Grade 8
Falcon Creek Middle School, CO

This House of Mine

This house of mine,
it's loud and crazy,
but there is no other,
quite like it.

This house of mine,
it's where family comes,
to talk, to have fun, to eat,
to play, to do nothing,
but laugh.

This house of mine,
is full of love,
of laughter, of happiness.
It is full of nothing
but family.

This house of mine,
I won't ever leave,
it really means the world to me.
This house is now,
and will forever be mine.

Francine Morales, Grade 8
Richardson PREP HI Middle School, CA

Beautiful City of Night

Oh, a beautiful city of night,
in a place faraway,
such beauty it brings.
A tower that is so tall,
it could be a castle all lit up.
There are many other towers in that beautiful city of night,
that make it so grand.
And to hear and see a beautifully lit clock tower,
is a wondrous sight.
And every so often a few lights can be seen,
and few cars can be heard.
The river that flows under the bridge is quiet,
and the boats have stopped and parked under the bridge,
at the docks that are under the bridge.
The city isn't too loud,
and it isn't too quiet,
it's just right.
And that's what makes a beautiful city of night.
Now if you'll excuse me, I have to go find my family,
and usher them to the airport. We're going on a family trip!

Janae Shannon, Grade 7
Daniel Savage Middle School, CA

Nature's Cruelty

Nature with her constant changing has wiped out countless
Without remorse, regret, mercy, or hesitation
Not even slowing for the grief she has and will cause to everyone
Whoever she has taken, whether family or friend, was just gone
Few fear her yet all should with her various ways to vent her fury
Volcanoes and wildfires to burn the world to the ground
Earthquakes to tear the world from its very foundation
Landslides to bury the wold and tsunamis to drown it
Tornadoes to rip the earth apart piece by piece
All of these just for offending her even the smallest bit
Yet she can be warm and beautiful at times
Changing from a harsh, deadly winter to a warm, lively spring
Allowing flowers to grow and blossom with a quiet beauty
Allowing majestic trees to sprout and reach the sky
So nature can be cruel and warm when needed

Tyler Orr, Grade 9
New Plymouth High School, ID

Day at the Beach

As you walk through the sandy beach
You hear the water coming towards your feet
People surfing over the crashing waves
The ocean blue calms down as the day goes by
The hot humid air makes you want to jump in the water
Kids building sand castles
People swimming in the freezing clear blue water
Seagulls trying to get a bit of your food
Seaweed laying on the shore
Seashells broken on the sand as people are walking by
As the sun starts to set people are leaving the beach

Janet Gonzalez, Grade 8
Monte Vista Christian School, CA

Today

Today was the day.
Today was the day my life began again.
Before the days went by and owned the sky,
And fled when it became night.
Life had no meaning, no laughter.
Until today.

Today was the day,
You stood in the shadows and drew no light.
I stood in the light and tried to see, ready to take flight.
You are the hunter and I am the prey.
You captured me and I decided to stay.

Today was the day…
I fell in love. I fell in love with you.
Life is laughter, life is humble, and life is pure.
Not the empty shell that I used to know.
Today is the day I live again.

Heather Howell, Grade 9
Pine Creek High School, CO

The Magic of a Moment

When times of chaos came and stood,
Your devoid song chorused through the wood,
All who found you did not regret,
Remarkable intellect they all met,
Yet, soon as you came, you were gone,
Your devotees did not blaspheme you, however forlorn,
The emblem of virtue stands by your side,
Embedded in those who have no lies,
Your amber glow envelopes all,
Who have come to find truth in your hall,
Every maelstrom that crosses your path,
Becomes diluted and can never last,
But when you leave, and strike up pain,
All the turmoil starts again,
And as the twilight hour set,
Your time has come, or has it yet?
The magic of a moment, bound to be afar,
Has come again, return abode, as an unblemished star.

Anjan Kolla, Grade 7
Foothills Middle School, CA

Beauty

Beauty is nature, growing all around us.
Beauty is love, showing in a kiss.
Beauty is music, prancing in our ears with its joyful beats.
Beauty is a soul, giving and asking nothing in return.
Beauty is a friend, helping you when you fall down.
Beauty is art, adding color to our eyes.
Beauty is a dream, giving us something to work hard for.
Beauty is belief, reminding us of the best we can do.
Beauty is knowledge, lighting up our minds with ideas.
Beauty is trust, teaching our hearts what we must do.

Alexis Cooley, Grade 7
St John's Episcopal School, CA

The Black
His mane as dark as night,
his eyes so gentle, but wild

His spirit is so strong, he can never be caught
He fights his enemies one by one

He is polite with fillies and colts
He doesn't back away with fear,
but runs with anger in his eyes

He is the strongest of them all
And protective of his herd

His heart is strong and wild,
He will never be caught

He will never be mine
Maggie Haun, Grade 7
Monte Vista Christian School, CA

The Weather Decided to Be Weird Today
The weather decided to be weird today
I guess it wanted to come out and play
The principal basked in warm sunlight
The teachers were surrounded by a breeze fresh and light
While us students were soaking, drenched in rain
The assistant faculty found the wind such a pain
My mom was being scorched, so her cooking wasn't right
My dad had to listen to sounds of sleet all night
Next morning the school had been crushed with hail
A huge boulder of it, stuck with papers and mail
The beach was having its sand turned into snow
And down in the desert temperatures dropped way too low
Up on top of the peaks of the mountains
Something had started to form, an ice water fountain
Nobody had a clue of what to do
And I'll never find out what really happened
Soon enough to tell you
Kaitlyn Vu, Grade 7
Sarah McGarvin Intermediate School, CA

The Fall
The cold fall breeze brings a chill to the body
And the scent of leaves,
The cold fall breeze brings the smell of pumpkins
And the water starts to freeze,
The cold fall breeze blows the leaves into orbit
And winter stares me in the face,
The cold fall breeze brings Halloween
And even astronauts know from space
That the cold fall breeze always blows
When fall comes around,
The cold fall breeze brings the rain down to Earth,
And will never cease to blow summer down.
Parker Hathaway, Grade 7
Monte Vista Christian School, CA

Oh, My Dear…
You infected me with that so called love;
Oh, my dear love I cannot believe it;
You made me fall in love with that white dove;
Oh, my dear love you got me in your bit.

My friend or my foe, tell me who you are;
Oh, my dear friend tell me why you said that;
My foe, oh my foe, you made me go far;
Oh, my dear lovely friend, I love your hat.

My love, Love of my life why did you leave?
Oh, my dear love you have got me star struck;
You made me fall, fall down like a dead leaf;
Oh, my dear love, you have gotten my luck.

As my dear love tells me I got to leave;
Because the love I love is the one piece.
Liliana Kale, Grade 8
Sequoia Village School, AZ

World Within a Child's Hand
For me
The world within a child's hand
Is a map of life.
It can tell the past and the many memories
That child has.
The world within a child's hand is a storybook
Just waiting to be read.
Every child has a story
And it will never end.
It goes on forever, from generation to generation,
Adding more and more
Leaving behind an endless book of memories,
Sorrow, love, and adventures.
The world within a child's hand is a treasure
To be treasured and it will be.
For every hand is different,
For every hand there is a world.
Natasha Taylor, Grade 7
Tenaya Middle School, CA

Oliver
On the 24th of May
a kitten came to stay.
He loves to run and play
though he likes to sleep all day.
At times, he's fun and crazy
other times he's tired and lazy.
He loves to eat his favorite fish
in the little kitty dish.
Although he sometimes makes me mad
he almost always makes me glad.
Sometimes, he hurts me with a scratch
but in my heart there is no match.
Alexandra Browning, Grade 7
Monte Vista Christian School, CA

Should I?

I'm trapped, torn. My people make me choose.
Stay here, some say, to protect us.
Go now, few say, to him, your love.
Should I stay or should I go?
I don't know.
He calls me over, like a cry for help.
I love him and he loves me.
But my people, they cry, needing me, too.
Should I stay or should I go?
I don't know.
Leaving the strife of my birthplace. An unresolved problem.
Only to find to him, my love, who waits.
In a world of freedom, I can be. But my people, they keep me.
Should I stay or should I go?
I don't know.
If I leave, I betray my family. The ones who raised me up to now.
If I stay, I betray him. The one who showed me color, life, love.
I'm torn, torn, torn.
Should I stay or should I go?
I don't know.

Desmarie Jackson, Grade 7
Mitchell Intermediate School, CA

Spider Spider

Spider, spider in our Christmas tree
Very hidden probably from me
Where are you in all that green
Please come out so you can be seen
Such a little ornament that I can't find
Because all the others are so intertwined
Oh, Mom, how you hide it so well
Makes me wish it were as big as the Liberty Bell
You'll bring me luck for the entire new year
If I find you first, so please just appear
I feel like I'm closer, I'm getting so near
I can almost see you crystal clear
Are you a she or even a he
Spider, spider, where could you be

Gracely Speth, Grade 8
Headwaters Academy, MT

Darkness

It is not known.
It's shrouded in darkness, never to be seen.
It disappears when you look, and when you don't.
A thing of mystery.
It's dark matter, and yet, it isn't.
Like when you were little
and you screeched that there was a monster.
It was real to you, but it wasn't real to them.
Like when you're on an empty street.
You feel like you're being followed.
It's not paranormal activity.
It just is.

Valentina Lavrentjev, Grade 7
Daniel Savage Middle School, CA

Baseball Bat

I am strong and loud.
I wonder why they don't hold me upside down
I hear the sand brush against the ground
I see the metal cage
I want a ball to hit
I am strong and loud.

I pretend I'm a ball
I feel fingers rub against me
I touch the laces of the ball
I worry when I don't make contact
I cry when I hear "Out!"
I am strong and loud.

I understand 3 and you're done
I say ding, not zing
I dream for a 400 footer
I try going for the fence
I hope I don't get the three
I am strong and loud.

Daniel Quezada, Grade 7
Falcon Creek Middle School, CO

My Domino Set

It was Christmas Day when I got my Domino set
I opened up the wrapping to see my name engraved
I knew it was special
But when I saw that it was a Domino set
I knew this was much more special than a normal gift
It matched my Dad's but it had my name
It was so meaningful to me
I opened it up and emptied the white rectangle Dominoes
The black dots were glistening
As the Dominoes were falling out of the case
One by one
Piece by piece
All tumbling out of the box
This was my Domino set.

Henry Walsh, Grade 8
Headwaters Academy, MT

I Am Thankful For

My Wonderful Parents who love me
Wonderful house built for my liking
Games and electronics for those boring days
Makeup to cover my imperfections
Holidays to gather around with family
My life and beautiful surroundings
Taylor Swift to keep my voice company
My relatives who care enough to love me
My Wonderful dogs who love me
Kitty Cat who bites and loves me
Plants to keep your heart warm
My love and others for company in hearts

Karla Woolard, Grade 7
Daniel Savage Middle School, CA

Ode to Seuss

Dr. Seuss was a lyrical king.
To the heart of children his rhymes would bring,
Joy, of which the youngsters would sing,
Of *Cat in the Hat*, *The Grinch*, and that Lorax thing.
The children cannot escape his words
That clump up like milk in old curds.
He told of Funicular goats that roam in herds,
But not funicular goats who scream their words.
He created Horton who hatched the egg
Or the who's who caught upon his leg.
Little people whose whole world could fit upon a peg
In which a speck of dust could be a crag.
His writing style was totally brand new.
Baadhi ya vitabu vyake ni favorite yangu.
Swahili translation is a clue,
To know what I said stanza five, line two.
Reading in the summer sun.
How many books three, two, or one.
How many doesn't matter though,
As long as Dr. Seuss's greatness is known.

Christopher Huebner, Grade 9
University Preparatory School, CA

Where I'm From

I am from sausage, bacon, and ham
Sizzling in the frying pan.
I am from a grandma and
Grandpa who love me so
Much that they let me come
To their house and let me play
Video games.

I am from treat others as
You want to be treated
And I love you have a good
Day at school and be good.
I am from sitting around the
Television watching Thanksgiving
Day Football and the parade.

I am from Naomi Shaffer and Brian Anderson.
I am from Native Americans,
Englishmen and Irishmen and that is
Where I am from and that makes me who I am.

Carson Anderson, Grade 7
White Pine Middle School, UT

Sensory

Calm is blue.
It sounds like palm trees swaying in the breeze.
It smells like marshmallows.
It tastes like a mango.
It looks like the ocean.
Calm feels like a warm breeze.

Elliott Rondash, Grade 7
White Pine Middle School, UT

Stresser of Worries

I am a stresser and a worrier.
I wonder what my blood pressure will be.
I hear my heart pound out of my chest a mile a minute.
I see the vibration of my skin.
I want to be calm and depowerize my brain.
I am a stresser and a worrier.

I pretend I am relaxed and happy.
I feel petrified after turning in tests.
I touch the button for relaxation, but it doesn't work.
I worry about the grade I will receive.
I cry about my starkness of the unexpected.
I am a stresser and a worrier.

I understand I will probably fail.
I say what's on paper.
I dream of succeeding.
I hope to pass.
I am a stresser and a worrier.

Tess Inhelder, Grade 7
Falcon Creek Middle School, CO

Skipping Seasons

Sun's baking your skin
for your long waited tan
with the warm breeze
slowly circling around you
then it hits you
the wind flies you over into a winter wonderland
the trees are dying rapidly
what happened to the green leaves
that never turned gold
or the flowers slowly wilt
its like a nature cemetery
did everything just die
or they waiting to be open again
with these skipping seasons

Hannah Fox, Grade 9
Agua Fria Union High School South Campus, AZ

Best Friends

Best friends are the people you tell something to,
That you don't want your parents to know.
They are always there for you, no matter what the situation is.
They know you better than just about anyone!
They scream when they see you for the first time in 3 days!
Best friends can bring out the side of you,
That has been hidden for a long time.
they know what to say at the right time.
Best friends aren't afraid of calling your parents mom and dad,
Or just walking in like they live at your house.
They even take up half of your closet with their clothes,
shoes, school work, and whatever junk they throw in there.
But best of all, they are also known as your brother/sister.

Haylee Shahan, Grade 7
Young Scholar's Academy, AZ

Night

The evening turns into a crisp fall night
With the moon high in the sky
Lights turned out in most buildings
People sleeping in their houses
Unaware of the night noises
The world spinning around them
Owls hooting
Mice running
Stars shining against the darkness
A full moon making things peaceful
A rustling in the leaves
Wind disturbing the ground
A howling at the moon
By a wary wolf
A town at the center
With woods all around
People peacefully dreaming
Glorious, happy things filling their minds
The stars start to fade as the sun rises
People start waking up
Preparing for another busy day
Mia Buak, Grade 8
Monte Vista Christian School, CA

Guilt

You're speechless
You don't know what to say
The feeling is so different
Guilt is on its way.

You want to hold back
But you can't anymore
Guilt is now knocking on the door.

Your eyes give it away
Something is wrong
The guilt is coming right along.

Your lips start to move
But no words come about
The guilt is showing
It's coming right out.

With eyes that tell
And lips that speak
Guilt is not safe to be inside of me.
Bianca Burkhart, Grade 8
St Francis School, CA

Sky

Blue as blue can be,
Clouds puffy as cotton balls,
Stretches forever.
Olivia Brooks, Grade 8
Desert Hills Middle School, UT

Enchanted Moon

Long ago, the moon used to shine.
She was brilliant, just like last night.

She illuminated the mystical dazzling lakeside:
Pale pink roses, Calming blue waters,
Butterflies flying to their haven.

She glowed as stupendous as a diamond in the twilight.

It was a genuine experience
To circle the glimmering lake
And walk on the sparkling, sandy shore.

The sweet smell of fruit and honey
Kissed the noses of the passersby.

But when the moon does not shine,
Out come the creatures that live
in the immense, crystalline forest.

They playfully pounced into the water,
Making it look like a vibrant firework,
Instead of a majestic lake.

The sound of the satisfied animals is very exuberant, in a soothing, musical way.

Milky white jaguars, orchid monkeys, saffron bears,
Sapphire elephants, and bronze ligers all saunter about
on the nights when the moon does not shine.
Grace Miller, Grade 7
Stapley Jr High School, AZ

Where's She From? She's From...

I'm from a reservation of traditional singing and dancing.
From tourists roaming the reservation
Taking pictures and asking questions.
I'm from waking up to a red star making the mountains all sorts of colors
To trying to go to sleep while coyotes howl around my house at night.

I'm from a beautiful mother to a handsome father.
To my brothers saying, "Stay away from them boys!"
And sisters being there always.
I'm from a little old basketball sitting outside my house,
To loving to go to our Hualapai Recreation Gym,
And playing basketball all the time.

I'm from the elders teaching how to sing the song
"One little, two little, three little Indians!"
To the teaching of how to make delicious, mouthwatering fry bread!
I'm from a good life, to an amazing life.
I'm from "I can't do it," to "I could do it!"
I'm from never giving up.
I'm from an incredible reservation.
I'm from the Hualapai Tribe.
Jaylenne Quasula, Grade 9
Seligman High School, AZ

Home

So many memories,
Playing in my room,
Candy Land to
Watching TV in my parent's room.

So many memories,
Looking out the window on a cold and rainy day,
Wishing it would stop to go out to play.

So many memories,
Fighting with my sister,
Sad to be fighting, and make up again.

So many memories,
Its not over yet,
We'll have more adventures,
Are you ready to play?

Bianca Delgadillo, Grade 8
Richardson PREP HI Middle School, CA

Winds of Fate

At its very best, it seems a flower,
Floating through the mighty ocean of fate,
Forever in its great controlling power,
Drifting along easily without hate,

At its worst, it seems an eternal flame,
Crushing your spirit in its burnt wake,
A horrid thought that you may be to blame,
Leaving you drowning beneath sorrow's lake,

But at most times it seems a riverboat,
Drifting neutrally along the riverbank,
You do not feel as if you have to gloat,
But you also don't feel crushed beneath a tank,

But in this seemingly endless great strife,
The point of existing is simply life.

Joshua Carlyon, Grade 8
Sequoia Village School, AZ

Emerald Road

Like the moss collecting
In the crannies of a carelessly carved cobblestone road,
Chloroplasts colorize columns of elodea canadensis cells
Cramped, like bland rooms of glass
Occupied by circles of grass and
Collecting water from a placid pond,
The housing complex
Absorbs refracted rays from the shining sun.
Under the glossed liquid top,
Waving along, not about to stop.
I cannot help but wonder more
Why you shimmer, emerald floor?

Kesten Solomon, Grade 8
The Mirman School, CA

Sunrise

As the sun rose
I got onto my toes.
So like my brothers
I, too, could see the wonders
Just outside my window pane.
Now tall enough
To be with the rough, tall, and tough,
I, too, could say I saw the wonders
Of the sun as it rose
Over the vast plain
Some call lame,
But I call home.
This place where the sun never ceases to roam,
Here in *this* place
Where I can see the sun rise,
No judgment in its eyes,
This is my home.

Kaitlyn Smith, Grade 8
Christ the King School, AZ

If Not for Night

Would tiny, golden lamps then blink in summertime?
And would the strings of unseen crickets gently chime
Nostalgic ballads to the upbeat fairy dance,
The glow bugs' spinning waltz in pairs of bright romance?

Would piercing winter air retain its fresh, cold scent?
Would bleak reflections shiv'ring on the pavement
Of gleaming rainy streetlights ever look so wet?
Would there be dreams of love for us to near forget?

Would we have silver gems to pluck from the dark sky?
And tapestries to draw the constellations by?
A place where none can see the fall of our cold tears
And wind to which we whisper secret fears?

Without the silent night, how could the light of morn'
Bestow upon our souls the hope to be reborn?

Kayla Keener, Grade 9
Valley Christian High School, CA

Thanks for These

I am thankful for the food I eat,
I am thankful for the people I see,
I am thankful for my education,
I am thankful for my generation,
I am thankful for being happy,
I am thankful for people who stand up for me,
I am thankful for scientists everywhere,
I am thankful for teachers who care,
I am thankful for the annoying things,
I am thankful for the search engine Bing,
I am thankful for the things I have,
But the most important, my mom and dad

Neilkevin Alejandre, Grade 7
Daniel Savage Middle School, CA

Home

I have a home
where I grew up with my parents.
Where I play with my brother and our dog joyfully.
I have a home
sometimes I feel sorrow when I get in trouble.
I will be happy when I have fun with my family.
I have a home
where I watch television,
and sleep in my bed peacefully.
That place is called home.

Kevin Diaz, Grade 8
Richardson PREP HI Middle School, CA

Green

Green is the grass, covering the land
Green are the leaves, blowing down the street
Green are the trees, covering the sun
Green is the nature, growing in my garden
Green is growth, increasing in the flowers
Green is the emerald, sparkling in the princess's necklace
Green is money, paying for clothes
Green are the elves, working hard on Christmas presents
Green are the Christmas lights, decorating my house
Green is the Christmas tree, illuminating my room

Romina Fimbres, Grade 7
St John's Episcopal School, CA

The Arms of a Bad Dream

The arms of a bad dream may be scary and frightful:
Full of evil laughs and devilish games,
Full of heart-racing pounces and bloody screams,
Full of coldness and violent wind,
Full of loneliness and fear,
Full of fire and hot steam,
Full of disparity and much unfairness,
Full of falling and never returning.
But don't look away from the arms of a bad dream,
Remember, you're only sleeping...

Tiana Modrzejewski, Grade 7
Salida Middle School, CO

Skyfall

As quickly as it began
My board leaves the ground in a leaping motion,
The sky closes in on my head in seconds.
I twist the lower part of my body.
I bring my heels up to my back.
My board slams to the ground.
And my feet leave where they're supposed to be put.
I catch my heel edge and tumble drastically.
The sky re-emerges and sinks back into space.

Matthew Fisher, Grade 7
Salida Middle School, CO

The Breeze

I leave my window open in the night
so I can feel the cool air in the night breeze.
I have the music really loud,
so the breeze can carry it around.
I open the car window,
just to feel the wind in my hair.
It makes me feel free.

The way the leaves move in the breeze,
looks just like a dance before my eyes.
I can watch for hours,
and not get bored of their movement.
I put on some music, and watch some more.
So serene and peaceful,
that I seem to forget everything around me.

As I look outside my window,
I feel so free and peaceful.
The wind in my hair,
with a breath of fresh air.
Better than yoga or a massage,
and calmer like when you have peace of mind.
The breeze can make you feel a lot of things.

Marissa Flores, Grade 7
St Helen Catholic School, CA

The Last Whistle

I can feel the rush going through me again,
And...
Uh Oh
I can't believe I'm going through this again!

I'm running down the sideline,
Straight into the corner.
I'm running on the grass,
And it gets hotter and hotter!

The coach was yelling from the sideline,
While the parents were cheering me on,
I can't believe that I,
I scored the final goal!

The score was 5-4,
And the whistle blew,
Tweet! Tweet! Tweet!

While the parents cheered me on,
We gave out our last and final cheer!
We high-fived the other team,
When no one could see my last tear...

Rheannon Hill, Grade 7
Joe Walker Middle School, CA

Nature's Fury
The leaves danced in the wind.
Happily as ever but unbeknownst to their plight.
The wind whistled through the trees.
Warning those who could see.

The trees shook in fear.
As the storm was so near.
The wind pushed through the trees
as if they were as insignificant as a pound

Limbs broke easily
as lightning struck out of anger.
The clouds wept tears
as the valiant trees fell

As a calm arose
the forest grew past the sorrow.
Saplings grew big and tall
to replace those who had fallen.

Sidharth Kumar, Grade 7
Gale Ranch Middle School, CA

Music
Music is
a collection of memories
another getaway to paradise
a replay of your life

every song, a different emotion
every genre, a different trip
every lyric, a different perspective
every beat, a different story

my headphones intertwine my memories together
my iPod stores all my thoughts
my interpretation snapshots my perspective
my voice captures every detail

music is my past, present, and future
music fills my empty pages
music is my
Scrapbook

Julia Han, Grade 8
Falcon Creek Middle School, CO

Here
Here is where the lonely eighth grade boy sat
and silently did his schoolwork.
Here is where he sincerely prayed
that he would find a place to fit in.
Here is where he was tortured
and taunted and bullied severely.
Here is where after eight years of being called fat
or obese…he snapped.
Here is the place where he decided he
had to leave this prison of sorrow
and start over, hopefully changing from prison…to paradise.
Here is where the bullies run wild
like lions feasting on defenseless antelope!
Here…is modern day middle school!

Spencer Crane, Grade 8
Bear Lake Middle School, ID

A Reason to Wake Up
Friendship is all around us,
Hugging us and giving us warmth
It is what holds all of us together,
And creates bonds between us
It is the invisible, smooth and lush force that entwines all of us
It is a velvet blanket
Washing over all
Like water slowly flowing down a stream
Friendship is like a hallway of doors
No matter how many of them close,
Another will open right next to it
Friendship is what keeps us running,
Because without it
All would be lonely, melancholy, and lonesome.

Will Turner, Grade 7
The Mirman School, CA

Musical Notes
On my sheet are black and white dots
With strange lines and curves everywhere
Each resembling a plinking note
That glides along the page
Connecting with one another
Forming many parts into one
Allowing a tune to sing in a soprano to bass voice
As I play, the notes transform into words
At times it's gentle
Sometimes it's powerful
It commands me to keep playing
As a sweet, melodic sound floats into my ear
And I'm deep into the music

Crystal Huynh, Grade 7
Challenger Middle School, CA

Life
Birth, a life begins
From baby to child we start the sins
The purpose of life has been erased
An untold story no ways to change
led through lies I want the truth
I'll seek, I'll find, set my mind on sooth
As we grow we choose our path mine seems
more because of difficult tasks
You can't relate our lives aren't the same
stop, the sympathy I'm too tough to break
grow old to whither life only comes to an end
but wait it's a new beginning no hurt no pain
I'm gone to attend

Violeta Carrillo, Grade 8
Daniel Savage Middle School, CA

Shooting Star

I lay on the black, burnt branch
of my tired tree
look upon the sweet, shimmering stars
full of light
oh, so bright
like a bullet
one shoots across the sky
snatching me from my tree
escaping the atmosphere
released from the cuffs of society
completely delivered to the universe.
Finally breathing
awakened.

Jeneen Ibrahim, Grade 8
Weldon Valley Jr High School, CO

Basketball

Screeching floor
Running
Up
Down
Screaming names
Like seagulls
Bouncing balls
Soaring through the air
Ball b-b-ball
Pivot, pivot, lay-up
SWISH!!!
Hollering people
Like a flock of geese

Brittney Leist, Grade 7
Weldon Valley Jr High School, CO

Thoughts on Escher's "Bond of Union"

I see two
People who love each other
But, something keeps
On breaking them apart every
Time
They want to be together.
They are pulled back;
But, they can't be permanently separated
Because of the bond
That holds them.

Jennifer Moreno, Grade 7
Tenaya Middle School, CA

Bob

There once was a kid named Bob.
He wanted a really nice job.
So he went to school
But never followed a rule
Then off to unemployment he did sob.

Alex Khukhua, Grade 7
Beacon Country Day School, CO

The Equestrian Horse

I think I must have lived once before not as a boy
but as an equestrian horse.
Strong, tall, and proud, anxiously awaiting,
with bundles of energy and enthusiasm for the upcoming race.
This would explain my love
for the outdoors, for running, and my passion to compete.
It would explain my determination
to finish a tennis match strong, to read a book fervently, to play a song loudly,
all of which require demanding skills,
a sharp intellect,
and absolute concentration.

It would explain my handsome pedigree,
my strong agility and movement and my desire for attention
to be an across the board the frontrunner.
It would also explain my speed and endurance as I finish a race, any race,
with the same amount of energy from the first leg to the last.
It would explain my bucking stubbornness
and my ability to whine because I don't get my way.
Yes, I must have been that agile horse racing to the finish line
galloping as a royal thoroughbred into the sunset.

Adam Sraberg, Grade 8
Harvard-Westlake School, CA

The Field

I dreamed of playing on the baseball field
I always wanted to play on the fresh, cut green grass
I could hear the screams of all of the fans in the seats
I dreamed of playing on the field
I could see the flashing fireworks go up as someone hits a home run
I could smell the odor of hot dogs coming from the stands
I could feel the rough, hard dirt as I ran
I dreamed of playing on the field
As I stepped into the batter's box I could hear the crowd roaring
I could hear the ball whiz right past my body as the pitcher threw it
The roar of the umpire calling the pitch a strike
I dreamed of playing on the field
As I walked to the mound to pitch I could hear the crowd yelling my name
As I began to windup I felt the pitching rubber touch my foot
I watched as the ball went into the catcher's mitt for a strike
I dreamed of playing on the field

Jake Helm, Grade 8
Palm Desert Charter Middle School, CA

My Color

Pink,
It's the sunset that kisses goodnight to the beach
It's a sign of love
It's a sun kissed hibiscus
It's a butterfly that comes to play on a hot summer day
It's the pink lemonade the children drink as they play in the sprinklers
It's the cute little piggy playing in the mud
It's the beautiful dresses at the proms
But most of all it's the color of this poem, you just read.

Taryn Brinton, Grade 7
Daniel Savage Middle School, CA

Angel Light

Although you may not see them
You are always in their sight
They bring the gift of love and guidance
It is called the Angel Light
You know they always hear you
To them your voice is dear
With the comfort that they bring to you
You need not ever fear
So here's a place for to come
To do with angels what must be done
To make our world whole and bright
And share with all, the Angel Light

Taylor Atchison, Grade 9
Valley Union High School, AZ

Reflection on Escher's "Relativity"

When I look at
this puzzle,
I see one man
and
all his life
memories going
by,
different, and unique
in may ways,
but the only similarity
I see
Is in that one strange man.

Hannah Louden, Grade 7
Tenaya Middle School, CA

Jesus

This is Jesus
The son of God
He makes miracles happen
He can calm storms
Walk on water
and make trees grow on oceans
He can cure the sick
with a few words
Let the blind see
with a touch of his hand
This is Jesus
The son of God

Andrew Ding, Grade 8
Sinaloa Middle School, CA

The Girl

Take a look at the girl.
Do you see her?
She is sitting on your left.
The one who is always smiling.
Take a closer look. I dare you.
Do you see it now?
The plastered on smile?
The fire behind her eyes?
Now go up to her. It's fine, She doesn't bite.
She'll greet you with a smile and a cheery hello.
Ask her a question. Please? For me?
Ask her this, just three words,
"Are you okay?"
Watch her closely. Did you see it?
The flicker in her eyes?
The twitch in her fingers?
The clench in her jaw?
"Yes," she will reply.
Lies. She isn't fine. Trust me, I know.
Now you will just nod your head, smile politely, turn your back, and walk away.
Everybody does.

Corenna Council, Grade 8
South Lake Middle School, CA

Serving the Colors

Fear and excitement filled the room.
We may not come back, but I am still serving the red, white and blue,
Honoring and protecting my faith in the nation.

The base is loaded with crying goodbyes.
Tears are filling the eyes of our families,
Since they know their loved ones are leaving.
Happy faces on the children are no longer visible.

Bang and boom was all I heard
After landing and unloading.
The gun shots and explosions
Made my ears hurt like I had been hit across the head.
Within the blink of an eye, I was blown into the air.
I felt the heavens comb my hair with their uncertainty.
When the smoke cleared and time passed,
I thought I had kicked the bucket as I looked through the debris.

My wife and children stand with pride and joy now.
Their happy spirits could bring the fallen back.
I have come back, knowing I protected the red, white and blue.

Lance Nua, Grade 7
Joe Walker Middle School, CA

At the Piano Bench

With its sheet music, the seemingly endless amount of keys, and the trembling hands
The sounds of the turning pages and the changing notes
Feels like thunder and lightning in a night sky
A chance to leave this world and enter a new one.

Nikita Bair, Grade 8
Ripona Elementary School, CA

Riding a Roller Coaster

I hear the rickety, rambunctious clanking of the coaster
As I lurch forward my heart feels like it's going to burst
I'm ascending to the top for an eternity
The anxiety is slowly eating away at me
I'm at the top, and my stomach is telling me not to do it
But it's too late now, WHIZZ!
The roller coaster is a raging bull
Trying to fling me off at every twist and loop
My hair is flying wildly in the wind
My eyes are being shoved into the back of my head
Adrenaline is rushing through by body
I get that funny feeling in my stomach
Ahh, it feels like I'm going to be sick!
It almost feels as if I will fall off
But I manage to hang in there like a pro
And before I know it, the ride comes to a halt
Wow, it's already over, that was faster than I expected
What do you know, I really could do it!
Then I hear the rickety, rambunctious clanking of the coaster
I think to myself, Ah! Darn! I forgot to get off!

Michael Backlund, Grade 7
Stapley Jr High School, AZ

The California Coast

It is early in the morning, as the sun rises.
I feel the waves pass by, as I am watching.
The ocean sounds beautiful.
I'm at the edge of a cliff.
The wind blows on me, very nice and cool.
I look at the beautiful waves as they get closer.
This looks like a fantastic seashore.
I feel so free.
The waves crash against the cliff,
Very gently and smoothly.
The ocean smells very salty.
The air smells fresh, like never before.
When I look further away, I see a desert of water.
I don't want to leave this place.
I feel like crying, because I am in paradise.

Bayaar Syed, Grade 7
Daniel Savage Middle School, CA

Ode to Papa John's Pizza

O' pizza, you, are marvelous.
When I pick you up from Papa John's
Those rare occasions, the world is good.
You crispy, cheesy devil.
I didn't think that a recipe could be perfect,
But yours is.
Your intoxicating smell,
The warm touch of your breath.
The king of deliciousness.

Brandon Harrison, Grade 7
Rolling Hills Country Day School, CA

Dark Times

Twisted faces controlling my dreams
Causing tears upon my bedsheets
Ugly beasts roaming the streets
As horrified faces lose everything
Dark lonesome streets, full of muck and trash
Not a soul left to help with what's left
Hidden faces due to the fear
Begging creatures, pleading for a single meal
Endless chaos leaving nothing around
As mischievous critters steal hope from what's left of people
Death is strolls from home to home
Like it never has in time before
Not a friendly neighbor who lends a hand
while disgusting smoke slays all types of beauty
and all living wonder becomes extinct
Sad beings stroll without faces
as ignorance has become a main trait
As a fog seems to dissolve it all
Was it just a dream
Or is it our reality?

Hasibe Caballero Gomez, Grade 8
Sepulveda Middle School, CA

Empty the Stones

The stones in my bag,
they are getting heavy.
Many times along the rough trail,
I have been weighed down by these stones.
Most of the stones are stones of others;
they give the rocks to me in many different ways.
People tease me, torment me, and shove me,
as they are mean they add…
…they add their rocks to my collection.
I will not keep other's rocks.
Their rocks are falling
down,
down,
down,
out of my bag.

Makenzie Stevens, Grade 8
Bear Lake Middle School, ID

Thanksgiving Is to Be Thankful For…

I am thankful for…
My family, who is my world,
Maui and Nightmare, my two pit bulls,
Konah, my beautiful horse,
The house I call home,
My crazy little sister, Clover and my big brother Beau,
The people always at my side, my friends,
My parents who care for me,
Me being as strong and loved as I am,
The school I go to every day,
I am thankful for being able to be thankful.

Kaely Grinstead, Grade 7
Daniel Savage Middle School, CA

London (Dream Happens)

Where lies my castle in the sky?
Will hopes disappear at,
The end of the rainbow near?
Or become buoyant—lighter than water?
What above smells of lilacs and perfume?
Or of a freshly baked chocolate chip cookie?
Maybe expectations rise above like a balloon?
Drifting in clouds
Flying high overhead.
Soaring above rooftops, then,
This is mysteriously when,
I find my fantasy.
My dream does come true.
Time to dream a new one.

Sophie Rolls, Grade 8
Rolling Hills Country Day School, CA

Nature and Peace

Trees grow as the sun rises and falls.
You hear the wind and you answer its call.
Nature will be around when we want it to be.
Peace will come when we decide our destiny.
We watch the world suffering through our eyes.
We see people survive and thrive.
If we could figure out a way to have a place.
Where suffering is not fast paced.
We could live in a world of peace.
A place where our emotions can release.
When people are free of will.
We can see peace over the hill.
Nature is trying to blend with the bright and the dull
Nature and Peace are two parts to the exact same whole.

Griffin Abrams, Grade 9
Woodbridge High School, CA

What I Do Not Understand

I do not understand
 Why homework on weekends is necessary
 Why other students don't try at school
 Why people have to be scared of each other.
But I really don't understand
 Why student teachers have to pay to teach
 Why we drive on parkways and park in driveways
 Why people have to work on weekends
 Why snow can't be warm
 Why people don't like reading.
What I do understand is building things
 I can picture stuff in my head
 And then put it into life
 Using Legos or other blocks.

Brandon Carroll, Grade 7
White Pine Middle School, UT

Backstage

The anticipation of the events to come
While getting my hair and make-up done
Getting into costume, preparing for the night
Watching the audience come into sight
Filling up the theater while it gets late at night
Going over dance moves as the nerves settle in
When the lights on the stage go dim
The curtains sweep across the floor
Then the set is revealed
And the characters come into the light
When the curtains close for the night
The applause can be heard from all the way backstage
And the actors hear the audience roar
And feel their ultimate reward

Adrienne Chavez, Grade 7
Christ the King School, AZ

The Betrayal of Love

We live in a time where freedom turns to hate,
Where hate and power become betrayal,
It is as if you're being locked behind a gate,
Where you and I will always share one pain.
When push turns to shove we turn to one thing,
A place where hate and fear overcome life,
Where the human eye can't see your true feelings,
Has my life turned into one big lie?
Am I going to die living this life?
Will I ever get to fly free again?
Seems to me that I'll never get to be me,
With this hatred hanging over me.
And that is when love turns to pure hate,
And that's when I will meet you at the gate.

Trena Johnson, Grade 7
Sequoia Village School, AZ

Christmas Joy

Snowflakes are falling in the winter snow,
Without snow boots, where can you go?
Instead stay inside by the brilliant fire,
While warm hot cocoa is desired.
Finish up your delicious drink,
Put it in the dishwasher or sink,
"What should I do next?" you think.
You decide to get, yet, another drink.
While preparing it, you look outside.
You have a view of far and wide.
But your focus is on kids in the snow,
Delight on their faces, they emit a glow.
The decoration on houses give even more cheer,
And all you can think is, "Christmas is here!"

Darlene Do, Grade 7
Sarah McGarvin Intermediate School, CA

Pain

Pain is sharp.
Pain is hard.
Pain is sudden.
Pain is you.

Why hurt me so?
Why pretend
To be a friend,
Then stab me, in the back?
I wish to cry but my tears you mock…

Do I hate you?
Do I love you?
Yes!
Why do you double-cross between
Friend and enemy?

Pain is sharp.
Pain is hard.
Pain is sudden.
Pain is love.
Pain is you.

Sage Stratton, Grade 8
Vallivue Middle School, ID

Ballet

It is beautiful
Spins and leaps it's so joyful
It's so wonderful

Dressed in pink and black
With a leotard and tights
With a perfect bun

It is beautiful
Flex and point it's filled with joy
It is so joyful

A ballerina
Leaps across the studio
Just so gracefully

Rebecca Salinas, Grade 7
Monte Vista Christian School, CA

If the Whole World Cared

If the whole world cared
About each other
If no one dared
To put down another

But instead showed
Love and forgiveness
We would all carry each other's load
And find pure happiness

Ashley Pearce, Grade 9
New Plymouth High School, ID

For My Family

For my loving family that loves to play,
    All doing their hobbies happily as time passes,
    Laughing at one another's jokes,
    And being very silly.

For my loving family who has the greatest abilities;
    Kalaila and her ability of intelligence and Kaleel with athletics,
    Devon and his ability with art and my parents with real estate,
    All with great talent and skill.

For my loving family and their great hopes for their futures;
    Champagne and her desire to become a fashion designer,
    Kaleel wants to be a professional basketball player,
    And Devon wants to be a game designer,
    All within their wonderful skills.

Let my people be successful in their fields, to be wise in their crafts,
    Let them be the best there will be, to change it into something better;
To recreate history into another meaning, to be heroes of the 21st century,
    And most of all, to be happy doing it.

Deivah Johnson, Grade 8
Ernest Becker Middle School, NV

Iceberg

The dark water laps hungrily at the base of the ice
Frozen water that means a certain death for any who fall afoul of the sea
Rising above the tumultuous ocean is a gleaming white tower
A behemoth of cloudy marble whose savage beauty is unrivaled
By any made by the hands of men
Cold and stern it belittles every other by comparison
Casting its shadow over all and sundry
Hidden by the fog in the dawn
The ship's doom is not yet revealed
Until the fateful moment when the fog clears
Unmasking the bane of the vessel
Then panic spreads through the passengers like a wave
Rendering many hysterical and others weeping anew
Scrambling for safety or any means of escape
Many people trampled as they all rush for the lifeboats
But too few make it to salvation
As the bow of the ship crashes into the pillar of ice
The craft tilts, leaning…sloping…slanting…
And the remaining passengers utter a last, desperate prayer
Before they plunge into the midnight blue murk of the sea

Lillian Nguyen, Grade 8
South Lake Middle School, CA

Friendship

Friendship is…the bear I used to tell all my secrets to when I was little
Friendship is like…finding gold in a cave and keeping the gold forever.
Friendship is as…painful like breaking a leg.
Friendship sounds like…laughter and happiness.
Friendship feels like…love, but sometimes it feels like getting a shot.
Friendship looks like…One Million Dollars.

Isabel Felix, Grade 7
Daniel Savage Middle School, CA

Mozi

Mozi, my French kitty
he diligently prances around
with the air of royalty
roaming the streets, for the ladies
Mozi
Mozi, my French kitty
travels like a valiant knight
with the best of all whiskers and fur,
that has never known a speck of dirt
Mozi
Mozi, my French kitty
who has 18 lives, unlike most...
and who purrs for hours on end
for he knows he is the best kitty
Mozi, my French kitty
Caleb Richardson, Grade 7
Salida Middle School, CO

Soda

I feel an urge of thirst
Like a crack of thunder
I hold the sweaty can
Lift tongue it cracks
Spits and then sizzles
Sweet syrupy smell
I bring to my lips
Then gulp
Like a cup of heaven
Sweet taste
I cannot bear
Once more I see
Drops of dew sliding
Down the slimy
Can
Jacob Roper, Grade 7
Weldon Valley Jr High School, CO

Forget

The owner walks in
Ready and Fresh
Hair flies
Women are waiting
a new style they claim
Reality says otherwise
wanting the void to be concealed
attempting to erase their horrors
They hide it well
but...
their eyes
it's seeping through
different times and places
stories
Never to be heard
Riley Moran, Grade 8
South Lake Middle School, CA

Promises

When they were young,
they promised eternal friendship.
Two friends,
always made promises.

When they dated,
they promised to be in love
till the end and
to never forget it.

When they got married
they promised to stay
by each other for eternity.
But not all promises can be kept.

Things always change,
Promises sometimes break,
Love can never be promised
and nothing lasts forever.
Melissa Valencia, Grade 8
Joe Walker Middle School, CA

The Great Outdoors

The sun shines through the meadows,
The flowers start to bloom.
The great outdoors is a world of wonders,
Where nature is very true.

The grass starts to sing,
As the rushing wind came to be.
Tiny sprouts came to life,
And will very soon become trees.

The wind blows,
Through the glowing green fields,
As it cuts through,
The light blue sky.

The flowers bloom,
Where sun shines through,
In a world of wonders,
Where nature is true.
Jose Elizarraras, Grade 8
Joe Walker Middle School, CA

Baseball Magic

I hit the ball so far it soared
The game-winning ball is mine
Congratulated by the team
The best day of my life
The bat is now hanging in my room
The ball on my dresser
I wake up from that great dream
That game is today
Crew Robinson, Grade 7
Mountain Ridge Jr High School, UT

Higher Than the Moon

I was born on a leaf
Shards of silver on the grass
Spider silk that hung like lace
Water, clear like glass.

I was put in a cocoon
With wonders inside
Transformed from rags to riches,
I was free now
Higher than the moon

I became a butterfly
With delicate wings of every color
Here I am,
Now I disappear.

So beautiful
So flittery
So glittery
There is nothing you can do to stop me.

I enter the room and everything stops
My energy like a bursting balloon
Soaring above you
Higher than the moon.
Rosa Llanto, Grade 8
Chandler School, CA

Oh So Quiet

Oh so quiet the house is now,
with rooms dark and unlit.
The silence is threatening;
foreign and empty.
I'm all alone, except for my pets.

One mutters a whimper,
whispered and low.
They know something's amiss.
They knew a different time.
They miss that time of late.

Oh so quiet the house is now,
with empty unused rooms.
Once filled with chatter,
with life and laughter.
All so different it is now.

No one is here;
no sense of family.
But they'll visit soon,
they always do.
But it's just a tease

A small taste, of what used to be.
Allison Raymundo, Grade 8
Richardson PREP HI Middle School, CA

Winter Rain

The cold winter rain
That falls like ice upon my face
Glitters like teardrops
From the weeping heavens.

The water flows
Into the gaping gutter
And collects in pools
On the ground.

Some people see
A lonely gray world.
They miss the colors of summer.

But I see
A world of promise
That spring will come again
And flowers that turn their heads up to the sun
Who cannot live without the rain.

Nuan-Yu Pan, Grade 9
Henry M Gunn High School, CA

Green Door

I wonder what's inside the old green door,
It's not kept up, grass makes up the floor.
The handle is worthless the window is broken,
It's hard to believe it was ever a token.

Back in the day it was worth more than we know,
It protected who lived there from wind, rain, and snow.
But the crack up the side may have formed an issue,
It made it so cold they all needed a tissue.

I would love to see it in its prime,
I bet it was a mansion of its time.
What looks to us like a beaten old door,
Really has so much more in store...

Katelynne Keezer, Grade 8
Bear Lake Middle School, ID

Reflections on Edvard Munch's Painting, "The Scream"

The lake started to fill with big waves,
The sky turned orange and yellow,
Which meant it was dawn.
A man, left out, lonely and ignored
Shouted a sharp scream
Because of what he saw;
A swamp of ghosts coming at him
With big, long chains.
The thought of me floating around with chains
Hanging off me
Gave me goose bumps
And a loud screech.
Wouldn't you scream, too?

Naomi Kaptryan, Grade 7
Tenaya Middle School, CA

The Haunter

It lives in dark, waiting for its prey,
It smiles, looking at its dinner with eyes so grey.
It rushes down the corner, invisible to the eye,
And with a terrible screech, somebody dies.

So many fell to the Haunter without a try,
Nobody who saw it ever survives.
It laughs at them, people believe,
Acting so foolish and naive.

It is everywhere from here to there
It can be as quiet as a hare.
Feared by many, it roars with delight,
Filling people's hearts with deathly fright.

The word "Haunter," gives people the chills,
Making them think of the way it kills.
But alas, trying to stop it is impossible to do,
Watch out, or it will get you!

Wesley Tsai, Grade 8
Stratford Elementary/Middle School, CA

The Final Battle

This was the soldier's greatest battle
It was the hardest by far, but he didn't care
He fought the battle knowing the pain it would bring
But only so much pain an old man can bear

In the end it was no bullet that ended his life
It was a stroke that gave the final blow
The battle was long and hard
But the soldier would not let the pain show

He knew this would be his last fight
Because he could not take much more
The brave soldier lost the battle
But he won the war

Cassidy Cable, Grade 9
Westlake High School, UT

Star My Boxer (My Dog)

Star waits for me to come home from school at four o'clock.
As I come up the driveway I can see her
Slobber, tail wag, and pouncing to play.
My dog is old, because she is nine to ten years old.
When we get inside out of the freezing weather,
We play, she bites my arm, but not that hard
Because she barely has any teeth.
Later that night she is tired and warn out.
So she sneaks to my room surreptitiously.
She begs to get on my bed, and when she does she is very warm.
She keeps me safe and sound.
I say "I love you and goodnight"
She just moans, groans, and snores!

Sierra Reed, Grade 7
Salida Middle School, CO

Morning Metamorphosis

Yaaawwwwwnnnnnn…
I slowly
turn
over
trying to keep the dream in my mind
just a while longer
but
it doesn't stay
it skitters out of my grasp
like a lonely balloon drifting high above the trees

the insistent beeps of the alarm
interrupt
my warm hazy halo

I finally drag myself out of my cocoon
sleep still crusted in the corners of my eyes.

Angelina Z. Wang, Grade 7
Jane Lathrop Stanford Middle School, CA

Winter Night

Dark winter clouds came near,
Thunder was the only thing I could hear;
I walked as silent as a mouse down the street,
Taking light steps with my feet.
Then it started to rain,
Water rushed like a river down the drain.
Birds flew silently into the trees,
Catching a slight breeze as they flew.

Then I reached my home,
And suddenly the rain stopped.
I opened up my door,
And put my back pack on the floor.
I took off my jacket and my shoes,
And started to watch a show called hidden clues.
Then I turned off the TV and went to bed,
Singing my favorite song in my head.

Jared Perez, Grade 7
Joe Walker Middle School, CA

Cheerleaders Have to Be…

The nicest of all,
The best at caring,
Always sweet lady's,
Always understanding,
The best while performing,
Never lying,
Nor stealing,
They're always appealing,
But please don't forget the most important thing..
They always have a smile worth sharing because they are caring.

Trinity Lampman, Grade 7
Monte Vista Christian School, CA

Wings

In the middle of two different worlds
I settle for a dream in the sky
With the ground at my feet

A war rages inside of me
As I reach for the for the clouds
Only to feel the tugging of gravity
Forcing me to be
A prisoner in my own haven

Too afraid to be free
And too afraid to break the chains that bind me
I am a coward in the face of bravery
But a dreamer
In the face of freedom

If only my feet were like feathers
Instead of heavy rocks
I might be able to grow beautiful wings
And fly towards my dreams with the wind at my back
And finally
In a word
Be
Free.

Abby Chen, Grade 7
Lawson Middle School, CA

You Won't Ever Forget Me

I know that you will always think of me
When you are in the dark and can't find a light
Remember the day I let myself be free

Oh how I fell in love so easily
I thought of you as my knight
I know that you will always think of me

When I saw you, my heart would race with glee
And how we would meet at our pond at night
Remember the day I let myself be free

In my heart, I felt the change of our destiny
But it was you who thought it would be all right
I know that you will always think of me

Your words killed and got nasty
They ignited the flames that started the fight
Remember the day I let myself be free

Our love drifted out, far into the sea
I ran so you couldn't see me in your sight
I know that you will always think of me
Remember the day I let myself be free

Caroline Mahoney, Grade 8
San Elijo Middle School, CA

Green

Green is the sweet grass
On a beautiful day,
The meadows alive with colors;
The highlight is green, green is a tart,
But sweet apple,
Green is an emerald sparkling in the sunshine,
It's a face after going on a roller coaster,
Green is a little frog near a murky pond
It's a young tomato's unripe skin,
Green is a crisp $100 bill
Folded neatly in my pocket
And a turtle's rock-hard shell,
Green is a juicy watermelon's
Tough outer casing,
It's the foul stench
From a desperate skunk,
It's the color of pears,
Peas, and vegetables galore,
Green are the hot chilies
Setting my mouth on fire,
Green is my favorite color.

Sehaj Sharma, Grade 7
Gale Ranch Middle School, CA

Where Poetry Hides for Me

Poetry hides
In the screen of my TV
Where I watch all of my favorite shows.
It hides
In my computer
Which is like a second life.
Poetry hides
In my cat.
It hides
In my headphones that provide the music
that gives me life.
It hides
In the school
That gives me an education.
These are the places where poetry hides for me.

Isac Herrera, Grade 7
Tenaya Middle School, CA

Pismo Beach

Golden, sandy beaches, sparkling blue water
Gigantic, frightening hills with steep, curving edges
The sight and smell of the salty Pacific Ocean
Annoying, nagging seagulls, little, vicious crabs and
Bombastic noises all live in Pismo
Happy family camps out on the beach
Everyone rides on loud, speedy quads and dirtbikes
The bright, yellow sun shines down on us transforming
Everything into a golden paradise
Pismo is deep love and family tradition that is never forgotten

Rebekah Esteves, Grade 8
Ripona Elementary School, CA

Surfing

The anxiety as I feel the sand between my toes
I set down my board and push into the water
The cold is tickling my neck but I still attempt to smile

Then the wave comes
I fall and tumble as I feel the cold hug my shoulders
I stay under the water, safe for a moment

I burst up with pride to try again
Reaching for my board I get on

I manage to get past all the waves and wait once I get there
I see a swell

I'm riding the wave and I'm in stance

The smooth ride it was, is now a bumpy and rocky ride
And the power was too much for me and I tumble into the water
I wait for the wave to pass over my head

The final chance for the wave I have been waiting for
I get back on the board with confidence
I wait for the wave. I see it. I start paddling; it's coming closer
It is sucking me in

I ride and get in stance
A feeling of joy is spreading inside me

Samantha Delurgio, Grade 7
Rolling Hills Country Day School, CA

My Changed Life

July 18th 2012 my life changed
Unexpected move from Newmarket, Ontario, Canada to Santa Cruz
New school, new friends
Different curriculum
Higher expectations

July 18th 2012 my life changed
Living with Grandma
Dad still in Canada waiting to come
Mom flying to and from
Parents put my dog down and didn't tell me

July 18th 2012
Brother changed…too nice now
Very emotional…I cry a lot
Miss my friends, miss my life
No space to call my own

July 18th 2012
Get to live near my family
Met new nice friends
I want to be a marine biologist and now I live near the ocean
I want to go back to Canada!

Kaitlyn Calverley, Grade 7
Monte Vista Christian School, CA

My Day at the Beach

Here I stand
In the sand
With the sand in my toes
And sunscreen on my nose
The waves are crashing
And the kids are splashing
I watch the kids
As I hear my soda fizz
Pelicans swooping
And seagulls snooping
Around people dropped food
Beach balls flying
Ice cream buying by people wrapped
In towels
I hear Will.I.Am rapping
My foot is tapping
With the music I must say
"I'm having a wonderful day!"
So much fun in the sun
I have only just begun
This is my day at the beach
Amira Satah, Grade 7
Sarah McGarvin Intermediate School, CA

Egyptian Pyramids

Tall structures,
The tombs of pharaohs,
They build them to honor the ruler.

Easily farmers build them,
A good archaeologist will tell you.
As you may already know,
The pharaohs have them built.
To get them steps to heaven,
They, with no hesitation,
Farmer and farmer,
Take the Nile to the unbuilt pyramid.

Perfect structures,
By one count 118.
War has not toppled them,
But all have suffered damage,
Some might be better than others,
But white coating has decayed.
That undertaking of the pharaohs,
To them is all credit given.
Lee Keslerwest, Grade 7
Sarah McGarvin Intermediate School, CA

Da Vinci's Secret

The Mona Lisa hangs in the Louvre.
Da Vinci painted her when in his groove.
We'll never know why she has a smile
To make us wonder was Leo's style.
Jonathan Bingham, Grade 8
Beacon Country Day School, CO

Within My Heart

I remember that fateful day.
Being a curious one the puppy crawled under the shed.
My dog automatically ran after him; motherly instincts kicking in.
Father got the tow truck and lifted the shed
Grabbed both of the dogs from where they lay.
I remember the next morning I went out to check on my dogs.
I saw where she was lying by the shed.
I called her as I always do. She didn't respond so I ran to her instead
I knelt beside her and noticed something was wrong.
Back inside I ran, and told my sister.
I remember her going to see what was wrong.
She knelt beside her, there she sat for a long time, it seemed.
Then, she looked at me and told me
With sorrow in her voice and tears in her eyes…
That my dog was dead.
At that moment I felt my world break apart around me;
I cried and I cried letting the tears flow.
I remember when they buried her.
It was a sunny day nice and warm with a little breeze.
I stood next to the tree watching them bury her.
Silent tears fell once more; to this day, I will always remember.
Azteka Tejeda, Grade 7
Tenaya Middle School, CA

Dreadful Happiness

The happiest and most dreadful day of my life…
The day my baby brother was born.
I remember the day vividly
Like a clear sky on a sunny day
As soon as I found out that my mom was going to have a baby
"BAM" I instantly wanted a sister.
The day our baby was born I had on my
"I am going to be a BIG sister" T-shirt.
It had little stains because I had worn it for the past 3 days
And the fact I was a toddler also played in.
Once my mom went in to the creepy crawly delivery room. The waiting began!
Thoughts raced through my head.
Then finally, finally, finally the moment we have all been waiting for…
To see my new baby sister!
Unfortunately, my baby brother wasn't a girl at all!
I was upset, angry and completely horrified
That our precious baby was a BOY!
I even told my parents to take him back…(that didn't go over very well)
The day ended with balloons and pushing my mom back to the car in a wheel chair.
And back home it was with my new baby sister!
— I mean brother. I was not looking forward to the dreadful dreary days ahead.
Emma Preston, Grade 7
Stapley Jr High School, AZ

Emotions of War

The pain of running away from bullets a penny away from you as sweat smothers your face.
The sadness that sweeps your mind as your best friend falls.
The cheering of happiness from your family as you walk toward them.
War has many emotions. Thank you veterans!
Thomas Stevens, Grade 7
St Francis School, CA

Old Man

Old man on the corner, dressed in rags
Smiling at the little boys playing tag
Grinning your gap-toothed, crinkly-eyed grin
Oblivious to the fact that your time runs thin.
How did you get here? Where are you going?
Did you too once have a life worth living?
A dream for the future, a hope to hold on to;
They said you weren't like the rest, told you you'd make it through
Be the exception, the one with the sense
To show the whole world that you could make a difference.
And yet, here you sit with your cardboard sign
Offering a sad smile to passersby
Who hurry past you, too busy to care
Embarrassed by their fortune, yet unwilling to share.
Should they look into your face, in your eyes they'd behold
A century's worth of emotions, a story waiting to be told.
For in every last line in that face of yours lies
A memory, a heartbreak, a sad lullaby,
Timeless love, hope, and joy
With the pure, raw hope of a little boy.

Cassidy Angell, Grade 9
University Preparatory School, CA

Three Lives Lost

Solemn turned his face to mourn
for a lifeless child, his, was born
longing for a soft caress
he strode weeping to her bed
only to bring more tears to his face he said,
"Why do you choose to, with my child, forever rest?"
to the ground he fell, and bawled and wept
tightly he gripped her coldness in hand
he choked, he sobbed, then gently cried
for once again, his jovial hopes lied
on that wet cold floor happiness he banned

As the day came to let them go
he bade the diggers to halt
then leaped and bounded toward their chasm
and to the ground he knelt into their grave to bawl
saying, "Take me under, dead or not, take me breath and all."
then as he finished, he lay beside them in sorrow
and before his last image above the ground, he quoted,
"There will be no joy tomorrow."

Anika Howe, Grade 8
Charter Home Study Academy, CA

Muggle

M eets me at the bus stop right when I get home
U nderfoot, jumping, so excited that I've come back
G oing in circles, prancing all about
G iving grateful glances, hoping for affection
L icking me with love
E veryone needs a dog so sweet

Maddie Cook, Grade 9
Trinity High School, CA

When You Left

When you left, I didn't know what to do.
Everything that I do reminds me of you.
You've moved on, found someone new.
I guess I should too
Do you think of me?
When you look out into the sea?

You said you were as busy as a bee.
And had no time for me.
Like the sky misses the sun at night.
I think of what we would've done on summer nights.
Now I'm all alone, and on my own.
Don't come back crying on the phone.

Why'd you turn away?
When everything was okay?
Remember all those things you said?
They're running crazy in my head.
When you left, everything was a mess.
Don't be upset that now you're in distress.

Kristen Valencia, Grade 7
Joe Walker Middle School, CA

Amazing Flowers They Are

A flower,
A flower of sun,
A flower that looks at the sky,
Has petals of gold and leaves of emerald,
And watches the sun pass by.
A bright sunflower it is.

A flower,
A flower of love,
A flower that is so romantic,
Has red petals like ruby and thorns so sharp,
And all together it looks fantastic.
A beautiful rose it is.

A flower,
A flower of tea,
A flower so pretty and sweet,
Is white like opal and as small as a dime,
But it can also be made into tea.
A shining jasmine it is.

Annikka Rodriguez, Grade 7
Joe Walker Middle School, CA

Stillness

Stillness pauses me.
He is a tall, statuesque figure.
Unflinching and motionless, he waits for time to pass.
Mysteriously, he fades into the ebony shadows.
He whispers smooth, soft, hushes.
I sigh in relief; my eyes open, alert and ready.

Nicole Mah, Grade 9
Monarch High School, CO

I Have Seen So Many Things
I have seen the trees sway
I have seen a robin lay her eggs
I have heard the creek's song sing
I have felt the mossy leaves.

I do know the forest paths
I have knowledge of their pasts.
I have walked the miles near,
I have talked to nature's dear.

I have lived so many lives,
I have kissed the far away skies
I do walk with silent stealth
I have stalked the butterflies.

I am the great wolf gray
I am here or far away,
And with each step I do take
I will always be in your wake.
Dayna Lamb, Grade 9
Kootenai Jr/Sr High School, ID

Katie Lou
I know a girl with bright blue eyes
Her hair is like the sun.
I am her aunt and she my niece
She is the only one.

She walks and talks and twirls around
A singer she may be.
She shouts the sounds of animals
How random can they be?

A dog, a cow, a peacock,
Believe it or not, a lion,
An elephant and a monkey,
And there's more that she's still tryin'.

I love my little niece.
She is one unique girl.
She'll be a cutie when she's older,
The Pixie Lou I adore.
Emma Whiting, Grade 8
Lowell Scott Middle School, ID

The One for Me
When I first met you, I stood in awe.
I couldn't believe what I had saw.
Something beautiful, something sweet.
I was happy for us to meet.
You stated your name and said hello,
Then later that night you started to glow.
In a special way I cannot describe.
I will never forget those soft brown eyes.
Naila Hernandez, Grade 7
Clement Middle School, CA

Chaotic Order
Trapped in a personal prison
Each an individual upon their group
Cells odd but beautiful
Like a mossy, green brick wall

Your movements random but perfect
A disfigured oddity
The strange intensity of mixed shades
Each in its own, different

The united singles
Moving on their individual's ways
Yet sharing a trail
Forever stuck with each other

Elodea Canadenis
Unique and odd
Separate but together
Unified
Milena DeGuere, Grade 7
The Mirman School, CA

The Woods
The fox trots
The deer hides,
The bird sings
The raccoon spies,

The beaver builds
The toad moans,
The ant runs
The owl sleeps,

The tree listens
The squirrel scatters,
The bunny skips
The lizard scampers,

The turtle rests
The duck strides,
The bear seeks
The woods sigh.
Aliyah Hubbard, Grade 7
Joe Walker Middle School, CA

Thoughts on Escher's "Bond of Union"
Two people abound in air,
Bouncy balls everywhere,
Can opener cut,
Nobody knows what.
Their bodies are gone,
Their lives have left;
But
Their love is long.
Madison Acker, Grade 7
Tenaya Middle School, CA

Passion
The spark inside of me
Like a glistening firework
Rolling waves in the sea
Silky colors of blue and green

A fight raging in you
Desire burns hot like a flame
Alive eyes are so true
You do everything you can do

Falling, but not smashin'
Glimmers of the light far away
So close to crashin'
But it shows all of your passion
Lauren Bown, Grade 9
Air Academy High School, CO

Snow
Crisp, white snow
Falling through the air
Yearning for the ground
Dropping here and there

A small boom
As it hits the glass
A small smile
Knowing it won't last

Hours have passed
A puddle forms
Outside your house
A big snowstorm
Linda Nguyen, Grade 7
Sarah McGarvin Intermediate School, CA

Reflections on Rodin's Sculpture
In this sculpture
I see a woman who is lost
From the real world;
She is trapped from reality,
But, reality
Is just a dream.
Is she trapped by her thoughts
Or is she trapped by the real world?
It seems like she is trying to get out
But she can't.
She is halfway out, but
She can't finish.
She will never be awakened from
Her thoughts of the real world.
Mikayla Flenory, Grade 7
Tenaya Middle School, CA

My Pain

No one knows the pain I feel deep inside,
I want to scream, shout, runaway and hide.
Why did you go, why did you leave?
Life without you is so hard to conceive.

My thoughts and feelings are so hard to explain,
Multiplied by infinity, my sorrow and pain.
I'll miss him so much, my tears say it all.
I cry when I see his old dirty ball.

Tears falling continuously into my open palm
This pain I feel from the loss of my dear dog.
I refuse to believe this horrible fate
My world lost its sun, my soul felt the weight.

I simply couldn't imagine the days and nights ahead.
My soul will be empty, my heart has had plenty.
I remember him bringing joy to me since day one
But now our happy days are done.
It's just so hard to say goodbye,
To some one you never expected to die.

Precious Lozano, Grade 8
John Adams Middle School, CA

Running

I pick up my feet to the beat of my mind
As my thoughts linger in the morning air
Watching the sunrise, my arms pump energy to keep me stable
My head is clear, and I can watch the world wake up.

This is my passion, my reliever of stress
It is my safeguard from my everyday pain
My excuse to engorge myself on chocolate milk
And build my legs for my outdoor adventures
I never once regret my morning runs. Never.

My heart beats as fast as a roller coaster's speed
I can see the finish line now
the green pathway to my house
My leg takes one last spring
as I stop my watch.

Summer Smith, Grade 8
Stapley Jr High School, AZ

Universal Studios

Cool, colorful, many things to explore
Smells of zebra popcorn and fresh cinnamon buns
Shrek and Fiona taking pictures with little children
Rides with long lines that everyone was waiting in
People walking around thinking about what to do next
Or if to take a break to eat
People taking pictures in front of the Simpson ride
This is a place that people create movies
For people to have memories.

Dakayla Dabney, Grade 8
Ripona Elementary School, CA

Pleasant Ride

Dirt goes flying, trees swish as I pass
Lovely smooth terrain
I turn easily
Music soothes my ears softly, my mind calm
Steady over all focus
Trail speaks with soft delight
Slow gust whistles
As rain drizzles, I am engulfed in mud
My wheels turn
Still I go
Rain makes my breathing easier
Still I flow
Tristan close behind, swishing along the trail
Ear buds dangling
Little epic jumps, quietly waiting to be hit
They're always ahead
Only clouds, no sun, perfect day to be riding
Our minds soothed
Little buzzing following behind us, it's our tires
Loving the terrain
But then they cry knowing, the ride is over.

Caleb Hallett, Grade 7
Salida Middle School, CO

A Dream

Somewhere over the rainbow
People have love for other races
Leaving no room for discrimination.
Where everyone goes to sleep with a full belly
And don't eat rice from bags.
A place where people have plenty of water
That is not wasted on watering lawns or cleaning cars.
Where the air is almost too fresh.
Where animals and man live in peace,
And children grow happily and live a happy life.
People don't kill or get killed:
Where everyone lives in peace and don't drop
Bombs, and people are not consumed by money
Or selfishness, and where negative images aren't the main criteria.
Where forests and jungles live in harmony,
And are not destroyed for buildings and farming.
Where people recycle and take care of the Earth,
Who don't litter or use resources to the extreme;
A place where people care and work out the problems.
But we live on this side of the rainbow,
Where the perfect world is only just a dream…

Kelsi Gradisar, Grade 9
Pueblo West High School, CO

Free Song

I'm in the ocean during a thunderstorm.
The air is cool but the water is warm.
I don't care about the lightning striking me,
Because right now I feel so free.

Alexa Suydam, Grade 7
Thurgood Marshall Middle School, CA

Tower of Terror

Excited when I get my FastPass
Waiting to see a preview
Jumping when the window smashes
Waiting nervously in line with others
Getting scared when they assign us to our row
Finally taking my seat in the 1st row
Screaming at the top of my lungs
Imagining that this is not real
Seeing some ghosts on the 13th floor
Feeling like I can't grab on to anything
Taking a 2-second picture
Seeing my bag floating in the air
Arriving at the 1st floor again
Not walking straight
Looking at my face in the picture
Reminding myself I have done this 9 times
At California Adventure

Jeanette Gonzalez, Grade 8
St John's Episcopal School, CA

My Room Is My Shrine

My room is my shrine
It keeps my deepest secrets
Nobody else will ever know
My room is my shrine
Everything in it describes me
It is my little place
No body will ever take
My room is a part of me
It is dark place with no light
The darkness of my room relaxes me
It also calms me down and lets me think
My room is my shrine
I could cry and laugh and my room will only know
I can scream and shout and my room will only hear
My room is my best friend
I know that he will never betray me
My room is my shrine

Marlen Huerta, Grade 8
Richardson PREP HI Middle School, CA

Rain

Drop, drop, drop
I hear the rain descend from the hole in the roof
Into the bowl in the kitchen
Drop, drop, drop
I listen to the rain pound on the window
Drop, drop. drop
As it falls from the pitch-black sky
Tapping on my window
Like someone trying to get in
Drop, drop, drop
That's the sound of rain.

Kyla Campbell, Grade 7
Salida Middle School, CO

First Crush

I was eight when I saw his bright, blue eyes,
His garish, blonde hairs, and his thin, stick arms.
I swear when he stood, he was six feet tall,
And he smelled as pleasant as a fresh, picked rose.

I will never forget that euphoric, shy grin,
And his special, comedic, blaring guffaw.
Whenever he looked at the gleaming, dark sky,
The stars seemed to fill up his beautiful, lush face.

He has big, red braces, and pale, white skin,
And has gargantuan, stinky feet.
But if you forget those crazy, weird things,
You will see his generous, soft, kind heart.

He's a unique, special person,
With a lot of kind, passionate love.
I'll never forget that old, first crush,
And he'll be in my late, nightfall dreams.

Lindsey Burdick, Grade 8
Joe Walker Middle School, CA

Lost Your Way

The first signs of winter show themselves.
Clouds dark as night, cloud my judgment.
The last of the leaves blow away with the wind.
A great storm has come but some friend's leave.

White light snow covered the trees like lies.
White lies bring up more lies which make up they're life.
The night sky cluttered with cloud's covered the stars.
The path had no moon or stars to show the way up ahead.

The dark storm came with snow to cover the way.
Trees stand thin and weary as snow beat down upon them.
The dark stormy clouds rained down ice with each second.
The cold night made birds leave their nests and homes.

With the sky so dark and the ground so light is it a lie.
Do my eyes deceive me or is that a light or is it my foe.
Is it a light, no it was a house with colorful lights.
The house seemed so close but so far at the same time.

Kevin Diego, Grade 8
John Adams Middle School, CA

My Little Dog

Coco is my crazy little mutt
He is very funny and silly
Most of his time is spent playing with me outside
When he is done, beware, he smells like wet dog
If you stand still and don't play with him he will bark at you
Never sleep with your mouth open or he will lick your tongue
Even though he's a crazy thing, he's my dog and I love him

Alannah Pringle, Grade 7
Daniel Savage Middle School, CA

I Am Swift and Stealthy

I am swift and stealthy
I wonder if the antelope can spot me
I hear the grass rustle
I spot the innocent zebra chew the grass
I want to feast
I am swift and stealthy

I pretend to hunt with my fellow companions
I feel the brush rub against my fur
I touch the dirt softly
I worry the other animal will sense my presence
I cry because my prey escaped
I am swift and stealthy

I understand I too could be hunted
I say "Rawr"
I dream of hunting and roaming freely
I try to stalk quietly
I hope when I catch my prey
no other thing will try to devour it
I am swift and stealthy

Darius Tucker, Grade 7
Falcon Creek Middle School, CO

Strawberry

The smooth, yet bumpy texture
Tingles my fingers as I hold it.
Thousands of tiny seeds
Squinting at me.
Firm at first touch,
Yet gives away
To soft, cotton candy bruises.
The deep crimson fades,
Like a sunset overlooking the ocean.
The fragrance is ineffable;
Sweet, sour, and mysterious.
I hold the small ruby
By its lush, emerald leaves.
A burst of sweet and sour juice
Sends a chill through my body.
Tiny fibers of flesh pull,
Microscopic seeds crunch as I savor the taste.
The exhilarating zest
Dances around my mouth.
A river of juice flows through,
Not a single bud left out.

Alice Yang, Grade 7
Gale Ranch Middle School, CA

The Night Sky

The dark black sky, with stars shining bright.
They all are different but share the same light.
They are much like us, each in their own way.
We should be like them each and every day.

Tiani Salanoa, Grade 8
Canyon View Jr High School, UT

The Written Word

There are few things in our world
As powerful as the written word
What other thing could take you places
You might never see
Bring nations crashing to their knees
Weave impossible tales
Stab as hard as knives
Douse a roaring fire
Coax furious flames from plain paper sheets
A big bang can take place
In a drop of midnight ink
Forming and destroying worlds
As fast as you can think
The words can sing their stories
With rhythms in your head
From the ages long past
To the many days ahead
In every time and every age
We have given these books form
And through their whispered words
They have breathed back worlds

Kathryn Harlan, Grade 9
The Mirman School, CA

A New Page

A white, clean sheet of paper,
A new opportunity,
Crisp in its neatness.
To soon be filled with blocky letters,
Or maybe round curlicues.

A doodle of an alien —
Or your math teacher might appear.
Maybe scrawled notes,
Or an essay,
Maybe even a poem will form.

Someone crumples an old paper,
Its sound echoes in the stillness of the room.
Someone else flips a page and begins to write again.
Oh the possibilities of a new sheet of paper!

You may do whatever you wish with it,
For it belongs to you.
Creativity awaits…
On a new page.

Jameson McEnany, Grade 7
Salida Middle School, CO

Nicolas Tesla

There once was a scientist named Nicolas Tesla.
Using alternating current he did wrestle.
Tesla tried and tried to send raw power.
Instead, he made a death ray tower.

Quinnan Gill, Grade 8
Beacon Country Day School, CO

I Am

I come from a little reservation
Where boringness was all born, born in Kingman, Arizona.

I come from a house full of happiness and hate,
A house full of good memories that have been kept.

I come a truthful family.
I come from a mother full of confusion,
A dad full of mixed emotions,
Brothers and sisters full of rudeness.

I come from a loving, caring grandma.
I come from a saying my grandpa always told me,
"When you're mad, let it go, it's water under the bridge."

I come from a room full of things that are bright and dark,
Full of so many memories. Full of laughter and depression,
The only place where I could really be alone.

I come from a court, a goal, the sound of the ball,
The Nikes and Jordans squeaking, trying to go for it all.
This is who I am.

Tahne Siyuja, Grade 9
Seligman High School, AZ

I Wish

He said to me, "Don't rush, go slow,"
He took his time; I didn't.
I tripped and fell; he helped me up,
But not before he repeated; "Don't rush, go slow,"
I didn't listen.

He said to me, "Details matter,"
He knew what he was doing; I failed the test,
Details matter.
He helped me study for the next,
But not before he repeated; "Details matter."
I didn't listen.

Now that he has passed away,
I think of what he said; and everything he taught to me,
I wish that I had listened.
Many times I've sat and thought,
I wish that he was here,
There is so much that I know I've missed,
I wish,
That I had listened.

Elisha Smith, Grade 8
Cody Middle School, WY

The Mind Game

the last two seconds of the game.
the buzzer buzzed as I shot and cashed it right in.
to have won the game of my mind.

Jayson Roberts, Grade 7
Salida Middle School, CO

Christmas

Christmas is the time when I get to see all of my family.
It makes me sing carols so happily.
The carols we sing describe Santa as a big jolly old fellow,
"Merry Christmas to all," we hear him bellow.
We give him cookies that taste sugary and sweet,
We wait all night to hear the pitter-patter of his feet.

I wait all year for the presents my family brings,
I know they're here when the doorbell rings.
My family is kind and loving,
Except when my sister and brother are pushing and shoving.
We look at each bright light as it twinkles on the Christmas tree,
Each color seems to flow beautifully.

I look outside as the snow comes down,
Like a blanket it covers our town.
It makes me shiver as I sit inside,
I cuddle up and watch the kids go on a sled ride.
I think of Santa's beard as fluffy as the snow,
All the lights glisten and glow,
The image of Christmas fills my mind,
I wish it was Christmas all the time.

Sinead Heaney, Grade 9
Monarch High School, CO

Pismo

Pismo Beach is a fun place to be,
we ride our quads around by the sea.
We make a fire every night,
I cook my hot dog until it's just right.
It's fun when my dog plays with us in the sand,
until he starts digging and steps on my hand.
We go up a hill and then we go down,
when we're at the top, we see the whole town.
When I ride quads, my hand gets really sore
and it hurts when I try to open the door.
It's a three hour drive to get to the fun,
and it is really sad when we are all done.
When we get home, we have to unpack
all the things we put in the back.
I can't wait until the next time we go,
and ride our quads on the dunes in Pismo.

Jody McFate, Grade 7
Monte Vista Christian School, CA

Fireworks

Spectacular
Amazing scenery
A few seconds of gorgeous lights
Brighter than the sun
A symbol of justice
Inspiring
A message to us all
To be joyful and happy throughout your life.

Drew Poweleit, Grade 8
Christ the King School, AZ

Not So Smart

I am stupid and don't listen
I wonder about nothing
I hear the vacant echo in my head
I see the odd scribbles on paper
I want to learn something new
I am stupid and can't listen

I pretend to be deaf and blind
I feel like I don't know a single thing
I touch the power button on the TV
I worry I'm getting the few things I know tugged from my head
I cry that I will forever be this way
I am stupid and can't listen

I understand all words
I say I can do it if I put my mind to it
I dream about being the new Einstein
I try to learn and listen
I hope I will get better soon
I am intelligent and listen

Vincent Schuldies, Grade 7
Falcon Creek Middle School, CO

Your Favorite Food Critic

Dear McDonald's
I would like to tell you
Your food is atrocious
You tell me
It's mouthwatering
You tell me
It's cheap
I would like to tell you
Your fries make a greasy trail at the bottom of the box.
So during our next encounter
When you have three customers
And Subway has 15
And the cars will not
Enter your parking lot
Then you know, you need to change.

Morgan Quimby, Grade 7
Falcon Creek Middle School, CO

Confusion

I do not understand
Why people use violence to control other people.
Why almost everybody needs to be rude and mean.
Why people don't want to make this world a better place.
But most of all I do not understand
Why school has to be at 7:30 in the morning.
Why people think what others think about them matters most.
Why drugs were made and why we don't throw them all away.
What I do understand is basketball.
Every box out and rebound.
Every pass and shot.

Samantha Shumway, Grade 7
White Pine Middle School, UT

The Message

There once was a boy, his life was so grand,
He knew yonder woods like the back of his hand.
Well, let's hope so, for he raised himself there,
Living off of what the woods have to spare.

He fled home nine months ago,
When he and his father banged heads,
Declaring he would not come home
Until the forest was dead.

While running from home, he thought what to do,
He would use a large tree just like an igloo,
To keep himself from turning blue,
And to stay warm all winter through.

The next five months were the best of his life,
But he did end up missing the good ol' strife.
That is when his dad showed up,
Stating that the boy had won…
And he wanted his son!

Garrett Cregier, Grade 8
Joe Walker Middle School, CA

Life Is a Roller Coaster

To some, life is like a lollipop.
So sweet, and full of sugar.
But to me, life is a roller coaster.
What happens on the ride is unpredictable.
You are unable to control what happens.
Sometimes there may be ups, downs, twists, and turns.
In the ride there will be scary moments,
When all you want to do is close your eyes,
And wait for it to be over.
Sometimes there will be enjoyable moments,
Which are usually at the beginning.
There will be times when the world is spinning right in front of you,
And you are unsure of what to do.
But before you know it, the ride is over,
And you must get off.

Jenny Le, Grade 7
Sarah McGarvin Intermediate School, CA

Blue

Blue is a cloudless sky
The burst of fresh blueberries in my mouth
The shine of a robin's egg
Newly washed denim jeans
The flash of wings from a blue jay in flight
Blue is the pain I don't want to feel on a sad day
Loyalty, a part of our flag
And the scent of the Caribbean Sea
But most of all,
Blue is certainty and courage
The qualities I want to have.

Gabrielle Nguyen, Grade 7
Gale Ranch Middle School, CA

Christmas

The best time of the year,
everyone's in the Christmas cheer.
Is it the happiness in the air,
or the snow in your hair?
The smell of holly,
laughs so jolly,
make us happy and full of love.
Falling asleep is such a chore,
snore, snore, snore,
waking up to presents galore.
Kallie Dunkleberger, Grade 8
Christ the King School, AZ

Blue

Blue is the ocean, embracing the sand
Blue is the water, splashing the rocks
Blue is the sky, covered with clouds
Blue is a flower, smelling fresh and clean
Blue is a car, racing the streets
Blue are the waves, rippling the shore
Blue is a dolphin, swimming in the ocean
Blue is the Earth, floating in space
Blue is the moon, sparkling in the night
Blue is a bird, flying free and high
Omar Martinez, Grade 7
St John's Episcopal School, CA

Space Sky

Vast, deep, dark
and yet buzzing with life
like a forest under the night sky.
A star dies,
another is born.
The circle of life is
forever going around
and around and around
until it spins into a
black hole.
Alea Valadez, Grade 7
Prescott Mile High Middle School, AZ

Autumn

Autumn is my favorite season.
Winter is cold, spring is rainy,
Summer is hot, but fall is not.
Pumpkin pie, roasted turkey,
Golden leaves, early evenings.
Gatherings with the family,
Chasing turkeys in the fields.
Halloween is around the corner;
Thanksgiving comes and warms my heart.
Oh, how I love autumn!
Jamie Back, Grade 7
Monte Vista Christian School, CA

Present Individualism

The time to act is now
The future is in our hands
We have so much more potential, than doing nothing but following commands
There's a world of possibilities, just waiting to be tried
We have the right to go explore them, we cannot be denied!
History's in the making, let's make it something great,
We should be the ones deciding, the way we live out our fate
Yes, maybe God decides it, but we make it what it is
We make our own decisions, when it comes down to the end

To be followed, or not followed
To lead or not to lead
Who says we're the ones who must give in, who says we must pay heed!
Who says there's a way to do things right, and a way to do things wrong,
We're the ones who write the lyrics, to our life's own song
God writes the melody, and puts it on a track
But we make our own decisions, and hope we're not out of whack
We could make history, as we're doing right now
We can hope that one day, they'll look up our names, and remember what we did to help
Because you can make a difference, each and every day
Make an impact on a person's life
It all depends, on what you say
Madelynn Turner, Grade 8
Sequoia Village School, AZ

Realness*

What is real
Real is not a real thing
Real is whatever you make it, what is real to you and your heart alone
Real is rare
Real is being honest with yourself no matter how hard
Real is a leaf that falls in the fall
Real is a lion that doesn't want to kill
Real is like a kite that doesn't want to soar
Real is like a nonviolent war
Real is a kid that wants to dream
Real is like mortal enemies becoming a team
Real is like a butterfly that cannot fly
Real is living life as a lie
Real is being scared to try
Real is like a stuck window, you have to work to open it
Reyna Kocarslan, Grade 8
Rolling Hills Country Day School, CA
*In response to the poem "Famous" by Naomi Shihab Nye.

Fear

Running and running, all I can do. Panting heavily, looking back every second.
I hide in a bush. Am I being watched, am I being hunted, or am I the hunter?
I hear footsteps. Leaves crunching. I hold my breath,
nothing. Not a sound. Just wind blowing, silent and chilling, like a cold winter night,
It feels dead. Am I alone, I peek my head out.
Nothing. I get tackled, I fall to the ground with a thud.
I stagger to my feet, and face my opponent.
Fear.
Ben Cotton, Grade 7
Gale Ranch Middle School, CA

Magic

A world beyond the imagination,
Of mere mortals and their strife,
The bringer of the world of death
And of course, the world of life.

Like a breath of pure air,
Deep under the water dark,
The power of gods divine,
That forever the world will mark.

The power must be harnessed,
Through one thing alone,
The heart of the purest,
That will freely give it a home.

Magic is the power that from day to day,
Will keep us alive and free,
I beg this humble plight,
Please always stay with me.

Celeste Hompstead-Dudley, Grade 8
Rio Rancho Cyber Academy, NM

It's Just That Grandma Feeling…

My grandma doesn't smile much,
but when she does it's gentle and soft,
she's 70 and smells like strawberries,
though she never eats them that much,
her hair smells like lilac shampoo,
and is colored black as the night sky,
her eyes twinkle like stars when she laughs,
and it warms my heart,
she never complains much,
never disrespects anyone,
never makes anyone mad,
she always puts others in front of herself,
I can still remember sitting on her lap,
those good old days,
they'll never fade away,
she's completely caring,
and lovingly lovely,
it's just that grandma feeling,
and nobody will ever take it away…

Gabrielle Chan, Grade 7
Daniel Savage Middle School, CA

The Moon

The moon shines bright
It shines through my window
The beams creep into the cracks
All remains still
I hear sirens of silence
My heart feels content of loneliness
Although as I breathe the darkest air
I'm glad the moon is still there

Dominique Saldana, Grade 7
Sarah McGarvin Intermediate School, CA

Ideas Are…

Ideas are…
buildings
carefully constructed
with a plan
a theory

buildings
soar to the sky
limitless

buildings
come in all forms
tall or short
skinny or wide

buildings
if assembled the wrong way
they can crumble
but try again
with a new perspective

Emma Rarden, Grade 8
Falcon Creek Middle School, CO

Forgotten

What are you afraid of?
Me, being forgotten.
I can't wander forever within
The minds of the unknown.

I'm scared to death that I'll be
A blur, a painted face.
I refuse to disappear
Into the abyss of normality.

Our lives belong to those who know us
And we have to hold on tight
Or we'll slip away
Into the oblivion of insignificance.

If no one ever knows us
Do we disappear? Did we ever exist?
Do we need someone to remind us

That we're here?

Maggie Hart, Grade 9
Pine Creek High School, CO

Me, Myself, and I

Allie
Pleasant, caring, responsible, kind
A sister of Ashley
Lover of swimming and the summer
Traveling with family
And always being with friends and family

Allie Crook, Grade 8
Daniel Savage Middle School, CA

Winter Wonderland

Winter Wonderland,
Crisp, cool, climate
Pricks my skin
Stimulating my senses.

Winter Wonderland,
Fragile snowflakes twirl
Like delicate dancers
I realize their beauty.

Winter Wonderland,
Fresh, fallen snow
White as clouds
"Crunch" and sink under my feet.

Winter Wonderland,
The breeze hums a soft tune
Through the evergreen treetops
A pleasant melody.

Winter Wonderland,
Everything works together
Showing the season's finest
In perfect harmony.

Emily Pennell, Grade 7
Stapley Jr High School, AZ

How Not to Die

Dance is a beating heart,
If ever to fail,
Life would be nonexistent.
It's what drives every breath.
What makes us love.
Without it, I'd be dead.

"5…6…5, 6, 7, 8"
The music starts,
Steady beat pulsing
Keeping us alive.

Dance is what makes me, me
To live, to breath,
To face every day with a smile,
What makes me happy.

Dance is life itself,
A beating heart.
Loving,
Caring,
Believing,
Beating.
Dance is everything.

Katelynn Eckles, Grade 8
Falcon Creek Middle School, CO

The Little Bird

He follows me
Almost everywhere.
He's in the left-hand corner,
Suspended in the air.

His feathers are bright blue,
As if a wild berry.
If he ever chirped,
His sound would be quite merry.

The bird he is not real,
And he will never speak.
He's busy flying back and forth,
Delivering humans' "tweets."

As I got on my iPad
After eating dinner,
I went to visit my little bird.
"I'm back again, Twitter!"
Sydney Green, Grade 7
Joe Walker Middle School, CA

The Last Bark

I lost a treasured friend today.
The type of friend who used to lay
His gentle paw upon my knee
Who shared his silent thoughts with me.

The time has come for him to go.
Although my eyes are wet not dry,
I'll still remember him inside and
Thank him for the happy years.

I'll hold those memories
In my mind like a star in the sky.
Although I didn't want memories
I only wanted you.

My tears will make a stairway
And my pain will make a lane.
That will bring you back from Heaven
And back home again.
Esmeralda Olivares, Grade 8
John Adams Middle School, CA

Pie Is the Best

Pie is the best
In all of the land.
I will not rest.
These pies are all mine.
Apple, lemon, or even grape pie,
If I don't have some
I think I will cry.
Lloyd Nguyen, Grade 7
Sarah McGarvin Intermediate School, CA

The Love of the Orangutan

I looked up into the tree
And wondered what I had found
At first I didn't know what it could be
Until it came down to the ground

He was very peaceful and calm
Without a trace of danger or fear
He had something in his palm
Something that almost made me tear

In his hand was a note from his owner
Requesting that he could have a home
And no longer be a loner
And no longer need to roam

I knew he would never bring me pain
That sweet old orangutan
Daniel G. Laird, Grade 9
Heritage Christian High School, CA

Softball

When we win we feel so great
But when we lose we feel defeat.
We never stop trying to compete.

We hit the ball
Not the mall.

Try to put us down it's impossible
We made the team
So we're not going to stop
We want to make it to the top.

We get bruises
We break bones
But it doesn't matter
When we go home.
Haley Castro, Grade 7
Monte Vista Christian School, CA

Words

Words are hurtful
Words cause pain
They make you angry
They make you cry
They make you feel empty inside
But
Words can make your day
Words can make you laugh
Words can turn things around
At the end of it all words are words
Don't let them touch you
Because you are you
And you are perfect
Vivie Ly, Grade 7
Sarah McGarvin Intermediate School, CA

One Day at a Time

One day at a time
Step by step
Inch by inch
One day at a time
We grow
We mature
We learn
One day at a time
Life gives us lessons
It gives us its ups
And its downs
One day at a time
Our future is shaped
Our destiny unfolds
One day at a time
We become our true selves
One day at a time
Everyone meets the real you
Callie Trautner, Grade 9
Pine Creek High School, CO

Someone to Care

All I want is someone to care,
Someone who wouldn't leave my side,
All I want is someone to care,
Someone who fights my fears,
Someone who makes sure I'm all right,
All I want is someone to care,
Someone who listens to my words,
to hold my hand,
to brighten my day,
All I want is someone to care,
Someone who helps me when I'm sad,
telling me to forget the past,
Someone to hug me till I feel better,
who really wants my heart,
but when I think I found that someone,

they're always the missing one.
Carolinne Biorggio, Grade 7
Falcon Creek Middle School, CO

Mask of Smiles

Callous remarks are whispered,
A heart wrenching cacophony,
To where do they go?
My bulwark of the soul,
Fades away,
In the darkness of my heart.
My cache of sorrow,
I futilely try to cajole,
To smile,
Never to let the tears stream,
As does my heart.
Colin Wu, Grade 8
Gale Ranch Middle School, CA

I Wish You Were Not Leaving

A tear drop for every memory
A sob for every laugh
I wish you were not leaving
The year's not even done
All the memories
Everything we've done
I wish you were not leaving
High school's only begun
Yet it won't be the same once you are gone
I will miss you, Katy

Maddi Kobuth, Grade 9
Monarch High School, CO

U.S.C. Game

You walk in and see yellow and red
"Fight on" is all that is said
The torch is lit, fifteen minutes on the clock
The other team's fans sit and mock
It's fourth quarter and the scores are tied
He throws to his player on the outside
Into the end zone he goes
We cheer because everyone knows
The celebration has begun
The Trojans have won

Julianna Morton, Grade 8
St Francis School, CA

Autumn

The leaves are changing,
Fading and falling,
Autumn is on its way.
The hills are golden,
The temperature is growing,
Colder and colder
Each day.
The food is ready,
The night is steady,
Autumn is on it's way.

Abbey Lynch, Grade 7
Monte Vista Christian School, CA

The One I Admire

She is graceful as an eagle
Floating on the wind
Swift as a cheetah
Running through the field
She's demanding like a small boy
Wanting his toy truck
She is wild like a monkey
In danger in his jungle
A swan floating on a lake
Is not as lovely as she is

Ashley Porter, Grade 7
Daniel Savage Middle School, CA

Regretful Dreams

Iron cage, iron bars,
Broken wings, I only dream of flying.
I can talk with a rusty voice, nobody listens.
I can't scream, my throat becomes blocked.
Tears flow freely down my cheeks, making paths through the grime.
If I couldn't cry, this would be the end.
Darkness surrounds me, crushing my hopes,
I'm suffocating in the pressure of another day.
I want to tell them all to stop! Expectations get too high,
Can't go on, I need to cry, I'm all dried up,
I need some help, I can't go on. This world is hard, it's cruel and tough, but I'm not soft.
I don't fit in, the people judge me, but I can't, I won't, stop.
I need a key to unlock my cage, and fix my wings, and try to fly.
I can only dream, of one day flying over the dull gray crowd.
I just need your help to heal my broken confidence.
I've survived through all of this, and all the pain,
To let you fix my wings. If you can light a match, to brighten up my dark world,
A small hope might live to see through this twisted place.
If I can succeed here, then I might just get high enough to fly,
Away to another world,
Where my dreams are a reality.

Alexis Harper, Grade 7
Vista Heights Middle School, UT

My Hero

My hero
Is my father
Because he was in the army and fought for our country.
He was my role model because he taught me everything
I need to know about life and everything I need to know about growing up.
He was always there for me
When I needed someone to talk to.
He took care of me when I was sick.
He showed me how to be a good and caring person and
How to be my best.
He taught me to work as hard as I can and to give my best effort when applying myself.
He was my best friend and I miss him very much each day.
I will always cherish everything that he ever taught me.
That is why
He will always be my hero.

Tawni Forston, Grade 7
Tenaya Middle School, CA

These Little Stars

Looking up at the black veil that covers the earth,
What do you see?
You see stars, planets, and occasional airplanes
I see not only beautiful stars,
I see pictures and animals and dreams
Whales, dogs, or a baby squirrel
A little boy or an American girl
A mansion, an apartment, or a beach house
We may not know it but these images may show our true hopes and desires
Some just cannot seem to find them

Oniya Valencia, Grade 7
St Elizabeth Ann Seton Catholic School, AZ

Dream

Dreams: beautiful, epic, divine.
Staring out a window — stars falling, time passing
Making a wish for white and cold,
Hoping upon the sunrise.

Reality: unchangeable, dream-shattering, uptide.
Watching people walk by without a glance,
The world and life flying past,
Alone, again, with time.

Everlasting: a dream, a reality, ablaze.
Something reaching out — unfamiliar yet warm,
Seeing a strange look — happy yet foreign,
Awakening from a daze — refreshing yet confusing.

Ablaze: hope, will, way, a race against time
Turning away from the window, sunlight falling gently
Corners lifting into a mirror image — a smile,
Washing away the bittersweet life all around.

Memories: the past, the future, the now.
Tears hiding in shadows, window far too small now,
Alone again, but now a different thing in mind,
An eternal smile found.

Tiffany Park and Hyewon Seong, Grade 9
Torrey Pines High School, CA

The Truth About Lying

Lying can destroy,
It will steal my joy.
Telling the truth is like building a castle,
Lying just knocks it down.

Lying means distrust,
Telling truth means trust,
Making me as murky as muddy water,
Only truth purifies.

Liars have no friends,
Only lonely ends.
A liar's heart is a deserted island,
Scared and isolated.

Lying gets you jailed,
Sometimes with no bail.
Fear whispers, "Lie," when you're scared and afraid,
Don't let fear control you.

Truth is hard sometimes,
Worth it over time,
It gets you off the deserted island.
Truth will restore your life.

Cody Williams, Grade 7
Joe Walker Middle School, CA

Lonely Then Found

I am a calm, sensitive book.
I see many people passing by me.
I hear people talking to their friends and laughing.
I feel sad that nobody wants me.
I am a sad and lonely book.

I dream that somebody will read me.
I worry that I will be lonely forever.
I love to be grasped in people's hands.
I hope that I will be read very soon.
I am a lonely book.

I understand that there are many other books to read.
I try to be seen with my beautiful cover.
I say constantly read me, read me!
I touch someone's warm and clammy hands.
I am so excited to be read.

Savannah Nelson, Grade 8
Palm Desert Charter Middle School, CA

I Don't Understand

I do not understand
Why we have to wake up for school so early
Why people have to cut in line
Why people have to be so mean

But most of all I do not understand
Why kids bully other kids
Why kids can't work hard to get good careers
Why kids can't be quiet when the teacher tells them to
Why people rob other people
Why people kill others

What I do understand is homework and studying
When people can't wear fancy clothes like others
Why people work so hard
The excitement of going to fun places like the fair and Lagoon
And other places in the world.

Cristina Saenz, Grade 7
White Pine Middle School, UT

Veterans

Flying high above a foreign land.
Sailing over tortured seas, quite missing the sight of sand.
Trudging through a marshy hell,
Shooting at people, they scream and yell.
Saving those of woe-filled homes.
You then walk through a capitol building, that has a dome.
Because of your courage, as fine as art,
You get a golden medal,
A wondrous golden medal,
On which bears a purple heart.

Bridget Gill, Grade 7
St Francis School, CA

Love Is a Thing of the Past

Love is a thing of the past,
It will never last;
Love will leave you broken-hearted,
So might as well not get started.

Love is a thing of the past,
It will go by too fast;
Because when you realize that you're in love,
It will already be over and done.

Love is a thing of the past,
Although some people will think it's a blast;
They will think that love will be like a song,
But unfortunately, they will be wrong.

Love is a thing of the past,
Some people will think that they need it to last;
That without love, they would want to die,
But single people can survive.

Itzeli Garcia, Grade 8
Joe Walker Middle School, CA

Diamond in the Rough

I sparkle in the moonlight as I lay on velvet cushions,
Trapped in a jewelry box. Pieces of broken pearl necklaces
And miss-matched buttons keep me company
And hide my existence. Cob webs and dust
Pile up like fresh snow on the antique chest.
How could my owner forget me like this?
All of our memories are kept inside this single stone.
I reflect the old bliss of her marriage as they promised
Each other their love would never abolish.
Their two souls kept in me. I used to be worn on young hands
That would hold another. I had that exact spot,
On the left hand, ring finger.
Now I am empty, nobody to wear me,
Nothing to grasp onto, but the sweet relics.

Hannah Rutter, Grade 9
La Reina High School, CA

Afraid

In my bed all snuggled up,
The day suddenly ends, very abrupt.

I look out my window and I fear I see things in the night,
But I'm too scared so I snuggle up tight.

I feel like a child,
I haven't felt like this in a while.
I grab my bedtime friend,
That I discarded because I felt that my childhood was at an end.

I realize now,
It's okay to be afraid.

Isabella Dossola, Grade 7
Charlotte Wood Middle School, CA

Colors of Fall

A rain of leaves,
Colored red and yellow,
Fluttering and flying around the meadow.
The birds chirping and hopping with glee,
While the wind sings about all that is and could be.
A red carpet covers the floor,
With crunches as mice run on all fours.
And suddenly a gust,
Rips through the trees,
Yellow, red, green,
All dancing in the breeze.
Trees reach up straight and high,
Stretching for the blue empty sky.
And buzzing around are dragonflies,
As the fox tries to find where berries lie.
A robin flies above the clearing,
The warm singing wind is all he is hearing.
Everything beneath him seeming so small,
Yet still admiring the delicate colors of fall.

Eric Zhao, Grade 8
Gale Ranch Middle School, CA

The Pain of Dusk

Why does the dusk invoke such fear in us,
The fear of death from another man's hand?
The very strange fear of dusk is still just,
Although the feeling is still in demand.
Death has a queer and seductive feeling
Of course, this is but one feeling of dusk
Yet, through this affect, new life is raining,
Life that steps out hiding in a dark husk.
When I lay down, the night again shrouds me.
My mentor came and sat down near my bed
"Listen to the new sounds dusk brings," said he.
He sat and let his hands cradle his head
Reminding me the truth behind the musk,
Truth, being the unholy pain of dusk.

Pete Raschke, Grade 9
Lucerne Valley Middle/Sr High School, CA

The Color of Renewal

Green the symbol of spring
Entices you to its sweet color
A calm gentleness flows throughout
And envelops you with memories
Of newborn flowers exploding
From the ground

Green the color of healthy leaves
Falling here and there
Whispering their hidden secrets
Of a distant past
Where colors change and the dying fall
Where they are covered in an ocean of white

Katherine Duncombe, Grade 9
New Plymouth High School, ID

Someone's There

Someone's there, someone's there,
With a mysterious stare.
I should head back to town,
But I know someone's around.
Someone's there, someone's there.

As I creep deeper in the woods,
It seems darker than a demon's heart.
Feeling surrounded by people in hoods,
My body shakes like a quake;
Someone's there, Someone's there.

I ran as fast as a flash;
Then I see something dash.
Tripping on a branch,
I knew I should get snatched.
As it came closer and closer.
I just knew it was over.
My soul was seized in a breeze.
I'm pretty sure it had a pumpkin for a head;
But all I know is that I'm dead.

Chad Valladares, Grade 7
Joe Walker Middle School, CA

Isolation

If there was something I could have said,
Or something I could have done,
Would you still have gone and run?

My best friend found someone new.
Am I just like nothing to you?

Off you went, like I don't even matter.
I was lonely, isolated, for hours and hours.
You deleted me from your life.
You stabbed me in the back with an icy knife.

If we are done, could you please let me know?
I'm tired of fighting, it's time to let you go.
Since we are done, don't ever come back.
I'm finally moving on, I'm free, and that's a fact!

Have a good life, hope it's swell.
I won't be there to catch you when you fall.
When you stop and think about me, just always know,
Though we've moved on, don't worry, because I'm doing just well.

Brooke Walsh, Grade 7
Joe Walker Middle School, CA

Rain

The clouds rumble in,
the sky fades from blue to a dark spine-chilling gray.
The sun no longer appears
but its light still shines through
as though it won't give in.
The rain softly taps on the ground
quickly tumbling down faster with every drop
that falls from the dark sky.
Thunder crashes
shaking me with all of its strength.
It all stops
as if someone turned it off like a switch.
All that it leaves are puddles
and a rainbow that stretches across the sky.
Soon it will fade
only resembling the sweet smell of rain.

Hannah DeKing, Grade 7
Salida Middle School, CO

Where Poetry Hides for Me

Poetry hides
In the pencil I use,
It hides
In the book I always read.
It hides in the poems I write.
Poetry hides
In the old picture of me when I was eight.
Poetry hides
In the library at my school.
It hides in my old hat.
Poetry hides
In my sixth grade class picture.
It hides in my computer and in my old school I.D.
Poetry hides
In my old blue jacket and in my room.
It even hides in my big, blue folder.

Jack Lu, Grade 7
Tenaya Middle School, CA

Cousin

Elegant, sweet, beautiful all describe my cousin,
she spreads her kindness to everyone
whenever I need her she's there
she never lets me
or anyone else down
she reminds me of a hibiscus
spreading her kindness to everyone
she would help anyone even if she didn't know them.
I love my cousin

Kaitlyn Byers, Grade 7
Daniel Savage Middle School, CA

Ode to Laughter

In movies everyone loves the sound of the little children's laughter.
Well I love to laugh too.
Without laughter I'd be nothing.
You always cheer me up, and you never disappoint.
You're there with my friends, with me at home, school, and practice
It doesn't matter where…you're there.
So thank you laughter for sticking around,
Even when you make my ribs hurt,
But I'd rather hurt so thank you laughter.

Bailey Comstock, Grade 7
Daniel Savage Middle School, CA

Gymnastics Sonnet
Walking in and feeling like it's your home
The smell of chalk roams through out the big gym
The gym outside looks like it is a dome
I always think that I might break a limb

I know that I can get hurt doing what I love
In gymnastics I feel invincible
When tumbling I always fly like a dove
Making sure you land is the principle

I love that my team always cheers for me
In return I always cheer for them too
Gymnastics is so difficult you see
Our coach yells at us when we "boo and hoo"

Gymnastics is always what I live for
The point is to try to get the best score
Mikie Kasten, Grade 9
Monarch High School, CO

Life!
Life has heaven and life has hell;
Whether we live, time will tell.
The loved ones we lost,
My heart has been tossed,
But somehow my soul is still well.

The "L" is for love for the loved ones we lost;
The "I" is for interests for the ones we have;
The "F" is for family for the care we share;
The "E" is for eternity,
eternal love we bear;

The life we have
Has wandered the sea's,
And space in the air
That I cannot see;
The life that I have I've cherished in me.
Aubrey Petersen, Grade 8
Joe Walker Middle School, CA

Reflections on Rodin's Sculpture, "Thought"
I
See a woman
Who look stuck in her own world.
It looks like she can do something about it,
But,
How does she get out?
The lady has a problem
And she feels she will be there forever.
She needs help
And
I bet her parents
Feel sick about it.
Samara Douglas, Grade 7
Tenaya Middle School, CA

Bountiful Barbies
Dolls dolls everywhere
Always yearning for more,
But nothing ever to spare.
Lovable enough for everyone to share.

Dolls dolls everywhere
The more you see, the more you gasp for air.
In astonishment or amazement?
I just can't seem to fair!

Dolls dolls everywhere
How I love their silky hair.
Flowing in the wind without a care.
Like turning around in a swivel chair.

Dolls dolls everywhere
To sleep without one — a nightmare.
With one, we make a perfect pair,
Lovable enough for everyone to share.
Lindsay Annabelle Collins, Grade 8
Richardson PREP HI Middle School, CA

Standing on a Cliff
I stand on a cliff
six green trees surround me
each tree bending backwards by the wind like a gymnast
the smell of the trees are unexplainable
the sky is cloudy, with only small sections of blue throughout it
sharp, cold winds shoot at my face like glass
there isn't an animal for miles
and I'm guessing that I'm the only human for miles
a storm is on its way
I can feel drops of water hit my forehead
and many dark clouds fill the sky
this cliff takes me to another world, a magical world
but when it all comes back to it I'm only doing one thing
standing on a cliff
Taylor Smith, Grade 7
Daniel Savage Middle School, CA

Ode to Basketball
Oh basketball
what would I do without you
every time I get mad, sad, or angry
I go outside to dribble or shoot you

When I am in a game, you score for me
you help me at the tricks I try
you slide through my hands like butter
you also make me feel wonderful when I am holding you
you make me feel like I can do anything

Oh basketball,
what would I do without you
Caleb Whorton, Grade 7
Daniel Savage Middle School, CA

I Never Learn

I never learn
I cruise along the sidewalk when suddenly...
My lips dry;
my stomach begs for a snack.
I see a small Shell gas station
I take a sharp turn to the even smaller convenience store
and instantly grab
two candy bars
I go to the counter
and plonk down my items
A lady looks up at me
with her evil eye and says,
"It's gunna be...3 dollars and 79 cents plus tax."
That's crazy!
I pay for it anyway, dying for those delicious teeth-rotters.
As I walk out,
I caught sight of the CVS
across the street a sign advertises:
"1.50 for two candy bars for a limited time only!"
I sink down to my knees and shout
No! Why do I never learn?

Brian Huebner, Grade 7
St Stephen Lutheran School, CA

The Devil Within

The devil within is a cunning figure
Never in sight but always in mind
Cloaked in mystery and deception
Concealed within the internal abyss

He is a nasty creature
Full of spite and malevolence
Who only comes out to play
When the tidal wave of anger arises

A cousin to death
He arises when least wanted
Destroying lives and reputations
Sending them to the grave
Wished away with the snap of his decaying fingers

Sierra Westmoreland, Grade 9
Eaton High School, CO

The Ballerina

Leap, jump, twirl, spin
Her tutu flows in the wind
She leaps so high she touches the sky
She lands with grace, a smile on her face
When she goes on point she says it's easy
Her kicks are so high they're above her head
She is so flexible, she has all her splits
She works so hard for a lot of reasons
She is good at dance she would never quit
Dancing is her passion forever and always

Danielle Simpson, Grade 7
Monte Vista Christian School, CA

The Thickest of Material

I see many things.
Things that many people do not wish to see.
They fog my mind
Like the pages of a thrilling book that I can't close.
The faces
They flash through my mind
Like a fight sequence from an action film.
These faces
They remind me of my past.
They scream at me
Making me see all my insecurities.
They come from the smallest fragment of my mind.
They are frightening faces.
They make me cringe in fear.
But these ghouls that fog my mind
Are hidden from me.
They are behind a large wall
Created by the thickest of material.
They are bound by chain
Only to be unlocked by a key.
A key that shall never be found.

Michael Ellis, Grade 9
Las Vegas Academy, NV

Thunder

Cracks of majestic strides
Pounds on dark intimidating masses
charges with its grumbling thuds
Sounding the ferocious war cry
Sending out warnings to life all around
Its depression is seen from everywhere
Roaring its sobs with regret
Crying for every strike to the earth
And groaning for every miniscule drop
Earth sees its sorrow
The foe falters for loss of support
Then all is quiet
Life peeks out of its perches
The enemy has retreated
Bright rays of sun fight through the weak clouds
Warmth embraces the cold wet earth

Nick Leavitt, Grade 9
Pine Creek High School, CO

Home

The light bulb turned off in the hall for the last time
As thoughts of things
Things I love splash through my mind
The tangy smell of nail polish
The blue green sea
The dust left after erasing
The ringing sound of laughter
Things I will miss
Home

Olivia Webb, Grade 7
Canyon View Jr High School, UT

I Call This Home

When I came here I was happy,
What a beautiful place.
Icy mountains, very pale
Wispy winds burn your skin,
I call this home.

Going camping in the wilderness,
Going fishing by the lakes,
Going hunting in the forests,
Going swimming in the river,
In this wild, adventurous place.

I call this home.
Mahlanie Cartlidge, Grade 7
Salida Middle School, CO

Change

Time is turning
People changing
Thoughts running
Why can't things stay the same?
Childhood memories flash like lightning
Friends and people I once knew disappear
I need to grasp on to something, anything
Why does it have to be this way?
My head is burning
I lose focus
Memories become like fog
Why can't I stay,
Frozen in time?
Morgan Beus, Grade 7
Stapley Jr High School, AZ

Be You

Roses are red
Violets are blue
Whatever you do
Just be you
Who cares what others say
This is you and don't let it get away
Don't ever feel insecure
You are beautiful, that's for sure
Shine bright and don't back down
Because you are you and be proud!
Lani Tran, Grade 7
Sarah McGarvin Intermediate School, CA

Rob

There once was a boy named Rob.
All through the day he did sob.
But then at school
A cute girl said, "He's cool"
So now girls surround him like a mob.
Brison Owens, Grade 7
Beacon Country Day School, CO

Friends Come and Go

I remember a time not long ago
When we stood there
When we laughed and shared it all
We were very best of friends

You are a great person
I had so much respect for you
I thought our friendship was going to last
But that is what I thought

When the day came
I sat there and cried
And in a blink of an eye
I saw you said goodbye

Something happened to me when our friendship died
Something happened to me when we said goodbye
Friends are hard to come by
I needed to be the wise guy to find someone new

Juan Salazar, Grade 8
John Adams Middle School, CA

Death

Death surrounds you with his summoning howls and lacerating claws
You think you may have escaped him, but you never will
He comes clashing into your life, claiming cherishing moments
You may not be the next on his scheme
But you soon will be

I mourn for all of the things that Death has trapped
I mourn for the trees
With their colorful leaves and sculptured trunks
I mourn for the sun
When it falls to its knees getting caught in Death's pathway
Darkness is whispered upon you,
Pretending to defeat the purpose of life

But last I mourn for our family and friends
When Death has wrapped our kinsmen
With a soft naked sand, being enfolded in earth's hand
There isn't a way of escaping pain when Death is on your front step
Only mourning for those who have already been visited
Kennedy Overly, Grade 9
Gunnison Valley High School, UT

Christmas

Oh how beautiful the lights on the tree are,
How elegantly the presents are wrapped,
And how my heart melts at the sound of children singing Christmas carols.
All of these things bring joy to my heart on Christmas day,
But most of all, I love the smiles on everybody's face,
And the joy of a child opening a gift from Santa Claus.
Christmas is a time for everyone to tell each other how much they love one another,
And a time for joy.
Brandon Skinner, Grade 8
Christ the King School, AZ

Hope

Hope is something that helps you believe,
hope is something that you cannot see.
Hope helps you stand strong and tall,
hope helps you get up when you fall.

Hope is something that everyone needs,
hope fills all the people who breathe.
Hope fills Haiti, Japan, and more,
hope fills the children whose parents are no more.

And looking at this hope you start to wonder,
what keeps them going farther and farther?
A person can instill hope in a young child's route,
for hope is what keep us going without a doubt.

Adriana Osorio, Grade 8
Christ the King School, AZ

Veterans

Those brave men and women
Who've gone to fight for our country,
Protect us at all costs,
And defend our valued freedom.

They did something no one else could.
They risked their lives just to protect us,
Who sit here back home in the safety of America.
It's safe here because of them.

They are the heart and soul of America.
They've answered the call of duty
And stepped up in the face of danger.
They are true Americans.

Eric Inman, Grade 8
St Francis School, CA

Grandma's Lovely House

Grandma, oh I love your house!
I sneak in everywhere around this house
From one room to another like a mouse
A hole I poked in that painting of those cows

Peaceful, quiet rooms like a library
Warm, relaxing with a scent of raspberry
The kitchen, painted the color of jelly
Delicious food that feed my belly

Beautiful, clear sky, stars shine bright
Feeling warmth of a bonfire on a cool night
Pleasant scent of roses linger on my blouse
Grandma, oh I love your house!

Tiffany Garcia, Grade 8
Richardson PREP HI Middle School, CA

Autumn Sunset

The blazing sun hangs low in the sky,
Moments from touching the horizon.
The lengthening shadows stretch their fingers,
About to grasp the last shreds of light.
Autumn leaves spiral through the air,
Floating down to the Earth below.
A cool, gentle breeze wraps around you,
Before releasing you and drifting way.
The blue sky tinged with pinks and oranges
Slowly fades into a dark, cool black.
Darkness pushes the light away,
The night like an inky blanket.
Frosty swirls of glittering stars twinkle in the sky,
The beautiful sunset has disappeared, the night begins its reign.

Amy Hatfield, Grade 7
Sarah McGarvin Intermediate School, CA

Popsicles

Summer time heat like the cold, blowing snow
Melting cold ice on warm hands
Juicy candy filled with caramel
Sour lemons biting taste buds
Sweet as apples kissing cheeks
Yummy like hot, tasty spaghetti
Cold like snow that falls in winter
Sticky cotton candy on fingertips
Wet like Atlantic Ocean waves
"slurp, slurp" you drink soda pop
"crunch, crunch" you eat chips
Sweet bananas that hug my tongue
Delicious sweet, sour, squishy Skittles
Bye, bye is me eating the popsicles all by myself

Britney Filter, Grade 7
Weldon Valley Jr High School, CO

Seven Years

Seven years,
from five to twelve,
kinder to sixth,
why, it's the preparation years!
elementary school—preparing for the later years,
one class throughout the day, many subjects taught by one,
the years whom many sorrowfully miss,
once you move beyond, you can't come back,
middle and high await,
six more years beyond the seven,
but one never forgets,
the wonderful years
one will experience,
through seven years.

Christopher Mai, Grade 7
Sarah McGarvin Intermediate School, CA

Dream of Insecurity

All I see is a shattered conscious,
Staring right back at me.
I wish I had covered all my tracks completely,
Because I am so afraid of being seen.

Lift your arms, only heaven knows,
Whether danger grows.
It's safe to say,
"There's a bright light up
Ahead and help is on the way."

I forgot the last time I felt brave,
I just recall insecurity.
Something came down like a tidal wave,
And swept over me with guilt.

Depression please cut to the chase,
And cut the long story short.
Fate looks sharp, severs all my ties,
And breaks whatever doesn't bend.
Sadly then, my heavy hopes just fall,
Right back down again.

Sophia Nguyen, Grade 7
Sarah McGarvin Intermediate School, CA

Wishes Upon Dreams

A wish upon a shooting star.
A penny in a fountain.
A secret tied to a blue balloon.
An eyelash blown away.
A dandelion taken away by the wind,
Or a rainbow on your special day.
They are all wishes, hopes, and dreams.
They are a desire for something that will never happen.
So why do we do them?
Why do people wish?
Because it gives us a reason to still have hope in our eyes.
To dream about the unthinkable.
To move on, keep going.
It's our pot of gold at the end of a never ending rainbow.
It's who we are.
And who I am.

Ashley Coulston and Jaylene Solis, Grade 8
Palm Desert Charter Middle School, CA

Untouched

I have struggled all my life.
Trying to make a different path than the one layed before me.

I have seen death conquer the ones I love,
leaving me untouched.

The pain not only tearing a hole in my heart,
has left my inmost being, shattered back to the start.

Lakota Lawson, Grade 9
Shelby High School, MT

What Is a True Friend?

All I want is someone to understand me.
Someone to always be there through thick and thin.

All I want is someone to understand me.
Someone to listen to my childish jokes.
Someone to die of laughter with me.

All I want is someone to understand me.
Someone to listen to what I have to say.
Someone to talk about problems and get each others' feelings.
Someone to be able to tell secrets with and
trust one another with them.

All I want is someone to understand me.
Someone to fight with but always make up.
Someone to watch movies with and end up falling
asleep together.

Someone to be able to hold a serious conversation with.
While they're on the toilet.

All I want is someone to be able to always be friends with.

Clarissa Garza, Grade 7
Falcon Creek Middle School, CO

Where Poetry Hides for Me

Poetry hides in the crystal-blue eyes of my grandma
Poetry hides in your way of life,
It hides in the palm of a little baby
In the wrinkles on my grandma's face
In the smiles on my mom's face
It hides in the bright, blue sky,
Poetry hides on the writing paper
It hides in the bright sun
In the wet, green grass
In the walls on the classroom
It hides in a person's soul
In a person's mind
In a person's heart
It hides in the bright fire
Poetry hides
Everywhere.

Lily Tamazyan, Grade 7
Tenaya Middle School, CA

A Letter to My Younger Self

My darling,
Don't let time pass you by.
Don't let your future end with a sigh.
Explore the world, don't be shy.
But don't be afraid to say some goodbyes.
Your life will be great, don't you cry.
It's time for me to go; keep your head up high.
Tell yourself, reach farther than the skies.

Aira Valera, Grade 8
Christ the King School, AZ

Sheltered Love

Sheltered love —
My house, the one and only
Where my dreams soared beyond the yonder
The place I sleep soundly in, night after night
A place where I can call my own now
And in the future

Sheltered love —
The dark coffee cooling in the kitchen
The cookies cooking in the oven
The place where love grows and never dies
Time has ticked and tocked
To make the ages move on

Sheltered love —
Where time is never taken for granted
And my love for one never becomes old
This time in the century,
All are welcome to my throne

Leilani Negrete, Grade 8
Richardson PREP HI Middle School, CA

Life, Joy, Dream

Loving each day
Imagining each day
Flying through each day
Enjoying each day

Joyful and happy
Only you can spread happiness! So…
You should be happy too!

Dreaming is to living as living is to breathing.
Remember to dream!
Every day is a new adventure
Always dream
Memories are like dreams

Alyson Ely, Grade 7
Monte Vista Christian School, CA

A Good Dog

Sadie was a good dog.
She was sweet, cuddly, and fun.
There was no dog like her.
Her smallness made her cute.
Her white fur was just like snow.
Even her barking wasn't a bother to me.
Petting her when I was sad made me happy again.
Running with her and playing with her was fun.
Her snoring was funny.
It made me laugh.
Now since she is gone it makes me cry.
I couldn't always be with her because I was focused on school.
There will never be a dog like Sadie.

Mack Lewis, Grade 8
Palm Desert Charter Middle School, CA

Athletic and Determined

I am athletic and determined.
I wonder what it takes to play at a high level.
I hear the net go "swish."
I see the ball's rotation in the air.
I want to be the best I can be.
I am athletic and determined.

I pretend I can shoot like Ray Allen.
I feel the butterflies before a huge game.
I touch the leather basketball.
I worry about having an off shooting day.
I cry when I give my all and lose it.
I am athletic and determined.

I understand the game and love for it.
I say "Let's go baby!"
I dream of being as good as Kobe.
I try to work 110% 100% of the time.
I hope the NBA will find me.
I am athletic and determined.

Noah Lewis, Grade 7
Falcon Creek Middle School, CO

Understand

All I want is someone to understand.
Someone to listen to my opinion.
All I want is someone to understand.
Someone to agree.
Someone to disagree.
All I want is someone to understand.
Someone to listen.
Someone to think.
Someone to speak their mind.
All I want is someone to understand.
Someone to wonder.
Someone to know.
Someone to aid.
Someone to assist me.

All I want is someone to understand how I think.

Hayden Nickles, Grade 7
Falcon Creek Middle School, CO

True Friends

True friends are your peanut to your butter,
The cheese to your stick,
The tic to your toe,
They are with you wherever you go.
Even though you get in fights,
You're still tight,
Your true friends it's all right.
When it's at night,
And your praying to yourself,
You start praying for your friends, not yourself.

Mattea Romo, Grade 7
Monte Vista Christian School, CA

Go in Peace

I stood there waiting.
The clock was ticking.
There wasn't much time
For me to go on.
I was always cold;
Goose bumps up my arms,
Shivers up my spine,
Yet, I was happy.
My whole life I knew,
That one day would come.
It will end my pain,
And my suffering.
There was no one here.
Thankfully, no one.
I wouldn't want to
Hurt my beloved.
I felt it coming.
There was a smile.
Now I knew I could,
I could go in peace.

Grace Kang, Grade 8
Joe Walker Middle School, CA

Alone

I walk alone,
On this lonely path,
With nobody to talk to.
The trees ignore me,
Not even moving.

I walk alone,
On this lonely path,
Surrounded, but isolated,
I talk but nobody listens.

I walk alone,
On this lonely path,
Only hearing the leaves rustle,
And the wind whistle.

I walk alone,
On this lonely path,
Wondering,
When will it end?

Brian Eskenazi, Grade 7
Joe Walker Middle School, CA

The Reward Is Ours

Dribbling down the court
He shoots to score,
Swish
It falls down through
The hoop
The reward is ours

Dakota Moncivaiz-Likes, Grade 7
Salida Middle School, CO

The Fire of Bonds

A relationship is a fire
trying to blaze.
Getting it started can be difficult,
for there are no lighters in this world.
All you can do
is rub two things together, and see if you can get some sparks.
The sparks might catch and start a small fire, but you are not done yet.
This small fire is very delicate and can be blown out with a slight breeze,
but when different pieces start to catch
Hold on…
Because you can think whatever you want
but there is no way to control a fire.
Things are going to catch ablaze that shouldn't have
and pieces are going to be added that are unwanted.
But this.
This is what makes it fun, this is what really keeps it going.
Sometimes it flickers and pops, catching you off guard.
The fire will not go on forever though,
you might have to put it out yourself, or it dies off on its own.
No matter how it goes out though, after you always feel empty and lifeless;
but the most terrifying thing, is the darkness that follows.

Gavin Livingston, Grade 8
Falcon Creek Middle School, CO

Didn't You Ever Stop to Think?

You degraded her because you thought her odd,
Because she did not fit into your mould of ideal,
But didn't you ever stop to think
That she heard every whisper and every cursed word,
And although she showed no outward sign,
Didn't you ever stop to think
That she was breaking on the inside
For the lack of fitting in,
For being nothing but misunderstood,
For every word of your cruel ridicule,
Didn't you ever stop to think
That she cried herself to sleep every single night,
Sobbing with your words echoing clear in her mind,
Didn't you ever stop and see the pain and hurt
That shone only in her dark, saddened eyes,
Didn't you ever stop to think
That your words and actions were the only reason
That she could not face herself in the mirror?
Didn't you ever stop to think that after a while
The only her she saw was the her you made her out to be,
Didn't you ever stop to think?

Victoria Hoaglin, Grade 9
Arizona Agribusiness & Equine Center - Paradise Valley Campus, AZ

Stouffer Park

With its green grass fields, cracked baseball diamonds, and luscious underbrush
Smells of cut grass, food cooking, and sweet blackberries
Reminds me of a meadow right before a storm
A place to be free

Derek Rosendin, Grade 8
Ripona Elementary School, CA

A Tiny Rose

She awakes to the morning light,
While she's misted by a water sprite.
She blows her light fragrance into the air,
As the breeze flows through her emerald hair.

She wears an elegant ruby gown,
And is donned in a pointed crown.
She clothes herself in transparent jewels,
And relaxes amongst spacious pools.

Her beauty attracts many to her,
But constantly leaves her in a blur.
She resides in many vases,
And on desks in various places.

She is the queen amongst the flowers,
And is often admired for hours.
But as time flies her time comes to a close,
Because she is merely a tiny rose.

Leana Sottile, Grade 9
La Reina High School, CA

I Am Thankful

I am thankful for
the smiles that brighten my day
a shelter to keep me safe
water to keeps me healthy
parents that are always there for me
police to keep the world safe
cars to transport us to places we need to go
a sister to talk to
teachers to help me learn
money to buy necessary items
clothes to keep me warm
an education to be smart and knowledgeable
a pencil to write with and get things done
a baby cousin to make my day great

Meridian Jaques, Grade 7
Daniel Savage Middle School, CA

Reflections on Edvard Munch's Painting, "The Scream"

This painting
Tells a story each and every way you look at it.
It tells a story
Of anguish,
A story of excitement,
A story of ooh…and ah…moments.
It tells a story
Of a painting of a man screaming in a sea of different emotions,
And scenery that just doesn't care.
He screams so loud that his voice is silent.
This painting
Has so many stories and so much light
With one voice, one sound, one scream.

Jayden Jefferson, Grade 7
Tenaya Middle School, CA

Life of the Wild

The forest is calm as the morning rays of light hit the tree tops.
Wild life begins to awake,
Dew hits the river as the sun comes into view.
The flowers on the trees open as rays of sun
Appear in shafts of light between the trees.
Birds hop from branch to branch,
Gathering nuts and fruit.
Water flows silently and swiftly in the river.
Dew slides along the spiders web.
Sun fills the meadow with light as the deer eat.
The day moves on and the heat becomes stronger.
Animals stop by the river to cool down from the heat of the day.
Beautiful birds sing as raccoons rest high above the forest floor.
Fish jump and dive in the rivers making small splashes.
As the day comes to an end, the forest starts to cool down,
Small animals scurry into their dens and prepare to sleep.
Animals watch from their dens as night falls on the forest.
As the darkness engulfs the forest,
The sun disappears behind the mountains.
The meadow is lit by the moonlight.
The animals drift off into a peaceful slumber along with the forest.

Katie Minarik, Grade 7
Monte Vista Christian School, CA

Shark Bait

As I am floating in the middle of nowhere
I feel the cold water and waves bobbing.
I hear only the waves crashing and swishing.
I only see the night sky reflecting off the water.
I feel a cold giant body skim my leg.
Everything is too dark.
I wonder:
What is happening?
Will I die?
Will the world end?
What is down there?
Will I die?

No. I am dragged down
into a dark abyss. Never to
be seen again. I am shark bait.

Lucas Ansel, Grade 7
Falcon Creek Middle School, CO

Ode to Grandpa

There he stood in green and brown
He worked in the USMC
He enlisted when he was 18
He fought the Koreans in the Korean War
He is retired now and is skilled with a hammer
He built many things in my house and his
Every day he climbs his tree, to get his physical therapy
His old-fashion words give me a smile
I haven't seen him in a while.

Michael Schoonmaker, Grade 7
Daniel Savage Middle School, CA

The Dream

Sleeping soundly on my pillow,
Starts a whirlwind of dreams,
Taking me to a magical land,
Full of sweet sounds.
The waterfalls,
As if soothing pebbles were dropping.
The clouds,
Looking as fluffy as mouthwatering marshmallows,
Good enough to eat.
The clouds melt,
Into dark, dreary, creatures,
Calling me in.
Fear, I could feel it,
Zipping through my mind and body.
At that moment,
I felt I was dead.
Until the blaring sound of my alarm wakes me.
I open my eyes,
To see the familiar sight of my wallpaper.
A dream,
It was just a dream.

Emma Santiago, Grade 7
Canyon View Jr High School, UT

I Do Not Understand

Why is there hatred
Why is there starvation
Why are there feelings

But most of all I do not understand
Why there is poison
Why people die
Why people judge
Why everything is expensive
Why there is hunger

But what I do understand is friends
They are always there for you
They help you when you're feeling down
They trust you and it makes you feel good to have friends

Brook Jenkins, Grade 7
White Pine Middle School, UT

Winter

It's wet, cold, and white.
What is this?
Could it be?
The season of winter
Which comes in December after fall?
This cannot be vanished, but, it may not be seen.
Many people like it,
Many people don't
It's just one of those seasons
That you cannot control

Denise Mondragon, Grade 7
Isbell Middle School, CA

Something Great

Overwhelmed.
Depressed.
And still no one listens
Angry.
Upset.
And no one seems to care
They say they want to help
And yet they never pay attention
They say just let it out
And yet they criticize
But one day I'll have it all
Freedom.
Power.
And they will want to listen
Happiness.
Friends.
Who really do care
Then they won't need to help
Or even pay attention
Because one day I'll be something great
And I will have only them to thank

Talia Gardner, Grade 9
Encore Jr/Sr High School for the Performing & Visual Arts, CA

Daily

As we walk on that same path,
Past empty faces,
Beside blurring cars,
And beyond still trees:
We are silent

In that large grey building,
We meet with weary handshakes,
Laugh at each others jokes, and chat about local news.
Still we are silent

Time and again,
We're in that same place,
We don't think,
We don't care,
We stay silent.

Nhan Le, Grade 8
Joe Walker Middle School, CA

Reflections on Rodin's Sculpture, "Thought"

I see a woman
Her feelings are trapping her,
But her mind is open.
She's sad because her feelings
Are holding her back.
She is on the edge,
Ready to give up,
But, there is one thing
Preventing her from quitting life.

David Turner, Grade 7
Tenaya Middle School, CA

Once I Leave

When I first arrived
I would have never thought of the pain inside
That I would have to face
Once I leave my wonderful place

All the days that flew by
Where I would watch the beautiful sky
All of that will disappear
Once I leave my wonderful place

When I would yell throughout the night
And with my brother I would fight
I will still miss those good ol' times
Once I leave my wonderful place

All the feelings that are inside
Come out even when they try to hide
It will truly hurt my heart
Once I leave my wonderful place

Angel Garcia, Grade 8
Richardson PREP HI Middle School, CA

Hidden Feelings

All is blurry, unseeingly far, not meant to reach for
Separate you are, from the rest
A simple thing blown apart by the breeze
A soul fragile and so soft
But somehow solid enough to cry
Tears hot, salty-cold, tasteless
So far, them and I,
I have faded against the scene, watching
Seeing, sobbing quietly,
Sorrow is the darkness of the caves
Dripping, dripping down on cold earth
A grave of stone, solid, full of forever
Yes, mourning is darker still
And death even darker

Varesh Gorabi, Grade 8
Salt Lake Center for Science Education, UT

Does Anyone Know?

There is a girl who walks these streets
Her eyes are filled with sorrow so deep
Her past has plenty of despair
From it you will see a lot of pain and misery.
The past shows her parents leaving her at birth
No one cares or loves her or thinks of what she is worth
She is capable of more than they could ever know
She sits and watches everything like a crow
In the winter as she sits alone in the snow
Her lightened skin and darkened hair
Glisten mournfully in the pale blue sky
As she walks unnoticed through this unknown town
One might ask, "Does anyone know?"

Alysa Prather, Grade 9
Plevna High School, MT

Just a Little Happiness Can Make a Better World

All I want is someone to be happy
Someone to think only positive thoughts,

All I want is someone to be happy
Someone to laugh or giggle every day
Someone to smile every part of their day,

All I want is someone to be happy
Someone to always love life
Someone to always be proud of themselves
Someone to have wonderful memories,

All I want is someone to be happy
Someone to not be afraid to express themselves
Someone to feel safe and to have peace in life
Someone to relax and stay calm
Someone to be glad they were born and are alive

All I want is a happy, peaceful world of people.

Kitana Piansiaksone, Grade 7
Falcon Creek Middle School, CO

Slow, Silent Snow

Snowflakes land softly on the ground.
I stick out my tongue to catch the frozen water droplets.
White specks float through the air.
The snow is silent and slow.
The frozen ground is imprinted upon by footsteps.
The sky grows darker and darker and yet the snow continues to fall.
Snowflakes jump from the clouds and are caught by the black sky.
I study a smidgen of white that is like an intricate design.
More flakes descend from above.
Frozen vapor slides down a dreary backdrop.
The cozy fluff that covers the land blankets my being.
Chill continues to flow from the sky to the pavement.
The deepening dark of the night continues as angels cry.
One night of winter passes away under the stars.

Katherine Johnson, Grade 9
Monarch High School, CO

Ode to Music

O', music, you bring joy to me and the world.
With different kinds of you.
Rock, classical, country, hip hop.
You calm people down and sometimes even make them upbeat.
Some people say you are just rhythm or even just words,
but to me, you're everything.
Your upbeat pace, your calm soothing rhythm,
your clever words.
Considered annoying and unnecessary
by some, some think you are critical for living.
The sun shines.
The bells ring.
You bring warmth, comfort, and love.

Jordan Yarak, Grade 7
Rolling Hills Country Day School, CA

Light Source

Silent, still, quiet, ominous.
Bright, loud, teaming with life.
One day.
One night.
One happy.
One sad.
They both have one thing in common.

Light.
Silver and glowing or bright and golden.
The sun and the moon.
Both sources of light.
Both connected.
Both filled with questions.

Does one spark romance?
Does one make a person happy?
Is one meant for sorrow and pain, the other happiness and joy?
Is that their true intent?
Is one good and one evil?
It's up to you to decide.

Christena Smith, Grade 8
Vista Heights Middle School, UT

That Is My Dream

Splash,
splash,
splash,
the swimmers are in rhythm
silence
they are in the flip, turn, and push off
splash,
splash,
hollers and cheers from teammates
as the rhythm quickens
in the last stretch
and then cries of success
swimmers wiping water from their eyes
tingling limbs just on the brink of exhaustion
that is my dream

Alexis Russell, Grade 7
White Pine Middle School, UT

The Sensation of Speed

Speed oh speed, how I love you so.
You throw me about then leave me lying in the snow!
When you throw me back then forward again,
My love for you grows again and again.
The sense of speed is loathed by some
But to me you're as good as a motor's hum.
Oh give me more, I can never have enough.
Your feeling is matched by no one.
Speed oh speed, how I love you so.
You throw me about then leave me lying in the snow!

Michael Ekstrom, Grade 7
Mountain Ridge Jr High School, UT

The Championship

I listen to the sound of the basketball bouncing down the court
Bang, Bang, Bang, Bang
It mimics the beat of my racing heart
The score is tied and we have never worked so hard in our lives
The crowd is screaming their heads off
Cheering for their favorite team
But as our center takes a shot
The crowd falls silent, holding their breath
The ball floats through space
Hurtling towards the basket
And the shot is made
There are thirty seconds left on the clock
And we are winning by two points
We continue to fight
Our opponent throws in the ball
But we won't let them pass half-court
We steal the ball
And shoot
The buzzer goes off, my heart skips a beat
The basket is made
We did it, we did it, our team won the championship

Nicole Mason, Grade 8
Sts Peter and Paul Catholic School, CO

Get Back Up

When you fall, it's tough to get back up
Find your footing, use your strength
And then you just get knocked back down
With barely enough energy to blink
Your hands come out in front of you
And you push off until you're on your feet
Now it's just a matter of bracing yourself for the next blow
And people are starting to wonder why you're still trying
Because it's obvious you're not going to win
But it's a matter of finding your limits and yourself
Someone gives you a shove
And you find out what you're made of
Who we are is not defined by how we act when everything is okay
Who we are is defined by challenges and obstacles
What sets us apart, is how many times we're willing to get back up
Even if it's tough to get back up after you fall

Sarah Scott, Grade 9
La Reina High School, CA

Best Friends

Best friends are meant to be
No matter what happens they are always by your side
When you are sad they make you smile
When you are in trouble they help you out
When you start crying they say, "Those are tears of joy"
No matter if you cry, laugh, smile
They are always on your side
That's what best friends are for
That describes my best friend

Jessica Juarez, Grade 7
Meridian Elementary School, CA

Music, a River

Music is a river
its rippling sound echoing.
Listen to its gentle waves.

Waterfalls of music
cascade into
a stream leading
to your future.

Decide your path,
and know that
your choice
is right.

Listen to the music,
but don't let
them decide
which path to take.

When you are the one taking it.
Tu-Khuyen Nguyen, Grade 8
Falcon Creek Middle School, CO

The Sea Horse

A small, shy figure,
Avoiding confrontation,
With unwanted foes.

A colorful, spotted being,
Blending in with its surroundings.

Happy and unnoticed,
Moving through its habitat,
With grace and elegance.

A marvel in life,
Crowned with colors,
A fantastic creature.

Outwitting opponents,
Fighting with camouflage and wits.

An underwater majesty,
Living as an unrecognized masterpiece.
Scott Fordham, Grade 8
Chandler School, CA

Believe

Heaven's got a plan for you
So don't worry if something goes wrong
Obstacles will always stand in your way
Because in the end
You will succeed
Kate Solis, Grade 8
Young Scholar's Academy, AZ

Lost Necklace

The necklace was a present from a boy.
I felt like a child with a new toy.
I was so grateful,
I could scream for joy.

When I wore it I felt bold.
I didn't care if it was new or old.
I felt as if power was within my grasp.
Without it I felt so cold.

Lost it at a movie about true love.
There were dark skies above,
I was eaten up by sadness.
I felt like wings without its dove.

I thought I would go mad,
I was so sad.
Darkness came upon me,
But was calmed down by my dad.
Leslie Santos, Grade 8
John Adams Middle School, CA

In the Shadows

He lurks in the shadows
Day and night.
But he can't get you,
Unless you're tucked in tight.
Watch your children
Or save yourselves,
Because he watches all
So don't fall fast asleep.

He's pretty ugly,
Do not be alarmed,
He will not hurt you
If you're not armed.

But that's all wrong,
He'll hunt you down.
With a Bang! You'll be taken out,
When he comes along
In the shadows.
Cassie Barnett, Grade 7
Joe Walker Middle School, CA

True Friends

true friends are always there for you,
not talking behind your back,
or loving you one second,
and hating you the next,
so when you choose your friends,
choose them carefully,
because once you find a true friend,
you will truly be happy.
Izabela Anna Kudasik, Grade 7
Salida Middle School, CO

Summer Blaze

The sun's so bright
Have to use lots of fans
Go to the beach to fly my kite
Get to make my own plans

Every day put on sunscreen
Flowers are blooming
Don't have to stay on a routine
Don't have to do any more brooming

Freedom from school
Get to do lots of sleeping
Go have fun in the pool
No more waking up to beeping

Get to go on vacations
Go hang out with lots of friends
Get to use my imagination
Oh, why does summer have to end
Ciena Steinbeck, Grade 7
St Martin-in-the-Fields School, CA

The Man Who Wrote That Book

Honest, so brutally true
You learn something new every day
People come and people go
But the lessons are here to stay

This wisdom is not heavenly
His words are a relic
It's what we're needed to know
To see everything's not so angelic

You're given a new pair of eyes
A new world to hear
For the things that you once knew
Was nothing, but your fear

So here comes a new day
For everything is so new
I look down and turn the page
So I can learn more from you
Alaya Hubbard, Grade 9
Turlock High School, CA

Winter Snow

Down in the winter snow
Is where we stand
Making snow angels
In the fluffy white sand
Snowball fights and snowmen
When we're done there we stand
In the fluffy white sand
Hand in hand
Nina Leal, Grade 8
Meridian Elementary School, CA

Football

As the ball is snapped
The line surges forward
A fight of the strong

The game has started
The outcomes are unknown
It comes down to heart

As the game endures
The victor starts to show
The strong over weak

The coach knows his men
He knows their strengths and flaws
As all coaches should

He knows what to do
Slowly and steadily
The team bounces back

The team knows they must
They start to pull ahead
Their confidence returns

The final buzzer
It signals the game's end
And the team has won
Seraphim Therianos, Grade 9
Pine Creek High School, CO

An Ordinary Onion

Allium cepa
An ordinary onion
Yet mystical up close

Each layer
Its own world
Intricately inextricably intertwined

The nuclei
Little black dots
Controlling our every movement

Eyeballs looking
Observing the world
What do they see?

Peering into
Our daily lives
Silent and sneaky

Allium cepa
An ordinary onion
A surreptitious spy
Calyx Liu, Grade 8
The Mirman School, CA

Maize Maze

We are lost, dizzy
Hearts beating in our ears like music
The glow sticks on our chests
Dancing to the beat
Of our scared feet
I see him
His mask white as snow
Holes like a dark night
He revs the chain-saw engine
"RUNNNNNNN"
It yells at us
We freak and flee
Everything dark as coal
We cannot see
Then as if magic we are out and
FREE
Kelsey Criswell, Grade 8
Weldon Valley Jr High School, CO

Gone

Saras, Bills, Joes, and Emmas
Names of humans gone
Forever.
But.
6 billion, 6.5, 7 billion people
Every day
More and more.

Majorcan Hares, Syrian Elephants,
Red Gazelles, and Barbary Lions
Names of species gone
Forever.
And.
They are never
Ever
Coming back.
Nithika Arunkumar, Grade 9
Saratoga High School, CA

Brooklyn Sidewalks

She walks invisibly
through the Brooklyn sidewalks
looking at the buildings
wondering
why she's here
why she was made
why she looks the way she does
why she laughs the way she does
the way she feels insecure
almost scared to look at her reflection
but, she'll find her purpose one day
and someone to love her so
she just needs a little faith
in the Brooklyn sidewalks
Mikayla Kvislen, Grade 7
Daniel Savage Middle School, CA

World Series

Derek Jeter,
Up to bat,
Crowded around,
The TV,
Everyone's staring,
Silently,
Runner on third,
Jeter cracks it,
Base knock,
Runner scores,
Everyone roars,
Tonight,
We sleep proud,
Of the,
Yankees
Tracy Wheeler, Grade 9
New Plymouth High School, ID

Ode to Ocean

The wind and gust blew
And brought chilly waves
Up the sandy shore
When you feel like relaxing
Staring at the crashing waves
And the blazing sun at you
It makes you peaceful
Yawing with joy
The warm soft sand
Surrounds your hand
Under the warm land
As the waves crash
I get a rash
And then goes
The waves splash
Antony Lan, Grade 8
South Lake Middle School, CA

Winter

On the ice
I'm like a newborn deer,
slipping and falling in the frosty cold

In the snow
I'm like a little white mouse,
Building a home in the fluffy powder

By a fire
I'm like a squirrel,
curious and energetic

In my bed
I'm a little boy,
As warm and content as can be.
Matthew Luthy, Grade 7
White Pine Middle School, UT

I Am Me

What is wrong with being me?
For me to change is
like for you to change.
You can't judge me because of
your opinion. The world is very
opinionated, what makes you special?
I may be loud and impatient,
but you are serious and brutal.
You and I are merely a bug
on this small planet, so
what if one of it changes?
I will decide whether or not to
change. So best if the
greatest, most powerful creator
named God tells you the
best of all the uniqueness
in all of us.

Anas Ullah, Grade 7
Sarah McGarvin Intermediate School, CA

Thanksgiving Day

We prepare the food:
Turkey and ham,
Mashed potatoes and gravy,
Then the yams,
On Thanksgiving Day.

We sit together,
At the dining table,
were the turkey is displayed,
The delicious aroma in the air,
On Thanksgiving Day.

Next we all pray,
All the food displayed,
We eat like pigs,
As we all dig in,
On Thanksgiving Day.

David Castillo, Grade 8
Joe Walker Middle School, CA

Winter

The snowflakes fall
softly down
landing on my rosy cheeks.
I close my eyes
and take a breath
listening to the peaceful earth.
I slowly fall
into the powder
and feel the hot tears on my cheeks.
I now understand
how it feels
to lose the one you love the most.

Jenny Lucke, Grade 9
Monarch High School, CO

Tree

I am a tree
Branches extended,
I embrace and shelter friends and family, and welcome many

My branches provide a safe haven
When my siblings are in need, they come to me
I have refuge and security in my strong branches

I am rooted in many ways: athletics, family, academics
I am constantly seeking nutrition
Breaking through rocks to find new experiences and knowledge

Brutal storms of insults and self-doubt
Will sway and bend my branches to their limits,
But I will never break; my trunk has built me solid and stable

My bark shows my scars and scrapes
From times of hardship; but that is just my splintered, rough outer shell
Inside, my wood gleams smooth and sleek, shining its inner beauty

Branches reaching to new heights, growing taller, wiser
Stretching towards the sun
Seeking both nutrients and memories to come

Scarred but beautiful, strong and safe,
Solid but gentle,
I am a tree

Josie Johnson, Grade 7
Sagewood Middle School, CO

Anthem for the FIFA World Cup

A celebration to honor the reigning king, the ruler of all latter-day sports
In homage to this quadrennial blessing
The soldier sheaths his bloody weapon; the despondent seeks another sunrise
Zealous fans pour in from near and far
To witness a celebration of the globe's finest footballers
They pack full the stadium tier by tier, countries connecting for a common cause
The stands are a sea of red and yellow as fans wave their flags back and forth

A striker braces to boot the ball hearing the perpetual buzz, buzz of vuvuzelas
He inhales and exhales, focusing on his form
Knowing he has practiced this kick a billion times
Wham! Silence settles suddenly in the arena
Restless supporters emanate nervous energy, teetering upon the edge of their chairs
A blanket of tension falls over the spectators
Not a trace of oxygen is left in the air as one and all hold their breath — together

The ball is a black and white bullet shooting across the field like a meteor
Number 7 leaps upward, his forehead connecting with the ball
Swish! The projectile locates its target, slamming into the back of the goal
Olé, olé! Spectators roar like proud lions for the "victory heard 'round the world"
Red and yellow confetti pours down like a cleansing rain
Over a planet now more united and unified
This is the FIFA World Cup

Maya Flannery, Grade 9
The Mirman School, CA

Lying Lips

Beating.
My heart is beating in its boney cage.
But it beats in fear,
fear of the lacerations of spite,
the arrows of ice that are malicious hate.
Its shield are my lips…my cold, lying lips.
No emotion.
No pain.
You cannot feel what you ward away.
Lying lips.
Door to the cage of my heart.
It is a sin to lie.
But suicide is also a sin.
So tell me: which is the greater evil?
To lock away emotion,
To not say what you feel;
Or to willingly bleed,
To kneel before the ravening wolves.
Are you okay?
Yes. Fine.
No one wants to hear my lying, lying lips.
                Bailey Collins, Grade 9
                C M Russell High School, MT

The Masters of the World

He enters quietly
Eagerly waiting
His fingers out stretched
Hide the light
His breath blowing
Cools the warmth
He comes silently
Eagerly waiting
For the shadows to be complete
For the world to be
His, the Darkness
Just as quickly
She walks in
Eagerly waiting
Her hands pushing
Weakens the darkness
Her breath blowing
Warms the cold
She waits happily for the world
To be hers again, Light
                Yasaman Lorkalantari, Grade 7
                South Lake Middle School, CA

Billy and His Voices

Many voices, high and low, Billy would use.
His teacher thought language he did abuse.
One day Billy growled
And then he howled.
Then to Billy's delight he made the news.
                Michael Tennis, Grade 7
                Beacon Country Day School, CO

My Room

Baby blue walls, fish tank, a comfy bed
A laptop filled with memories of the past
The smell of Victoria's Secret perfume and dirty volleyball clothes on the ground
My fish, swimming around their fish tank freely
There I do my homework and read my magazines about One Direction
The sun peeks through my colorful curtains
It transforms my room into a peaceful heaven
This room is love and beautiful and perfect for me
                Alejandra Gutierrez, Grade 8
                Ripona Elementary School, CA

God

God, who or what is God
God is a special being that gives us hope, wonder, and happiness.
God helps us overcome our fears and passed loved ones.
God also gave us the happiness and the wonder of earth and all its glories
Life
                Hilario Zavala, Grade 7
                Meridian Elementary School, CA

Gabrielle

fun, bright, full of delight
daughter of Ralph and Tonya Torres
lover of
music, world's greatest discovery,
who feels happy, sad
and sometimes
mad
who fears
being home alone
in the darkest hour of
the night
who would like to see
a change in the world like
world peace and a change
in me
resident of
Modesto, California, USA
on the planet Earth and in
the Milky Way Galaxy
Torres
                Gabrielle Torres, Grade 7
                Daniel Savage Middle School, CA

Star in the Sky

the star in the sky
way up high
calls me every night
It shines so brightly
but don't take it lightly
cause that is
when the fighting
ends
                Alex Tran, Grade 7
                Sarah McGarvin Intermediate School, CA

On The Ice

An ice rink
A peaceful sanctuary
An environment
Where I don't have to think
My mind roaming freely

My feet effortlessly working
Gliding gracefully across the ice
With speed I swiftly do a three turn
Landing a salchow
Stunning

I lift my left leg high into the air
Perfecting an arabesque
Magnificent

Relaxed.
Joyful.
Happy.
Welcome to my world.
                Amy Wong, Grade 7
                Carmel Valley Middle School, CA

Just Believe

Roses are red
Violets are blue
Dreams do come true
Just be you
If it doesn't
Don't be blue
Try again
And you'll be new
                Amy Dang, Grade 7
                Sarah McGarvin Intermediate School, CA

Rainbows...

They're there, magnificent and mocking.
What do they mean?
They hold a promise of illusion,
The trick of the eye, the mind's delusion.
"I'll keep these colors for you," it says,
Then it fades, leaving behind the lingering empty promise.
The promise that keeps you walking forever.
Walk, dear friend, walk and search,
Search fruitlessly for the pot of gold that ceases to exist.
Some seem to last longer,
Others, disappearing as fast as they appear.
They give you something to hope in,
Then shatter it with a silent goodbye.
In the darkest hours you won't find them,
But they're there after the storm
As if they were taunting your hardships
Oh—this reminds me.
Isn't friendship just as fake as a rainbow?

Hien Phan, Grade 7
Sarah McGarvin Intermediate School, CA

Much More Than Brother

You're my big brother and I love you so much,
Your punches and wrestling are your affectionate touch.
One brother with five girls in our big family,
This makes you unique and special to me.
You have a bigger heart than anyone I know,
And that makes me so happy to call you my bro.
Now that I am older I can surely see,
That you are much more than a brother to me.
You're my pal, my secret holder, my role model, and my best friend,
And I hope our close-knit relationship will never end.
I love the laughs we've had and the things we have done.
I love your smile, your personality, and you are second to none.
I always enjoy when I get to see you.
The years we lived at home together, time flew.
I love all the moments and memories we share.
A brother like you is definitely rare.
I just want to thank you for impacting my life in such a positive way,
And I thank God for you every time I pray.

Jennifer Wirth, Grade 8
Christ the King School, AZ

The World Within a Child's Hand

In a child's hand
I see lots of adventures and room to learn,
Making memories with the people who are there;
making mistakes and learning from them,
Doing things you're not supposed to,
Hearing old stories from your elders,
Playing outside,
Getting dirty and then washing it all away.
If only we could be like this forever.
All of these things I see in the world within a child's hand.

Evan Hevle, Grade 7
Tenaya Middle School, CA

Someone to Love

All I want is someone to love.
Someone to be concerned about my feelings.
All I want is someone to love.
Someone to love me, for me.
Someone to say, "I love you," without
regretting it.
All I want is someone to love.
Someone to have manners.
Someone to say, "You're the only thing
that's on my mind."
All I want is someone to love.
Someone who would do anything for me.
Someone to be just, plain, charming.
Someone who is not afraid to tell the
truth, no matter what.
Someone to be romantic in every
way he can.
All I want is someone to love.

Mikala Nguyen, Grade 7
Falcon Creek Middle School, CO

I Am Me

Clean, crisp...
Fresh, untouched,
Waiting for my heart to spill its contents.
Its simpleness beckons me.
Once again, this infinite world has begun again,
The key turned in the lock,
The skies have opened.
Here come the soft rains of tear drops.
Each a rainstorm upon the waiting page.
The pen glides,
Across the white expanse like a dove soaring.
An eagle.
A lion.
Peaceful, strong, fearless.
I am these three.
All at once, and not at all.
I am free.
I am me.

Olivia Deveau, Grade 9
La Reina High School, CA

Niente e Vero, Tutto e Permesso

Nothing is true, everything is permitted.
Quite a bold statement to the common man.
It sends chills down the back of your neck.

It means, what we know can change humanity,
That we are the architects of our own lives,
And we choose how to direct it.
Just be careful with what you know.

Nothing is true, everything is permitted.

Chris Boggs, Grade 8
Young Scholar's Academy, AZ

Life, Earth, and My Oatmeal

Pretty little butterfly
Swift, beautiful, and full of glee.
Incredible big sky
Blue, huge, and full of trees.
Small little me
Impractical, unimaginable, and full of dreams.

Flying around, a fly.
Walking around, a hound.
Leisurely around the park.

Complicated, unpredictable, extraordinary
Life.
Large, simple, healthy
Nature.
Unstoppable, self-destructive, constructive
Earth.

All around us.
Under our beds.
In our hair.

Melanie Jarbeau, Grade 8
Joe Walker Middle School, CA

The Unknown

My heart hurts and its burning my chest
The Ambassador of pain has my heart under arrest,
Under control, did he also take my soul?
Your heart is supposed to be a whole
And your soul holds the deepest feelings within,
All I feel is pain and restlessness
Right now I'm going down Stress Rd. not knowing which way to go
There's him, they, she, he, but ME is all I need to worry about
I'm trying not to be filled with doubt
UH! I wish I could take another route
But for now, I'm going down here
The road where most people disappear
I wish I could close my eyes and see my life crystal clear
but
Have no fear, sooner or later I'll get outta here

Jane't Cooksie, Grade 9
Will C Wood High School, CA

Blue

Blue is the soft sky, shining upon the grass
Blue is the clam wind, whispering through the night
Blue is the cold ice, breaking in the pond
Blue are the ocean's waves, hitting the sand
Blue is the boy, running through the park
Blue is the ocean, flowing all around the world
Blue is the dream, passing through my head
Blue is the vein, helping my brain
Blue is the calm balloon, floating at noon
Blue is the universe, surrounding me

Francisco Saracho, Grade 7
St John's Episcopal School, CA

Yellow

Yellow is the color of happiness, and cheer.
It is the color that sparks a light bulb,
generating a new invention.
Yellow is the color of lions' fur, roaring in all directions.
It is the lightning that strikes in a storm,
like a predator that strikes its prey.
It is the smooth caramel that flows down your ice cream,
like a river flowing down a mountain.
Yellow is a primary color,
blending with others to create anew.
It is the streak of light,
that makes a sunset true.
Yellow is the color of honey,
pollinated from the buzz of bees.
Yellow is the color of ice-cold lemonade,
that chills you on a dreadfully hot summer day.
It is the smile that permeates you face with bliss,
Yellow is and will always be the light
that guides you and your journey in life.
It is the spark of hope that will never befriend you.

Nandu Vudumula, Grade 7
Gale Ranch Middle School, CA

Lovely and Beautiful

I am lovely and beautiful
I wonder if my color is deep and soft
I hear the breeze whistle
I see a bee's wings
I want to bloom forever
I am lovely and beautiful

I pretend I don't have thorns
I feel the warm sunrise
I touch the Earth with my long stem
I worry someone will pick me
I cry when winter comes
I am lovely and beautiful

I understand seasons have to change
I say nothing when dew drops roll off my petals
I dream about the fresh air
I try to soak up the sun's light
I hope the sun will always come
I am lovely and beautiful

Ivy Nickles, Grade 7
Falcon Creek Middle School, CO

What Is Love?

Yesterday I woke up with a hole in my heart,
Today I opened my eyes and saw through the dark.
Yesterday I had every reason to cry,
Today I'm sitting here and wondering why.
Yesterday I didn't know what love meant,
Today I'd say it's Heaven sent.

Mykal-Ann Gomez, Grade 9
Colorado Connections Academy, CO

Leaves Fall Like Tears Across the Sky...

Thy season of fall comes near,
To recognize all of the skeptical, sympathetic tears,
As leaves fall from the distant sky, with a tree sparkling in orange light,
A tear is shed about the relationships and unfortunate heartbreaking events,
I walk amongst the autumn, view of the cascading leaves in the sky,
Whilst I crush the leaves, that have fallen, and sigh.
For every crushed leaf, lays a instant thought of a misfortunate event.
For each leaf fallen, lays the thought of the hourglass, as the universe provides a precious surprise.
For the hoping and happiness every family shares,
Alas, we know not of the pinpointed time of the end of those years,
For all misfortunate events that we emotionally share,
Each day a heart will be torn.
Contradictions and doubtful thoughts don't revoke nature's reality.
The presence of accurate events will always bestow.
Those emotional times, will never outgrow.
The loss of our loved ones, is outgrown with the seasonal delusions, and beauty of the bestowed events.
But own the thought, for every leaf that seeps through the sky, giving it's formal appreciative goodbye,
A new leaf will grow, with past symphony that will stand by.
Winds, shiver, a holiday and snow come as fall's primary conclusion,
As winter approaches cautiously, without her proper collusion.
Whilst, and truthfully, alas, leaves fall like tears across the sky...

Zyyad Roache, Grade 8
Julian Charter School, CA

The Colors of Autumn

Red, yellow, orange, brown, and a wave of green.
These are the colors of autumn, they affect us in different ways like our emotions.
They bring upon a mood change, that everyone seems to appreciate with gratitude.
The change is slow, but soon slaps you in the face with the sudden rush of chill in the daytime.
The flow of leaves that cross your path, overwhelm you with the caress of former memories.
These memories bring you back to a happier time, where your worries seem to melt away from you.
All of your loved ones flood in, ready to bring you joy and peace.
No one can bring you down, you are untouchable by the evil that lies within your day.
The kindness of others protects you, like a shield protects a knight in shining armor.
The colors of autumn once again bring a nicer, calmness to everyone it affects.

Chelsey Carns, Grade 8
Palm Desert Charter Middle School, CA

My 'Not So Empty' Canvas

My dirty water color pallet lay on the floor next to a evenly folded napkin.
My only brush has bristles falling to the floor when you glide it across the air.
My cup of water is filled halfway with some tap water, tainted from the previous use of dark colors.
My canvas, empty.
I take my bubble gum pink nails over my brush and snatch it.
I close my eyes and take a breath.
Crossing my legs on my rug, I dip the frizzy brush to some water, and then a dirty color.
Vivid flowers, baby blue rivers, and fluffy white clouds.
All come together to make a beautiful landscape, the opposite of what I was creating.
The strokes of color on the canvas would occasionally fly off and land on my rug.
A tree in the sky and a bird on the floor; making an opposite world.
Different and unusual colors fill my empty white space.
When I'm done, I wipe my forehead on my sleeve and take pride in my work.
My imagination is now in front of me; breathtaking.
No one can tell me otherwise.

Alesik Valdez, Grade 8
Palm Desert Charter Middle School, CA

Dance Is Like

Dance is a way to express yourself through movement
A way to share your story and inspire others
A way to let out your built up emotions
A way to let your worries go

Dance helps you let out emotions
And the audience is like your therapist
They just sit there: sit, sit
Listening and watching the magic ahead

Dance can be a jumbled mess
The routine can be too confusing
The audience may not understand
But the dancer understands

Dance will always be in my life
It helps me relax
And sometimes makes me even more mad
Technique builds up, but emotion is a day to day thing

No matter who you are, you can dance
Just get up and move how you feel

Dance is like life, it exists as you move through
To me dance is powerful, what is it to you?

Shayla Anderson, Grade 9
University Preparatory School, CA

Music

Music. It has a rhythm,
It has a beat. It has a
Beauty, you can't defeat.

Music has lyrics.
The lyrics can speak of love or happiness.
They may even speak of reality or loneliness.

Music can be expressed in many ways.
Singing or dancing. Even by acting.

There are many genres
Of music. Reggae, jazz, pop,
And classical. Each one is so
Magical!

How can you listen to music?
You can listen from your iPod,
Your phone, a cassette, or a
Radio.

Music is such a beautiful
Way to express yourself.
It will always have a place
In my heart.

Angelina Porras, Grade 8
St Helen Catholic School, CA

She Wishes She Stayed

She wishes she stayed with you
Comforted you, loved you, told you stories like you would do
Seeing you in pain
Brought sorrow and pain into her heart
Desire to help you pull through
Crying tears you would be ashamed of her for crying
Tears stained her shirt, her face streaked red
What could she have done to help
You laying there coughing, heaving, gasping for air
Shutting your eyes waiting for a white light
To take you to your new destination
A destination your daughter would never choose for you
Wanting to be your angel not being able to
Her seeing your lifeless body made her go numb
She wished she could still hug you, receive your Eskimo kisses
Hear your rusty ol' voice that would sing her to sleep at night
Smell the whiskey and coffee on your breath one last time
2-step with her tiny feet on your boots
One last time to see her daddy in his prime
She wishes she stayed with you

Cherokee Leppert, Grade 9
New Plymouth High School, ID

Soccer Ball

I bought you in May,
Played with you every day,
Until I kicked you up, up, and away,
I haven't seen you since that day.

You went round and round like a wheel,
And you were softer than a baby's meal,
You were gray as steel,
But not as big as Shaquille O'Neal.

If I sat on you, I would hurt you,
I didn't want to hurt you, because I had one soccer ball, not two,
If I did you were going to get a bump,
So instead of rolling you would jump.

To me you were like a brother,
Even though we didn't have the same mother,
You were my favorite toy and I won't trade you for another,
You left me and didn't bother, to say goodbye.

Alex Delgado, Grade 8
John Adams Middle School, CA

My Dear Love

Let us shovel our way to happiness.
Let me destroy this debt.
Let us die in piece and happiness.
Let me protect you and our children.
Let my fist thicken when they threaten you.
Let me give you a chance to move on when I die.
Please. Please. Let me die with a clear conscience when I die.

Herbert L. Scott, Grade 7
Salida Middle School, CO

Love Is Life

Love is life
And life does hurt
When you like someone
They leave you alert

Love is like music to me
It can be quiet or loud
It can try to warn you
Or make you proud

Your heart does not lie
But your mind tries to trick you
Don't fall into the trap
Follow what you want to do

Love can hurt
Or turn out great
But when it comes to love for me
I don't try to hesitate

Sharmin Raza, Grade 8
Orville Wright Middle School, CA

Gymnastics

Beam:
Flip, jump, turn on beam
16 feet and 4 inches
What fun is the beam

Bars:
Flying flying high
The bars make you touch the sky
Land it with a stick

Floor:
Tumbling is the best
Dance and jumps are fun also
Harder every day

Vault:
Running running run
Hit the board with a hard jump
You got a good score

Leah Hamilton, Grade 7
Monte Vista Christian School, CA

Love

Love runs deep
So deep
You don't know
When to stop
That you would do anything
Say anything
To make that person happy

Channel Bryant, Grade 8
Meridian Elementary School, CA

The Sad Days of World War 1

In the year of 1914 the days of World War 1 had just begun.
The cold days of winter made the trials last longer and harder.
It was mostly the beginning, but for those who died it was the end.

I was in the mines that our army had just made.
We could hear the tanks swaying back and forth.
That's when I heard the first cry of attack
and the captains screaming get back get back.
I was running from the scene and trying to get away
that's when I started to get on my knees and pray.

Then I felt the surge to get back on my feet and join my troop.
I knew that if I stopped trying nothing would be possible.
I grabbed my gun and I went to find my friend who was on the ground.
I helped him get back onto his feet though his feet were still shaking.
He had blood dripping from his lip and had a cut on his arm,
but he held strong and so did I.

There were countless of us fighting, but we did it for the ones we loved.
I knew our God was watching from above,
For our Nation had won
and every man and woman had won too!

Adam Rookstool, Grade 7
Mountain Ridge Jr High School, UT

Star Test

Everyone in school and I
Are finishing eighth grade without a black eye.
We aren't trying just to get by,
And Star Test is coming faster than you could spell Mediterranean fruit fly.
I can't just wait for it to show up at the front door like a bad guy.
I'm studying all day and all night.
My room is so messy it looks like a bomb site.
My head hurts so much it might blow out tonight.
Reading so much I can only see black and white.
"I'm going to fly through this test at the speed of light!"
Star Test is as long as a light year.
Feels like I'm in the Final Frontier.
I'm hanging from a string like a chandelier,
But all my work seems to reappear
In my mind like a volunteer
Without fear.
When I get home I parade around.
Eighth grade has just boiled down
To a piece of ground
In my past like a burial mound,
And now I can slow down.

Adam Boney, Grade 9
San Diego High School of International Studies, CA

Christmas Morning

The crisp smell of cookies and hot chocolate in the air, wakes me up with a pleasant smile.
Surrounded by family, opening gifts, laughing, everyone is happy.
Christmas morning, who would have known, it would be my happiest memory.

Kailani Lucas, Grade 7
St. Francis School, CA

Death

I ponder the idea and word at times
Tentatively wondering about it
Up and into my head the idea climbs
Reality frightens me, I must admit

I push it away for the fear of truth
Scary, dark and patient, it will persist
It's been waiting since your innocent youth
Always lurking, waiting to coexist

Living within you the day your time comes
Nothing to fear, nothing left to live for
That peaceful point in life when life succumbs
Sinking, deep in sleep, ending the cold war

When your time is expired, you won't fear
You'll face reality with a grateful cheer
Henry Harris, Grade 9
Monarch High School, CO

Bright

I wish I could find my place in this world,
Because for now I know that it's not here.
My wishes and dreams have been since curled,
I want to conquer the Earth and this fear.

Life is full and beautiful, so live!
Take your time for time itself is needed.
Be kind, be patient, and let yourself give.
That's what they tell me, my mind is seeded.

I should feel young, happy, completely free.
Groping around blindly, needing the light,
World, open my eyes and let me see!
Folding in, closing the gap out of fright.

And yet, through the dark I can see a glow.
Down this new road, this rocky path, I go.
Ali Harford, Grade 9
Monarch High School, CO

Christmas

Sitting by the fire
Drinking hot chocolate
Singing Christmas carols
Laughing and playing in the snow
Wrapping gifts, opening gifts
Decorating trees with amazing ornaments
Putting green and red lights around the house
Staying awake to witness Santa Claus
Celebrating Jesus' birth
Spending time with family
This is Christmas
Maryssa Agnes, Grade 7
Christ the King Catholic School, AZ

You

I was a fool to love you like I did.
I thought we would be together forever.
All you did was play around like a kid,
And all you ever said was "whatever."

I know you never really did love me.
The only thing you cared about was you.
Blind by your selfishness, you could not see,
Like a poor animal trapped in a zoo.

But I know that you have another side,
A side full of love that you never show.
But why don't you show it, all of that pride,
Because without it, you just fall so low?

I know things will work out some other day,
Even if that day is far, far away.
Mailys Steiblen, Grade 9
Monarch High School, CO

On the Inside

The pressure is building up around me.
This sweet, pretty, perfect little lady
That the other kids perceive me to be,
A role model to kids who are shady.

The clouds hover over my tender heart.
I put on a smile and be who I'm not.
I'm just like you; please give me a fresh start.
I'm fighting a fight that just can't be fought.

You will not hold me back any longer
For my personality will shine through.
I will be the real me, who is stronger.
I can be someone that nobody knew.

Now I'm myself; I'm feeling quite merry;
The typical me I can now bury.
Aspen Fabrizio, Grade 9
Monarch High School, CO

Lonely Heart

You were the missing piece to my loveless heart
I wish we had never grown apart
You were the stars to my endless night sky
A smile on my face suddenly appeared
It finally became vividly clear
I loved you and you loved me
Was this really meant to be?
I'm alone in the dark
Yet we are so far apart
I'd wish you'd let me back into your arms
But instead I was left with a broken heart
Joanna Morales, Grade 8
Sepulveda Middle School, CA

Home

That was the place.
The place of happiness and joy
A place I called home,
Tijuana

That was the place
Where I first rode my bike
Where I woke up every day to the smell of eggs
In the place I called kitchen

That was the place
Where I first learned to trace
From a channel I watched on Saturdays
On what was the best of my memories, my television.
In what I surely know was my living room

That was the place
Where I lived half of my life.
Desperately waiting I am
To go back to my home, Tijuana

Jesus Carreon, Grade 8
Richardson PREP HI Middle School, CA

Warrior

On the adobe rock
rests a painting.
That painting is of a
mighty Ute warrior.

The warrior tells his story
sitting on that rock.
The story of how he
became a man.

He fought bravely,
he led his troops,
He conquered thousands,
but the day he really became a man
was when he learned how to forgive.

He forgave his sisters.
He forgave his brothers.
He even forgave his enemies.
That is the story of the Ute warrior on the rock.

Sheven Andersen, Grade 8
Bear Lake Middle School, ID

Angry

Anger is black.
It sounds like rocket thrusters.
It smells like smoke.
It tastes like hot magma.
It looks like holes in the wall.
Anger feels like getting cut by a jagged, dull knife.

Ostin Jensen, Grade 7
White Pine Middle School, UT

My Grandma

My grandma,
always smiling and always happy.
Her laugh was contagious.
It made everyone happy.

Her smile lit up the room.
I never saw her sad.
Always giving, and never expecting anything back.

We needed more bonding time,
more storytelling time.
I was eight years old,
and I didn't understand.

My mom was crying,
tears ran down her face constantly,
but I only wondered why.

I wish I could go back in time,
and tell my grandma, once again, that I love her,
and that she means everything to me.

That day, I was expecting to see her.
But before I knew it, she was gone.
Completely gone.

Alondra Ackerman, Grade 8
St John's Episcopal School, CA

Light

It spreads everywhere at sunrise
And can only be murdered at night
It doesn't seem important
Unless it goes dormant

It overcomes the evils of the night
And it is faster than any flight
During the day a ball of fire embodies it
And at night it is a celestial body

Sight is the most pleasing sense
But can only be used when it is present
With only darkness the eye could not see
The world and its many breathtaking beauties

The smell of a cleome cannot compare
To the sight of a rainforest with water falling from the air
The sound of wind whispering to the waves
"Whoosh, whoosh"
Is nothing without the sight of the water's clear blue caves

It brings bliss to a bunny or human being
And provides warmth which keeps us breathing
Taking it away is like taking away air
It is something that you or I could never bear

Dharan Kumar, Grade 8
The Mirman School, CA

Ramblings Through Insanity

Stumbling through this desert land,
The bleeding plane had crashed.
Rummaging through a suitcase,
I'll be sorting with a gnash.

At first there are black plants,
Reminding me of berries,
Followed by a dress shirt,
Like whipped cream from a dairy.

Thirdly, a red bow tie,
Just like apple pie.
Then, a fitted bleach-blonde wig.
Please don't ask me why.

Next, brown leather shoes,
Reminding me of steak.
Afterwards, a Hawaiian shirt,
Colored like fruit cake.

I feel my sanity's slipping,
I really can't decide.
You'd better get me to a hospital;
I've gone by the wayside.

Darrius Estigoy, Grade 8
South Lake Middle School, CA

Mistake

I can't believe what I did,
Though I'd rather never say.
I feel like a selfish kid,
I won't go out and play.

Never once did I listen
To the other person there.
Then tears started to glisten,
Verbal fights are never fair.

We both wanted the same thing,
I would not, could not, give in.
Ev'ry mem'ry like a sting,
I've committed a great sin.

I'm in a permanent pout.
Until this awful mess ends.
I hope that things will work out,
That just maybe we'll be friends?

I pray this never happens
To me or you ever again.
I hope that some door opens,
And we'll get along again.

Emily DeBusschere, Grade 9
La Reina High School, CA

My Great Loss

I was in third grade on that April day,
When my favorite aunt passed away,
Don't cry over me when I'm gone,
Were the words she would always say.

When I heard the news I tried,
To contain my tears but I still cried,
I felt a big part of me was missing,
I wished my aunt was still by my side.

It was hard to deal with the pain I felt,
It was as if my heart had begun to melt,
But I had to get back up on my feet,
And do away with my face that was pale.

My aunt will be forever missed,
If she can hear me from wherever she is,
I want her to know that I love her,
And that I send her a big kiss.

Noe Martinon, Grade 8
John Adams Middle School, CA

Grandma

When everyone left me,
You stayed by my side.
You wiped away my tears,
And told me not to cry.

I had given up all hope,
But you told me not to quit.
You had so much faith in me,
You knew I'd get through it.

You saw the good in me,
That no one else could see.
It took you dying for me to realize,
How much I needed you in my life.

You are the only person I trust,
From here and beyond.
I believe in myself because,
You believed in me.

Heidi Castro, Grade 8
John Adams Middle School, CA

Ear Piercing

Sat in the chair.
Don't know what
To expect. Click.
Click. Earrings shot
Through my ear lobes.
It didn't even hurt.
I am so happy!

Emma Goulart, Grade 8
St Francis of Assisi Parish School, CA

Time Flies

It's Sunday,
I look out the window and see sun light,
I look again it's dark,
I go to sleep and wake the next morning,
Its time for school,
The weekend comes Saturday, Sunday,
I look out the window and see light
I look again it's dark,
Time is a hawk, flying, never stopping

Every day,
Every night,
Every second,
Every minute,
Every hour,
Forever.

Nicholas Arroyo, Grade 7
Monte Vista Christian School, CA

Writer's Block

Do you have writer's block?
I sure do.
Writer's Block,
Thinking about a dirty rock,
Or maybe even an old, ripped sock.
Don't know what to write,
Maybe about an old grey bike?
Do you have this problem?
Thinking about a possum?
Do you know what to write?
Maybe ask your uncle Mike.
Do you have writer's block?
I sure do.
Now thinking about a trip to the zoo.
Oh! Hey, look! I wrote. Writer's block?
Please, I sure don't.

Alicia Perez, Grade 8
Ogden Preparatory Academy, UT

Final Goodbye

A baby,
Born a day earlier, lies sleeping.
Dark flowers decorate her room.
Her parents sit at the foot of her bed.
They listen to the trees thrashing
And her soft snores.
They stare at her little scarlet head
And wish they could prepare her
For the fight that will soon be hers.
They watch as the light
Of the moon settles on her
Like beautiful feathers.
Kissing her head,
They say their final goodbyes.

London Feher, Grade 8
Mancos Middle School, CO

All I Want Is Something to Change

All I want is someone to take a stand
Someone to say, "No."

All I want is someone to take a stand
Someone to be honest
Someone to be brave

All I want is someone to take a stand
Someone to know that words can stab you
right in the heart
Someone to wipe the tears off their face
Someone just to listen

All I want is someone to take a stand
Someone to say, "You're not ugly, you're
beautiful."
Someone to know that society is a monster
Someone to hold them tight like a teddy bear
Someone to say "You're worth it"

All I want is bullying to stop

Orlie Suverza, Grade 7
Falcon Creek Middle School, CO

Trees Are Awesome!!!

Trees are awesome in their own ways.
A tree stand still
As firm and tall as the other trees around it.
It has red, yellow, and green leaves
Like the colors of a sleeve.
Its leaves fall as we sin.
As the wind blows slowly, the leaves fall
It falls with great sadness
No sun rises upon it, only darkness
What a dark and a cloudy sky.
If you hurt this tree, it shall wither more and more.
Then if you hurt it again, you shall hurt its core.
Unless with love,
You water that tree each and every day.
This tree will beautifully grow — outgrow decay.

Megan Khong, Grade 7
St Peter and Paul School, CO

The Day at the Park

The artist paints,
The author writes,
The birds fly higher than the kites,
The children play while the sun burns down,
On this beautiful day in the town,
The trees all sway while the children play,
Laughter fills the air,
And as I walk home that day I think to myself,
What a wonderful day I had today,
I wouldn't be anywhere else!

Trevor Watkins, Grade 7
Young Scholar's Academy, AZ

Finally Found

Pushed with eyes of hate and words of resent
There I was paralyzed on the cold, hard ground
Tears poured out of my doleful eyes
To make a puddle beneath my head
Trapped in a world of darkness
I lay there forced to stare at their pleasure
The pleasure I had once experienced with them
My body blue and purple from the coldness
My face red from tears
I screamed for help but no one cared to listen
The puddle I had noticed before
Had turned into a death trap
My death trap
Not realizing I was drowning in my own cries
I took another breath
But it was to late
I look down at those heartless fools
From this white, luminous world I am now apart of
A figure wraps her arms around my emotionless body
Right then I felt loved and cared for
A feeling I had forgotten

Amaya Frutkoff, Grade 8
California Virtual Academy, CA

Sheer Coverings

One blow.
That's all it takes,
Only one huff of breath, and
Everything is revealed.
Years and years of stillness denied,
After a single swipe,
Discoveries are made,
Not just new surprises,
But secrets of the past.
Some things are just meant to be unnoticed,
Kept hidden by a layer of time.
There is no turning back.
Time is the only thing that can erase one's mistakes.
Mistake is movement.
Movement is evidence.
Evidence is existence.

Kate Fischer, Grade 9
Pine Creek High School, CO

Homework

You're just a stack of paper
That piles on my desk
Held together by a stapler
You're the source of my distress
Through day and night you boggle my mind
The missing answer is what you make me find
The best word that defines you is just plain boring,
And after 5 seconds of seeing you...
Anyone can hear me snoring

Larry Lam, Grade 7
Sarah McGarvin Intermediate School, CA

When I Got a Note

When I got the note I felt suffocated!
My legs rattled.
I felt like crying even though that never works.

I felt sad,
Knowing that when I got home my mother would be mad.
She might even be furious.

I felt mad,
At my teacher who gave me the note,
But, as I thought, mostly at myself.

I know of kids
Who take that piece of paper as any other,
Whose parents care little to none, but I'm glad I have one who does.

When I told my mother,
She was furious, and shocked.
I've always been a good student

She was mad with me.
I could see it in her eyes,
And in the way she signed the paper.

Yet I am partially glad that I got that piece of paper,
Because it gave me something to write about.
Thank you, Mrs. Windsor (in a sarcastic and realistic way).
Anthony Guevara, Grade 7
St Helen Catholic School, CA

Magic in the Air

Magic in the air,
snow in the sky and children sledding.
Hot cocoa warming up their chilling bodies,
watching carolers sing songs and eat fruitcake.

Magic in the air,
deep in the snow.
Skiers and snowboarders rushing down
steep,
sleek,
slopes…
swish, swish, swish!

Magic in the air,
in the lights,
and the trees,
and in the laughing people,
accompanied by the chill of a cold winter day.

Magic in the air,
can you feel it?
The love, the joy, the fun
all the things that make winter great!
Melody Ornelas, Grade 8
The Connect Charter School, CO

Fantasy

What if I was in the Hunger Games?
I would be a killing machine!
What if I was a demigod?
I would fall in love with Percy Jackson.
What if I was number four?
Sertikus Ka better watch out.
What if I was a shadow hunter?
Monsters should stay away.
What if I was a victor?
I would have a lifetime of riches.
What if I were Poseidon?
I could walk on water and breathe underwater.
What if Lorien was destroyed?
There would be no point in fighting.
What if Jace died in the fire?
Clary wouldn't have a brother.
What is your fantasy?
Caitlin O'Donnell, Grade 7
Falcon Creek Middle School, CO

Forever to Go

I have all the miles in the world to walk,
Before I'm where I want to be.
I have every door to unlock,
Before I can finally say that I'm free.

I have so much happiness to pursue,
Before I can settle down and stay.
I have too much work to do,
Before I can call it a day.

I have every mountain to climb,
Before I can see what I want to see.
I don't have any time
To stop and smell a rosie.

I have forever to go
Before I end the journey that I now undergo
Ian Scott, Grade 9
Monarch High School, CO

The Portal

You're in the womb all warm and cozy,
hoping to never come out, the nurses so nosey.
You twist and turn all raveled up in a ball,
nothing can get better, nothing at all.
You hear a voice, your mom vibrates in your ears,
you can barely hear it so quiet and so queer.
As they tug and pull and insist you come out,
you twist and turn and begin to pout.
As you enter the world no longer warm and quiet,
you begin to cry no sight, but blinded.
Can't walk, can't talk, can't explain what's wrong,
you expect the nurses to understand, you want Mom.
Kamille Bauguess, Grade 7
Reformation Lutheran School, CA

Moving On

Oh, my love, do not despair
Wipe those tears from your eyes
What we had was real, I swear
But it's time to be moving on.

Remember that day, the day we both fell
And told ourselves we'd never get up
But look, I awaken to the call
I am now standing again.

You will always have a piece of my heart
I'll miss you when I'm gone
We've done all we could, we played our part
But now the play is done.

And it's time to be moving on.
Elizabeth Resendiz, Grade 7
Aurora Quest K-8 School, CO

Oblivious

Oblivious
Unseeing
I'm here
Look at me
Bright and shining
Yet unknown
Judged, for what I am not
Never given a second glance
See me
Find me
Know me
Before you discard me
Watch me
I'll prove you wrong
Chances
Never given
Mikaela Schiller, Grade 8
Whitehall Middle School, MT

Much More than a Tree

In front of me lies a tree,
So beautiful and free.
It glistens in the sunlight
Yet it's nothing but a tree.

It stands so proud and strong
With branches open and long.
Changing color with the seasons,
Bathed in the beauty of dawn.

In front of me lies a tree,
All it can do is "be."
I am astonished at its beauty,
For its much more than a tree.
Sophie Bryden, Grade 7
Joe Walker Middle School, CA

A Heavenly Breakfast

As I entered the Paris Buffet in Las Vegas
I could see steam rising up from the scrumptious food
An array of dazzling colors
Food in all shapes and sizes
I gazed at the fresh fruit with beads of sparkling water
My nose absorbed the sweet aroma of rich hot chocolate
And the buttery scent of pancakes and waffles
I could hear the sizzling of food on hot skillets
And the swish of ice in the cold beverages
Touching my warm mug sent shivers down my spine
The first sip of my chocolate immersed me in warmth
My fork dove in for a fluffy bite of crepe
And I experienced the sweetness of fresh bananas and creamy chocolate
Hot, crispy bacon and hash browns
Light and fluffy eggs sprinkled with cheese
All was cooked to perfection
By cooks in tall white hats
The fresh flavor of juicy pineapple, melons, and berries of all kinds
Made my tongue tingle with joy
I ate until I could barely breathe
And then we stayed for lunch!
Tori Ramirez, Grade 7
Christ the King School, AZ

Claustrophobia

Closing around me, this place ever-shrinking
Lost in my panic and worry
All I can think of is escaping out from
Under this heavy blanket of darkness
Slowly losing my breath, I
Try not to panic
Roving this space I feel nothing but the cold walls
Only those damn walls
Pacing, I let out an anxious, shaky breath
Hell, that's what this is; my own hell
Onwards I go, crawling now
Because the ceiling is shrinking with the walls
I see a light, an exit! But
All out of breath, and exhausted, I collapse and once again, I am plunged into darkness
Sierra Morrison, Grade 8
Young Scholar's Academy, AZ

Dance Shoes

Now I'm not talking about any dance shoes…I am talking about my old dance shoes

The ones that are so worn out they have dirt marks from where I point my feet.
The ribbons that are fraying from being tied so much.
The ones that have holes at the tip of the toes.
The pointed shoes that squeak every time I go on toe,
The shoes that are missing screws from dancing in competitions.
The shoes that helped me win in competitions.
The shoes that had a pin in them when I was dancing on stage.
The shoes that are so old they are fraying.
It is amazing that these inanimate objects can hold such a special place in my heart.
Alexandra Rennie, Grade 7
Rolling Hills Country Day School, CA

Dominic

Dominic
funny, joyful, happy, caring
Son of Mandy
lover of dub step
lover of football
lover of video games
Who feels pain
Who feels happy on my birthday
Who feels sad when family passes
Who fears heights
Who fears clowns
Who fears snakes
Who would like to see a flying car
Who would like to see a koala bear
Who would like to see a bald eagle
Resident of Modesto, CA USA on planet Earth in Milky Way galaxy
Huesca

Dominic Huesca, Grade 7
Daniel Savage Middle School, CA

Nervous

Butterflies.
Dance in my stomach.
I pull my fire suit on.
Safe in its shields, I slide my hand over the warm metal of the car.
I climb in.
I smell the old burnt rubber from the past days.
The five arms of my belt soothe me and tell me I'll be safe.
It's like a lion.
The car.
Low breathing, motor rumbling softly,
Swallows me up.
I push my foot down and immediately scare the butterflies away.
The swiftly shaking cylinders of the steel block growl at me.
Now it's all over.
I give my lion one last burst of life before rest.
VROOOM!
Then an empty silence.

Cody Hall, Grade 7
Weldon Valley Jr High School, CO

Teardrop

She is a teardrop.
Gliding down the crease of my face.
In a coat of sorrow,
She dances quietly back and forth.
Expressing her emotions to all those around her.
Her saddest moments are those of her companions.
As her dreams slide along with her she thinks about her life.
Down by the mouth she kissed her companion goodbye.
Landing softly she rolls away, taking away the sorrow.
As she leaves, the only thing left is the streak she made.
Her brothers and sisters come flowing down next landing,
Swiftly beside her as she leaps away.

Abigail Adcock, Grade 9
La Reina High School, CA

The Author's Christmas

The holly leaves begin to fall in sight
The Christmas trees are decked with many lights
The snow sprinkles down in bits and dots,
His pen writes across the page in words and jots.

The author. At his desk, he takes a moment to stare —
The halcyon scene, the fierce wintry glare.
He sips his warming drink, looks way beyond
The children playing; over snowmen they bond.

He smiles. And scrambles to get the words down, fast.
He's seen the scene that truly matters, at last!
The golden star, the symbol of Christmas
And all the presents bound, the children restless.

It's all a culmination, the end of the season
It's everyone's favorite holiday for that reason

Robert Miranda, Grade 9
Schurr High School, CA

Marine Journey

As I stood in the cold December air,
The Downtown Aquarium shone electric blue.
I couldn't wait to adventure around.
To discover new scenes of beauty and disguise.
So much to ponder,
So much to love.
The turtles swam above,
The sharks swam under.
Jellyfish looked vibrant,
While starfish appeared flamboyant.
An octopus clung to its tank,
And the stingrays swiftly moved past each other.
A gift shop that was dreaded,
For it was the last stop of the experience.
To an end the thrill seemed to come,
But wait!
The Cheesecake Factory was too close to miss.

Madison Bodmer, Grade 9
Pueblo West High School, CO

Myself

I am not perfect, I know I am not, but who is?
I have my faults, I can admit that,
But I know who I am.
I don't need people to tell me if I am popular.

I know some people dislike me but I'm trying to focus on the good.
I may argue but that doesn't mean I dislike you.
I am just myself.

I have my interests and people have theirs,
But if they do not like my interests I'm not going to change.
All I want to be and will be is myself.

Alex Contreras, Grade 7
St. Helen Catholic School, CA

Moon

Endless darkness in the sky
That is all brightened with this
Large, lunar, light.

A faint outline by day,
But by night it
Gleams a glorious glimmer.

The moon is like a lens,
And the sun is like a light.
A team of two that shine day and night.

Our moon is bright.
It is one big light.
Shining every single night.

So we do not have to fright.
We have our moon
As our night light.

Right?

Lanafaye Kovacs, Grade 7
Joe Walker Middle School, CA

Love

Love is like leaves in the wind.
Love is like a flower opening.
Love is like the sun.
Love is like lightning.
Love is like a candle.
Love is a net.
Love is joy.
Love is good.
Love is like fireworks.
Love is a bomb exploding.
Love is the stars and moon.
Love is birds singing.
Love is kind.
Love will find you.

Mariah Moosman, Grade 8
Canyon View Jr High School, UT

Blank

There are things that have no name
people say it's all the same
that some just can't think
or they forget to make one
but for every time I didn't write one
it all would weigh a ton!
so they throw it away
or they will title it
untitled,
blank,
or no name.

Julian Gonzales, Grade 7
Salida Middle School, CO

Cold Wind Blowing

The cold winds blowing through the night, all across the cities lights,
You can hear it, but you can't see it, try to run from it, you can't beat it
Hope all the candles in your house are lit
Everything is blown out on your lawn
When it comes everything is gone
It comes and goes as the city flows
Just trying to blow
In comes the snow
It grows and grows
At the time when the cold wind blows

Kieran Christopher Hall, Grade 7
Monte Vista Christian School, CA

Hero

Tony Najera Jr., is my hero.
Not only is he my hero, he is my little brother.
He is my inspiration, the one I can go to.
I know he may be younger than me,
But he will always have a huge space in my heart.
He inspires me to be myself and not care what anybody thinks of me.
He truly is one of the people I can be myself around.
He is a kid and I am a kid at heart.
We have our arguments but get along in the end.
I love my hero, and my hero loves me.

Sierra Najera, Grade 7
Tenaya Middle School, CA

My Hero

My hero is my mom;
There are many great reasons.
My mom has been there for me every time my dad went to jail, every time he yelled, but most
Importantly when he went to Arizona to never be seen again.
She is my father and my mom all in one.
She is the most important person in my life and always will be.
She is always there for me in the good and bad.
She is a wonderful person and makes me smile every day.
And that's why
She is my hero.

Sabrina M. Velasquez, Grade 7
Tenaya Middle School, CA

Lost with Doubt

Transportation is just a small fishing boat.
Traveling across the open sea, hopeless, lost, hungry, and desperate.
Finally arriving at a refugee camp, but what happens then, will we ever leave?
Depression and hopelessness settle into their eyes and scar them for life.
Surrounded by others that have also lost everything, just like you.
A thought burns in the back of your head, knowing you may never leave.
On a plane, heading to a new, safe, home,
Wondering if you have made the right decision for you and your family.

Jacqueline Nguyen, Grade 8
South Lake Middle School, CA

The Reason

World has been changing you'd say.
Everything, from the way you live, and I live.
Things have developed so much in such a short time.
What, in two hundred years?

Our life is short, including yours and my own.
During our brief magnificence, what can you change dramatically?
Maybe in your lifetime, you might have invented something,
something that might have changed other generation's lives, forever.

It is proud to help other generation, for it might save countless other lives.
It might help your descendants, your family, and make them feel proud.
One day, they might say, "I have such a great ancestor; he changed our lives!"

It will make you soul to feel proud, if your body cannot feel it anymore.
Heaven will rejoice, and maybe the devils might be pardoned of their wrong doings because of you.
Every people might respect you forever for what you had done for your lifetime.
But what is good for you?

You will not remember any of this.
You will not enjoy any of your achievements that will make you famous after your death.
But you cannot remember any of this.
Why would you do it then?
Because, my fella,
Your soul, the very soul of yours, will be all in our hearts.

Yejoo Lee, Grade 7
Huntington Middle School, CA

Ode to the Sweatshirt

Oh you sweatshirt you, believing that the category of sweater will forever define your existence!
The navy blue of the cotton-polyester draping your baggy form outstands all crocheted knits.
For a final touch comes the hood adorning your back while the sweater stays abandoned and bare.
Oh sweatshirt, how I love you, more than any sweater that came before.

The oceanic hue of your cloth brings about our adventures together,
Across many seas and the compacted cabins enclosed in planes flying about in the air.
Symbolizing comfort and safety,
You tower above all clothing like the last beacon in sight on a journey home.

When pulling your pilling material over my head, a weak mess of floral and sweets fills my senses,
Reminding myself of the day previous,
In which a tour through Macy's cosmetics was pertinent above all else.

One of your favorable traits, oh sweatshirt of mine, is the thick layers that cover me,
The coziness and unforgettable velvet of touch easing my skin
While warmth emits like the glow of a fireplace on a dark and stormy night.

Oh sweatshirt, you will never leave my side, though you will wear.
The gashes on your sleeves from impatiently pulled strings
Like a master of frivolous puppets.
I woe that, alas, your time will come,
The golden string symbolizing your life will be cut
And I will be forced to turn you in.
But until then, thank you for it all.

Riley Ng, Grade 7
Rolling Hills Country Day School, CA

Hope and Fear

As the wind sings a song of joy,
Here lay a glorious newborn boy.
As it starts to cry and weep,
There lay a lifeless insensible sheep.

When the Sea's lips lick the silver sand,
The children laugh all across the land.
But when she simmers with uncontrollable power,
The world is filled with abundant sorrow.

The wood around with dappled shades of emerald,
While the lovely white paper lay uncrumpled.
But when the snarling wolves come out to bite,
A child is crying within the night.

While the blue bird sings its lovely song,
The teenager feels as though she belongs.
As the bird starts to lose its gorgeous voice,
A bullied girl makes a terrible choice.

Samantha Blanchard, Grade 7
Joe Walker Middle School, CA

Seasons and Trees

In autumn my leaves are kissed gently by the cold;
They turn very crispy, crunchy, and golden brown.
Some turn red, yellow, and orange as they turn old.
The wind takes them for a gentle ride around town.

In the winter the cold comes and harshly bites me,
my skin peels off and my trunk is left bare.
The frost is the meanest the wind will ever be.
Now I do not have anything not even a hair.

In spring the sun comes and happily greets me,
my leaves start to blossom and turn a luscious green.
I'm dressed and the happiest I could ever be;
now I can't wait till when the rain will come to clean.

In summer the sun comes out to play every single day.
Except for when the rain ever so kindly washes me.
I like when the children come to me and play.
It's finally summer, I can relax…Oh geez, it's a bee!

Averi Calder, Grade 7
Joe Walker Middle School, CA

Agony

Agony is like tears in your eyes
you ask what got you there
it hurts for a little bit
then it heals
it happens over and over like rain from the sky
one drop at a time
agony is tears in your eyes

Darrion Hogge and Gabe Garibay, Grade 8
Johnson Jr High School, WY

Volleyball

My feet stick to the shiny floor
The opponents look tired, weak
The net
A barrier between
Two teams, fighting hard
Coaches throwing orders
Back up, get back to base
Tip toe tip toe
Thump, swish, smack
Smooth, silky leather on my sand paper hands
I glance at the scoreboard
24 to 24
Crack, mine, thump
Out
The crowd jumps like fire doused in gasoline
As we gather in a huddle
It smells like sweat and victory
It's over
Until we meet again

Kit Baugh, Grade 7
Weldon Valley Jr High School, CO

More Than Words

What could be more divine
Then the sound of a sweet tune?
Expressing emotion on each line,
Each word making your heart swoon,
Is it the way it conveys a message of love,
Or how each instrument makes your heart flutter?
Is it how the words seem to be sent from above,
Or how it makes your soul melt like butter?
It is able to sing what cannot be said;
It conveys from deep within.
It takes mixed feelings found in your head
And gives them a beat and a spin.
Music is not simply words that sound good together;
Music is an emotion deep, yet sung lighter than a feather.

Natalie Bastawros, Grade 9
Heritage Christian School, CA

Thankful

I'm thankful for…
my parents that care
and the tasty food I eat.
Video games for entertainment
and TV shows that make me laugh.
Friends that help me
and cars for transportation.
eyes to see the world
and ears to listen to the world.
School for education
and technology that makes life easier.
I'm thankful for everything good in the world.

Zachary Bates, Grade 7
Daniel Savage Middle School, CA

Lost Childhood

A little old melody,
Keeps on singing to me,
Waiting to be heard,

A little old memory,
Wanders memory lane,
Trying to find it's way back home,

A little old story book,
Spins its tales,
Hoping to be read,

All these waiting,
For somebody,
To pick them up

Dust them off,
To remember how it was,
Before we grew up,
Before we forgot all those memories,
To reminisce about.

Theyanna Imacseng, Grade 9
Stockton Collegiate Int'l High School, CA

The Tree

I view the tree,
sturdy and towering in the breeze.
Its tallness,
greatness,
and triumph.
The mighty winds
come,
they are too faint,
the tree
does not budge.

Lumberjacks come.
Instead of cutting it down,
I notice them applauding it
and see them leave it there.
Isolated
with me.
Standing firm
and tall,
I see
the tree.

Ryan Laurenzano, Grade 7
St Stephen Lutheran School, CA

Winter Wonderland

Cold snow trickles down
Blanketing the frozen ground
Wintertime is here

Lexi Timme, Grade 9
Pueblo West High School, CO

Food from Your Heart

There once was a boy who lived inside Costco
There was nothing he liked more than a taco.
So one day he sneaked inside the food stand
When strangely he found and old man
Then the old man said, "Why are bananas yellow?"
The boy said, "I don't know, why my good fellow?"
"Find out and you'll get a taco,
but you won't find the answer in Costco."
The boy was looking at him with distrust
Even a slight feeling of disgust,
The man said, "Do you not trust me?"
The boy said, "No you just came out randomly!"
The man was clapping and surprised
"The taco will be your prize!"
"How did I win this taco?
You said it won't be in Costco?"
The man said, "It came from your heart!"
"That's where everything starts!"
The boy said, "I don't know how I won this prize! It seems like blasphemy!"
The man said, "As you said it comes out randomly!"

Aaron Hiura, Grade 7
Monte Vista Christian School, CA

What Is a Hero?

To me, a hero is someone who you look up to.
A hero is someone who has changed your life.
A hero is someone you want to be like.
But, who is my hero?
My hero is my sister.
Not only has she been with me ever since I could remember,
She was the one who took care of me when our parents were at work.
She was the one who played with me even though I broke her toys.
She was the one who wiped my tears away when I tripped over my own feet.
She was the one who was by my side when our family was falling apart.
She was the one who sacrificed so much for me every day.
She was the one who held me whenever I cried at night.
She was the one who cried beside me.
She was the only one who understood everything I felt.
But, not only is she my hero,
She is also my role model,
My shoulder to cry on,
My best friend,
My sister.
My hero.

Allianah Karlin Pingol, Grade 7
Tenaya Middle School, CA

My Friendships

Friendship is a seed that grows into a tree
Friendship is like two weirdos who don't care what people think
Friendship is as fun as jumping in a bounce house
Friendship sounds like waves crashing on rocks
Friendship feels like a time capsule that is saving every stupid, funny, and awesome memory
Friendship looks like a beautiful sunset setting the edge to the world

Delany Frates, Grade 7
Daniel Savage Middle School, CA

Never...

Forever is such a powerful word,
but sometimes, it's backwards,
Never...
Best friends is what we were,
but then along came "her."
I was nothing.
They did everything, without me.
Sometimes, I wonder, did I see?
Obviously I didn't, but I'm not going back.
Best friends is what we were,
I won't ever forget,
When my best friend forgot about me.
Best friends is what we were,
we thought it'd be forever,
but forever is such a powerful word,
but sometimes it means backwards,
Never...

Hannah Vander Poel, Grade 8
St Francis School, CA

Remember Our Love

Love and friendship awaits us each day
Waiting for us to hold it in our arms
Warm and inviting in every way
Knowing it will do us no harm;

It will not fade away unless you allow it
Ask yourself why? What will you change
To protect the love as you see fit
Will you remember the smiles we exchange;

Know our love was meant to be
When I give you my heart
Will you carve our names into a tree
Or will you throw it away like a dart;

Will you promise to cherish this love
Remember it as a white dove.

Tierra McGown, Grade 8
Sequoia Village School, AZ

Spring Is Here

the sun rose
the birds sing
flowers bloom
in the signs of spring
bears come out
foxes pounce on the prowl
deer, poking their head out of their den
bees busy working
the fog lifts
warmth fills the flower bed
goodbye winter
spring is here

Paul Tran, Grade 7
Sarah McGarvin Intermediate School, CA

Wind of Nostalgia

I look out into the distance
Into the barren land
Coated with glistening frost

I hear the gravel crunch under my feet
As the sharp wind burns my cheeks
The frozen river remains paralyzed, unable to speak

A while ago, I walked here
When the rolling river still sang
And when the aspen leaves waved their golden tipped arms in the wind

A while ago, I sat here
While the squirrels scampered around
And while the birds still chirped

But now I am alone
With only the wind to blow the cold, dry air to me
While silently saying, "Goodbye"

So much can change in an instant
Will anything ever be the same?
Only time knows its lies

A light breeze tickles my hair
Giving me hope
As if saying, "Spring is on its way."

Megan Cho, Grade 9
Pine Creek High School, CO

Skipping Rocks

We locked our knees but ran,
racing against the sunrise that would surely win.
Almost out of breath we jumped into summer;
The only place that we knew would always exist.

A quarter after eight we would trace stars in the backyard,
Using our hands to find a place where we could always find each other.

The times of laughing in the gullies and falling out of trees would be over.
We all knew that we would have to leave someday;
Just like everyone before us.
The leaves would fall but have nowhere to land,
And the rivers must run to other valleys and creeks.
The days were getting shorter,
Time was running out;
The world we created would just become a childhood memory;
Days of playing in the sandbox and stories told to my children.

The kingdom was now just an old dream we might be able to find one day,
Stored away in the back of our memories forever.

We were growing up, so we did the only thing we could do;
We locked our knees but ran.

Chervanna Givens, Grade 9
Center for Academic Success, AZ

Mothers

Mothers will always care,
No matter the challenge they bear,
Loving, honest, and gentle too,
Mothers will always love you for you.

They are there when we need them the most,
And when we are not all they do is boast,
They tell you the truth for everything that may brew,
Mothers will always love you for you.

Sweet, nourishing, kind, and more;
These are qualities they look for,
They were there for us when we grew,
Mothers will always love you for you.

Mothers have a special place in our hearts,
They will always play a key part,
They are the ones we turn to because,
Mothers will always love you for you.

Izabel Florez, Grade 8
Joe Walker Middle School, CA

Once Called Family

Back then when we were all together,
You and Mom where in love
I thought that would actually be forever
Did you guys forget what was so special?

There started all this arguing,
You didn't know how much it affected us
You were like cats and dogs
All we could do was just sit there and watch

One day I came home, it felt empty
I walked inside your room, everything was gone
I asked Mom, she was crying, telling me it was over
Even until now, I feel like this is all my fault

I look at families and I am just afraid
We are never going to be that again
Now you're gone somewhere far
And you make it seem like you don't care

Jennifer Valdes, Grade 8
John Adams Middle School, CA

12 Little Doves

Twelve doves bounded by pain
For they were vain
They dance for love
For they are twelve little doves
They're trapped in a cage on the dark side of the moon
Shining like flowers that blossom just once
For they are twelve little doves bounded by heart

Katyna Pham, Grade 7
Sarah McGarvin Intermediate School, CA

Childhood Goes Away

Have you ever wondered why we lost our childhood?
Those silly, fun games of tag and games of falsehood
Those warm, second grade days in the sun
Remember those days when everything was fun?

Now as we grow up, we play less childish game
And our minds begin to mature and tame
Now we are scared and timid in our new school
As we see the eighth graders of this school make the rule

We are now the new leaders of our school
We are now people the new students see as cool
We must do our best and play less
And hopefully, as we grow, there is no stress

We are now growing up and seeking our future
We are excited to begin high schools adventure
Our futures are just about to begin
But first I must finish eight grade with a flourish of my pen

Karla Garcia, Grade 8
John Adams Middle School, CA

Love Is the Key

Wonderful thing, it happens all the time,
I know it's great when it happens to me;
It is the answer to every unsolvable riddle,
Love is the key.

People around me bathe in its presence,
As happy as anyone could be;
It's just so enjoyable to have,
Love is the key.

Nothing could be better than this,
It is my cup of tea;
Everyone goes through it at one point in time,
Love is the key.

Falling in and out is hard,
When someone's in it its obvious to me;
Want it to happen again and again,
Love is the key.

Quetzali Garcia, Grade 8
Joe Walker Middle School, CA

Thoughts on Edvard Munch's Painting "The Scream"

This painting makes me think
He doesn't have anything, nothing, he's sad.
He is alone …by himself in the world,
Maybe he broke up with his love,
He is surprised at something…a thought?
He is desperate,
He is lonely.

Treyjhawn Hill, Grade 7
Tenaya Middle School, CA

To Beckon the Dark with a Trembling Hand
The shadows move across the dark wall
Watching
Waiting
Where are you, my dear?
I've been waiting
But days blur
And the dark creeps in

I miss the light
I miss dancing
I miss laughing
I miss flying so high I could paint the sky

Now the shadows edge closer
Crying out through bloodied veins
Staring through me
Dead on the walls
Lifeless in decay
I have found a family in them
As alone in life as most are in death
Tara Downey, Grade 8
A P Giannini Middle School, CA

Unwanted Pain
The ripping, shredding feel of unnecessary aggression
Born from the jealousy of one
Slowly pries apart our friendship
No need for it

The growl of anger tears at my ears
Pointless and unwanted
It causes pain and suffering
No need for it

The hate that covers my eyes with a red veil
Makes me forget the reason it was born
Happiness and joy are a thing of the past
No need for it
Clayton King, Grade 9
New Plymouth High School, ID

Reflections on Edvard Munch's Painting, "The Scream"
Silent
Sounds
come.

"Aah! Aah!" No one cares;
The hurt I feel inside cannot be repaired.
Hear, hear, hear me scream,
Random spats of paint near thee,
Alone now, I realize
Only I can hear me,
Because the screams are thoughts
Only heard within me.
Melea Murdock, Grade 7
Tenaya Middle School, CA

This Is Who I Am
I am shy yet kind
I wonder why is there war in the world?
I hear the ocean's waves crashing down
I see the warm tan sandy beach
I want peace in the world
I am shy yet kind

I pretend that I am a fish in a river
I feel at peace at the image of the ocean
I touch a small soft blue shell
I worry for my grandmother
I cry at the thought of losing a loved one
I am shy yet kind

I understand that I should be grateful
I say that two wrongs don't make a right
I dream of living in a mystical place
I try my best to express my feelings
I hope that one day I will soar above the clouds
I am shy yet kind
Tori Rogers, Grade 7
Falcon Creek Middle School, CO

A World Without Second Chances
There was a place
Where no one had a second chance.

You could be the most passive of kids
But one little slip up and that was it.

You could try to make up for it, try to do better
But it didn't matter
No one had a second chance.

The prisons were full, the enforcement was small
Until there was no one left at all.
Everyone had been locked up
No one had a second chance.
Jaden Taylor, Grade 8
Desert Hills Middle School, UT

Just Take a Few Seconds and Realize
The crashing of waves on the shore
The wind blowing as if wanting more
Not sure of what to think
As the sand below me starts to sink
Laps of water in a row
In a rhythm that starts to flow
The warm sun beats on my skin
When I realize that life is just too thin
That's when I start to see
That there's beauty in everything
And hold to what you've got
For it might leave you without another thought
Cinnamin McDonald, Grade 8
Young Scholar's Academy, AZ

A While with Me

Come walk with me,
Come talk with me,
Come spend a while with me,
Chit with me,
Chat with me,
Sit with me,
Laugh with me,
Let's watch the sun set,
Let's feel the wind,
For a day,
For a year,
For a life,
Come spend a while with me.

Mattie Lagan, Grade 7
Monte Vista Christian School, CA

Chocolate

It is made fresh
From cocoa beans
It comes in different flavors
If you know what I mean
It melts in your mouth
As it melts on your hand
You won't be like a baby
And will never pout
There's nothing about chocolate
That you would not like
So eat it right now
You know you want some
You cannot lie.

Jennifer Nguyen, Grade 7
Sarah McGarvin Intermediate School, CA

Stains

A drop of coffee on the wall
Slowly drying
Stretching longer and larger
Like a tornado
Falling slowly
Fading fast
Then ends right after a midnight storm
Leaving stains of pain and hurt
It's a burning sensation
Like pins pricking and poking at my heart

Dameion Cowan, Grade 8
Weldon Valley Jr High School, CO

Doing My Best

I was taking a very long test.
I really wanted to rest.
Then there was lunch.
I ate a bunch.
Now it's good; I'm doing my best.

Trey Lantzy, Grade 7
Beacon Country Day School, CO

Silence

Silence is that moment. . .
Right after a child is born
When everyone stares at the little miracle wrapped up tightly in a blanket
Silence is that moment. . .
When that child grows up and goes to school for the first time
When he learns to drive and turns sixteen
When she graduates and goes off to college
Silence is happiness.
It is also the tears of loss.
Silence is that moment when that child, grown and with children themselves,
Kneels by a hospital bed wishing for another day
Standing around a grave, remembering every moment
As he watch his parents leave the world and meet in a world unknown to the living
Silence is the moments that matter most
Silence is that moment when everything changes
The moments that we live for
Silence. . .

Grace Stumpo, Grade 9
Grandview High School, CO

Nature

I lean against a tree observing nature, the wild
There are squirrels leaping from branch to branch
Deer wading through a stream plucking tubers and vines.
I shift to get a better view and they vanish
I gaze at the swaying rushes and notice red winged blackbirds building nests
I take in their red shoulders, their glossy feathers.
Their nests look like baskets woven out of straw and hair.
A sparrow flies by and I watch it hop from branch to branch, from stalk to stalk
It pauses on a blackberry bush and starts to trill.
I wonder what it is singing about.
Maybe about his love, maybe about how many blackberries there are.
he flies over the bush and lands outside of my sight
A bat flies overhead and I realize it is getting late
The sun is at the horizon
I stand up and jog towards home
I wonder what the animals will do tomorrow
I vow to come back and find out

Sonya Churkin, Grade 7
Meridian Elementary School, CA

Shades of Life

In your life there are shades,
made of colors that always stay.
Green represents a calm soul that's as calm as the wind,
and blue stands for a kind soul that has always grinned.
Red means you are as angry as a swarm of bees,
and orange means you have a great responsibility but it's as easy as a breeze.
Yellow symbolizes a person as joyful as the sun,
and gold corresponds to a person with courage equal to the bravest son.
Black stands for selfishness you can't rid yourself of,
but only change with a deed filled with love.
The shades of life decide your fate,
and decide if you slide or skate.

Brian Vuong, Grade 7
Sarah McGarvin Intermediate School, CA

Someone to Do What's Right

All I want is someone to be focused
Someone to stay on task
Someone to get straight A's.
Someone to graduate high school
All I want is someone to get into a good college
Someone to graduate all 4 years
Someone to get a really good job that I want
Someone to really focus and make all of the money.
But all I want is someone to work hard.
All I want is someone to be the owner of a really good company.
Someone to do what's right
Always on top of it not matter what.
Someone to always succeed at whatever they are doing
if they are a manager
if they work at a restaurant.
All I want is someone to never give up
Someone to keep trying even if they constantly fail
because you will eventually succeed no matter what.
Someone to become a hero
Someone to make a stance
Someone to do what's right.

Tanner Peterson, Grade 7
Falcon Creek Middle School, CO

Restart Button

I'm not willing
I'm not willing to be "sponged out, erased, canceled, made nothing."
No I'm not willing to be dipped into oblivion either
I don't care if I will never really change
Who said I had to?
Who said I ever wanted to?
I don't need to be reborn
Life is all about mistakes
If it wasn't then there would be a button
A restart button
If I pressed it, it would change my life
But I won't press it
I'm not willing, I'm unable, and I refuse to press this button
This restart button
I'm not willing to be "burnt, burnt alive, and burnt down"
I'm not willing to do any of that and I never will because
I've made up my mind
I won't press this restart button
I refuse to change.
Because who said I had to?
Who said I ever wanted to?

Kyle Olinger, Grade 8
Rolling Hills Country Day School, CA

Just Dream

Pride is hidden beneath,
Love can be expressed in more ways than speech,
You can dream farther than what is in reach,
So dream, and may God give you peace.

Latrice White, Grade 9
California Virtual Academies, CA

I've Got to Study Every Day

I am studying for school,
To get good grades on my work.
I need to get one-hundred percent on my work.
I would love to be a good student by studying.

That's why I've got to study every day.
Always work hard in school,
Do my best work, and study every day.

I would make something happen with my scores,
The highest score can make something happen.
I can improve my score today.
It is for my report card.

That's why I've got to study every day.
Always work hard in school,
Do my best work, and study every day.

So I do my best,
And make my move, to grades I haven't gotten,
And make my teachers impressed.

That's why I've got to study every day.
Always work hard in school,
Do my best work, and study every day.

Michael Gomez, Grade 7
St Helen Catholic School, CA

Dear Doctors — A Hope Message for Kids Everywhere

Dear Doctors
Please don't let my mom die
If she does I am not ready
To say good-bye

Dear Doctors
Don't let my mom lose herself in sleep
If she does I will most likely
Forever weep

Dear Doctors
You better not let my mom fade
If she does I will certainly
Feel betrayed

Dear Doctors
Stop right there and don't let my mom fail
If she does I will always
Pitifully wail

Dear Doctors
You let me down, my mom is done
Another day is passed, come at dawn
I'll see her again someday, for sure
At least I can say this: thank you that her new life's begun

Zoe Dunning, Grade 8
The Daniel Academy, CO

Freedom

Gray, black, and blue,
Are you getting a clue?
Fighting winds over seas.
To just keep us safe please.

Soldiers die with honor and glory,
That might be a good end to their story.
Heroes they will always be,
Perishing overseas to let me be me.

Green, pink, and yellow.
Are you a lucky fellow?
To be able to go back home?
To have freedom to roam?

Soldiers who live to tell the tale,
To share how they might have failed.
But to see the sun shine over the trees,
Proves that we won, have the freedom to be free.

Lyndsay Hanson, Grade 8
Bear Lake Middle School, ID

Mount SAC

The millions of feet on the floor,
Coming out of the school bus door,
The runners making lots of noise,
In the tunnel from parking lot four.

Just the feeling of being there brought me joys,
Getting to run with all of the boys,
Seeing those mighty switchbacks,
Made me know I needed to have poise.

The starter's gun screamed crack,
And the runners went by the track,
Finishing back by the airstrip
After a two-mile run at Mount SAC.

It was an experimental trip,
And was worth the signature on a slip,
And I'll give you this free running tip:
Drink lots of water and don't trip.

Jonah Purcell, Grade 7
Joe Walker Middle School, CA

The Wonders of Christmas

Christmas is a time to rejoice and be glad
It's a time for families to come together
And enjoy each other's company
There are the bright lights and the Christmas cheer
There are the children, the laughing, and the playing
There's the holiday spirit and sweet hymns
It's all so lovely and beautiful
Christmas is the best time of year

Addison Fairbanks, Grade 8
Christ the King School, AZ

Losing a Baby Tooth

As I ate my apple, my tooth started twisting.
My tooth moved left and right, for it was shifting.
It was so loose, it was holding on by a pinky.
I was so scared, for my eating was just assisting.

With another bite, my tooth was gone.
I ran to tell my dad, who said, "Right on!"
This was my first tooth, the only one that I lost.
There were no actions, I could act on.

I was so sad, for I looked like a bum.
Every time I smiled, you can see my tongue.
My mother told me not to worry and relax.
I could not relax, for the gap was the size of my thumb.

After a week, I was no longer blue.
I felt a new tooth, which whom grew.
I ran to the mirror, and saw it there.
I thought, out with the old and in with the new.

Eduardo Martinez, Grade 8
John Adams Middle School, CA

Season of Seasons

While the winners of the Super Bowl are cocky,
They're dropping the puck for hockey.
As the legends of the hardwood are shooting their threes,
The excitement of Lord Stanley Cup brings us to our knees.

The ice has melted and now it's raining.
For the boys of summer it's time to report for spring training.
The NBA comes to an end
Just as the curve balls start to bend.

The boys of summer are now in full swing,
Keeping their eye on the ball and the ring,
Because we all know it's not over until we hear the fat lady sing.

The leaves are changing color, and falling to the ground.
Fall is among us, and America's past time is quickly winding down.
America's passion is getting ready to pound,
Hearing the whistle signal,
First down.

Colt Serrano, Grade 7
Joe Walker Middle School, CA

A Christmas Season

The Christmas season has lots of cheer,
It only comes but once a year.
Everyone sings to the Christmas beat,
And thinks about what they're going to eat.
All of the children play in the snow,
While the parents dance under the mistletoe.
The children's smiles began to lift,
After they've opened all their gifts.

Kyle Koliboski, Grade 8
Christ the King School, AZ

A Childhood

Early life as simple as basic math
Do not have to worry about the right path
Your favorite blanket is like a cloud
Your tantrums pierce the silence all around

Riding a bike is like learning to talk
Your first words are as colorful as chalk
Walking is not as fast a rocket
Dusty are the garments in the closet

Life is hardly a bowl of ripe cherries
Homework is difficult to the plenty
Responsibilities come more frequently
You will be glad you are not too merry

There is a bright light we have to embrace
Lust starts to rust as truth shines in our face
All the good memories start to erase
Hopefully a childhood was not a waste

Omar Gomez, Grade 8
John Adams Middle School, CA

Fall

I dwell with my brothers
Dangling from a tree
The breeze of the wind
Making me sway

When it's hot, the sun beats down on me
Keeping my master cool
When it rains, it rains on me
Keeping my master dry

Autumn was here, the parting season
We all knew what was soon to happen
As I watched my brothers fall from their master
I noticed I was falling with them

Ever so slowly, ever so gently
I watched as my brothers fell so lightly
And as I was looking, I hit the ground
And gazed up at my brothers, cascading around me

Frederic Mulbarger, Grade 9
Viewpoint School, CA

Books

Books are the greatest creation,
Books give people such wonder and fascination.
They will make you smarter,
And in knowledge you shall go farther.
Books are great when you are at home.
Books are great when you are alone.
The thing you do when you are in need.
The thing that is, you need to read.

Leon Kha, Grade 7
Sarah McGarvin Intermediate School, CA

My Grandfather

I know you are dead and gone for good
It's hard to accept but now I understood
Not everything last forever even if its good or bad
Now that you're in heaven that makes me feel glad.

You were a hard working man, busy as a bee,
But never in your life did you drank tea.
You raised a beautiful and special family
That is why I feel so gladly.

Although we still feel sad together
We will always remember him forever.
Never had we cried a river of tears
The emptiness we feel, hold so many fears.

Now watching from above with a smile in his face
Trying to tell us he is resting in a special place.
Tonight and tomorrow when I go to sleep
I will always remember him as the alarms beeps.

Arturo Pena, Grade 8
John Adams Middle School, CA

The Best Dog in the World

We got him when I was seven.
His light brown eyes looked up to heaven.
He cried and cried with a siren yell.
He smelled like my newborn brother Evan.

He ran around the house like crazy.
We thought since he was a puppy, he would be lazy.
He had no self control
See we seem to be a little crazy.

He grew and grew like a well-watered tree.
We could no longer keep him inside, you see.
He ran around the back yard all day.
He was like a hurricane with teeth.

We came home one day like we always did.
We could no longer find my dog, where had he hid?
His chocolate coat no longer moved.
My precious dog was not kidding.

Michael Torres, Grade 8
John Adams Middle School, CA

Cookies on Christmas Night

On Christmas night a plate full of warm gooey cookies
Just sitting there taunting me
I slowly extend my arm to grab one
But I'm too short, I will never give up
I yell in my head
I grab a chair and climb up like a monkey
But as slow as a snail
"Yes I got one!" I say in a whisper.

Sara Buckingham, Grade 7
Salida Middle School, CO

The Masterpiece

I am creative
I wonder what will materialize
I hear voices on which way to go
I see colors running together smoothly
I want them to stop clashing
I am creative

I pretend my imagination explodes
I feel joy
I touch. Is it dry?
I worry about mistakes
I cry to the big mistakes
I am creative

I understand it's not always perfect
I say let it not be destroyed
I dream of becoming a professional
I try to make it possible
I hope one day I am at the top
I am creative

Jaiden Kelly, Grade 7
Falcon Creek Middle School, CO

My Home

In my room so lonely, yet feeling so homey
I always stayed.
To hear my own music, to be free
Out of the way
Always quiet, but never silent,
That is how I played.
That is home.

Smells from the kitchen
Drifting to my nose,
Making my mouth water
And my eyes close.
I always roam because;
That is home.

Place where I grew up,
To the yelling of my sisters,
Barking of my dogs, and
Hugs from my mom,
That is home.

Chelsea Hidalgo, Grade 8
Richardson PREP HI Middle School, CA

Light

I am bright
I am warm
But sometimes I am not there in a storm
When you look at me I am white
Can you guess what I am?
I am light

Michael Hafferty, Grade 8
Meridian Elementary School, CA

The River

Lingering about the forest
Seeking out a mouse or two,
Is a creature as graceful
As a moon of blue.

She wanders toward her den
In search of her kits.
Tiny paw prints lead her
To a river filled with fish.

A desperate wail calls out
Into the star lit field.
With eyes the size of buttons
She runs for her kits, all three.

With a parrot like cry
Her children go under.
As many have done before her
She leaves to hide forever.

Siena Avila, Grade 7
Joe Walker Middle School, CA

Missing You

I came into this life
You held me in your arms
You kept me safe
So no one could harm

You taught me values
Lessons in life I would learn
You taught me to respect
I gave you love in return

You have always been in my life
Through thick and thin
And now my lonely journey
Without you will unfortunately begin.

I miss you so much
The pain does not ease
I pray you are happy
And finally at peace

Andrew Barrios, Grade 8
John Adams Middle School, CA

Be You...

Life is a shining star
The peanuts in a Planters jar
But it depends on who we are
Whether we'll stay close or go far
If we can hold the heavy bar
Whether we play piano or rock guitar
Be yourself, that's who you are
You're amazin', that you are

Hibaq Osman, Grade 8
Thomas Jefferson High School, CO

Love

Since you left,
my heart has been broken.
For your love to me,
was a special token.

Everything you did,
everything you will do,
you were the rabbit in my hat,
I loved you.

Now every time I think of love,
you pop into my head.
You flew away,
as a small white dove,
and now my eyes are red.

But now you are gone,
as I have spoken.
Still, since you left,
my heart has been broken.

Jane Earley, Grade 7
Joe Walker Middle School, CA

The Loss of the Rose

Away with the wind
The petals fly
Along with it, the hope
The thorns are here
Sickenly stuck in your side
It won't go away
The months pass
The petals wilt into the sun
No more earth-shattering love
No more heavenly light
Off into the wind
the faith fades
The petals have fallen off
The rose is shedding its tears
They won't be back
But don't over worry
Even though it pulls at your heart
And the tears seem never-ending
Remember one thing
Petals always grow back.

Brittany Mangus, Grade 8
Lovell Middle School, WY

Life

Life is a gift that God gave to us
Life is a gift to take and to give
We all have a destiny from birth to death
Without this there's no point to live
The best way to live is to live a great life
And die a great death

Jonathan Hemming, Grade 7
Cinnamon Hills School, UT

This Painted Smile

When I Laugh – I Laugh The Loudest. When I Smile – I Smile The Brightest
When I Speak – I Speak The Merriest But In Reality – I Cry The Fastest.
My Smile Camouflages My Tormented Soul Which Is Torn Into Pieces, Never Again To Be Whole
With My Smile The Truth Never To Be Revealed My Fear Of Allowing The World The See The Me That Is Real
I Overcast My Fears Of Not Being Accepted Of Being Hated Or Scorned And Of Being Rejected A Painted Smile On My Face
This Is Just A Big Fat Lie I Pretend That Everything Is Okay When In Reality I Want To Die
I Front And I Pretend No One Knows This Smile Isn't Real I Live A Life Of Concealment Hiding My Shattered Soul – Unable To Heal
I Put On A Show So Well Rehearsed Yet Every Single Day I Think That I'm Cursed
I Paint On A Smile To Make People Think I'm Okay This Is Just For A While Till I'm Dead And Gone Anyway
But When I'm Alone, Alone In My Room The Smile Of Paint Is Removed And I Face My Private Doom
Only The Walls Know Only The Walls See Only The Walls I Trust They Will Never Betray Me Cause They Know Who I Really Am
The Person I Will Always Be The Person Beneath The Painted Smile Never To Reveal My True Identity
The Mirror Also Knows The Person Deep Inside I Conceal Her From The World But With The Mirror – I Cannot Hide
All Of My Depression All Of My Confusion Only, And Only The Mirror Alone
Has This Kind Of X-Ray Vision It Sees Beyond The Surface
It Sees Deep Within My Eyes Beyond All The Pretense
To Where The Pain And Sorrow Lie But The Moment I Leave My Room
There Is This Painted Smile Of Lies Never To Show That My Gloom Even Though It Never Meets My Eyes
My Life Is A Masquerade I Hide The Tears That I Cry
You Can't Imagine The Tears And Sorrow Behind This Painted Smile
behind this painted smile.

Valerie Cornwell, Grade 8
Payson Jr. High School, UT

What If

What if is a question that makes you wonder, a question that makes you think. Like, what if the stars could dance with us or what if the stars could sing? What if people could sunbathe at night or what if people could star gaze in day light? What if the Earth spins because it was once a dancer or what if the earth is green because it has cancer? What if humans grew wings and could fly or what if fish could actually cry? What if, what if I ask of you, what if, what if I pray to you. So dear neighbor, or friend, or even stranger, I end this by asking you, what if?

Selena Rossi, Grade 8
Sierra Middle School, NM

Goodbye Lucky

I once had a dog named Lucky
He was a white colored puppy
He always liked to run and play
He was happy until the end of the day

Then one day he got sick
Lucky did not want to run or play
He was laying in his bed all day
I tried to imagine that it was all just a trick

When he died I was sad
I wished it wasn't this bad
I tried to smile with glee
But it won't be the same without him

Lucky was my best friend
I know he would want me to be happy
For him I always cried
But I knew it was time to say goodbye

Anthony Bueno, Grade 8
John Adams Middle School, CA

Forever Lost

My life has been passing by like a river,
On and beyond all the known hither.
To the great beyond I dare not go,
For fear of my fate I do now show.

Though my life has been full of sorrow,
I wish it not to become tomorrow.
For my root has borne so much fruit,
I fear for its future downhill route.

My marvelous life is heading to an end,
And great big tears I do now shed.
My youth has already quickly fled
Like a kid downhill on a winter sled.

But it is as though I have been born all over
For my life has proved to be much far from over;
For it is just simply the new beginning
Of a whole new strange life full of meaning.

Juan Toledo, Grade 8
John Adams Middle School, CA

When You Thought I Wasn't Looking

When You thought I wasn't looking, I saw you cleaning the house, and I learned that we need to care for what we have.

When you thought I wasn't looking, I saw you make food for the neighbors after they found their baby had a brain tumor, and I realized that we should help those in need of help.

When you thought I wasn't looking, I saw you do yard work for people who couldn't do it themselves, and I learned that serving others is a great thing.

When you thought I wasn't looking, I saw you go to work every day, and I learned that you have to work in life to get what you want.

When you thought I wasn't looking, I saw you praise someone who felt like they didn't do something right, and I learned that you have to look at the good things in a person, not the bad.

When you thought I wasn't looking, I saw you make my favorite food even though it wasn't easy, and I learned that sometimes it's the small things you do that people remember the most.

When you thought I wasn't looking, I saw you help a sick person, and I learned that I should help sick people with things they can't do themselves.

When you thought I wasn't looking, I saw you go to Grandma's to help her, and I learned family is a great thing and it is good to help your family.

When you thought I wasn't looking, I saw you make a cake for someone's birthday, and I learned that people really appreciate things you do that are nice for them.

When you thought I wasn't looking, I learned some of life's most valuable lessons, so I'd like to thank you for the things you did when you thought I wasn't looking.

Evan Jarvis, Grade 7
Canyon View Jr High School, UT

Without Limits

Leaving behind the shackles of our reality
And after the rules that tie and bind us are broken—
Freedom is ours.
Undefined, we have no purpose
Like Sisyphus' stone seated.
Purple panic pools over us, paralyzing our souls.

But extraordinary events will help us
Unearth the purer essence of us that lies within.
The honest truth of the world will slap us in the face now that our eyes are open.
Barriers and unexpected, twists may conspire to confuse
But in the end the light of the sun
Will illuminate what was not seen before.
If this hindrance is overcome, our bodies will tap into a well spring of energy.
This infinite fuel will let us do the impossible
With absolute control,
While the limitations of our self we thought were steel, vanish as fog does when hit by the light of day.
We are invincible…without limits.

Spencer Levy, Grade 8
Rolling Hills Country Day School, CA

Hawaii

I remember the long, and fun airplane ride with my family
I remember when I was in the beautiful country, Hawaii
I could still feel the hot humid air, I'd walk through every day
I still remember the smell of the Hawaiian food we would eat every day
Or the fun times me and my family had whenever we would have at the beach or even the pool side
And the sunny days we would go shopping and buy a lot of things to remember our fun trip
Or the happy moments when me and my cousin saw crazy things throughout the city
I still remember the scary moments I had when I didn't want to do anything or when I saw fish
But I will always remember the memories me and my family made

Gabriella Cavazos, Grade 8
Daniel Savage Middle School, CA

Bird

If I were a bird,
I would fly high beyond the blue sky.
The so blue, so clear blue sky.

If I were a bird, I would fly
Beyond the clouds,
And never come down.

If I were a bird,
I would fly beyond the heavens,
And beyond the starry sky.

If I were a bird,
I would fly beyond the seas
And fly beyond the trees.

If I were a bird,
I would fly with no cage
And no boundaries.

I would fly beyond
The sky, the mountains
And the seas.

But sadly, I am not
A bird so I have to stay
In this cold cruel world of mine.
Aldair Bardales, Grade 8
St Helen Catholic School, CA

Boredom

Boredom is a shadow
that pursues you
and never goes away

It mocks you, plays with you
like an annoying lyrebird.
You try neglecting it,
but it mostly doesn't work

It's there during the day,
suspending over your head
until the night falls and
it vanishes

It changes size
depending on what you're doing.
Some days there's a lot,
some days there's a little

It eventually goes away
only to come back later.
It'll always be there
and you can't do anything about it.
Shannelle Yick, Grade 8
Falcon Creek Middle School, CO

The Thief

A lone wanderer he is called
making wagers he can't hold
Wondering how to live he steals
without a conscience
through the stormy night

Then when the dawn comes
over the mountains
he moves out of sight
not knowing why he's here
At last a light comes and guides
him through all his fear

Then in the end his conscience is clear
Aaron Bottorff, Grade 7
Salida Middle School, CO

Streetlight

The woman
With the basketball stomach
sipped frothy,
foamy,
hot chocolate,
the streetlight sparks,
and pops,
illuminating her profile,
as it dawned on her that
she was soon to be a mother.
like a hooded ostrich
sinking in the dirt,
in a calm panic
she wandered.
Emily Colton, Grade 7
Canyon View Jr High School, UT

Run Away

Run, run, away
Far, far, from here
Dear run and don't come back
This country lacks

Don't you fear
Dear I'll be with you forever
However long it may be
You can see

Run, run, away
Far, far, from here
Do not fear
I shall hear you
Jennifer Collins, Grade 8
Branson Undivided High School, CO

Night in the Woods

As darkness falls on the campsite
All is quiet, still —
Shrouded in a blanket of night
The birds stop their trill.

As I lay silently in my tent
The wind blows through the trees.
Everything in its path is swept
In the howling breeze.

I listen as far in the hills
A wolf calls to the moon.
And down my back it sends some chills
His cold wailing tune

Nighttime in the woods
Is anything but deafening
It is calm and good
It is honest and all-telling
Callan Buechsenschuetz, Grade 9
La Reina High School, CA

Ellis Island

Off the boat,
down a ramp,
through heavy doors I walk.

I emerge into a plain, white room,
the sounds of screams, hopeless screams,
echo through the hall.

I stand frozen with fear,
but a dream for freedom
pushes on.

The masked ghosts do what they want,
they care not for me,
but for the money, for the greed.

I sit in a white chair,
will I make it? Will I die?
I shall at least try.
Trevor Wood, Grade 7
The Connect Charter School, CO

Basketball Player

We were down by two,
I had just made a free throw, one
More and we'd be going to states,
I looked into the crowd, I
Felt my heart beating, I got into
Shooting position and swoosh,
The crowd went wild
Dylan Ngo, Grade 7
Sarah McGarvin Intermediate School, CA

The Life of a Tree

A seed
Engulfed in dirt
Sprouts.
A new tree is welcomed into our world.

It gropes for the sky
Growing taller by the minute
Now it is a sapling.

Audacious and strong
It won't stop climbing until it gets
A gulp of Heaven

Now
A wise, noble giant,
It overlooks
Our world.
Vasey Stephens, Grade 7
Salida Middle School, CO

Sharks

Sharks are mean
Sharks are fierce
With teeth unafraid to pierce
Fast and lean
A true killing machine
Not wanting to be tampered with
They rule the seas
They hunt with ease
Though violent they are
Sometimes even bizarre
They are beautiful creatures
And excellent teachers
To teach their young
To live for fun
Nearly invincible
These predators are
Although covered they are with scars!
Zac Ingalls, Grade 7
Sarah McGarvin Intermediate School, CA

Twinkle

Stars shine so bright,
They twinkle with their light.
They shine like diamonds,
Amaze us in seconds.
Stars beam from up so high,
Glowing throughout the night sky.
They look oh so beautiful,
And make us feel joyful.
Late at night,
They glow in our wonderful sight.
Stars, as you can see,
Radiate upon us and fill us with glee.
Karen Pham, Grade 7
Sarah McGarvin Intermediate School, CA

Nature

The trees blow in the soft wind
Grasses breathe like rain
The cold air will soon be here

Turtles sunbathe on the rocks
Fish swim in the pond
Where all the lily pads grow

Horses breathe in the cold air
Then breathe in the warmth
They are beautiful and strong

Quiet whispers in the air
In forests they call
Listen before they are gone
Sean Woock, Grade 7
Monte Vista Christian School, CA

Cheer

Cheerleading is a sport,
It is very hard to do.
On the track or on the court,
You have to cheer on cue.

You hide your pain inside,
As if nobody knew.
A smile you must find,
And your spirit will shine through.

Encouragement is the key,
If your love for cheer is true.
If this is who you want to be,
Then join the chosen few!
Sara Swing, Grade 7
Monte Vista Christian School, CA

The Mountain Peaks

I awake to the feeling of bitter cold
Fear spreads its pestilent hold
The snowy peaks reach glorious heights
And behind them is a glowing light

Tentatively emerging from its lair
Warming me with it sunny glare
I feel the ice melting away
As the sun casts its shining rays

The grass peeks out from under the snow
Yellow light sets the land aglow
And with the snow melts away my fears
I feel safe and peaceful here
Anushi Patel, Grade 7
South Lake Middle School, CA

The Room and the Kitchen

The room
Where I was scared to sleep
Where I would hide in the deep
Where all I heard was the door

The kitchen
Where everyone met up
Where everyone named their cup
Where I would be ignored

The room
Where everything was dark
Where all the dogs would smell and bark
Where all things belonged to the floor

The kitchen
Where I burnt the toast
Where I thought I saw a ghost
Where I always asked for more
Millie Hernandez, Grade 8
Richardson PREP HI Middle School, CA

My Home

I'm petting two kittens away from the rain
Under a barn, close to some hay
Off to my side some horses roam
This could not feel more like home

The trees whisper ever so soft
Streaking skies, hint at frost
In front of me so colts run and play
On this dark, damp winter day

Soon the rain has turned to snow
Now it's loud, the wind blows
After a minute the storm slows down
The sun peeks from behind the clouds

Some of the horses neigh with glee
Peacefulness is restored to me
And again I say with a happy tone
"This could not feel more like home."
Aubree Blanchard, Grade 7
Canyon View Jr High School, UT

Tonight

I will follow you
To the end of the world
Just to tell you
A secret
Four words, one voice
Unite to say
I love you tonight.
Dayana Cortez, Grade 9
East High School, UT

A Tribute

Broken-hearted, body shaking, eyes crying a flood of tears, grief
Blaming myself for lack of time spent together and lack of appreciation for the times we did, regret
The cancer spread throughout his body, sending sharp and merciless pangs all over
I can't even begin to imagine what he went through, but the grief spreading throughout me was painful
His situation was fatal and he kept fighting on and on, but now he's gone
Shock was sent down my spine, causing me to shudder in disbelief
My friend, my friend that I had known for so many years is dead. He's gone

I was inundated and weighed down by feelings of grief and regret
It was as if I constantly had an anchor tied to my heart.
I kept feeling deep inside that I could've been there for him more
Pondering the coulda, shoulda, wouldas of our friendship

He told his friends and family to live the life you want to
He didn't want all his loved ones to be swallowed by feelings of grief
He wanted everyone to keep living the lives that they wanted to
For him I will keep smiling and have a positive outlook on my life, just like he did
I will live the life I want to, by overcoming grief and doing what I love with those I love
I'm sure he's looking down on all his friends and family with favor, elated that we are fulfilling his wish
We will always have the sadness, but it hasn't stopped us from living our lives
We are happy, just like he intended

Ellie Taylor, Grade 8
Rolling Hills Country Day School, CA

Winter

The great golden ball of tremendous flame begins to turn out the light with a soft golden glow,
A pure and moist scent of fine, freshly fallen white powder fills the air with no blow.

Trees stand silently, awaiting that moment they can finally shed their heavy white cloaks,
A hole filled with a clear liquid turns rock-solid, making the transformation without so much as a croak.

Oozing from some great woody pines is a sap sweeter than a triple chocolate cake,
Overhangs of a mysterious substance that's as bright as the sun twinkle for their own sake.

Great grey masses of chill take over all of the massive space in the air above
Cool, crisp water is a mirror, a perfect reflection of a moment as peaceful as a dove.

Hannah Hatheway, Grade 7
Cedaredge Middle School, CO

Snow Capped Beasts

There are big mountains.
The majestic mountains rise into the sky and out of sight.
Snow capped giants shoot into the sea of blue overhead.
Enormous pyramids break new barriers of the endless blank page.
Titanic globs of rock touch the celestial sphere, towering over the whole enchilada of the human population.
The seductive heaven invites the heaps of stone to accompany her on a never-ending journey of pirouettes.
Cliffs caress dreams of quixotic people that have drifted miles above.
Peaks ponder on the heavily guarded gates of the universe.
Alps fit into the grooves of the aquamarine vaults like it was meant to be.
The mountains paw at the azure envelope softly.
Forbidding summits rise to dangerously provoking heights.
Incredible beasts snarl down at the sea, daring her to disturb their quiet.
Steep slopes execute any being not strong enough to take the rigorous ultimatum.
The angelic, yet rugged domes take control of your breath the moment you inhale their crisp, fresh fragrance.

Micaela Marquez, Grade 9
Monarch High School, CO

Pink

Pink comes from the dribble of juice running down your chin,
Pink comes from children's cheeks on a cold winter day, and from a mother blowing her kids a good night kiss,
Pink comes from blush and from lip gloss,
Pink comes from an untold crush,
Pink bubbles from jealousy and from sweetness,
Pink is that tiny bottle of expensive perfume,
Pink is the smell of bubble gum and Valentine's Day chocolate,
Pink comes from little girls' giggles and piglet squeals.

Tatum Lenberg, Grade 7
Gale Ranch Middle School, CA

Gazing

Standing out and looking up, the reflection of the universe is on my eyes.
The entire world around was blocked out, as the entire world above was brought in.
Gazing up into the colossal universe and knowing that I am small.
The immense space above me holds so many secrets, while it has nothing to hide.
Knowing that there are planets and stars, but also not knowing what else space holds.
Our home planet may seem vast, but while looking into the cosmos above, you realize that it is minuscule.
Beholding a clouded canvas invaded by flickering silver droplets,
I am forced to cast my eyes downward and be yanked back to reality.

Erin Smith, Grade 9
Monarch High School, CO

Dave and Buster's

I remember when I went to Dave and Buster's.
I remember all the games, and all the fun I had.
I remember playing against my sister in the games that we played.
I remember all the food I ate.
I remember all the shouting of excitement when people won a game.
I remember my sister winning the jackpot on the Sea Bass game, making everyone want to play.
I remember the long drive home, and talking about all the fun we had.
I remember that day just like it was yesterday, and can't wait to go back!!!

Amanda Miller-Blaylock, Grade 8
Daniel Savage Middle School, CA

Sunset

The sun sets with a wash of colors:
Pink outlines the clouds, purple surrounding the sphere of bright orange and soft red.
A soft breeze brushes past as the dandelions dance in the wind, the seeds shooting from its stem, finding a place to settle.
As the fiery orange sun slowly sinks down, the breeze turns into a cold chill, the sky dimming at the loss of light.
Finally, the sun is no longer in sight, and the stars start to twinkle in and out of existence, flashing in all kinds of colors.
At first, it looks like it's just a random pattern, but as more stars blink into sight, the stars seem to make a flowing river pattern, snaking through the center of the infinite skies.

Micah Rapelje, Grade 7
Westside Neighborhood School, CA

I Am a Book

I may be boring in the beginning and you may want to move on, but then you won't understand me.
I can get lonely if all you do is look at me and leave me lying around in your bookshelf.
If only you wait, you will soon find out how interesting I can be.
I can be fun, just give me a try.
Don't give up on me and you will see the results.
In the end you will be happy to have read me and you will find out it was worth it.
As you have heard many times, "Don't judge a book by its cover."

Paola Yazmin Perez Duran, Grade 8
Palm Desert Charter Middle School, CA

Behind Her Smile

Behind her smile,
There is self-loathing,
There is pain.
She looks in the mirror,
Here it comes again.

Behind her smile,
She wishes,
She dreams.
She thinks to herself,
"Why do I have to be me?"

Behind her smile,
There is envy,
There is jealousy.
She walks past girls thinking,
"Why can't I be that pretty?"

Behind her smile,
She is clueless,
She cannot see
What other people see,
Which is her inner beauty.
Genevieve Knott, Grade 7
Joe Walker Middle School, CA

Rainbow

I am a rainbow
Conflicting personalities
Different shapes and sizes
I can never make up my mind.

I am red,
Hotter and nastier each day
Stubborn and cross
Fiery and hateful.

I am green,
Crazy, disobedient,
Spunky and unpredictable
Mischievous.

I am blue,
Dark, mysterious
Quiet but wise
Shielding many secrets.

I am a rainbow
Conflicting personalities
Different shapes and sizes
I can never make up my mind.
Rachel Higinbotham, Grade 7
Canyon View Jr High School, UT

Hope

Amazing, how a few
Words of
Love
Can bring sunshine
In through the
Never ending
Rain
Clouds

Even the darkest,
Thickest clouds
Must yield to
The kindness and
Love of
Another

Though it is still raining,
That one ray of sunshine
Breeds hope that,
One day,
The rain will
Finally
Stop
Arianna Martinez, Grade 9
Centennial High School, NM

Basketball

Basketball is an airplane
It may have turbulence
along its journey

I can turn and fly through the air
with one turn in command

My main goal is to
get to my destination
Without my passengers
getting injured

Woosh! I made it through
the white cloud

If I get a loss of air I can
drop the masks
and fill up with air

Now I have reached my goal
with many similar to come

If I want to fly the "big journey"
I will have to prove I am worthy
Hunter Allen, Grade 8
Falcon Creek Middle School, CO

That Is Mendicino

Natural, rough, with
green moss everywhere
That is Mendicino

Mountain lion screams as
the campfire sings
That is Mendicino

Tiny creatures and giant trees
look up and down upon you
That is Mendicino

Families going to the beach
while others set up camp
That is Mendicino

Sunlight peering through the clouds
watching the children play
That is Mendicino

This is just a place for some people,
but for me it feels like home
That is Mendicino
Mikaela Ferreira, Grade 8
Ripona Elementary School, CA

Our Story

Turn page

Models thin pretty face
Beautiful undeniable grace

Turn page

Boy and girl sweet embrace
True love's kiss princesses wake

Turn page

Dollar signs money trees
Happiness bought no mistakes

Turn page

Summary society's pressure
Be like this or be unhappy

Tear pages

THIS IS FAKE
Sophie Cardin, Grade 7
Stanley British Primary School, CO

Spark

Everyone has a spark.
They choose whether they go out,
Or whether they start

Your spark lets others know who you are.
Let yours shine like a star.
Make it bright, not dark.
Don't let other people take your spark.

Let your spark shine for all to see.
Remember who you want to be.
Be who you are.

Bam! Pow!
Once people see your spark, they'll say, "Wow!"
Don't frown,
Turn that upside-down.

Everyone has a spark.
They choose whether they go out,
Or whether they start.

Delaney Johnson, Grade 7
Joe Walker Middle School, CA

Fun

The fun has only just begun
What is to be done
With the fun that has just begun
Can this get any more confusing
Fun is fun
But without fun what can be done
To be or not to be or to see the seeing
Fun is not dumb for it can be done
To be the most annoying thing
Is to have fun with the most fun thing
So with what is done when having fun
To be or not to be
Is what I wish I can say
But for what I know and what I see
Fun is only to be me
And if you saw me then you would see
How much fun my life could be
With what am I
If I wasn't fun
Then what would my life become
When there is everything fun that hasn't begun

Stephanie Amstutz, Grade 8
Monte Vista Christian School, CA

The Famous Detective

Blood stains the clothes of Mr. Sherlock Holmes.
He lurks in the shadows of catacombs.
He and his partner keep Moriarty in line.
Sherlock Holmes as a person is well…quite divine.

Katie Lennon, Grade 8
Beacon Country Day School, CO

Somnambulist

Dawn turned to dusk and I fell asleep
The fireflies stars, however, woke me up
Not all of me though
Just my feet…
Soon my hands…
My face but not my mind
A drowsy sweeping motion threw the blanket off me
I rolled over
Slowly my upper body came up
My lower body came down
I stood without thought
Right, left, right, left…
Right, left, right, left…
I gradually opened my eyes
Surprise made them suddenly burst open
My jaw dropped
I shook my head in disbelief
How did I get from…
Brooklyn
…To…
Central Park!

Akilan Murugesan, Grade 9
Sacramento Country Day School, CA

Swordplay*

Those innocently brown eyes stared hopefully,
screaming, "Play with me!"

As we clashed our stick-swords,
and as he fell onto the lush, green, bed of grass,
he was laughing.
He fell, thinking himself a soldier.
He fell, not knowing.
But I knew.

I knew the battlefield where soldiers toppled.
But they never giggled.
They never got back up to play some more,
and they certainly didn't yell "Again! Again!"

They didn't have a second chance;
there is no second chance.

But for now, I help him up,
and we begin Round Two.

Claire Kim-Narita, Grade 8
Rolling Hills Country Day School, CA
In response to Gwendolyn Brooks' "The Boy Died in My Alley."

Carol Burnett

There once was a comedian named Carol Burnett.
In some of her shows, she sang in a quartet.
If she wasn't a comedian, it wouldn't be the same.
An era of comedy never told, what a shame.

Nicolas Gianos, Grade 8
Beacon Country Day School, CO

Music Blows Like the Wind
Music blows like the wind
Whispering in your ear

Bouncing through your head
Gives Happiness
Sadness
Nostalgia

Music flows all around
Makes you dance
Sing

Music is colorful
Gives life to everything
Is essential for living

Music is irresistible
Makes you want to let your hair down

Music is always there
All you have to do is listen
Shelby Lee, Grade 8
Falcon Creek Middle School, CO

Sun
Every morning
When I wake up
I see the sun rise.

And every time
I go to bed
I see the sun die.

Its blinding light
Shines about
Like a firework show.

But when I stare
Its blinding light
Hurts my eyes you know.

And every morning or every night
When the sun rises or falls

Everybody on this Earth declares
Thank you sun, thank you for all.
Ryan McCammon, Grade 7
White Pine Middle School, UT

Waterfalls
A relaxing sight
Water gushing very fast
Falling cool water
Harrison Sun, Grade 7
Young Scholar's Academy, AZ

Forever*
Gone forever,
It can't be so,
The light of your joy,
Will always show,
I should have remembered every word,
For they all disappeared,
On October third,
To your thoughts,
I will hold on forever,
Even in the stormy weather.
Alena Robinson, Grade 7
Monte Vista Christian School, CA
*Dedicated to Miss Carrie McCoid, October 3, 2012. I love you Carrie! RIP

Best Friend
He is a playful puppy waiting to follow the older sibling
He is a loud train passing by a group of kids
He is his dad, a blonde waiting for his moment
He is baseball every day
He is a special gift you get and do not want to give away
He is the kitten curled up in my lap
He is the freckles that sit upon his face different in every way
He is my teddy bear the one you do everything with
He is my heart always growing and fast
He is my cup of tea when I do not feel good, always making me smile
He is my brother and my best friend
Bari Agnes, Grade 9
Pueblo West High School, CO

Friendship
True friendship may be hard to find but once you have it's undefined
Friendship's a bright, shining star, always there to lead your way
Friends may be far apart but they will never leave your heart
You can count on one another and always make your good times last
You may imagine, sing, or play, they will love you anyway
They keep your secrets and share your dreams and love you for who you are
It's hard to survive without friends they help through beginnings, mourn the sad ends
They warm you with their presence, always help you through hard times
Friendship is like a hot, sunny day, it makes you happy in every way
The laughs and smiles spent with friends will always last a lifetime
Wide, beaming smiles all day long with your friends, you belong
Katie Donenfeld, Grade 7
The Mirman School, CA

The Gate
Standing at the gate,
a power overcomes me, as if an avalanche is tumbling down on top of me.
Then I feel at ease as I walk through the gates.
Everything is joyful, I feel at peace like I have found my rightful place in this world.
Many other people are surrounding me, greeting me.
Abruptly, I feel warmth come upon me.
Suddenly I miss being outside the gates, but I have to move on now.
I am home now with my Father, where I will be forever.
Georgie Morris, Grade 8
Muirlands Middle School, CA

Detention

I want out, out today!
I really want to go play.
This place is like a cage.
I am full of rage!

This is, absolutely terrible.
It is, truly unbearable.
I have been here for days!
This is torture in a different way.

The clock is ticking.
the bell has rung
I run and jump and play!
uh oh I'm late!

I run to my class.
I run very fast.
I got there at last.
oh did I forget to mention
I got another detention
Tanner Idleman, Grade 7
Joe Walker Middle School, CA

My Puppy

She is a devil in an angel costume,
Whom everyone adores and loves.
She chews my socks and steals my slippers,
And still expects forgiveness.
She holds her head high,
Her nose in the sky,
As if she were ten times her size.
If I leave her alone,
She's bored of her bone,
And she'll steal something of mine.

Yet if I walk by,
She'll look right at me,
And thump the tail on her rump.
Right then I believe,
Maybe, or possibly,
She may not be what I had thought.
For she is my beloved puppy,
With that troublesome look,
Who loves me more than I had dreamed.
Sheena Eustice, Grade 7
Joe Walker Middle School, CA

My Little Sister

We went to the hospital
Where my sister was born,
She was so tiny and cute,
When I held her for the first time,
She looked into my eyes and I
Knew we would be best friends.
Maggie Waguespack, Grade 7
St Francis School, CA

The Leap of Faith

On a warm, sunny afternoon, my courage had been built up
To jump the Leap of Faith

To the tallest rock I climbed
One of my greatest endeavors approaching
To jump the Leap of Faith

I knew not how it would end
The great tidal wave of anxiety had overcome me
As to jump the Leap of Faith

The brown, murky water seemed to be calling to me
The suspense was growing stronger
Should I jump the Leap of Faith?

As I sprinted towards the perilous spot, my great bravery abandoned me
But now there was no turning back
As I jumped the Leap of Faith

The water hurtled toward me like a jet
I became a bird in the spacious sky
Aware of all, but really nothing

I was full of pride as the impact of water surrounded me with a "Splash!"
My fears were no longer; my strength was stronger
I had jumped the leap of faith
Talmage Knight, Grade 7
Stapley Jr High School, AZ

My Tribute

Bring the coffin, fold the flag
Tears escape me as the honor guard slowly performs the military honors
The 21 gun salute shakes the ground;
And the echo rings out with a thundering pound

'Taps' plays and the trumpets whine
Then the flood gates burst and tears flow
As I stand there solemnly, hand over my heart
And listen to that trumpet blow

I know he is in a better place,
But it is hard to lose someone who you love so much
I remember his big smile, his flannel shirts, cowboy hat, suspenders
And his laugh

He was my neighbor, my friend, and someone who was there for me
Then the cancer came
This strong warrior began to fade
And my heart sank more and more with each passing day

To my dismay, it ate him away
Until he was in so much pain he couldn't take it
Hospice came in and he withered away until one day we got the news
He passed away today at noon
Nichole Lindstrand, Grade 9
University Preparatory School, CA

Happiness

Sitting there,
dreaming,
dreaming of dark,
empty eyes
staring,
they are staring
at me, but
then a radiant
light appears
in those eyes
I think of every happy moment
running toward me.
the trees,
tipped with snow,
reaching up
and taking all happiness,
putting it
in my heart
mine,
to keep
forever.

Zach Hubert, Grade 7
Canyon View Jr High School, UT

Song of Storms

When the sunshine has gone
We all know what will come…
From the sky, to the ground
Rain comes pouring down
With thunder, rain, and wind
The song of storms begins…
First comes the aqueous rain
Then the ferocious wind
Next a thundering hurricane,
With lightning striking the waves.
Hear the song, feel its cry
Teardrops continue falling from the sky…
Come along, sing the song,
Until the gray clouds have gone.
Now you've heard the song…of storms.

Kelsea Nguyen, Grade 7
Sarah McGarvin Intermediate School, CA

Us

You are so smart,
I love you with all my heart.
I know that you are true,
And that's why I love you.
You are as sweet as a honeybee.
As we stand a tree,
I show you all my love,
You are gentle like a dove.
I won't make a fuss,
It's just about us.

Mya Craig, Grade 8
Canyon View Jr High School, UT

Our Hero: Sestina

The horrible time that has been long dreaded has come
Where greed, lust, and misery have taken over without, toward the poor, a single blessing;
The powerful and the corrupt of the ages hold the reins,
While the weak cower in fear, while they watch with hopes and a dream
That a hero will come and save them from this terror;
Will they fall alone without any help, or will a hero draw the ancient blade?

Suddenly a hero emerges who holds the legendary blade;
A savior has finally come!
She has arrived to save the citizens from terror,
Over the land, she has put her blessing,
She has answered the devoted inhabitants' dream;
Coming on a white horse, our savior is at the reins.

Now the rich don't hold the reins,
For peace has come due to the warrior with the legendary blade.
The grief and poverty only seem like a faraway dream;
A time of peace and forgiveness has finally come,
For we always had the hero's blessing,
And we will never know again of fear or terror.

The hero has finally given the blessing needed while holding the white horse's reins,
And we know no more of terror — as if it never had come;
The dream of all children is to meet the hero wielding the legendary blade!

Megha Natarajan, Grade 7
Stratford Elementary/Middle School, CA

Sounds

I walked through the eerie mansion, holding my breath;
The stairs creaked, and the wind howled;
I heard a noise upstairs and called out, "Who's there?"
But all that responded was a tapping noise.
I hid under a table and nervously waited,
And the noise came ever so close, and then there was silence.

I waited for it to come closer — but still, silence.
The cold air in front of me fogged from my breath,
And still, I waited.
Then a noise emitted from the creature; it howled.
I waited still through the gruesome noise;
I peered out, and a black cat was there.

I laughed nervously, and for a moment the cat stayed there.
But it left, and again I was left in silence;
I waited for a sound, anything, but still no noise —
Not a tap, a thump, or even a breath;
All sounds ceased, but before I darted out the door, something howled:
It wasn't the cat, I was sure, since it left while I waited.

I stayed there, but again reigned a creepy silence;
The noise began again but abruptly stopped when I released a breath;
Once more it howled, but this time I had not waited.

Saikeerthana Sunkara, Grade 7
Stratford Elementary/Middle School, CA

In the Night Sky

In the night sky,
is something up high,
something that shines very bright.

It is a beam of light,
that makes you smile,
and makes you feel just right.

It is a luminous star,
that twinkles in the night,
right before your very eyes.

No one knows what they really are,
but they give you a sense of comfort.
They make you feel so close even if you are so far.

You can wish upon a star,
but it makes no difference who you are,
it just keeps you from falling apart.

They fly and soar through the sky.
Through the sky in a dark night,
but only sometimes, for you have to believe.

You can't just think the sky is blue,
you have to believe your wish will come true,
and when your wish comes true, just be you!

Kelsyann Cervera, Grade 8
St Helen Catholic School, CA

One Direction

There are five boys, they have hit songs,
They sing their hearts out,
They have millions of fans.

My first favorite is Harry. Harry is the guy I would marry,
He's funny, cute, and flirty
But he is 18 years old so too old.

My other favorite is Liam, he is so cute, and nice,
He always knows what to say,
But he is 19 years old so too old.

My third favorite is Louis, he is the funny one in the band,
He makes people laugh always,
But he is 20 so that is way too old.

My fourth favorite is Zayne, he is the mysterious one in the band,
You never know what he is thinking,
But he is 19 so way too old.

My fifth favor is Niall, he is the Irish one in the band,
He is claustrophobic so he has to have space,
He is 18, soon to be 19, but still too old.

Melissa Garibaldi, Grade 7
St Helen Catholic School, CA

Ships at Bay

Sometimes we wish to just sail away,
Only to realize there are anchors aweigh;
Usually set just to keep us at bay

In the heart, in the mind
Where the mixed feelings intertwine,
We think of the place we are leaving behind

We dream of the promising foam
At another beach we are destined to roam,
Yet regret seeps in at the word "home"

We move away from our small town and all its promising dreamers
To the big city of lights, filled with winners and streamers

These anchors, these "roots," one day their ropes will sever
Halfheartedly wishing us luck on our promising endeavors
Yet deep inside, we cling to these anchors forever

Arni Dyan Daroy, Grade 9
University High School, CA

Daddy's Little Princess

When I was younger, I used to believe that
I was my daddy's little princess and that
I would live in the castle of my dreams,
In the land of my dreams, with the man of my dreams,
And that all of my dreams would come true.

But as I got a little older,
And I saw how hard it'd be for my dreams to come true,
I went to my dad and I said,
"Hey I see how hard it is,
So I don't think I'll ever be famous."

And he said, "Baby, that's okay,
I love you to the moon and back
And that's a long way.
But if that's not far enough,
I'll try and wrap my love for you
Around the universe."

Brianna Corbett, Grade 8
Ventura Missionary Christian School, CA

Photos

I love the way they look.
Always different, and never the same.
I love photos, the people in them never change,
Although in real life they might.
From photos of flowers to people, always amazing.
From tiny, little details to huge landscapes, they
Are always different.
When you look at them, memories flood into your mind.
That's what makes me happy about them.
Nothing about them ever changes.

Josephine Emory, Grade 7
Daniel Savage Middle School, CA

The Wounded Bird

I watched a bird fly down the sky
And search for something in the ground
It spread its wings about to fly
But then found out that he was bound

I was frozen on my bench
While he was struggling on the ground
I realized he was wounded
So he couldn't move around

I tenderly picked him up
And carried him above the ground
I held him very carefully
So he wouldn't feel impound

I took him home to heal his wounds
And saw him peering at the ground
I asked what he was doing
And was responded with no sound

I then saw what wounded him
It had been a heart shaped mound
He soared high above the ground
And I began to cry happily
You see, this bird was me
Denisse Suastegui, Grade 9
The Preuss School at UCSD, CA

Tall

Oh! But this is no compliment.
'Tis a curse,
Trapping me,
Locking me away in glass walls.

No one comes to free me,
How could they?
They do not see.
In their prejudice they are deaf to my cries.

Oh! They call it a blessing.
'Tis a brand mark,
Burned to my side by their ignorance.

Oh! Will no one come,
And teach me to fly?
Or do you all assume,
That I was born with the knowledge?

Oh! They have forgotten.
How even poor Paul with his axe,
Was alone with his ox.

Oh! Believe Me!
This is no compliment!
Morgan Carpenter, Grade 7
Ward School, AZ

Lucky Necklace

I got my necklace in a may
It made me happy every day.
I take it everywhere I go.
I even love it you could say.

The answers on tests I would know.
Some days classes would be a bore.
I got good grades that made me glad.
In my head my necklace would glow.

The day I lost it I was sad.
I knew the day would end up bad.
That day was very dark and cold.
For some reason I was not mad.

I would find it I was even told.
I had some dreams where it was sold.
They told me to be strong and bold.
But I still wish for one more hold.
Azalia Maravilla, Grade 8
John Adams Middle School, CA

Friendship

Friendship is like a string,
If you're parted, it will snap.
Friendship is like a balloon,
If you argue, it will pop.

Friendship is a delicate thing,
Like a feather, like a shell.
Friendship is a powerful force,
Like a bomb, like a storm.

But when friendship is stopped,
It's a power come to an end,
Like a vase that has smashed.
A popped balloon, a snapped string.

Don't let friendship fade away.
Let it flourish, let it blossom.
With friendship on your side,
Everything is possible.
Cooper Gower-Samples, Grade 7
The Mirman School, CA

Cold Sky

Snow, falling from the sky
Fluffy snowflakes landing on my tongue
Sprinkling lightly into my hair.
Rolling into a field of snow,
Watching my nose as it turns a bright red,
From the cold, cold air.
Hearing Christmas carols,
From many children in the town
Maharlika Amar, Grade 7
Sarah McGarvin Intermediate School, CA

Night and Day

As I move through the night,
The light will not appear,
Nor come to my hands,
It is only darkness.

The night will not end,
Nor blow away,
Nor go away,
Because it is here to stay.

The moon shining bright,
The stars hanging high,
It's almost like a dream.

But now the sun is rising,
And the moon is vanishing,
The trees are singing,
The flowers are dancing,
It is now day.
Zoë Takishita, Grade 7
Joe Walker Middle School, CA

Stutter King

Yeah, I stutter,
So what; I don't care.
If you really don't like it,
Go cry in your lair.

The comments really hurt,
I can't describe the pain;
You have no idea what it's like,
Until you've been me for a day.

People make fun of me,
They think I am weak;
Be me for a day,
You'll find out how hard it is to speak.

Although it is hard,
I blow the mean comments off;
Although it really hurts,
I only laugh and scoff.
Braxton Dothard, Grade 8
Joe Walker Middle School, CA

Bully

That guy making looks at you,
That guy making you a fool,
Do you think he has that right,
Stand up with all your might.
Don't even leave without a fight,
Please, you have the power,
He would be at the bottom
And you would be on the top of the power.
Quang Dao, Grade 7
Sarah McGarvin Intermediate School, CA

A Great Idea

All I want is for someone to listen to me,
Someone to actually listen for once!

All I want is for someone to listen to me,
Someone to believe in me,
Someone to agree and stand with me.

All I want is for someone to listen to me,
Someone to get the idea,
Someone to think it's the greatest idea ever,
Someone to actually think of ideas to go along with my idea!

All I want is for someone to listen to me,
Someone to love the idea,
Someone to already make a visual of my idea,
Someone to spread rumors about my idea,
Someone to top my idea and make it better!

All I want is to have an above and beyond idea!

Kyle Schwulst, Grade 7
Falcon Creek Middle School, CO

Exile Eyes

Eyes that have a voice of their own
The truth is whispered in how they are shown
With their old clothes and silent cries
The truth comes out in their exile eyes

Even when they smile and laugh
They can still feel the pain
The pain of the past that won't disappear
Living off hope that is nowhere near

Your eyes are a true opening into your soul
The burden of having to hold back your tears
Knowing you won't have a place to call home
Left in this cruel world all alone

Sophia Seraj, Grade 9
Woodbridge High School, CA

Senseless Violence

Bullets screech towards the innocent
Violence tears the children's dreams
The innocent prevail

Drugs fuel the anarchist
Children are tempted to follow others' mistakes
The innocent rebel against ill ideas
The innocent prevail

Corrupt ideas *cannot* determine lives
Challenge the poor judgment of others
Against all odds,
The innocent prevail

Andrew Xavier Gudino, Grade 8
Richardson PREP HI Middle School, CA

Now

Chatty and talkative were common terms,
Hearing all the stories that stuck like germs.
And when we laughed,
Not stopping to breathe,
Deciding to giggle endlessly.
Laughing was hard to stop,
Everything seems better,
Reviving all the jokes like some sane person.
All of the stuff we talked about,
Not choosing to ever forget,
Doing all these things.
Every day was like a masterpiece,
Loving every bit of it,
Lulling to sleep during class,
Illogical like certain things should they pass.
Ongoing days as if in a trance,
Totally like a complicated dance.
Timing it perfectly with the sound of life,
Like the elaborate sky.
Venture to that destiny,
Ending with my mind so free.

Katie Miller, Grade 7
White Pine Middle School, UT

On Our Own

On our own —
my Mom and I —
crying inside
yet struggling to smile on the outside

On our own —
mom sayin' "It's gonna be ok" —
knowing that it is not!
Why are there lies?

On our own —
Light at the end of the tunnel,
NOW-now-we are not sad nor faking our emotions

On our own —
Happy as happy can be!

Veronica Brundage, Grade 8
Richardson PREP HI Middle School, CA

Love

Love isn't just hope,
Love isn't just fate.
Love is how you use it and if you give or take.
Love is not just passion,
Love is pure.
Love isn't about the race, or rather the face.
It's about who you share it with and if you stay or break.
When you find someone who you may love, just remember
We were made to love, so love with all the love you can take.

Desiree Pelham, Grade 8
Palm Desert Charter Middle School, CA

Better

People say
That so much is going on around us
Vast solar systems fail, cosmic galaxies spinning and whirling, the sonic boom of stars exploding,
crest fallen clouds crying icy tears of hail
Why?
We think the world is so big it can't grow anymore
The world we see and know is the all-white door on the one story house, the purple flowerbed in the front yard,
businessmen walking and talking on their cellphones, sales at the store we covet,
the non-fat, decaf, iced, caramel macchiato with extra caramel we must bring to our boss at exactly 6:32 A.M. sharp.
But what?
What about what?
What about what is happening to this universe right now as words escape the creases of my mouth
As I speak this poem in front of you
Kids are thinking more than us
Kids are discovering more than us
Kids are doing more than us
Kids know more than us
"They know that if a man runs off the edge of a cliff he will not fall until
he notices his mistake"
Because they think differently…
Better

Molly Leimbach, Grade 8
Rolling Hills Country Day School, CA

The Beauty of Belief

In the end, all the pain and agony and sins we have committed turn into raindrops on your eyelashes.
They are forgotten, erased, never to be seen again in the rearview mirror of life.
Don't look for the darkness, look to the light.
We humans forget the good blessings and keep the memories of our sorrow from past, present and future.
So, put down that bottle and pick up your little girl who has been waiting to be proud to call you Dad.
Put down that knife, because it isn't the answer.
Pick up that pencil and present your story of happiness and joy to the world who loves you for you!
So be you, be the one and only, be the one who isn't plastic or just a copy of someone else.
You are an original.
You are who you were meant to be, and you have never looked more beautiful.

Kesney Faubion, Grade 8
Deer Creek Middle School, CO

My Parents

When you thought I wasn't looking, I saw you making me a peanut butter and jelly sandwich and I learned to serve the ones I love.
When you thought I wasn't looking, I saw you being helpful and I realized all you do for the world and I hope to do the same.
When you thought I wasn't looking, I saw you being kind to those in need and I learned that I need to do the same.
When you thought I wasn't looking, I saw you cleaning up the house and I realized how determined you are to make our home a
    welcoming place.
When you thought I wasn't looking, I saw you kneeling down to pray and I noticed how spiritual and faithful you really are.
When you thought I wasn't looking, I saw you reading in your bed and I noticed how smart you are.
When you thought I wasn't looking, I saw you having a positive attitude and I learned that you are the best parents.
When you thought I wasn't looking, I saw you being a leader and I will try to do the same in my life.
When you thought I wasn't looking, I saw you sad when we leave somewhere and I learned how much you love us.
When you thought I wasn't looking, I saw you putting up Christmas decorations and realized how much you love our family and
    the holidays.

Matthew Mella, Grade 7
Canyon View Jr High School, UT

Brian

His fur, dark as a chimney's smoke.
His eyes, yellow like an egg's yolk.
The cutest thing you would ever see.
So young, but his glare is mean.

Ah, time flew by so fast.
Is this warm embrace the last?
Everybody is becoming old.
Thank you for this time we've passed.

I hear a violin playing a sad song.
Why does it seem to be so long?
I feel the rain coming.
It is time to go where you belong.

As time goes by, I won't forget.
You were my beloved pet.
Such a cheerful feline.
Now it's time for you to rest.
Shaelly Flores, Grade 8
John Adams Middle School, CA

Ode to My Phone

My small black phone
You hold so much information
I could never remember.
Without you I would be lost.

I wouldn't be able to call anyone
I wouldn't be able to text
I would not know anyone's number
I would not be able to
Remember anyone's birthdays or special
Events.
I would not even know the
Date.

What would I do without you?
You remember the small and
Big things I would forget.
Thank you, my small black
Phone.

Estefania Pulido, Grade 7
Daniel Savage Middle School, CA

Winter

Winter where it's cold outside
Air is crisp and light outside
And in the frozen sky above
I see your face, I think of you
I miss your face, I miss your smile
Your big blue eyes, and mine
Your laughter lingers in the air
And your memory makes me cry
Claudia Wing, Grade 8
Meridian Elementary School, CA

Ode to Avocados

O, green, mushy, sweet avocado,
How you taste like pure heaven
With your mild sweet and salty flavor
When I add a sprinkle of salt to you.
You feel like velvet
And you melt in my mouth.
Although avocado
You have some funky skin
Like my dear old grandma
Who is welted and thin.
How avocado,
How do you do it?
Convince me to eat you,
Without persuading me with words.
O, sweet avocado you lure me towards you
Like a little girl when she spots a puppy.
Sometimes I ask myself,
Don't you just feel like having an avocado?
Emily Levin, Grade 7
Rolling Hills Country Day School, CA

Good Samaritan

Who helps the lost
When they are scared
Who leads them into the light
When they are stuck in the dark
Who comforts them
When they cry
Who laughs with them
When they need a friend
Who listens to them
When they need to talk
Who carries them
When they cannot stand
Who cares for them
When they are sick
Who loves them
When they are old
Who mourns them
When they are gone.
Ariel Pan, Grade 8
Jane Lathrop Stanford Middle School, CA

The Day You Left Me

I'll never forget the day you left me,
standing in the dust, all alone.
I was so very sad.
I sad there and cried,
doing nothing else for hours.
Oh how I wish you were here,
I am in so much pain without you.
If only I could hear your voice again,
it would mean the world to me because
I'll never stop wishing you were here.
Karie Russell, Grade 9
Encampment K-12 School, WY

The Four Seasons

Winter, cold and dark
Moonlight on the deep white snow
Holidays are near

Springtime, loud and clear
Delicate petals adorn
Everything I see

Summer in its blaze
Burning sand against my feet
Water as escape

Fall, brown and simple
Leaves crunch, days shorten, come school
Gone carefree allure
Abbie Mulmat, Grade 7
Carmel Valley Middle School, CA

The Joy of Water

Great waves skim the sea
Their power engulfing us
Repeating motion

Small fish in the stream
So majestic, lean, and swift
Abundant and scarce

Sparkly yet so plain
Is what water really is
Cold, yet wonderful

Sometimes falling hard
And other times so softly
Rain is essential
Madeline Jinks, Grade 7
Monte Vista Christian School, CA

A Clever Kind of Love

If I shall take this step
I shall take it with thee
For thou will be the eyes
Of all I cannot see
In this heart thou had given me love
In these hands thou has given me trust
Yet if this is all that may lay
A constant plead to know
Then let faith lead the way
In which I shall stay
Or I shall go
But for now I shall wait
But not forever
For you my love are smart
But I am very clever
Nicodee Clark, Grade 8
Canyon View Jr High School, UT

The Color of Life
The passionate green,
That fills the Earth.
The stem of a flower.

It's photosynthesis
It's jungles, rain forests, and seaweed.
Green is the color of money,
A necessity to live.

Green is the way environmentalists
Choose to abide.
Green is growing,
It's vines
It's new leaves
And fresh shoots of grass.

Green is life.
It's the beginning
Of a cycle
It's spring time
And it's hope.
Katherine Chretien, Grade 8
Daniel Savage Middle School, CA

I See It
I see it.
I see it.
As scary as could be,
screams, roars, and sometimes laughs
and usually scares me.

I see it.
I see it,
in my dreams and on my mind.
Black and bright,
but not very kind.

On one night,
not two,
I couldn't carry on.
It came unexpected
and grasped me by the arm.
It was pretty ugly.
I couldn't go on.
But suddenly I woke up,
and everything was gone.
Sheridan Hagle, Grade 7
Joe Walker Middle School, CA

Clouds
Clouds up in the sky
Looking like white cotton balls
Soaring way up high
Bulos Farah, Grade 7
St Martin-in-the-Fields School, CA

Autumn
I like how when fall comes,
All the trees change,
And all the butterflies and the birds go south.

It's a beautiful time of year,
With late dinners by the fire,
The laughter of family that fills the room.

Everyone gets this celebration spirit inside of them,
They become excited for the holidays.
It's such a warm feeling.

All the Christmas items are put on display,
Alongside the pumpkins and Halloween costumes,
While all the children get more and more thrilled for the presents and candy.

Different-colored leaves scatter on the floor,
Drizzles of rain fall every now and then,
While people watch the gloomy clouds outside dreamily.

The air has a cold but welcoming feeling to it,
It's just the entire atmosphere,
That makes everyone smile.

Maybe I like autumn because of the beauty.
I know I like autumn,
For its beauty most of all.
Crystal Perez, Grade 7
St Helen Catholic School, CA

Why Starting to Play Basketball Is a Baby Bird
Starting to play basketball is a baby bird.
At first when the baby bird enters the world,
it may seem bewildering,
But the baby bird has to take steps in its nest, made of comforting twigs, to learn how to fly.
The baby bird will fail numerous times and come crashing down in its nest,
but the baby bird cannot give up or it will never reach its goals.

Starting to play basketball is a baby bird.
Some days its wings just don't want to work.
Like human beings on Mondays.
But every day it gets better, getting higher and higher off the ground.
And it continues that way, more and more each day, higher and higher off the ground.
Its feathers are getting more defined, blue and black feathers expanding each day.
It learned from its past experiences, and whoosh! The baby bird flew for three seconds.
The baby bird kept getting bigger, better. Flying for more and more seconds each day,
Soon the baby bird excelled at flying.

Playing basketball is a bird.
The baby bird kept getting higher and higher off the ground until it was flying.
And sometimes you fly back to your nest when you've grown up,
just to see the place where you conquered
flying.
Dereck Helms, Grade 8
Falcon Creek Middle School, CO

Alone

In a room full of people
Everyone screaming
Phones buzzing
Radios blaring
Walls shouting back
"Silence, silence"
No one hears
This tiny box holds
All the people of the world
Here I sit quiet
Alone

Kelsey Rae, Grade 8
Weldon Valley Jr High School, CO

What I Do Best

I love painting my nails,
All night and day.
To paint in the details,
And pass the time away.
Swirls, sparkles and tips,
Shoes, Avengers and even lips!
I will never give up my hobby,
It's what I do best.
They may come out blobby,
But they're how I express.

Sarah Cadwallader, Grade 8
St Martin-in-the-Fields School, CA

The Perfect Guy

I hide behind my own shadow
Then I met him
Dirty dish blond hair cutie
My hands are clammy, cold
Afraid like a lost puppy on a winter day
I meander over to him and say hi
He flashes me his perfect smile
His sky blue eyes draw me in
I smile back
I think he is falling for me

McKayla Barber, Grade 8
Weldon Valley Jr High School, CO

Love Is Love

love
love is complicated
love is hard
love is like a flower
it dies
love can be strong
love can be fragile
but whatever happens
love is
love

Isabel Nguyen, Grade 7
Sarah McGarvin Intermediate School, CA

The Fallen Tree

I woke up by a fallen tree, the sky was blue, the grass was green.
Standing up, I looked around, my smile then turned into a frown.

Looking down the hill I saw, a scene that made my stomach crawl.
The sky was a depressing gray, no living thing could live and stay.

The towns were burned and fallen down, the houses were all on the ground.
I looked down at all familiar roads, I then remembered this is my home.

Tears were rolling down my face, running fast, like in a race.
Memories came flooding back, in time, I knew why I was left.

Armies came crashing through the town, they threw us all hard to the ground.
In chaos, my mom told me to run, she said, "Head towards the west, wait for the sun."

So I waited and waited, she didn't show, I started to worry as it got cold.
I remember lying down by that tree, so everyone's gone; there's no one but me.

Kenzie Blomquist, Grade 9
Pine Creek High School, CO

A Blank Canvas

A blank canvas, nothing to see, nothing to hold,
Fill in the world with your brushes, as the trees spread over the horizon

A stroke for the land, a wave for the sea, you paint it exactly as it should be,
With nothing to fight, no decisions to make, this is a world only you can create

Canvas the world, across an uneven page,
Dance with the colors of freedom and purity, you are the rainbows

When you paint, you are beautiful, no prejudice of the eye can hold you,
You tame the golden, savage lion of beauty, charm it to bow before you

Yet when you paint, you are delicate and graceful, like a flower borne from a storm,
Nothing can touch you, you are just to behold

As your creation comes to a close, you step to the side,
View from the distance, appraise this new life

Ava Dobbs, Grade 7
The Mirman School, CA

Home

I have a place
Where I learned how to walk.
Where I learned how to smile joyfully and playing enthusiastic

I have a place
Where I will be frightened in the dark
Be sad until my mom calms me down.

I have a place
Where my family takes care of me feeds me, hugs me, and feel happy

That place is called home

Ronald Diaz, Grade 8
Richardson PREP HI Middle School, CA

Labyrinth

Dear Life,
I would like to notify you
of your unpredictable nature.
You tell me you're not fair.
You tease me with things
I can never achieve.
You say you're impossible
like a labyrinth.
I would like to tell you
that I'll never stop trying.
So during our next encounter,
when you can't dim my light
and I don't give in like a
house of cards,
Then I will have defeated
you, even though I can never
truly win.
I will know you aren't
impossible, just difficult.
Then I will have uncovered
your secret.

Caecilia Sarnowski, Grade 7
Falcon Creek Middle School, CO

A Slice of Something I Can't Forget

Wishing I could still
Color outside the lines
Without being judged.

Wishing I could still
Not have a care in the world.
Be who I want.

Wishing I could still
See that light
In every day.

Fighting off monsters
Who live under our beds.
Making memories.
Dreaming big.

Playing in the rain.
Forgetting what hurts.
Dreaming everything in the world
Will be okay.

Audrey Klein, Grade 7
Salida Middle School, CO

Life

L ove
I ncidents
F right
E xcitement

Rawaan Khatib, Grade 7
Young Scholar's Academy, AZ

My Heart

Forever I give you my heart
But why should I?

You dropped it once on nails and glass
It shattered into a thousand pieces of regret, broken promises, and lies

I give you my heart
Because I trust you to do the right thing
I trust you to never drop it again but
To hold it close to yours
Forever

I trust you because you asked me to
Because you promised
Promised to never break my heart
Ever again

Saige Cannedy, Grade 7
Salida Middle School, CO

Puppies

Hey! Don't eat plants.
Don't steal food or underpants.

Don't eat my socks, don't grab my hair.
Don't rip the stuffing from that chair!

Don't eat those peas! Don't touch that bush! Don't chew my toes! What IS that mush?

Eat your cookies. Drink your drink,
Outta the toilet! Outta the sink!

Away from the cat box, it's for the cat!
And MUST you kiss me after that?

Yes, raising a puppy is not for the lazy!
Though puppies are funny, they're also quite crazy.

Justise Johnson, Grade 8
Christ the King School, AZ

No One Believed

No one believed in the rose that grew from concrete
Just as no one believed that man had grown from soil
We all show our struggles
Just as the rose shows the world its struggles
We fight to live
It fights to live, seeking nourishment from stone
We show our strength against our weaknesses
Just as a rose's bright flower is a contrast of strength and beauty
It is an inspiration to all who seek
It has shown its beauty through the petals but its strength from its thorns
It has proven every one wrong
When no one else believed in it
When no one else thought it could grow into the beauty it is now
They were wrong — it has grown to be the most beautiful flower of all

Joe Polack, Grade 8
Rolling Hills Country Day School, CA

Hurray!

I'm so small, I can't be seen.
She doesn't even know I'm me.

She knows I'm here!
I *can* be seen!
My eyes, my ears, my everything.

I wonder what it will be like.
I know she wonders too.
We will be happy and content,
Him and me and her.

There's more of me, but less of space.
It's way to tight!
I'm in a fright!

The day is here. It's finally here!
Today I will see her,
Her eyes, her ears, her nose, her everything!
Today, this day, is a special day.
Today is the day that I am born!
Hurray!
Renee Grambihler, Grade 8
Christ the King School, AZ

Seasons

Rain drops will soon fall
As fall turns into winter
Cold will turn to snow

The whispering winds
Will change winter into spring
The flowers will bloom

With blooming flowers
We will see Aprils showers
Which will bring summer

Summer means no school
Time to catch up on our rest
Rain drops will soon fall
Nathaniel Amaris, Grade 7
Monte Vista Christian School, CA

Wonder Mom

Works as a doctor's assistant in Turlock.
Always cares about people in need.
She always has a smile like a sunflower.
She is brave like a lion.
Smart as a nerd with glasses.
She is like Wonder Women without powers.
Cuddles like a stuffed animal.
Cooks good like a pot on a stove.
She is thin as water flowing in a stream.
Liliana Facio, Grade 7
Daniel Savage Middle School, CA

Friendship

A friend is someone who cheers you up
When you spirits are down
A friend is someone who holds you hand
When you have a frown
A friend is someone who wipes you tears away
When they start to flow
A friend is someone who gives you hope
When your meter is low
A friend is someone who picks you up
Whenever you may fall
A friend is someone who drops everything
When she gets your call
A friend is some who laughs at your jokes
Even when they're not funny
A friend is someone who radiates warmth
Even when it's not sunny
A friend is someone who shows you the way
When you get lost
A friend is someone who fights for you
No matter the cost
A friend is someone who stays by your side through all the dips and turns in life
Christina Tesarek, Grade 7
Stapley Jr High School, AZ

Just Because He Loves Us

Our family gathers inside one day
While us children whine and beg to go play
We all sit down, wondering what for, then Dad comes walking in through the door
On his face he wears a look of sorrow and despair
Right then, I knew, he must be going somewhere
He explains to us he'll be gone for a year
How can he not be overwhelmed with fear?
He has to, I know, but why, oh why?
I turn to see tears streaming down my family's eyes
A sense of silence and gloom slowly starts suffusing the room
My mind starts racing with thoughts of what he'll miss
From all the big holidays, to the simplest goodnight kiss
Our family will fight hard to stay strong, even though he'll be gone for so long
While he risks his life every day, not letting anything get in his way
It's amazing what things he does, just because he loves us.
Gabriella Gonzalez, Grade 9
Pine Creek High School, CO

Friendship

Friendship is a Christmas tree, and we are the ornaments
Friendship is a brilliant star, shining brighter when the sky turns darker
Friendship is your guardian angel, keeping an eye out to see if anybody wants to hurt you
Friendship is a guitar playing, and though the music may stop, the strings are forever
Friendship is medicine, curing your loneliness
Friendship is the list-topper, helping you survive through life
Friendship is going to a concert, crying to slow sad songs
Friendship is someone caring about how you feel
Friendship is someone who laughs when you fall but still cares for you,
Falling and laughing and you don't care that's when you realize that you have a best friend.
Valeria Fitch, Grade 7
St John's Episcopal School, CA

Memories Forgotten

As time faintly dwindled down,
Slow and so steady.
Painful memories of the past,
Guilty and very heavy,
Memories not forgotten.

Memories in the worn mind,
Soulless and immensely hollow.
Wrenched to the open heart,
Over encumbered and shallow,
Memories not forgotten.

Like moths to a flame,
Blackened and very faint.
The life quickly burned away,
Troubled and constant hate,
Memories not forgotten.

To the peak of endurance,
Death crept at long last,
Memories not forgotten.
Justin Truong, Grade 8
Joe Walker Middle School, CA

Family

Families stick together forever
They will always love you
They have unconditional love for you
They have a mom and a dad
And maybe a brother or a sister
Maybe grandpa, grandma
Aunts and uncles
Cousins, nieces and nephews
However big the family, the love is there
Always there
It's there in your heart
In the heart of your family
In the heart of God
Cause God is part of your family
And everyone's family
Isabella Alvarado, Grade 7
Monte Vista Christian School, CA

Scenes of Nature

As the blue sky turns red,
The clouds move over ahead.
The waterfall forever runs,
But the rock cliff stays still.
The sunset stuns,
As many lights still fill
The scene will only last a day,
As night extends.
Like how seasons go away,
But nature never ends.
Karina Duran, Grade 8
South Lake Middle School, CA

Where Poetry Hides for Me

Poetry hides everywhere.
Poetry hides in my old house where I spent almost half my life.
It hides in my old laptop that now gathers dust in a closet.
It hides in all my old school projects that now fill plastic tubs.
Poetry hides in my old GameCube, that sits in my closet aging with time.
Poetry hides with my grandmother who lives in Mexico.
Poetry hides in all my old toys that I had when I was little.
It hides in all my old books that I used to read when I was younger.
Poetry hides in my old dog who is no longer with me.
Poetry hides in my first bike that I learned to ride when I was 7.
Poetry hides in a special outfit I got when I was a baby that I was baptized in.
Poetry hides in all my old pictures that are displayed neatly in a photo album.
Poetry hides in the memories I have of all the vacations I've ever had.
Poetry hides with all my old teachers who have helped me get through school.
Poetry hides with all my family members who have helped me in life.
It hides with all the people I have ever met who made me who I am.
Ricardo Torres, Grade 7
Tenaya Middle School, CA

White Bliss

As I speed down the slope, I am surrounded by a snowy white bliss
I feel the cold, blistering wind gnawing at my face
As I become faster and faster, the world around me becomes blurred
I am focused only on the present
My future and past have been forgotten
The wind whirls around my body as it rushes past
The sound of it so loud it blocks out any other noise
Nothing around me matters
All I know is that I must finish, must get to the end
I feel like anything is possible, like an eagle spreading its wings
The finish becomes closer every second that goes by
I know this incredible journey must draw to a close
As I near the finish, I am gasping for breath and my legs are burning
Time to do it again
Kyle Gunzy, Grade 7
Christ the King School, AZ

Dark, Lonely Night

Intently following the dark tale, the hairs on my arm begin to stand at attention.
The beastly creature holds his victim tightly.
Lifting my eyes, I see dark shadows lurking in the distance.
Suddenly the echo of a hooting owl pierces the silence.
The whispering of spirits arises from afar.
Gusts of wind rattle the cracked panes of the window.
Cracks of lightning intermittently send the slightest glow.
Footsteps shuffle above me.
Voices start up again.
The heavy knocker bangs loudly three times.
Slowly my head returns down to the novel.
My thoughts jumble as I ponder,
Is this real? Or just my twisted imagination?
Cecilia Rossi, Grade 7
St Cecilia School, CA

Walking with Champions

Starting off in the morning dew,
Our trip was planned to fly through the blue
As we floated through the sky
With music in my ears
Looking for a crowd that will give me a cheer

Heading down to a land that I have never seen,
Full of riches and many shades of green
As we were waiting for our luggage we saw an old friend
And they help us get to the golf course played by many great men.
When the final day of the tournament came to an end
I learned that you can never get out of the harsh weather.

Traveling around on the island beauty
Waiting for the next round of perfect mutiny
There course try to bring me down to a tear,
But my dreams will have no fear.
After I found that perfect round
I walk among champions to their homeward bound

Charles Reiter, Grade 8
Palm Desert Charter Middle School, CA

A World Without Technology

Think back to the good ol' times,
No electricity to power the lines,
Long, long ago apple was a fruit,
Not a corporation run by men in suits.

How simple life could still be,
No emails to see,
Things saved on paper!
Not electronically.

Real world problems like sickness and death,
Not Facebook friends becoming less,
Ask around for the news,
Don't listen to a talking screen for a clue.

I suppose all is easier said than done,
It will be hard to turn off all that fun,
So I will start, I will be the one…
Oh wait, let me text my mum!

Simone Decker, Grade 7
Joe Walker Middle School, CA

December

Upon this cold December night,
I do not need a fireplace to keep me warm
His arms do that
I do not need a mirror to tell me I am beautiful
His eyes do that
I do not need a poem or song to say, "I love you"
His heart does that

Hana Ayoub, Grade 9
Centennial High School, CA

Catalina

I woke up that Sunday
Knowing it was gonna be sad.
It was our last day there;
I wanted to stay so very bad.

I put my shoes and jacket on,
And caught up with the pack.
We were one-fourth up the mountain
When I realized my friends were in the back.

The sunrise was beautiful,
On that Catalina day.
I couldn't believe it was time
To march back down and pack away.

Oh, how I miss that piece of land.
And someday I will return,
With a welcoming hand,
To the place I love called Catalina Island.

Aimee McPherson, Grade 7
Joe Walker Middle School, CA

Violin

Your shoulders straighten up,
Your wrist is relaxed.
The bow of your instrument sits on your strings.

Passion and talent rises like smoke in a chimney.
Plucking, pizzicato, pitch, and playing perfectly,
Is all combined, and each stroke is taken effectively.

An arm supports the hand,
The hand supports your wooden beauty.
You bow up and down flawlessly,
With lifting fingers that rise off of your strings,
One by one, they are popping kernels.

The vibration of your music sings,
Each note calls for an audience.
Lovely music is soothing,
And kind to the ear like the bible's words.
The violin produces harmony and happiness.

Cozette Montagut, Grade 7
Joe Walker Middle School, CA

Ode to a Snowy Night

Under the moon, snow
sparkles as it falls from the light puffy clouds
snow
like a dream
come true to every child in every home,
drifting down covering the
earth in a blanket of snow

Danielle Jensen, Grade 8
Mountain Ridge Jr High School, UT

Defy Everything

If today was your last
Would you go with the flow
Or defy everything
Give up
Or go on
Quit
Or play the game
Let time pass
Or use every second
If you have something to say
Say it
If you want to do something
Do it
Never let anyone
Do it for you
So if you like to play it safe
Or quit
I get that
But if you really want to live
You'll
Defy everything
Shade Hadley, Grade 7
Salida Middle School, CO

Baseball Cards

Baseball cards are determination
When you pursue an excellent one,
That is your high determination.

When you find a bad card,
That is your low determination.
Throw that inadequate card in your
Fireplace as it patiently waits to devour it
With the flames of disappointment.
Encounter a good card so,
you can succeed.

Some days you have no cards
so you're firm about obtaining more.

Keep those outstanding cards,
Because you may never get them again.

So open that binder again,
Take out that unique card
And keep it with you forever.
Ryan Herringshaw, Grade 8
Falcon Creek Middle School, CO

White

Beautiful flying doves
Shining full moon
Bright lights
Angel wings in heaven
Devin England, Grade 7
Daniel Savage Middle School, CA

Map to Eden

Meet me at the bright yellow house on Crespi Drive
Where a couple once brought home their newborn baby.
Find the immense apple tree near the front porch, where the baby once sat, under the shade
And try to find the pacifier she left on moving day
Then, follow the symphony of humming birds and blue-jays,
To another house nearby, on Canzonet Street.
See the vacant blanket and empty picnic basket
Where the toddler once sat with her father
And wait for the stars to shine. Go in the picnic basket, and find a camera
Find the picture of a little girl holding a fish tank
With her parents and even another baby
Right outside a house Birden Street.
Go to that house, and burst open the door!
Feed the fish, that the little girl had left for the new tenants
And find the jazz, tap, and ballet shoes
Neatly lined up in a row.
And lastly, travel to Friar Street.
And you will see ironically enough
I lay there, on the lawn, with a blanket, a picnic basket,
And a sky full of stars
It is then, you realize, you have just found, me.
Eden Burakoff, Grade 7
Archer School for Girls, CA

Leech

Darkness, I'm hiding on the bed in a blanket of fear and darkness.
I see a shadow moving on the ground below, I hug my pillow.
A mixture of fear and excitement floods my trembling body.

Movement…

The creature leaps on the bed.
I strike him with my pillow as I scream.
He grabs my leg and starts to pull me down to the dark abyss below me,
I shake him off just in time.

He slides off to the cold shadows on the ground.
Waiting for his next opportunity to attack.

Success! I have won this round.
This has been yet another thrilling round of Leech.
Anya Evaskovich, Grade 7
Salida Middle School, CO

Music

Click to your favorite song
Listen to the musician sing and hear each different tone in their voice
Hear as the trebles clasp in your ear
Feel the bass rock your head
Experience the highs bring light to the song
Sense every note as it roles off the singer's tongue
Sing along and enjoy every verse as it plays by
Think of every song as if it were a new one
Music, taking anyone who hears it into their own world
Andrew Piazza, Grade 8
Christ the King School, AZ

Where I Am From

I am from ice fishing, Bass and Trout
I am from games screaming and cheating
I am from deer meat, fish meat, and hamburgers
I am from green grass playgrounds and flowers
And the green grass daring me to lay in it

I am from popcorn, movies, and candy
I am from "stop it" and "knock it off"
From Brent Jeppesen and Wendy Anderson
I am from fresh Christmas trees and staying up late
From singing and playing to family history and caroling
And my great grandpa who was a Veteran

I am from Smithfield, Utah
I am from 5 people
I am from pink, purple, and lime green too
I am from traditions and my family tree

Kaylie Jeppesen, Grade 7
White Pine Middle School, UT

Alone

I stand amid the stillness.
of a land full of nothingness.
I look around,
to see nothing but pure ground.
Nobody in sight,
as far as the eye can see.
I am alone.
It is only me.

All I want is a friend.
Someone who would listen,
as I empty the thoughts deep inside my head.
Someone to love me.
Someone to hold me close,
when I need them most.
I stand amid the stillness,
of a land full of nothingness.

Cole Elliott, Grade 7
Joe Walker Middle School, CA

Ode to Volleyball

The game resumes after the time-out.
It starts with a hard serve.
The ball is spinning in the air like it's on fire.
Hoping it does not get stopped by the net.
The ball gets over as the other team hits the ball
It comes back.
One hit, second hit, and a spike.
The ball is fast in the air like lighting.
The ball crashes on the floor.
As we win our last point, the other team is out the door.
You hear the crowd cheer our last winning score.

Spoogmai Ahmad, Grade 7
Daniel Savage Middle School, CA

The Feelings

What do you feel,
When someone lets you down?
When someone leaves you all alone,
Or even breaks your heart?
That is the feeling of despair.

What do you feel,
When someone dies?
When you see people starving,
Or when someone is tortured?
That is the feeling of sadness.

What do you feel,
When you find the right person for you?
When you hang out with friends,
Or when you spend time with family?
That is the feeling of love and hope.

Luckily, it is the most powerful feeling of all.

Stacy Truong, Grade 7
Sarah McGarvin Intermediate School, CA

Love

What is love?
Is it an emotion
Or imagination?
Do we both feel it
Or just do I?
Am I just a friend?
She thinks so…
I wish she felt the same.
I don't want to be jealous anymore.
I want to spend that very special gift with her.
She thinks I'm a good friend
I wish she knew,
How I felt.
Love?

Devin Michael Read, Grade 7
Young Scholar's Academy, AZ

Fear

My worst fear,
My ferocious enemy,
If I were to disappear,
Would I be remembered?
Would I be a distant memory?
Would I still be precious to those who knew me,
Or would I lay to rest,
Forgotten, and

now forever

Alone.

Britney Vi, Grade 7
Sarah McGarvin Intermediate School, CA

My Grandpa's Death

Grandpa where can you be?
Are you somewhere around the sea?
I am like a broken glass missing my piece.
Soon it will be just you and me.

Grandpa are you somewhere in the air,
Like a bird soaring through the air?
When the sun shines are you there?
All the fun times that we share,
Every day and everywhere.

Only if I could see you now,
If there was a way somehow.
Through the hall way I go,
I see the memories I know

I can see your smile in the moon.
Do not worry about a thing,
I will see you soon,
I will see you soon someday.
Yesenia Alvarez, Grade 8
John Adams Middle School, CA

I Belong in the Sky

I belong in the sky,
High, high, high in the sky
Where all the hopes and dreams
Fly.
When I'm up in the sky I
Lose all my worries and
The things that burden me day to day.
As I fly higher and
Higher
I want to stay
But I just can't
Seem to fly high enough.
I need to let go,
Break the chains that hold me down
From the sky and the
Hopes and dreams.
Am I strong enough to
Break the chains
That keep me from my
Hopes and dreams?
Jacqueline Barsley, Grade 9
La Reina High School, CA

Color

Pink reminds me of nail polish,
glossy, shiny lip gloss,
sparkling jewelry,
blooming flowers,
soft, fuzzy slippers,
and a cozy blanket.
Erika Flores, Grade 7
Daniel Savage Middle School, CA

Until You Went Away

We played all day
The mess we left
Could be cleaned another day
But then you went away

The fun we had
The happiness we felt
I thought no one could take away
But then you went away

Just about every sunny day
I'd come over and play
It felt like our fun would last always
But then you went away

The days were always hot
The nights spent so cold
I remember those days
But then you went away
Joseph Palacios, Grade 8
Richardson PREP HI Middle School, CA

Three Houses from the Corner

Three houses from the corner,
Where the evil winds make a mess.
Far from the New York border
My house lays to rest

Three houses from the corner,
Where the silent door creaks open.
And where the food is being ordered,
My house lays to rest.

Three houses from the corner,
Where we play from dawn to dusk
And where my beautiful dog likes to fuss.
My house lays to rest.

To those who live before me,
From when the sun sets
To when the dark rises mysteriously.
My house lays to rest.
Samuel Michael Angelo Medina, Grade 8
Richardson PREP HI Middle School, CA

Change

Pencil
yellow, black
writes, erasers, tapping.
hits, throws, moves, lays.
Point, flies, weapon.
Black, white.
Pen.
Andy Fausto, Grade 8
Canyon View Jr High School, UT

Blinded

Tragedy is beauty dressed in rags.
Joy disguised as pain.
Deceiving,
tricking us because we're blind.
We can't see,
the beauty that hide's beneath.
Tragedy makes us lose hope.
It's a game,
to see how long you last.
How long until you say,
I give up!
I lose hope!
I won't play anymore!
So never lose hope.
Never give up,
and in the darkness that lost you,
you'll find the light that can guide you.
You'll see,
from tragedy emerges beauty,
we were just too blind to see it.
Kimberly Escalante, Grade 9
Anaheim High School, CA

Storms are Bullets

Storms are bullets
they move in fast
with no mercy

They kill the innocent
and destroy what they hit

Storms are bullets
they cut through the air like lightning
and can take everything you have

They don't care what they hit
and they can strike any time

Storms are bullets
they are unstoppable
and super powerful

Some don't do much
but there is always one that will
Jay Matheson, Grade 8
Falcon Creek Middle School, CO

The Widow's Bite

He drops in on our conversation,
like a ninja he crawls around,
he moves in slowly to take the bite,
closer and closer,
until finally,
he delivers the lethal injection
Joseph Ostlee, Grade 7
Salida Middle School, CO

Painful Expectations*

Her eloquence and wit disguised her pain at a great scale.
She talked with such beauty, the words melting from her lips.
Her eyes as bright as the tropic sea. Her ears keen, yet sensitive, her feet carried her far.
Her attitude? Delightfully uplifting. Her hair fell down her back caressing her delicate frame.
Her heart, pure gold. This girl, this girl was you.
Yet behind those dainty ears were memories of pure terror, imbedded with the thoughts of self-doubt.
Her optimism…because it was not used towards her.
The speed? She used to have to use it with her words. This girl is a symbol of beauty.
The world had made her believe she was ugly, not thin enough, too short.
That her eyes were too big, her lips too small. Not smart enough, too curious about nonsense.
But this girl knew better to think anyone was right about herself other than she.
She was not the ugly one, this was a trick society played well on her.
Many a time she wept, believing what she was told.
She looked in the mirror. Her perfect imperfections blurred. She was glittering, it was surreal.
Once she thought about it, she was beautiful.
She had brought herself far. What is truly beautiful is the ability to realize that she is just that, beautiful.
It were as if she were glowing with happiness.
She had defied the expectation of others.
She was not perfect, but because of that, she was.

Brooke Harman, Grade 9
Pine Creek High School, CO
A dedication to my aunt

Football

I love the sport with all my heart, everything about it makes me smile; the hitting, the throwing, the passing, the fans, and even the penalties. I love football because if I want to be a great player I have to work my hardest to earn that spot, nothing is given. I was born and raised around football, I've been watching and playing it since I could crawl. I love playing football in the rain, it makes the game more intense and feels like the stakes are more immense. This game has brought me so much joy and taught me much as a boy, as I grow older and older I look to this game for guidance and help, the game of football has never failed me and has taught me so many lessons, I am thankful for it and hope to keep on playing and start on the pro level. I cannot explain how happy I am that football was introduced to me at such a young age, it has molded me into a better person all around.

David Morales, Grade 8
Christ the King School, AZ

They're Gone*

Sheer cliff below
One by one they fell
Time was being swallowed away
Almost gone
Going slowly
Off they went
Twenty-foot fall
You don't know the grief
The grief of being responsible for a horrible thing
I want the one who dropped the blueberries
Kurplunk kurplunk kurplunk
Into the water
Gone forever
Forever no blueberries

Mimi Archuleta, Grade 8
Mancos Middle School, CO
Inspired by "The Maze Runner" by James Dashner
and "Blueberries for Sal" by Robert McCloskey

An Orchestra

An orchestra is really talented
With every sound together
With our bows we play across
Thick and thin strings all together
My teacher says we are getting smarter,
Our brain stems growing thicker,
That someday we could achieve
A goal impossible to reach
Though sometimes we would struggle,
With our pitch and our timing,
But we would always try again
Until we would succeed.
An orchestra has parts that fit like a piano,
Violins and violas are the right hand
While cellos and basses are the left.
An orchestra has sounds, like never before,
But at the end of every song,
A ring would echo out.

Kelly Hua, Grade 7
Sarah McGarvin Intermediate School, CA

A Childhood Memory

My family and I get in the car and drive off to the parade.
It takes a while to find a parking spot with many others also in search of one.
Once parked, we walk along the sidewalk to Danville Boulevard and join the crowd.
I enjoy myself watching the bright floats, bands, and people dancing like gazelles.
My favorite handout is a squishy cow on a key chain to promote 'Challenge butter'.
Loud bangs coming from the distance is cue for me and my mom to walk down the street.
The one part I hate in the parade is when people from the military shoot bullets into the air.
The noise hurts my ears and is an annual routine for me and my mom to leave at this time.
Though the thunderous sounds trouble me, I'm happy, for this occasion invites lots of joyful things too.
Overall, the parade was a success and gets me energized for the other activities we will do today.

The scrumptious smell of KFC's chicken filled my lungs as we drove to the park.
I hop out of the car and walk with my cousin to an open grassy-green area surrounded by trees.
Even in July the cold California night air nipped at my skin, making me pull on a jacket.
After the blanket was laid out, we sat down to eat our delicious dinner.
Everyone in my family loves to play soccer and enjoys playing together.
So, my aunt, uncle, brother, sisters, cousins, and I started a game.
A spark flew up in the dark sky and broke apart into an outburst of colors — the first firework.
We hurry to the blanket and bundle up as we watch the lights shoot across the sky.
My favorite is shaped like a giant yellow smiley face, to show 'This is a fun holiday'.
I want the fireworks to last forever, but there is always next year for another great 4th of July.

Aubrey Clark, Grade 7
Stapley Jr High School, AZ

Fruitless Efforts to Ripen

I am a seed on a tiny green strawberry,
Hardly worth noticing.
I am just a speck on a worthless fruit,
Not even ready to be picked.

I am only a seed without the power to change my fate,
Yet I have a fantasy, that one day I too can be a strawberry.
Grown and waiting to be picked,
But it can become a reality, only if I have enough courage to take a risk.

And fall hard into the earth, letting it swallow me whole,
So I can fight for a spot in this world,
A spot is this large plantation.

Seasons of disappointments have left me restless,
If I can lose hope all will be bearable.
Because without a dream I will not be hurt,

However dreams are worth dying for,
Since there is no reason to live without hopes.

But I am still only a small seed on a sour strawberry,
Only an ordinary speck in this field.
Yet I will never stop dreaming,
Even if my dream is left unfulfilled,
Because I can still cherish it in my heart.

Briana Shen, Grade 9
Arcadia High School, CA

Someone I Admire

My Aunt Amy
A tough and strong cowgirl
Never gives up
Pushes you toward your goals
No matter what
So sweet and joyful
In many ways
So sweet and caring
Any day

Trinity Mejias, Grade 7
Daniel Savage Middle School, CA

Broken Wings

I can no longer live without my wings
They take me to different places
Without them I am nothing
I walk while all the others set off to fly
Without my wings I am stronger
I will live without my wings
I will no longer fly
But no matter what happens
I'll always get by

Georgia Mora, Grade 7
Isbell Middle School, CA

The Dangerous Game

Screech!
We ground to a halt
Hoping for the best
Expecting the worst
Yelling rang in our ears
Our breathing came in massive gulps
The sight confirmed our greatest fears
 Medics crowded the figure lying prone on the ground
The referee was blowing his whistle like a mad man
An opposing player had shoved one of our players over his outstretched leg, onto the floor
The referee blew a final blast
His shout seemed to hang in the air
"Foul, two free throws!"
My limping teammate stumbled to the free throw line
The shot spun through the air in an amazing arc
"Swoosh!"
The net swayed as the ball passed through it
The second shot sprang from his hands
Again the ball passed through the hoop perfectly
The clock had five seconds left as I stole the ball from a boy's outstretched fingers as he yelled in protest
The ball flew through the air, hit the backboard, and the game was won.

Caleb Ostler, Grade 7
Stapley Jr High School, AZ

Holy Is Your Name

Darkness lurked in my life, and fear devoured me. I could never see beyond the shadows of sin. Then you came for me, you pushed away the fear and anxiety that held me captive. Like a cup of living water you filled my life with your grace and light. You destroyed all the wicked, you crushed all the fear, and you threw the evil away from me. You never let me out of your hands. You refuge me in your arms and your love drapes over my shoulders. You blanket me in love and drench me in faith. For I humble to your greatness and I bow to your holy name. I shall live every day praising you God. I am a servant to you and shall spend every moment I am alive singing to your precious name. May the darkness run away in terror and the evil fear your power. For you have set me free, you broke the chains that bound me. You laid your life down so that I may be free. How mighty you are! Knowing that you, the maker of heaven and earth, love a poor sinner like me fills me with wonder. Evil is powerless against your greatness. God, you are mighty! Forever I am your child and will serve you all of my days. For holy is your name!
Amen

Alicia Gomez, Grade 7
Carden Traditional School, AZ

What if Dreaming Was Real?

What if mankind lived on Mars?
I would learn to speak Alien.
What if our world froze over?
I would be a splendid ice skater.
What if we could fly?
I would walk.
What if our world was a dream,
and we woke up one day
beginning the day we were born?

Payton Wolf, Grade 7
Falcon Creek Middle School, CO

The Mockingjay

It can fly
It can hide
It's gorgeous with black and white feathers
It flies from branch to branch
Singing a beautiful song
When you look up
You can see its beautiful feathers
It brings happiness and joy
It's the Mockingjay

Angela Ramirez, Grade 7
Meridian Elementary School, CA

The Last Shot

I dribble the ball up the court.
Nothing is on my mind but this last shot.
I can see my teammate get open.
But I can tell he will be caught.

This is the last chance.
Until the next dawn.
Because if I don't make this last shot.
I will end up back on my lawn.

I can see the clock ticking down.
Five… Four… Three…
On the three point line I throw it up.
Nothing more or less excites me.

I made it, I did.
My opportunity sought.
I am happier then I have ever been.
About this last shot.

Caleb Hawkins, Grade 7
Monte Vista Christian School, CA

Index by Author

Index by School